Anonymus

Leading business men of Back Bay

South End, Boston Highlands, Jamaica Plain and Dorchester

Anonymus

Leading business men of Back Bay
South End, Boston Highlands, Jamaica Plain and Dorchester

ISBN/EAN: 9783742884305

Manufactured in Europe, USA, Canada, Australia, Japa

Cover: Foto ©Suzi / pixelio.de

Manufactured and distributed by brebook publishing software
(www.brebook.com)

Anonymus

Leading business men of Back Bay

LEADING

BUSINESS MEN

OF

BACK BAY, SOUTH END,

BOSTON HIGHLANDS, JAMAICA PLAIN

AND

DORCHESTER.

ILLUSTRATED.

BOSTON:
Copyright by
MERCANTILE PUBLISHING COMPANY,
1888.

PREFACE.

The name of Boston calls up numerous and interesting suggestions in every part of the country. Though there are other cities much larger, none has exercised a broader influence or gained a more lasting and deserved fame. In respect to historical associations and memorials, it can be justly said that no other place in this country is so rich and honored. To adequately represent the vast field here presented, would be a herculean task, which no single work, however large, could hope to accomplish. It has been our aim to present the most interesting features of five of the prominent sections of the Hub — the Back-Bay, representing the accumulated wealth and social élite of the city, the South End, the Highlands, and the outlying and delightful districts of Dorchester and Jamaica Plain. The large and valuable business interests have also been carefully studied and represented as fully as possible, and we take pleasure in presenting them herewith to all lovers of this beautiful and justly celebrated city.

THE PUBLISHERS.

Introduction to Business Notices.

In the following pages will be found brief notices of the principal Business firms of the sections under review. While the majority are old established houses and leaders in every sense of the word, we have mentioned others who, though recently established, are, through their enterprise and ability, deserving of notice. Abundant evidences of the energy and talent for which Bostonians are so distinguished have been met with in every department of commercial, professional and social life. We commend these firms as a whole, to the favorable attention of all into whose hands this volume may fall, believing that they well represent the business interests of this section.

THE PUBLISHERS.

LEADING BUSINESS MEN.

INDEX TO NOTICES.

BAKERS AND CONFECTIONERS.

	PAGE
Blunt, Harvey	71
Chace & Co	87
Dunbar, F. N.	85
Davis, M. L. Mrs	190
Ernst, I.	221
Goodnow, J. W.	218
Hatch, M. A.	37
Hart, Joseph A	42
Hickie, D. J.	80
Hausman & Cook	102
Keller, A	48
Keith & Hastings	164
Lang, J. P.	161
Martin, George E.	60
Marble, E. F. Mrs	97
McDonald, M. L. Mrs	83
Patch & Clark	86
Penule, J	166
Rich, Frederick L	107
Rutledge, Charles A	200
Seiler, H. J	176
Whitney, J. B. Jr	74
Young, C. L.	44

BELL HANGERS AND LOCKSMITHS.

	PAGE
Blackwood, Alex	180
Pierce, Charles	122
Sheffield, W. H.	65
Woodward, J	172

BOOTS AND SHOES.

	PAGE
Appleton, Samuel	123
Bouve, Crawford & Co	155
Chaplin, C. C.	35
Chaplin, Frank P	60
Day & Gould	172
Emmons, James N. W	176
Howard, J. B.	187
Howe, Alfred H	193
McLean, Charles	62
Mooar, C. T.	174
Mooar, O. G.	153
Rooney, William	219
Wright, E. W	163

BOOKS, STATIONERY AND PERIODICALS.

	PAGE
Bates, Amos E	40
Barton, A. W	165
Babb, E. Miss	197
Cox, C. M. & J. W	129
Cate, F. S.	196
McDormand, E. Miss	196
Nelson, J. H	60
Ochs, C. A. & Co	89
Osgood, M. E.	78
Ridler, C. E.	123
Stacey, G. W	135
Woodruff, John	57
Weston, H. G	61
Williams, Nicholas M. (Catholic)	76
Walker, J. B	170

CARPENTERS, MASONS AND BUILDERS.

	PAGE
Ballantyne, W	176
Boardman, Wm. H. (stair builder)	65
Butterfield, B. H	58
Burke Brothers	207
Brackett, G. A. & S. W. (jobbing)	195
Colcord, B. F. & Co	70
Fuller, C. C	197
Lanfair, L. H	44
Murphy, Stephen	83
Oliver, John	155
Soderbery, G. R	151
Shaw, J. P	222
Vallee, Francis	157
White, George H	62

CLOTHING AND GENTS' FURNISHINGS.

Norfolk Clothing Store (Snow & Merrick)	187
Riley, J. H. (Rugby)	177
Roxbury Clothing Co. (S. C. Hadley)	180
Rosenkranz, I	182

COAL AND WOOD.

Adams, J. E. & Co	40
Bradford, J. A. & Co	60
Davis, E. S	211
Langley, F. A. & Co	01
Morse. R. G. & Co	50

DRUGGISTS.

Adams, N	179
Bartlett, Charles A	35
Blake, George W	36
Benedict, John G	40
Barteaux, F. A	56
Babo, Eugene	167
Bartlet, Wm. W	150
Bolster, George A	156
Burnham, A. A. jr	158
Brooks, George P	208
Colton, J. B	58
Copley, A. H	200
Kayrs, Albert H. & Co	218
Fairfield, William H	93
Folger, W. S. & Co	44
Gale, Stephen	47
Gilson, A. P	67
Godding, J. G. & Co	118
Highland Drug Store (N. Adams)	179
Hadcock, Henry L	162
Knowlton, J. D	49
Kraushaar, E. G. W	221
Leach, Edwin T	51
McIntire, Martin J	59
Mott Walter (free dispensary)	170
Mowry, A. D. & Co	157
Marcy, A. D	210

DRUGGISTS — Continued.

	PAGE
Neilson, Herbert	54
Otis, Edward F	191
Paine, Newell	172
Rogers, C. B	220
Sheppard, S. A. D. & Co	34
Smith, Edward K	39
Siegemund, C. A	84
Sweet, Wm. I	192
Tower, Walter S	173
Whitney, Justin & Co	44
Woodruff, Galen	48
Webster, S. & Co	63
Woodbury, F. B	166
Whitcomb, F. L	173

DRY AND FANCY GOODS AND MILLINERY.

Anderson, J. A	170
Aiken, E. S. Mrs	161
Ferguson & Co	164
Farwell, M. F	203
Gillett, J. E	57
Gaul, W. Mrs	158
Hurd, W. J	41
Howard, B. E	181
Hatch, C. R	150
Kerr, A. M. Miss	163
Kerr, M	169
Lithbridge, M. M	88
Lovell, Charles B	3d
Lougee, G. H. & Co	58
Mulliken, E. M. Mrs	78
Mendum, T. M. Mrs	83
Newton, M. A	66
Newell, J. M	190
Parker, H. F. Miss	120
Randall, C. W	55
Riley, K. E. Miss	180
Shedd, E. S. Mrs	54

EMPLOYMENT AGENCIES.

Babb, E. Miss	197

FRUITS, CONFECTIONERY AND CIGARS.

Barton, A. W	155
Coney, S. F	40
Friedlander, S	71
Hayes, C. M. Mrs	194
McDormand, E. Miss	106

FLORISTS.

Curley, John J	173
Dolay, James	122
Norton Brothers	123
O'Brien, James	184
Rough, James	56
Severy, S	38

FURNITURE, ETO.

	PAGE
Beard, Edward	100
Bakeman, George R. & Co	162
Ferdinand, Frank	150
Goldthwait, W. F. & Co	88
Lamb, E. T.	68
Margeson, R. S.	151
Smith Brothers	91
Thompson, E.	70

FISH AND OYSTERS.

	PAGE
Burrows, H. J.	210
Curley, James F.	108
Crosby, Thomas	191
Clark, R. F. & Co	94
Dow, George F.	44
Freeman, J. E.	00
Haskard, F. P.	73
Hopkins, S. C.	83
Isaacs, S.	183
Jones, W. W.	47
Johnson, S. C.	54
Lambert, G. E.	42
Litchfield, H. S.	80
Newcomb, W. W.	45
Nason, Samuel C.	185
O'Brien Brothers	118
Spear, A.	57
Sweet, L. K.	60
Smith, J. & Son	70
Shine, H. J. & W. J.	186

GROCERS AND PROVISION DEALERS.

	PAGE
Addison, Richard	73
Adams, Charles A.	80
Agry, William H.	123
Andrews, G. W. & Co	181
Ames Brothers	185
Ansart, B. F.	174
Allbright, H. G.	205
Anderson, William	221
Banks & Harriman	41
Burghard, Charles	222
Bradford, A. W.	174
Boleman, Thos. F.	102
Bradford, H	170
Bonney, W. A.	179
Barnard, E. G.	68
Barnes, Walter G.	62
Berry, George A.	80
Chase, Charles H	82
Clark, R. F. & Co	94
Clement, W. H.	92
Centennial American Tea Co	155
Crosby, E. B.	45

GROCERS AND PROVISION DEALERS.
Continued.

	PAGE
Dow, George F.	44
Dowell, F. H. & W. F.	47
Duffield & Davis	54
Decatur, Thos. (People's Cold Blast Market)	216
Drew, Cephas	164
Davenport, H. A	183
Dudley Market (Jas. F. Wise)	178
Davis, G. F.	71
Edwards, P. & Son	117
Eldredge, F. S.	189
Everett, D. H	152
Fox Brothers	48
Faunce, C. B.	167
Gleason, Wm. H	88
Greene & Stevens	183
Goff & Randall	164
Griswold, M. M	206
Gould & Co	207
Ganter, Frank & Co	223
Hunting, H. R	184
Hannon Brothers	171
Howland, C. C.	88
Haines & Murphy	120
Johnson, J. P	66
Jewett, George F.	85
Johnson, J. F.	41
Jordan, E. W.	210
Jacques, Geo. E.	66
Kempton, J. B.	67
Knowles, W. S.	189
Krug & Beck (sausages)	171
Kingsley, J. C. (Cunard Market)	196
Keezer, D.	219
Kittredge, S. F.	48
Krim, Philip	52
Lamson Brothers	52
Lambert, G. E.	42
Littig, Andrew	196
Lowe, F. O.	174
Lowe, E. R. (Essex Market)	170
Lord, J. H. & Co	191
Lord, F. C. & Co	124
Long & Keeler	63
Mitten Brothers	61
Moulton, E.	84
McDonald, M. L. Mrs.	83
Macdonald, D. B.	183
Morse, William W	103
McGlanflin, H. G	165
Mitchell, Thomas J	169
May, J. J	156
Morse, L. W. & H. F.	160
Moore, J. B.	217
MacCorry, Chas. E. S.	34
Mayo, W. C.	83

GROCERS AND PROVISION DEALERS.
Continued.

	PAGE
Nelson, Eugene B	34
Nicholson, A	173
Newton, John F	199
Newcomb & Frost	121
Oakes, Geo. A	65
Powers, John T	45
Pearson, G. H	158
Putnam, Nelson S	199
Ryder, C. C	61
Risteen, F. S. & Co	68
Russell, J. C	69
Rollins, Geo. E	87
Ryder, John H	189
Robinson, E. & Co	159
Richardson, A. M	193
Reynolds, E	211
Rice, James P	39
Spear, A	57
Swan, W. A	210
Strout, S. S	103
Sturdivant Brothers	83
Stevenson & Co	85
Sweet, L. K	00
Smith, S. C	78
Stone, C. H. & Co	89
Toothaker, Charles F	74
Tighe & Burke	110
Towle, Henry & Co	199
Towle, J. A	50
Upham, A. N	55
Upham, J. H. & Co	208
Wilson, S. E. & Co	70
Wise, James F	178
Woolley, Chas. B	68
Woodbridge, J. B	88
Worster, C. B. & Co	122
Woods, E. D	172
Williams, F. J	152
Yerxa, E. J. & Co	91

HATS, CAPS AND GENTS' FURNISHINGS.

Barta, W. J	104
Ferguson & Co	160
Jones, D. L	192
Reed, W. N	82
Tannatt, W. C	78

HARNESS, TRUNKS, ETC.

Atkinson, Charles	39
Curry, M. C. & Co	125
Dolan, Thomas F	175
Hanlon, J. W	90
Miller & Fiske	70
Mackay, Kenneth	109
Robinson, T. W	220
Smith, H. B	181

HARDWARE DEALERS.

	PAGE
Chamberlin, C. E	103
Gardner, A. M	90
Horan Brothers	56
Hunter, J. B. & Co	60
Nichols, Charles H	219
Woodward, J	172
White, Cyrus & Co	217

INSURANCE AND REAL ESTATE.

Cate, Martin L. & Co	153
Foss, Edwin P	51
Harris, Henry S	51
Herthel, F. J. jr	166
Keene, S. W. & Son	161
Learned, F. M	38
Newton, John F. jr	194
Richards, E. E	159

JEWELRY AND OPTICAL GOODS.

Barton, William	159
Fairbanks, E. H	219
L'Heureux, S. H	154
Mumford, C. A	64
Tizley, James	104
West, Forrest L	42

LIVERY, BOARDING AND SALE STABLES.

Aldrich, J. H	165
Allard, Isaac H	207
Bryant, Parker	187
Chappell, C. H	82
Cassidy, J. B. & Brother	168
Conklin, E. D	160
Draper, Horace	79
Hall, Lewis	200
Henley, J. H. & Co	70
Kenny & Clark	118
Merrill, B. B	51
McDowell, J. F	81
May, John H	86
Papineau, A	222
Rogers, J. Austin	178
Smith, H. D	72
Spofford, S. W. (St. James' Stable)	65
Wood, Daniel	85

LAUNDRIES AND DYE-HOUSES.

Daloz, L. H. (dyeing and cleansing)	224
Glen Laundry (S. K. Poore)	194
Griffith's Steam Laundry	149
Sargent's Steam Laundry	60

MANUFACTURERS.

Ash, George H. & Co. (pianos)	150
Carter, Dinsmore & Co. (inks)	84
Chandler Water Motor Co	95
Reece Button Hole Machine Co., The	61
Rock & Forrest (copper, iron and zinc work)	85
Roxbury Novelty Works (O. J. Jordan)	190
Woodberry & Harris (church organs)	94

MISCELLANEOUS.
PAGE

Appleton, Samuel (agency for Dr. Pray, chiropodist and manicure).......... 128
Allen Gymnasium, The..................... 110
Ball, Willard D. (dentist)............ 87
Blair Camera Co., The.................... 46
Back Bay, Glimpses of the............. 97
Boston Highlands, History of............. 126
Cutter, W. B. (doors, windows, etc.) 182
Chase Refrigerating Co 175
Coughlin, F. G. & Co. (marble, etc.)..... 68
Cuddihy, John J. (stone and drain pipe)... 60
Coulan, P. T. (wood carver)........... 78
Chase & Co. (billiard hall)............... 67
Cotton, Geo. H. (Belmont Spring Water)... 116
Clarendon Hotel (F. S. Risteen)............ 74
Curtis & Pope (lumber)................... 81
Cyclorama (Battle of Bunker Hill).......... 75
Cyclorama (Battle of Gettysburg)......... 77
Dinkin, Chas. L. (engravings, etc.) 87
Delaney, J. J. & Co. (monumental works).. 87
Dorchester, Historical Sketch of.......... 198
Eayrs, Albert H. & Co. (surgical bandages) 218
Emond & Quinster (fine carriages)........ 183
Jamaica Plain, History of................ 212
Keefe, J. (express, and furniture mover)... 120
Kyle, P. (sculptor in stone and wood)...... 87
Loveay, Henry (rustic work)............. 221
McCormack, D. F. (horseshoer)............ 209
Mulrey, T. D. (marble and granite) 186
McPherson, W. J. (decorative stained glass) 72
McCafferty, J. H. & Son (brass founders)... 92
Macfarlane, F. J. (dentist)................ 154
New England Conservatory of Music, The.. 90
Newman, A. W. (carriage maker)........ 117
Norfolk Billiard Hall (E. B. Wood)......... 150
Reed, E. V. R. (crayon artist)............. 52
Reed's Block (general manufacturing)...... 93
Ryder, Gilman M. (Mexican Rheumat. Cure) 95
Summers, H. & Co. (repairer silver ware,&c.) 124
Sawyer, Wm. (crockery)................. 193
Sinder, Frederick (gas fixtures)............ 179
Thomas, John (practical horseshoer)...... 180

MERCHANT TAILORS.

Carroll, P. J........................... 128
Martin, John C 186
McDonald, J. F.......................... 164
Steeger, Henry........................... 208
Whitcomb, N. O. & Co.................... 161
Washington, B. F......................... 61

PAINTS, OILS AND PAPER HANGINGS.

Chamberlin, C. E......................... 163
Marshall, A. L........................... 63
Woodward, J............................ 172

PAINTERS, ETC.
PAGE

Alexander, Samuel........................ 53
Bell, Charles H........................... 92
Burke, Alan............................. 220
Campbell, C. G........................... 15
Downs, Geo. W........................... 183
Hentz & Bennett.......................... 69
Knox, C. H. & Co........................ 55
McCabe & Strange........................ 163
Richardson, C. W. (carriage painter)... ... 188
Sefton, Charles H......................... 102
Wild, Thomas............................ 179

PHOTOGRAPHERS.

Bradley, Alvin F.......................... 189
Beans, C. E.............................. 193
Gray, G. E.............................. 193
Pepper, Arthur F......................... 166
Partridge, W. H.......................... 185

PLUMBERS.

Buerkel & Co............................ 86
Baldwin, C. E. & Co...................... 55
Bramhall, Wm........................... 158
Boyd, R. E.............................. 157
Carey, Thomas........................... 195
Collins, M. & H. H....................... 152
Cunningham, Lawrence.................... 81
Duggan, T. H. & Co...................... 117
Fallon Brothers.......................... 172
Hayes, James H.......................... 35
Keane, M. J............................. 60
Keefe, D. J. & Co........................ 125
Kelley, J. P............................. 186
Kelley, John C.......................... 174
Murphy, P. H. & Co...................... 120
McCaffrey, Charles H..................... 221
Ratigan, Thomas......................... 64
Sheehan, J. M........................... 153
Tombe, Henry W......................... 71
Tralner, Wm. & Co....................... 121
Waltt, W. H. & Co....................... 175
Woods, J. F............................. 208
White, Cyrus & Co....................... 217

PRODUCE DEALERS AND CREAMERIES.

Davis, W. E. (Highland Creamery)......... 151
Kingsley, J. G. (Cunard Market).......... 195
Merrow, A. W........................... 59
Pratt, E. B.............................. 193
Worcester County Creamery (Geo. B. Bruce) 47
Smith, S. C............................. 78

RESTAURANTS.

	PAGE
Cafe Waquolt (Louis Frenkel)	46
Dierkes, August	52
Davis, M. M. Mrs	190
Kelley, P.	124
Olympian Cafe (W. H. Stevens)	40
Potter, Geo. M	165
Purnell, William H	207
Steven's Cafe	61

STOVES, RANGES AND FURNACES.

Bramball, Wm	138
Cate, N. S.	103
Danaby, D. & Son (tin and sheet iron ware)	184
Ells, William F	105
Felton, B. W	154
Lafreniere, J. O.	167
Martin, J. M	177
Nichols, Charles H	210
Taylor & Carey	173
Wadman, J. C	62
White, Cyrus & Co	217

UNDERTAKERS.

	PAGE
Fallon, James P	157
Manning, William	64
Murray, B. E.	220
Peak Brothers	83
Waterman, Joseph S. & Sons	179

UPHOLSTERERS, ETC.

Anderson, F. O	58
Hoeffner, Fred	152
King, E. W	188
Mansfield, George S	118
Rowe, John H	132
Ryan, J. E.	153
Scales, Henry	79
Snyder, F. P.	121
Schwartz, Frank	171
Sauer, George & Co	218
Trask, E. J. H	117
Waltt, J. M	57

WINES, BEERS, ETC.

Cordelia Wine Co	43
Gray, James O. (bottler)	72
Hazelton, F. L. & Co. (bottlers)	171
Krim, Philip	52
Robinson, H. H. (wine)	43

*,

POINTS IN THE SOUTH END.

THE Puritans were above all things methodical, and one of their first experiments after they had settled in Shawmut, was to divide it into East, West, North and South Ends, which divisions have held with considerable exactitude up to the present time. A vast transformation has come over the face of the South End since the early days of the city. From a narrow "Neck," amid immense tracts of flats it has become a spacious and elegant district, largely composed of handsome private residences, palatial flats and hotels, interspersed with charming little parks. Yet another change is now being witnessed, as the residences are gradually being pushed out into the Highlands, and the ever widening tide of business interests sweeps on over the district. Already marked evidences of this change are apparent, and at no very distant day the largest part of this section must inevitably succumb to the insatiable commercial interests of the city, a metamorphosis not very pleasing to the quiet old residents of the South End, but the city listens to no arguments nor entreaties in her onward march. The main thoroughfares of the South End, which is generally regarded as bounded on the north by Boylston, Tremont and Dover streets, on the west by the Boston & Albany Railroad, on the east by the bay, and on the south by the old Roxbury line, are Columbus avenue, Tremont and Washington streets, Shawmut and Harrison avenues. These are all now largely given up to business, the retail trade on Washington street and the others being very large, while many extensive manufactories are scattered throughout the region.

Columbus avenue, one of the most recent streets of the South End, is also the most popular. It is one of the longest straight streets anywhere in the city, and has many very beautiful buildings situated upon it. It extends in a straight line from Park square to Northampton street,, and being paved with asphalt makes a very attractive and popular driveway, for which it is celebrated. Though one of the busiest, it is also, from its structure, one of the quietest streets in Boston, and is, therefore, still a very desirable location for residences. It is only a matter of years, however, before it will be taken up entirely for business and become one of the most famous in the city. West Chester Square, which crosses the avenue, is a delightful spot, being cultivated and adorned with great care and talent, so that the whole region attracts one by its great beauty and refined atmosphere. Other well known and favorite parks are Chester Square, which is really a street with a long narrow park running

WEST CHESTER SQUARE, COR. COLUMBUS AVENUE.

through, and spreading out into a commodious square in the center, where to the great trees and odorous flowers is added the dancing stream of a fountain; Union Park, between Tremont street and Shawmut avenue, and Worcester Square, between Washington and Harrison streets, each about a third of an acre in extent; Blackstone Square, between Washington street and Shawmut avenue, also possesses a large and beautiful fountain, being about two and a third acres in size, as also does Franklin Sq., between Washington, East Newton, East Brookline and James streets. Quite a number of South End streets still possess a large number of shade trees, which add a great deal of comfort and beauty to the region, and are among its most treasured possessions.

The South End is remarkable for the exceptionally fine arrangements it offers for residing comfortably within the limit of the city and all its privileges. In addition to numerous private residences of a high order, the French "flat" system of late years has been very popular. Over a score of these large "hotels," so called, "*a la Francaise*," are situated in the various sections of the South End, each suite being all on one floor and entirely separate from the others, so it is well adapted for family occupancy. There are, beside, numerous "family" hotels, which are conducted on much the same plan, such as the Pelham, Continental, Berkeley, Cluny, Boylston, Hoffman, Edinburgh, Albemarle and the Commonwealth, worthy in every respect to represent this or any other great city in the country.

The church edifices in the South End are among the largest and most beautiful in the city. The Tremont Meth. Epis. Church, on Tremont, between Concord and Worcester streets, is a large and stately edifice, and is generally regarded as the handsomest in the denomination in Boston. It is in plain but strong old Gothic style, and is constructed of Roxbury stone, having been one of the first large buildings on which this popular stone was used. The building is 200 feet long by 100 feet deep, and cost, including land, $68,000. It was completed in January, 1862, replacing another built by the same society, formerly called the "Hedding Church," in 1848. The effect of the two large, unequal towers, placed at opposite corners is very pleasing, and adds immeasurably to the beauty of the church.

The Berkeley Street Church (Congregational), is and has been for many years one of the most powerful forces in the religious and spiritual life of the city. It was organized in 1827, and its first structure was located at the corner of Washington and Pine streets, and was known as the Pine Street Church. Its present edifice, on the corner of Warren avenue, Tremont, Berkeley and Dover streets, was erected in 1862, and the society has since been known by its present name. Its list of ministers contains some of the most justly revered names in the christian church in this country, among whom are those of the Revs. Thomas Skinner, D.D., H. M. Dexter, D.D., Austin Phelps, D.D., and the present pastor, the Rev. William Bennet Wright, who is known for his preaching and literary work, as one of the strongest thinkers of his denomination. The church celebrated its semi-centennial in 1877, and the following year its debt was cancelled once for all, relieving the church from a long-felt incubus. The society is one of the most active and generous in all lines of religious and benevolent work in Boston, and its edifice is said to be the largest protestant church building in New England.

The Church of the Unity, is another well known society at the South End. Its large and attractive edifice, seating one thousand people, is situated on the corner of Shawmut avenue and Canton street. The society was organized in 1857 by a number of liberally inclined christian thinkers, to promote "good morals and the cause of liberal christianity." The present pastor, Rev. M. J. Savage, was installed in September, 1874, and has become one of the most influential and powerful thinkers in the city. He has written several valuable books, besides contributing occasionally to periodical literature, and by his broad views and thorough frankness has gained a large and sympathetic audience, both within and without the city.

The Shawmut Congregational Church has one of the most attractive and prominent edifices in the South End. It was begun in 1863, and was completed in the following year. Its tower is very lofty, and presents a striking appearance. The society grew out of a small company of fifty persons, who in 1849 worshipped in a little chapel on Shawmut avenue. Since that time it has grown steadily in power and life, and has accomplished a large and beneficent work.

The Second Universalist Church on Columbus avenue has a very beautiful and attractive building, erected in 1872. It is constructed of Roxbury stone, in simple old Gothic style, with a most harmonious blending of effect. The cost was $160,000. The interior agrees perfectly with the pleasing exterior, and the stained glass win-

2

dows representing the " Man of Sorrows," the " Risen Lord," and the twelve apostles, also figures of Hope, Faith, Charity and Purity, in memoriam of its first pastor, Rev. Hosea Ballou, and other early benefactors, are very beautiful. This is one of the oldest Universalist societies in the country and has long been known as leader in every department of denominational and philanthropic work. Its last pastor, A. A. Miner, D.D., president of Tufts college from 1862 to 1875, and for many years a member of the State Board of Education, has achieved a wide and lasting work in the cause of reform in governmental, educational and religious affairs.

The South Congregational Church on Union Park street, is one of the best known and respected in the city, both for its own untiring efforts in every good cause, and the honor of its pastor, Rev. Edward Everett Hale, D.D., who has long been recognized as one of the most helpful and inspiring thinkers in the country. Through his literary fame and the influence of his great work during the war and since, the church has become widely known through the country. It was first organized in 1825, and its present beautiful edifice was erected during the turmoil of the civil war, at the same time that the church itself was so busily engaged in its " christian and sanitary" work. It was dedicated January 8, 1862.

The Union Church owns a large and magnificent structure on the corner of Columbus avenue and Newton street, which was completed in 1870, and adds much to the beauty of that already grand avenue. The society was organized in 1822, and has long been among the most prominent and active in the city. It is now entirely free from debt and earnestly engaged in the wide-reaching endeavors for the advancement of Christianity and the truth.

The Cathedral of the Holy Cross (Cath.) is one of the stateliest structures in the country. It is situated at the corner of Washington and Malden streets, and covers over 40,000 square feet, or more than an acre of ground, there being but few cathedrals larger than it in the world. The corner stone of the church was laid in 1867, and it was dedicated in 1875. The great tower at the south-west corner, when completed, will be 300 feet in height, without an equal in the city. The smaller tower at the north-west corner, will be 200 feet high, but since the distance from ground to ridgepole is 120 feet, and the immense walls are proportionately high, these grand towers will seem perfectly in keeping with the rest of the structure. The total length of the building is 364 feet; width of the transepts 170 feet; width of naves and aisle, 90 feet. The great interior of the church is almost one unbroken expanse of immense size, with the exception of two rows of columns supporting the central roof, and seating space is afforded for about 3,500 people. The elaborate wood-work which covers the ceiling, panels, and spanderls, is especially beautiful, several shades of oak being combined with African wood in magnificent designs. Among other grand works is the great cross of inlaid wood on the roof of the transept, and the painted angel-figures of Faith, Hope, Charity, and other graces and virtues standing out most strikingly from a background of gold in the ceiling of the chancel. The stained-glass windows are also of highest artistic beauty. The window over the principal entrance represents a magnificent aureole rose. Over the transepts are two great windows, representing the Emperor Hemetitus exalting the cross, and the miracle verifying the true cross of Christ. Also in the chancel are three memorial windows of the Crucifixion, the Ascension and the Nativity. There are also twenty-four small but lovely windows depicting Bible scenes and subjects. The magnificent high altar, constructed most elaborately of variegated marble, is beautifully overshadowed by an immense canopy. The great organ in the front gallery is one of the best ever made in this country. It is from the works of Hook & Hastings and is famed for its sweet clearness and sublimity of tone. It contains over 5,000 pipes, seventy-eight stops, twelve combinations of pedals and five pneumatic knobs. There are four large and handsome chapels connected with the cathedral: the chapel of St. Joseph, the chapel of St. Patrick, the chapel of the Blessed Sacrament, and the chapel of the Blessed Virgin, the latter containing a fine marble image of the Virgin. These, together with the stately residence of Archbishop Williams, in the rear of the cathedral, form a most impressive and magnificent series of edifices.

The Church of the Immaculate Conception is an older Catholic building, near the Cathedral. It is externally a plain, yet not unattractive granite structure, without tower or spire. The almost exquisite loveliness of the interior forms a striking contrast. The white setting of the walls is very quiet and attractive, and adds to the effect of the brilliant ornamentation about the great altar. The great organ is considered among the most harmonious and powerful in the city. The building is 208 feet long by 85 feet wide; it was begun by the Jesuit fathers in 1857, and completed in 1861, at a cost of more than $100,000. The painting of the Crucifixion by Girialdi of Rome is a great work of art.

This sketch of the leading churches in the South End, though it does not include them all, will suffice to show their high character and powerful influence.

Next to the Church of the Immaculate Conception, is the Boston College, a Catholic institution of higher education founded by the Jesuits in 1863. The instruction is high and thorough, the classics being given an important place, and the corps of sixteen professors, tutors, etc., is admirably qualified for the important work required. The present president is J. J. O'Connor. The college has made marked progress in recent years, and is steadily extending its influence and power.

The Boston City Hospital grew out of a movement inaugurated by many of the best citizens and leading physicians, over thirty years ago, and after long discussions and delay the legislature passed a bill, in 1858, giving the city authority to incorporate one. A plot of ground near the bay in the South End was appropriated to this purpose in December, 1860, and the building was commenced in the following fall. It was completed in May, 1864, and opened for patients in the following June. The lot on which the beautiful buildings stand is seven acres in extent, and bounded by Concord, Albany and Springfield streets, and Harrison avenue. The buildings face upon the latter avenue, and consist of a central building with a fine dome, used for administration offices; two long pavilions, for medical and surgical treatment, on each side; and auxiliary buildings in the rear, including isolating wards, morgue and autopsy rooms and laundries. The whole cost of buildings was about $610,000, not including furnishings and appliances. The city pays annually in the region of $100,000 for its maintenance. It will accommodate about four hundred patients, those who are residents of Boston not being obliged to pay, but those desiring to do so receive extra privileges and board. There is a great amphitheater where operations are performed in the presence of physicians, surgeons and students. The out-door service, chiefly through the South End section is very extensive, and the accident wards are constantly crowded with patients, the ambulance service being very effective. A large

training school for nurses has been established, and is one of the great departments of the institution. The largest benefactor in the history of the hospital, has been Mr. Elisha Goodnow, who bequeathed it $21,000. About five thousand cases are annually treated within the hospital, and about twice as many out patients; while a much larger number receive consultation and medicine upon application at the regular hours. This institution with its great equipment and noble work is one of the most honorable testimonials to the spirit and kindness of the Hub.

The Central Club is one of the prominent social features of the South End. It was first organized in 1809 to gratify a long recognized desire of leading people, and has proved a great success. The first meetings were held informally in the St. James Hotel, but the membership increased so rapidly that in a few months a suite of rooms on Concord street was leased; its growth was still so rapid that these soon became too small, and in 1871 the handsome and luxurious quaters on the corner of Washington street and Worcester square were leased for a term of seven years, which lease was renewed. At present the building which the club occupies is located elsewhere.

The Mercantile Library Association has been for more than half a century one of the most influential, literary and social institutions in the South End, toward the culture of whose residents it has contributed no small share. It was re-organized about seven years ago, and to its old advantages has added new and important ones. The building of the Association is situated on the corner of Tremont and Newton streets, and is very attractive, both without and within. The parlors are cosily and elegantly furnished and a classic air is given by the numerous and beautiful paintings and statues clustered around. The leading magazines and newspapers are always on hand here. The extensive library of the Association has been transferred to the basement, where it forms a part of the South End branch of the Boston Public Library situated here. On the second floor are pleasant rooms for social gathering and conversation smoking being also allowed. One of the best and most popular features of the Association is the series of lectures, literary and musical entertainments which are given every year during the winter season. The membership is very large and highly prized; the annual dues are $5.00.

The South End is now fairly well supplied with markets, the Washington market at 1883 Washington street taking the lead. It is the farthest up town of any, and is largely patronized by residents of the South End and the Highlands. The building was erected in 1870, and is about two hundred and fifty feet long by one hundred and twenty wide. The whole interior is very commodious and it has the reputation of being the neatest and best kept in the city. Its situation gives it great advantages for trading with the country and all its houses are first class in style and character.

The Boston University School of Medicine is one of the leading educational institutions and professional schools in the city. It is situated in a fine building opposite the City Hospital on East Concord Street, with beautiful and spacious grounds round about it. It was organized in 1873, and like the other departments of Boston University, has the special feature of being open to both sexes. The New England Female College, the first medical school for women in the country was annexed in 1874. This school has stood among the first of those in the country requiring a thoroughly fitting preparation, scientific knowledge, and practical evidences of capability, before granting its diplomas, so that they stand for sound worth in marked contrast to those of the majority of so-called medical schools. It was a leader in the movement to establish a graded course of instruction, and is one of the few in the country whose regular course requires four years. The degree of doctor of medicine, however, can be obtained at the end of three years if the candidate gives sure evidences of progress and fitness. The school has a large and carefully selected library of several thousand volumes, museums, and large collections of histological and other specimens, thoroughly equipped chemical and microscopical laboratories, and a full equipment of appliances and instruments for every department of instruction and work. The faculty of the school is about thirty in number, all eminent and skilled practitioners and investigators, and every line and school of medical duty receives careful attention. A number of distinguished homœopathic physicians are on the faculty, but all schools are represented. The success of the school has been marked and deserved from the start, and it has gained a wide reputation for worth and efficiency. The proximity of the hospitals, both city and homœopathic is a valuable aid in practical work and appreciated and improved thoroughly. Dr. I. M. Talbot is the dean of the school, and applications and inquiries should be directed to him.

The Massachusetts Homœopathic Hospital is situated near the Boston University School of Medicine, to which it forms a valued coadjutor. The building now occupied is an extensive four story building of stone, the architecture being very pleasing and beautiful. It cost, including land, in the neighborhood of $100,000, and was first thrown open to patients in 1876. It is remarkable and famed for its perfection of fitness in construction, ventilation, heating, light, and all the appurtenances that go to make up a highly sanitary and comfortable hospital. The mortality of the hospital has been kept at the exceedingly low average of about two per cent, which is the highest of tributes to its character and work. The severest as well as the lighter cases of both medical and surgical complaints receive equal and thorough attention, and the results even in the worst cases are very beneficial and encouraging. The cost is very low and it is thus maintained for the benefit of all, not by a narrow or sparing policy, but by a true and wise economy which consists of careful and studied methods. The association was incorporated in 1855, but did not occupy a permanent place until 1871. For five years thereafter they conducted a hospital in Burroughs Place, and then moved to their present building where they have met a large and deserved success.

Among the charitable institutions of the South End, St. Vincent's Orphan Asylum deserves honorable mention. It is situated on the corner of Shawmut avenue and Camden street, and is under the charge of thirteen tender-hearted Catholic sisters who serve voluntarily and without pay. It is designed for the rescue and training up to the right life of destitute girls, and has admirably performed its mission since it was first established in 1831. It was incorporated in 1845. No distinction of race, color or creed is made, but all are received and have equal and devoted care. As occasion warrants, those of the children deserving it are sent to be adopted into good families. The expenses are chiefly met by contributions taken in all the Catholic churches in the city, and amount to about $12,000 annually. Several children are supported here by each church, and a few receive the support of relatives. Two hundred and twenty-five children are received and cared for each year.

The Association for the Protection of Destitute Catholic Children is another worthy charitable institution at the South End. It occupies a beautiful and commodious building, costing with the land $150,000, and situated opposite the Church of the Immaculate Conception on Harrison avenue. It was incorporated in 1864, and its great work has been done chiefly among Catholic children, though those of all denominations are received. The number of children cared for annually is between three and four hundred, and all are attended and trained by Sisters of Charity, and homes are provided for those without them. The annual expenses amount to about $15,000, and are met by endowments, legacies, and contributions of the laity of the city. The work is an excellent one and admirably executed.

Among other well-known and estimable charities in the South End is the "Boffin's Bower," at 1031 Washington street, which though not as large or famous as some has accomplished a unique and wide work for good, which in its great helpfulness and power is unexcelled. The late Jennie Collins, a name well known to the poor and needy, as well as to all lovers of Boston, was the chief mover and worker in carrying on this institution, which was founded in 1874 chiefly through her efforts. It is designed to afford food, clothing and temporary shelter to poor, working women who are out of

WASHINGTON STREET, COR. NEWTON STREET.

employment, and between one and two thousand women and girls have been greatly helped every year since it was founded. Its support has been entirely derived from voluntary contributions, and as its practical and beneficial work has become widely known, many of the leading people of Boston have united in its support. The name of its chief benefactor will ever be tenderly remembered in Boston, and the grand and powerful effects of her life work can never be obliterated from the city's life.

The Boston Female Asylum is another helpful charity in the South End, having its building at 1008 Washington street. It is in reality an orphan asylum for girls alone, and for many years has been carrying on a much needed and valuable work among the orphan poor of the city. The asylum accommodates between seventy and eighty children, who are all under eighteen, homes being found for them after they have reached that age, and much valuable instruction being given.

The Children's Hospital at 1583 Washington street, has accomplished a beneficent work since its establishment in 1869. It was founded, and has since been maintained, by the Protestant Episcopal Sisterhood of St. Margaret's, whose original foundation was in East Grimstead, England. Among the most prominent of its early supporters were Chandler Robbins, Dr. Francis H. Brown, Geo. H. Kuhn, Albert Fearing and N. H. Emmons. The building is a commodious structure, and capable of maintaining thirty patients at one time. Children are admitted between the ages of two and twelve years, except when suffering from contagious diseases, and are treated gratuitously or for a moderate fee according to the condition of their parents. The greatest care and skill are shown and the results are eminently satisfactory. The wisdom of isolating these diseases of childhood has been thoroughly proven, and the work not only well serves a great charitable purpose, but it has contributed much to the advancement of this branch of scientific medicine. A branch of this hospital, in the form of a Convalescent Home, was established in 1875, at Wellesley, about fourteen miles distant, and has aided vastly in the good work of the hospital.

The Massachusetts College of Pharmacy is another representative institution of the South End, but known everywhere. It was incorporated in 1852, among the first in the country, and has maintained its position since as a leader in this profession. Its stated aims are the regulation of the instruction of pharmacy, the diffusion of scientific information among the members of this profession, and the discountenancing the sale of spurious and adulterated drugs. All desiring to become members must have been actively engaged in the wholesale or retail drug trade. A School of Pharmacy, under the direction of the College, is in session during the winter, and instruction of the highest order by lectures, recitations and experimentation is given. The students who attend the whole course and pass the examinations receive the degree of Graduate in Pharmacy. The laboratory is one of the finest and most extensive in the city, and the institution is especially famed for its library which contains a very large and valuable collection of books and pamphlets. In connection with the library of the President, which is near by and open to the college, this collection is the second largest of its kind in the United States. There are about sixty-five members of the college, and about ninety students attending the school. This department is recognized as a leader throughout the drug trade of the country, and its diplomas are on a par with the highest, safe testimonials of knowledge and efficiency. It has been largely instrumental in placing pharmacy on the recognized basis of a profession which it is fast and well becoming in this country. In all departments of its activity the Massachusetts College of Pharmacy has been a most helpful and honored agent in the growth of the city and state, and has added much to the stability and reliance of its particular branch of business.

The Homœopathic Medical Dispensary is a noble institution, and has been long known and blessed by the people of the South End. It was incorporated in 1856 and treated 195 patients during the first year of its work, which number has been increased to thousands since then, so that it now dispenses in the neighborhood of 50,000 prescriptions to 15,000 patients annually. Its main office is at 14 Burroughs place, but it has a college branch in the Boston University Medical School building, where clinical instruction is afforded students as well as much charitable work done. This branch is divided into nine departments: medical, surgical, dental, eye and ear, children's, chest, throat, and skin, and as can be seen a vast and varied amount of work is done. The good it has afforded to the poor and needy of Boston, it would be impossible to estimate. This work has been largely supported by the receipts of a great fair held at Music Hall in 1859, which cleared a profit of $18,000, the income of which has been entirely devoted to the dispensary. The great increase of patients during the last decade or two has been attended by generous contributions and aid, so that this good work has not lagged for want of support, and will still continue to increase, so long as the people of the Hub retain their kindly hearts.

COLUMBUS AVENUE, COR. CLARENDON STREET,
LOOKING SOUTH.

The Scots' Charitable Society is another interesting organization which has long been located in the South End. It dates its incorporation back to 1786, but was founded over a century before, in 1657, being one of the oldest orders of any kind, and the oldest private charitable organization in the city. It therefore has much of interest from its antiquity, not to speak of its wide and benevolent work. Its main purpose has been to help and rescue in all possible ways, Scotch emigrants and descendants who might be in need, and it has been supported and engaged since the start with that warmth of patriotism and activity which characterizes the kindly people of Caledonia. St. Andrew's Home, where needy Scotch people might find a temporary home, was established in 1869, by this society, at 73 West Concord street. In 1872, the work was transferred to 77 Camden street, and the Scots' Temporary Home permanently established there, where it has since been maintained. Among other property owned by the society is a lot in Mount Auburn cemetery, where Scots without means are afforded a christian burial.   The membership is now about two hundred and fifty, and a large income is derived from a permanent fund formed by many legacies left in the past, the annual assessments of members, and bequests.   Although only natives of Scotland or their direct descendants can become active members, honorary membership is not restricted to nationality.   Between two and three hundred recipients are helped by the charity of this society every year, and its good work is unsurpassed for its extent and wisely applied efforts.   It is a good example of the spirit shown by the people in providing for the unfortunate, and has had many emulators.

There are several large street railroad lines running through the South End, some being marked "to the Neck," though all traces of its original narrow dimensions have disappeared.   Two large railroad lines, the Boston & Albany, and Boston & Providence pass through this district, while the immense and beautiful depots of these two and of the Old Colony Railroad are situated near the limits of the South End.   There has been much talk in recent years of establishing an elevated railroad here, and when this is carried out, several petitions having already been sent to the legislature, the South End will be largely interested and benefited therein.   Its streets being the straightest and most regular of any large district in the city, and being so largely the center of residences, the opening for an elevated railway is most advantageous, and it can hardly be more than a matter of a few years before this great modern improvement is introduced here.

The new English High and Latin School is one of the more recent buildings of the South End, and is the largest building devoted exclusively to educational purposes in this country, and the largest free public school in the world.   It was commenced in 1877 and was ready for occupancy in 1880.   The cost of construction was $700,000, and it is contemplated to further enlarge it in the future.   The length of the completed building will be four hundred and twenty feet, the part at present completed is three hundred and thirty-nine feet long by two hundred and twenty feet wide.   There are three high stories, and the exterior of Philadelphia brick with terra-cotta friezes, is after the modern renaissance style.   The building is fire-proof throughout, each of the school-rooms being surrounded by brick walls, thus constituting fire-proof sections.   The staircases are of iron, and of unusual width, proportioned mathematically to the capacity of accommodation of their respective parts of the building.   The plan of the structure is after the German style, that of a hollow square with surrounding corridors.   The school-rooms all front on the street, and on the inside face on a corridor, so that perfect light and ventilation are secured.   Throughout the sanitary regulations are of the most advanced type.   The school-rooms are forty-eight in number, each accommodating forty scholars.   In the center of the great interior court-yard, which is transected by long corridors, is a large "theatre building," containing two lecture halls, each with a seating capacity of two hundred and twenty-five, and also rooms for the cabinets and libraries of the two schools.   The English high school faces on Montgomery street, and the Latin school on Warren avenue.   On the south side of the quadrangle is situated the drill hall and gymnasium used by both schools, and a chemical laboratory is added in another detached building.   The drill-hall is magnificent and, in fact, unparalleled.   Situated on the ground floor, one hundred and thirty feet long by sixty feet wide, and thirty feet high, is admirably adapted for the purposes of exercise and display. It has four entrances, one each from Clarendon and Montgomery streets, Warren avenue and the corridor. The floor, which is calked and polished like a ship's deck, is of thick plank and based upon solid concrete. It not only accommodates the battalions of the whole school combined, but can also be used for mounted drill. With its gallery it is able to seat the exceedingly large number of three thousand persons. From this some idea of its size and arrangement can be derived. The gymnasium is of the same size as the drill-hall, and fully equipped with every modern appliance and device. It is safe to say that it is unparalleled in the public school history of this or any other country. Both of these grand halls are finished in the natural materials so as to give the appearance of open timber work, which is very attractive. The wood used is hard pine, shellacked and varnished, and the Philadelphia brick of the walls is trimmed with sandstone. The basement of this same building is to be fitted up as a play-room for the younger pupils. Bostonians may congratulate themselves, not only upon the great beauty and thorough utility of this structure, but also upon the fact that the architect, Mr. George A. Clough, whose ability and wide knowledge are everywhere seen through the work, is a native artist. In no department has the training which Boston has given her sons, been more visible in recent years than in that of architecture, as this and many other recent buildings conclusively testify. Such a model structure as this English high and Latin school is essentially Bostonian in its spirit and construction, testifying to the world of the unsurpassed position which the "Hub" has long sustained and is constantly advancing in its educational history.

The Girls' High School, situated on the corner of West Newton and Pembroke streets, is one of the finest public buildings and educational institutions in this center of learning. Its front is 444 feet, and depth 181 feet, within a fine lot 200 feet by 164 feet. The total cost of the building and land was $310,717, and there are accommodations for 1225 pupils. It is five stories in height, and contains sixty-six separate rooms, providing admirably for every department of the higher school instruction. The ventilation, heat and light are especially and thoroughly provided for, and one of its features is its use of electricity to connect every room with that of the principals by electric bells in addition to air tubes. There are several valuable scientific collections, and a museum of considerable size is here preserved. The large upper hall is handsomely adorned with sculpture-casts and statuary. An astronomical tower on the top of the building affords good opportunities for practical observations. The standard of scholarship and instruction is very high, ranking with the best in the city or in the world. The young ladies are fitted directly for the special work of the Normal School, or for entrance into Wellesley, Smith, Vassar, Harvard Annex, and other leading female colleges.

The Massachusetts Normal Art-School is another educational institution of which Boston and the State may indeed well be proud. It was established by the state in 1873 for the purpose of preparing teachers and masters of industrial drawing to superintend this department in the industrial and public schools of the state. The act of the legislature, passed in 1870, makes this instruction obligatory in the public

schools of the state.   The facilities enjoyed by the school are first class, and the results most praiseworthy.   The terms for students, who must be over sixteen, is for
residents of the state $20, tuition being free, and for non-residents a tuition of $100.

FRANKLIN SQUARE.

This beautiful Square is situated between Washington, James, East Brookline,
and Newton streets.   It contains several
acres of cultivated park, through which beautifully shaded walks are laid out, crossing
it in every direction.   The center is adorned with a fountain.   The popular New
England Conservatory of Music, described on page 90, fronts on this park.   On the
opposite side of Washington street is Blackstone Square, another park of the same
size, and laid out in similar style to Franklin square.

As the Back-Bay represents the very richest part of our national population, so the
South End represents the great middle class of moderately wealthy and well-to-do
people which has formed the back-bone of this country, of England, and of all great
governments of modern times.   Never was there a class of people more rich in resources, more independent, stable and moral in character, and more progressive than
this great middle class by whom and upon whom the fortunes of this country have
been built up.   Being human, they have not been without their faults, but these are

lost to sight in their many virtues. In this respect the South End, as being the center and the home of this great class, has been, and is, and will be, until the tide of business has swept over it completely, the heart of the city. Although not possessing many features which beautify and adorn other regions, no part of the city possesses more of interest or value for the present or future historian. Here still live the quiet, sensible reliable people who most preserve and practice the strong virtues of our ancestors; from whose midst have sprung our greatest men, and who undoubtedly possess an education of culture and refinement which no collection of people in

Rear View of the Conservatory from Washington St.

the world's history have far surpassed. The great literary leaders, orators, statesmen and public men of our country have come almost entirely from this class, and they have been advancing themselves until they now thoroughly represent, though there of course is difference of opinion here, the "salt," the "remnant" of the nation as Matthew Arnold calls it. So long as in Boston and in this country, this great class continues to exist, forming a healthy and safe medium between the very rich and the very poor, so long may we have confidence that the institutions and ideas of our free government are destined to prevail, but with their extinction, which some dismal prophets are already predicting, perish indubitably the great principles which our country has represented. It is not the least important part of a study of life at the South End, that it clearly shows the yet vigorous character and stability of this part of our people who are chiefly represented here. The influences which are tending to lessen their number and impair their power are not more numerous or strong than the forces they themselves have inaugurated, and which ensure for them yet a long and great prosperity. The power of the liberal education, the strength of religious purpose and principle, the energy of sound moral character and wide culture, and the surety of abundant material resources which the work of past generations have secured, all these are fully and satisfactorily demonstrated in the life of the people of the South End.

Special points and institutions have been already described, but there are some general considerations apart and arising from these which furnish light on this interesting region, and are not without broad application and value. Boston has long been famed for its intellectual supremacy, and the center of this influence seems to be in the South End. Its highest and best schools are situated here; from this region come the majority of its best scholars, and though great institutions like the Public Library and Art Museum are situated just beyond its limits, from this region come the larger part of those who employ and enjoy their privileges. On its surface, the life in the South End is not so attractive as that of some other parts of the city, being somewhat lacking in "glare and glitter," in fact being thoroughly "Bostonian," but underneath are its rich pleasures and privileges. The intellectual life is broad and intensely active. In connection with the churches and numerous literary and other societies, the amount of study and intellectual work done is very large. Other places of a different turn of mind, sometimes wonder and even laugh at the "Browning Societies," and other intellectual movements of Boston, which have their center of origin in the South End. But in reality these represent a great fact and power. It is the evolution of the mind of New England working itself out in the environment and competition of city activity, and gaining new power and advancement from the accumulative force of numbers. When we remember the great importance that the results of such movements now possess in our national literature and life, we cannot but hope they will continue and increase, knowing thereby that the intellectual heritage of our country, its contributions to the literature, scientific knowledge, arts and industries of the human race will be vastly increased.

The social life of the South End, though quiet in tone and somewhat, yes, largely affected by the "pale cast of thought," is yet active, widely enjoyed and profitable to an unusual extent. Reason here is not entirely set aside by fashion, and consequently the enjoyment is increased while the expenditure of health and other resources is lessened. Simpler fashions and earlier hours than are often the case in "fashionable society" prevail, and the large number of old Boston families of quiet tastes here find most of congeniality and social enjoyment. One great feature of social life is that it not only is enjoyable but helpful, either in the way of intellectual advancement, or in that of charity. The charitable tendencies of the people of the South End have already been well shown by their numerous practical results. The many churches are all actively engaged in this work, and the avenues through which their efforts flow forth in all directions through the city to bless and uplift its people are too numerous and varied to admit of specification.   A glance over the list of institutions given above will serve to show the extent and activity of direct charitable endeavors in the South End.   Wide and great as these are, they by no means represent all of this work which is far too broad, and much of it too quiet and unobtrusive to be known to the public. If Boston is intellectual she is not cold, as her increasing and hearty endeavors to aid all suffering and need amply show.   While all parts of the city share in this work, a considerable part of it is carried on and supported at the South End.

TREMONT STREET, COR. DEDHAM STREET,
LOOKING SOUTH.

The religious life is one of the great features of South End existence, the large number of churches making it peculiarly the center of these spiritual interests, and the activity of the churches being even more remarkable than their size.   A glimpse of the old Puritan life which is far from unpleasant in these materialistic days, seems to remain in the tendency of church people here to carry religious life and work into every department of activity and thought.   The intellectual movements of New England and Boston, have been vitally connected with the churches and a study of those in the South End will soon show the reason of this.   Many of the pastors and members of these churches are leaders in the world of thought in this country, and not only does this tend to make the churches of all denominations unusually liberal and charitable to others, but makes them practical, more interested in good work, and in christianity applied to conduct and every day life.   The leaders in this work are men of rare ability and energy, and the dwellers in the South End who are interested in its moral as well as material welfare, cannot be too thankful that the work left by the fathers has fallen into such worthy hands.

The growth of business interests in the South End has been most significant and now presents questions of vital importance which any study of the South End is sure to find at the very start as well as at the end, having a critical bearing on the future of the district. The tide of business has been sweeping steadily forward up the main thoroughfares of the South End, and spreading out gradually into the side streets. To entirely swallow up the South End and transform it from a district of residences to one of stores must be a work of many decades at least. Whether it will ever be entirely accomplished yet remains to be shown. That it cannot help but affect in large measure the quiet life of the people who have long made the South End their home, and through them the city, is evident. That the same thoughtful care which has marked the growth of the city in the past will still attend it, affords no small ground of hope that this growth will tend to the yet greater prosperity of the South End, and the upbuilding of the dear old city of which it forms so integral and helpful a part.

LEADING BUSINESS MEN

SOUTH END.

EDWIN P. FOSS, Auctioneer and Dealer in Real Estate and Mortgages, 3 Berkeley St., Cor. Tremont. As an evidence of what can be accomplished by energy and perseverance we would refer to the business conducted by Mr. Edwin P. Foss, whose present office is located at 3 Berkeley Street, corner Tremont. This gentleman, who is a native of Strafford, N. H., came to Boston in 1870, at the age of fifteen, and entered Comer's Commercial College. On graduating from that institution his entire capital consisted of three dollars and twenty-three and one-half cents(which, by the way, Mr. Foss still carries with him as a remembrance of boyhood days). In 1878 he embarked in the Real Estate and Auction business on Washington Street. Owing to the rapid increase of trade, and for the purpose of being nearer to his large number of tenants and customers, he leased the present building, corner Tremont and Berkeley Streets, and remodeled it to suit his business; removing there in January, 1883. This is a very central location, fronting four thoroughfares and accessible by horse-cars to all parts of the city, and with his extensive knowledge of the Real Estate Business, he feels competent to satisfactorily transact any business entrusted to his care. He has now over three hundred tenants in this vicinity, which is a sufficient guarantee that his facilities for taking charge of Real Estate are satisfactory to both landlord and tenant. Mr. Foss has already built up a very large business, and is able to lend material assistance to anyone seeking to buy, sell, exchange or hire Real Estate of any description. Mr. Foss was the originator and is one of the directors of the "One Hundred Associates," a stock company formed for the purpose of purchasing and improving Real Estate, Loaning Money and other investments. He has charge of all the Real Estate of the "Eleven Associates." Also auction sales of Real and Personal Estate held in any part of Mass. where property is located; Real Estate bought, sold and exchanged; Titles to Real Estate examined; Deeds, Leases, Wills, Bills of Sale, and all Legal Documents drawn; Buildings remodeled and repaired; Estimates furnished and contracts solicited; Houses, Stores, Tenements and Buildings rented; Rents, Notes, Bills and Interest collected; Money to Loan secured by Mortgage at four, four and one-half and five per cent interest; Fire Insurance placed in the most reliable companies; all business transacted pertaining to a General Real Estate and Office Business. Justice of the Peace and Notary Public, office hours, 9 A.M. to 9 P.M. You are respectfully referred to the following Real Estate owners in this vicinity:—C. Brigham & Co., 386 Tremont Street; Frank E. Maguillon, 496 Tremont Street; Benj. T. Baker, 538 Tremont Street; William Timlin, 53 Warren Avenue; J. H. Lynch, 25 Franklin Street; J. Lee Frost, 109 Boylston Street; J. F. Johnson, 256 Shawmut Avenue; P. H. Sheehan, 53 Harvard Street; H. S. Libby, 202 Shawmut Avenue, and many others.

3

S. A. D. Sheppard & Co., Pharmacists, Washington, Corner Dover Street, also branch store cor. Union Park. It is now generally agreed among physicians, that faith and confidence exert a very powerful influence in assisting nature to throw off disease, and this being the case, it will be readily seen that it is of the the utmost importance for the patient to have confidence, not only in his physician, but also in the medicines or other remedial agents which he may prescribe. It is known to everybody nowadays, that the virtues of drugs are influenced to some degree by their freshness, as well as by the manner in which they are kept and therefore it is not surprising that those who are familiar with the methods in vogue in the establishment carried on by Messrs. S. A. D. Sheppard & Co., at the corner of Dover & Washington Streets, should place a reliance upon goods coming from there, that could not be felt unless there was a positive surety of careful and skilful handling. The Pharmacy in question, is without doubt, one of the most celebrated as well as one of the most reliable in the city, and there is no man better known or more highly respected in the Drug trade, than the principal owner, Mr. S. A. D. Sheppard. This gentleman is a native of Manchester-by-the-sea, and has been connected with the enterprise to which we have reference since 1868, the business being originally founded in 1853 under the firm name of McGowan & Co. The premises occupied are 25 x 70 feet in dimensions and comprise one floor and a basement. A large stock is carried of Fancy and Toilet articles, Cigars, Perfumery, etc., and an extensive business is done in this line, but for all that, it is never forgotten that this is first and last a Pharmacy, and nothing is allowed to interfere with the prompt and satisfactory accommodation of customers in this department. There are ten courteous and well-informed assistants employed and physician's prescriptions are compounded with the greatest care, every modern facility being provided for the carrying on of this work. The charges made are always fair and moderate and an immense business is done. This firm has also a branch store at the corner of Washington Street and Union Park.

Chas. E. S. MacCorry, Wholesale and Retail Dealer in Provisions and Produce, 549 Tremont Street, Corner Hanson. Boston is attaining so wide and so high a reputation as a desirable place of residence for men of means, that this class of its population is rapidly and steadily increasing, and as this volume will doubtless circulate extensively among those coming within this category, who are strangers to the "Hub" and its "institutions," we are happy to take advantage of the opportunity thus offered to call attention to an establishment which is exceptionally well prepared to cater to the very highest class of trade. We refer to that conducted by Mr. Chas. E. S. MacCorry at No. 549 Tremont Street, Corner Hanson, and feel confident that under its present excellent and liberal management, it only needs a proper trial to convince all that what we may say regarding it is fully warranted and sustained by the facts. This popular enterprise was inaugurated in 1852 by Messrs. Moli-

neux & Bullard, who carried it on for ten years, being succeeded in 1872 by Messrs. Bullard & MacCorry, which firm gave place to the present proprietor in 1879, who has a thorough and intimate acquaintance with the Provision business that enables him to serve his patrons with unusual intelligence, as well as fidelity. One floor and a basement are occupied, of the dimensions of 20 x 45 feet, and employment is given to five efficient assistants. Customers are assured prompt service and, it should be added, polite service too, for Mr. MacCorry insists on the strict observance of the courtesy too often lacking in city establishments. A very finely selected and varied stock is carried, and although every effort is made to furnish goods that will suit the most fastidious, the prices are reasonable and just. A telephone connection is maintained, and orders received in this way are assured accurate and prompt delivery.

Eugene B. Nelson, Grocer, and Dealer in Foreign and Domestic Fruits, 633 Tremont Street. Those familiar with the origin and development of the enterprise conducted by Mr. Eugene B. Nelson at No. 633 Tremont Street, need no better example of what may be accomplished by energy, pluck and perseverance. Nearly a score of years ago, a grocery store was opened on Harrison Avenue, a few doors from East Canton Street, under the firm name of H. H. Nelson & Co. The neighborhood was not a wealthy one by any means and such establishments as had previously been inaugurated in the vicinity had apparently been more successful in accumulating dirt than dollars. But not so the new one. Three brothers carried it on and as none of them was afraid to work and all of them believed in neatness and order the store became known as an attractive, even if small establishment. Trade steadily increased, reliable goods at low prices had their usual effect and in a few years a thriving business was built up. In course of time it became necessary to seek larger quarters and a spacious store on the corner of East Brookline Street and Harrison Avenue was fitted up and occupied, under the firm name of H. H. & E. B. Nelson. Continued prosperity was enjoyed but finally the changes which have come to pass at the South End within the last dozen years and which are too well known to require detailed mention here caused a removal to be had to the present store No. 633 Tremont Street. For some time past Mr. Eugene B. Nelson has been the sole proprietor of the business and his long and exceptional experience enables him to carry it on in a most satisfactory manner. He is a native of Hillsborough, New Hampshire and during his mercantile career has gained a large circle of friends in this city. One floor and a basement are occupied, measuring 18 x 80 feet and an immense assortment of fine groceries is carried including Teas, Coffee, Butter, Cheese, Flour, Foreign & Domestic Fruits, fresh, dry and preserved. Employment is afforded to four efficient assistants and as goods are sold at low rates, delivered promptly and guaranteed as to quality, it naturally follows that a very large business is done.

James H. Hayes, Plumber, Sanitary Drainage and Ventilation. Removed to Tremont and Camden Street. Gas Fitting. Globes, Burners and Fixtures, 703 Tremont Street, Boston. Residence, 66 Kendall Street. Particular attention given to House Drainage and Water Service. So much has been said and written of late years regarding the importance of perfect drainage, particularly in large cities, that it is safe to assert that no person of ordinary intelligence can fail to appreciate to some degree at least the great influence which drainage has upon the health of individuals and of the community at large. It is now conceded that something more than bolts and bars is required to keep enemies out of our homes especially at night for although thieves and burglars may be provided for by this means, there is a still more dangerous and insidious foe that laughs at such precautions and that attacks not the property but the very lives of the inmates of the house it enters. Need we say that this deadly foe is sewer-gas? But modern science has provided a sure means to keep even this enemy at bay and those who knowingly dispense with the precautions plainly suggested by everyday experience are, to speak without reserve, simply trifling with their own lives and those of the other members of their family. A call on Mr. James H. Hayes at his store No. 703 Tremont Street corner of Camden, will result in the visitor's being impressed with the knowledge of drainage etc., displayed by this gentleman if the conversation be brought around to that subject for Mr. Hayes is a practical plumber as he has worked at the business since 1867. Starting in business for himself in 1876 he thus adds experience to natural ability. He is prepared to undertake anything in the line of Plumbing, Sanitary Drainage and Ventilation, making a specialty of House Drainage and Water Service. Employment is given to ten skilled hands and jobbing of all kinds will be given prompt and satisfactory attention. Mr. Hayes does uniformly first-class work and his charges are very moderate for the character of the service rendered.

A. N. Upham, Dealer in Choice Family Groceries, 705 Tremont Street, Cor. Rutland Square; Summer Store near Steamboat Wharf, Hull, Mass. There has been such a decided increase in the number of what may be called fancy groceries in the market of late years, such for instance as canned goods, prepared foods and cereals etc., that it is necessary for a grocer to carry a much more varied stock than was formerly the case if he wishes to be prepared to meet all the wants of his patrons, and it is largely owing to the liberality shown in this respect that the establishment carried on by Mr. A. N. Upham at No. 705 Tremont Street, has gained so high a position in the favor of the public. This undertaking was originated by Mr. A. N. Webb several years ago, succeeded by Mr. C. O. Carter in 1831, and was carried on by him up to 1886, when the present proprietor came into possession. He was born in Connecticut and is a member of the Free Masons, Knights of Pythias and Royal Arcanum, having a large circle of friends in this community. The premises utilized include one floor and a basement, and are of the dimensions of 20 x 60 feet, a very heavy stock being carried and employment given to four courteous and skilled assistants. Butter, Cheese, Eggs, Hams etc., are handled very largely, and a specialty is made of fine Dairy and Creamery Butter, this commodity being sold at the lowest rates and warranted to prove as represented. In addition to the establishment mentioned, Mr. Upham conducts a summer store, at Hull, Mass., near the steamboat wharf, and the same honorable and enterprising methods are employed there as have gained him success in his city undertaking.

Chas. A. Bartlett, Apothecary, 507 Tremont, cor. Berkeley Street. One of the finest-appointed and most liberally managed Apothecary stores to be found in the entire city, is that carried on by Mr. Chas. A. Bartlett at the corner of Berkeley and Tremont Streets, numbered 507 on the latter thoroughfare. As many of our readers know, this establishment is located in the elegant Odd Fellows' building, and certainly it would be hard to improve its situation for it is both conspicuous and central and well adapted to subserve the convenience of both Back Bay and South End patrons. Under these circumstances (taken in conjunction with the fact that Mr. Bartlett has the well-earned reputation of being one of the most skillful pharmacists in the city) it is not to be wondered at that a very large amount of business is done, and what is even more indicative of prosperity is the fact that the patronage shows a rapid and steady increase. Mr. Bartlett is a native of Maine, and assumed control of the enterprise in question in 1886. He is a member of the Odd Fellows and is one of the best-known of our city pharmacists. His store is not only a handsome but a spacious one, for it measures 25 x 60 feet and a large basement is utilized in connection with it. Employing three courteous and efficient assistants and carrying one of the most thoroughly complete assortments of choice drugs, medicines and chemicals to be found within the precincts of the "Hub," Mr. Bartlett is most admirably prepared to guarantee satisfaction as regards the filling of prescriptions, etc., and to give all orders of the kind prompt and skillful attention. His prices are reasonable and the utmost care is exercised in the compounding of every prescription.

C. C. Chaplin's Family Shoe Store, 1085 Washington Street, Under Commonwealth Hotel. To so conduct a "Family Shoe Store" as to make it worthy of the name, is no light task for any man, however able or experienced, for the average family consumes all kinds and sizes of foot-wear, from the tiny slippers of the wee toddler to the heavy boots of its proud father. Between these extremes we have a variety too numerous to mention, comprising school shoes for boys and girls, finer goods for youths and misses, street and home boots for mothers and their "grown up" daughters, and last but not least, those natty but perhaps rather cramped shoes, the inconveniences of which are borne without a murmur by the young gentleman who puts them on preparatory to calling on her whose smile is more to him than any mere bodily comfort. Just such a store, however, is conducted by Mr. C. C. Chaplin at No. 1685 Washington Street, under the Commonwealth Hotel, and it is only natural that since he began operations here, in 1880, he should have built up a large trade, for his stock is large, his goods reliable, his assistants courteous and his prices low; and if anybody wants more than this, the chances are that they will have to seek it in a country as yet unknown. Mr. Chaplin was born in Maine, and was a member of the original firm of Chaplin & Son in South Boston, and later he carried on an establishment in Brookline for ten years, removing to his present store in 1886. He knows good shoes when he sees them, and if his customers have not the same facility, it is no fault of his, for he deals in no other goods, and sells nothing he is not able to warrant in every respect. His prices are positively as low as can be fixed on reliable articles, and his stock is so complete that the most difficult foot can be perfectly fitted.

Geo. W. Blake. Apothecary, Successor to Gordon and Hinkley, 531 Columbus Avenue, Corner Worcester Street. Enterprise is an excellent thing, so is courtesy, so is ability to forecast the probable future — all of these things are most admirable qualities in a business man, but after all, in such an undertaking as that carried on by the druggist, the main essential is reliability. All of us like to be served promptly, politely and intelligently; but, in the purchase of medicines at least, in the compounding of prescriptions more especially — what we like better than anything else, is to feel that these medicines are being sold to us, or these prescriptions being put up by a man who not only thoroughly understands his business, but who may be absolutely depended on to do all in his power to guard against the slightest mistake of any kind. Taking these facts into consideration, it is not difficult to form an intelligent idea of the reasons why the establishment of which Mr. Geo. W. Blake is the proprietor, located at No. 531 Columbus Avenue, should have attained the popularity it undoubtedly enjoys. The enterprise in question was founded by Messrs. Gordon and Hinkley, but has been under Mr. Blake's control for quite an extended period. He is a native of Boston and a member of the Odd Fellows, and cannot but feel gratified at the confidence placed in him by the public, as it has been fairly earned by faithful and continuous service. One floor and a basement are occupied, 20 x 45 feet in size, and a large and complete stock of Drugs, Medicines, Chemicals, etc., is always carried. Prescriptions are filled at very short notice, and the use of the choicest ingredients and the employment of the greatest care in their compounding, assure satisfactory results.

Buerkel & Co., Steam Fitters, Plumbers, and Gas Fitters, No. 28 Union Park Street, Corner of Washington Street. Although steam is without a doubt the most efficient and economical heating agent known at the present day, still the general introduction of steam heating apparatus has been greatly hindered by the incompetency of some of those making a business

of putting it up; for not only its economy, but also its safety is largely dependent upon the manner in which this is done. A well constructed and well adjusted steam-heating plant combines a maximum of heating power with a minimum of danger, and when put in position by skilled hands, accident from its use is practically impossible. Thus it will be seen that it is of great importance to entrust such work only to some reputable and responsible house, and there is none more sure to give perfect satisfaction than that of Buerkel & Co., doing business at No. 28 Union Park Street, corner of Washington. This concern was founded in 1873, and during the past ten years has fitted up many manufactories, workshops, and private dwellings with heating facilities at low prices and with such thoroughness and skill as to have attained an unsurpassed reputation. The Star House Heating Boiler is handled by this firm, who are also agents for the celebrated "Johnson Railway Heater." Both parties are natives of Boston, the concern being made up of Messrs. J. F. Buerkel and S. E. Bentley, the former residing at No. 1403 Washington Street, and the latter at No. 24 Union Park. Employment is afforded to twenty skilled mechanics, and a well appointed machine shop supplied with ample steam power is run in connection with the enterprise. Steam-fitting, Plumbing and Gas-fitting of all descriptions will be done at short notice, and estimates submitted or contracts entered into for the performance of any job, large or small, in these lines.

Charles B. Lovell, Ladies' and Gents' Furnishing Goods, 1939 Washington Street, cor. Derby Place. As a general thing it is much easier to get what you want in an establishment devoted to the sale of certain lines of goods, than it is in a store containing about everything from a paper of pins to a three-volume novel, and should any of our readers desire anything in the line of Furnishing Goods, they would do well to make a call at No. 1939 Washington Street, corner of Derby Place, as there they would find Mr. Charles B. Lovell who makes a specialty of Ladies' and Gents' Furnishings of all descriptions. One floor and a basement are occupied, of the dimensions of 20x35 feet and the assortment of goods in stock is so complete and varied as to seem to render it a certainty that everybody could find just what they wanted therein. Certainly no objections can be raised to the prices quoted, for Mr. Lovell makes it a point to sell as low as anybody, quality for quality, and he is a sufficiently experienced and careful buyer to enable him to purchase goods at the best possible advantage. Employment is afforded to two courteous assistants and customers are promised both prompt and respectful attention. Mr. Lovell was born in Boston and as a member of Company K, 35th Massachusetts, he took part in some of the most memorable and decisive engagements of the Rebellion, Antietam, Fredericksburg, Vicksburg — each of these famous fields he was present at and passed through experiences of a kind that are never forgotten. He is a member of the Grand Army and has many friends in this city and vicinity.

J. E. Gillett, Dry and Fancy Goods, 37 Clarendon St. Although Mr. J. E. Gillett, of No. 37 Clarendon Street, does not pretend to rival Jordan, Marsh & Co., or R. H. White & Co., in the magnitude and variety of his stock, still there are certain points in which he might well be imitated by both those mammoth enterprises. One of the most important of these is promptness of service. All Boston shoppers know from sad experience what it is to make their way through a struggling crowd to some counter in an immense store, only to be told that the "department" of which they are in search is somewhere in the vicinity of a half-mile or so farther along, and finally after having by persistent exertion reached the spot pointed out, had to wait anywhere from five minutes to half an hour before they transacted their business and received the goods. Who, familiar with the facts, will call that a fancy sketch? On the contrary, one may enter Mr. Gillett's store, select his goods, pay for them and be on the street again in less time than the first operation could be gone through with, such as is described above. When hunting for "bargains," don't forget that "time is money," and few of us can afford to waste it. Mr. Gillett opened his present establishment in 1887. He is a native of Boston and a member of the Odd Fellows, and has a very thorough acquaintance with the various goods he handles. One floor and a basement are occupied, and a finely-selected stock of Dry and Fancy Goods is open for inspection. This is a popular Laundry Agency, and work of this kind is done in the best manner and at short notice.

Chas. L. Dakin, Fine Art Store, Dealer in Artists' Materials, Engravings, Etchings and Photographs, 578 Tremont Street. There is nothing that will lend such a homelike and refined effect to an apartment as a well-executed Engraving, Etching, Autotype, or Photograph, and it is well known that the most elegantly furnished room seems incomplete and comparatively bare unless a few pictures adorn its walls. Of course a person of taste if forced to choose between a cheap chromo and nothing at all would prefer the latter, but in point of fact no such choice is necessary even to people in very moderate circumstances, for truly artistic pictures are sold nowadays at prices within the reach of all, and it is easy enough to find such if the right establishment be visited. A favorite store with the most careful buyers of art goods and pictures, is that carried on by Mr. Chas. L. Dakin at No. 578 Tremont Street, and this popularity has been won by the policy this gentleman pursues of "quick sales and small profits." He is a believer in the foregoing maxim and therefore ensures the constant renewal of his stock by offering the same at absolutely bottom rates. No sacrifice of quality is made, however, and purchasers may feel perfectly assured that everything sold by Mr. Dakin will prove just as represented. He is a native of Bangor Me., and started his present business in 1885. Two competent assistants are employed and Fine Art goods of many descriptions carried in great profusion. Artistic Framing is made a specialty and is done at short notice at considerably below the average rates.

Dr. Willard D. Ball, Dentist, 674½ Tremont Street, Entrance on West Newton Street. Although there is doubtless a very large number of Dentists in this city, still there are none too many good ones, for unfortunately the teeth of the Americans of this generation are principally conspicuous by their badness. We have not the space, even if we had the ability, to enter on any discussion as to what has brought this condition of affairs, about for there are almost as many theories on the subject as there are dentists and whether our teeth have been ruined by abuse, "starved" for lack of proper food, or are congenitally imperfect, it remains a fact that as a rule they are simply vile. Speaking of good dentists calls to mind Dr. Willard D. Ball of No. 674½ Tremont Street, for it is the unanimous opinion, so far as we have been able to learn, of those who have tested his skill that he combines gentleness with decision and firmness with careful avoidance of all unnecessary pain having unrivaled facilities for the administration of ether when extracting. Dr. Ball is a native of Walpole, N. H., and opened his present office in 1870. He occupies two conveniently located and well-equipped rooms at the address given above, entrance being had from West Newton Street. His office hours are from 9 a. m. to 4 p. m. and appointments made in advance will prove mutually advantageous as the doctor's practice is a very extensive one and his time is apt to be fully occupied. Every appliance and instrument called for by modern operative dentistry are at hand and thoroughness as well as gentleness characterizes all the work done.

M. A. Hatch, Manufacturer of fine Confectionery and Ice Cream Wholesale and Retail, No. 605 Tremont Street. We have not the figures at hand to give the exact annual production of confectionery in the city of Boston but it must reach a very imposing amount, for there are many manufacturers located here and the great majority of them seem to be prosperous and thriving. Among those whose confections hold an especially high place, Mr. M. A. Hatch deserves prominent mention, for since he inaugurated his business in 1882 he has steadily added to his reputation until now it ranks above that of many more pretentious houses. Mr. Hatch is a native of Maine and has won his success by strict and intelligent attention to business and making it a point to let no goods leave his premises which he could not fully warrant in every respect. Confectionery is handled both at wholesale and retail and is supplied at the lowest market rates in quantities to suit. Employment is afforded to three skilled assistants and orders are filled without delay and with entirely fresh and desirable goods. The advantages of purchasing direct from the manufacturers are sufficiently obvious in any business but particularly so as regards confectionery, for this commodity owes a great part of its value to its freshness and purity. In addition to his large trade in Confectionery Mr. Hatch makes a specialty of *Extra fine* Ice Cream, which he guarantees to be unexcelled in purity. This is delivered at residences, at short notice. Orders for Sunday delivery taken. Special terms for Church Fairs, Festivals and other large orders.

F. M. Learned, Real Estate and Insurance Agent, 674½ Tremont, corner West Newton Street, Mercantile Library Association Building (basement). The name of Learned is very familiar to those conversant with real-estate matters in this city and particularly so to those who have given special attention to transactions of this nature at the South End. Mr. F. H. Learned began operations in this line in the year 1864, and in 1878 was succeeded by Mr. F. M. Learned who added insurance to his business in 1881. This gentleman is a native of Boston and is very prominent in Fraternal Society circles being connected with the Free Masons, Odd Fellows, Knights of Pythias and Red Men. His office is located in the basement of the Mercantile Library Association Building, corner of Tremont and West Newton streets, and no one desiring to buy, sell, exchange, rent or lease real estate should neglect giving him a call as the chances are that a mutually advantageous arrangement could be consummated. Particular attention is paid to the handling of South End real estate and as Mr. Learned is universally conceded to be an authority on this subject, his advice regarding it will be found sound and profitable to follow. He has at all times desirable houses for either large or small families and also has the letting of many stores of various sizes and adapted to all kinds of business. In the matter of Insurance he is also prepared to furnish first-class and strictly reliable accommodations as he conducts a branch office of the New York Bowery Fire Insurance Co., of New York city, and also of the Phœnix Assurance Co., of London, England. This latter company was established in 1782 while the former was incorporated in 1843 and both of them are known throughout the country as reliable and liberally conducted organizations. Mr. Learned is in a position to write policies in either company at bottom rates and his facilities in this respect are well worthy of being taken advantage of.

W. F. Goldthwait & Co., Manufacturers of and Dealers in Furniture, Draperies, Window Shades and Upholstery Goods, No. 1294 Washington Street. That every man should have a home of his own, and not be content with bachelor life, or with a boarding house existence if he be married, is a rule that is only proved by the very exceptions that can be made to it, and anything that tends to make housekeeping more pleasant and popular and to put it within the reach of more people, is a genuine boon to the community, and hence worthy of prominent mention. To keep house one must have furniture and house-furnishing goods in general, and as the firm of W. F. Goldthwait & Co. is prepared to supply such articles at bottom prices, it may be said to be rendering efficient aid in the bringing about of the happy time when domestic life will be much more common than it now is. Commodious quarters are occupied, and employment is afforded to several courteous assistants, Furniture, Draperies, Window Shades and Upholstery Goods being very extensively dealt in. Although striving to quote bottom prices on the commodities handled, the firm take pains to avoid supplying unsatisfactory articles of any kind, and fully warrant that whatever they sell will prove just as represented. Owing to the steady continuance of such fair and square business methods, this house has attained a high position in the confidence of the public, and every effort will be made in the future to assure the steady maintenance of this good feeling. Many of the articles on sale are manufactured by the firm, and it is largely owing to this fact that they are able to offer the many pronounced bargains for which their establishment is noted.

S. Severy, Florist, 534 Tremont Street, and **L. F. Severy**, Boston & Providence Depot, have constantly on hand a large and choice assortment of Cut Flowers. The Florist fills so important and even indispensable a position nowadays, in the large cities at least, that all information regarding this subject must prove of wide interest, and more especially is this true when such information refers to one who announces prices lower by twenty per cent than those of any other Florist in Boston. The gentleman who makes this liberal and enterprising offer is Mr. S. Severy, of No. 434 Tremont Street, who, in connection with L. F. Severy, also carries on business at the Boston & Providence Depot, and who has built up a very extensive trade since the inception of his undertaking in 1876. Mr. Severy was born in the Pine Tree state, and is a member of the Legion of Honor, having a wide circle of friends that is steadily increasing, while Mr. L. F. Severy is a native of Melrose, Mass. A very large and choice assortment of Cut Flowers is kept constantly on hand, and Flowers suitable for use at either Parties, Weddings or Funerals are supplied in any desired quantity. The Messrs. Severy have gained an exceptionally high reputation for the taste shown in the arranging of Artistic Decorations of all kinds, and those who may wish to procure a tribute of this description for an occasion of either joy or sorrow and who distrust their own taste in such matters, may safely leave the selection of the emblem to these gentlemen, as they are admirably fitted both by experience and natural gifts to be authorities on such subjects. Choice Roses, Pinks and Violets are always in stock, and fine specimens for artists' use can be furnished at all times. Orders by express, mail or telegraph will be promptly filled with the same care as though given in person, and orders will be taken Saturday for Sunday delivery, the store being open Saturday evening until 10.30, and other evenings until 9.30. As before remarked, Messrs. Severy's prices are remarkably low, and their flowers are unexcelled for freshness. In addition to their large trade in flowers, Messrs. Severy are also proprietors of the Great Lung and Cough Remedy, Dr. Kanolah's Indian Vegetable Pulmonary Syrup, made of roots and herbs; a sure cure for coughs, colds, bronchitis, whooping-cough, asthma, croup, spitting blood, pain in the side, night sweats, humors, general debility, throat affections to which public speakers are liable, and all complaints leading to consumption. Price 50 cents and $1.00 per bottle. For sale by all druggists.

C. A. Ochs & Co., Stationers; Commonwealth Circulating Library; 1605 Washington Street. That there is abundant patronage at the South End for a fashionable Stationery and Periodical Store that is conducted as such an establishment should be, is amply proved by the experience of Messrs. C. A. Ochs & Co., since they inaugurated their present enterprise in 1897, for the liberal methods and wide knowledge of the business that this house has displayed, have been rewarded by the prompt appreciation and generous support of the residents of the vicinity. The premises utilized are of the dimensions of 20 x 90 feet, and include one floor and a basement, there being carried a very extensive and varied stock of Stationery, comprising the Latest Fashionable Novelties, as well as Standard Goods of every description. A well-selected Circulating Library is also maintained, and the latest works of Fiction, etc., are at once secured, it being the aim of the proprietors to afford their customers the opportunity to become conversant with the most popular Novels at a merely nominal expense. School Goods are dealt in very largely, and "Scholars' Companions" and all similar devices that cost so little, but mean so much to the childish heart, are at hand in many styles and suited to widely diverse tastes. Newspapers, Periodicals, etc., are dealt in very extensively, and subscriptions will be received here for all the leading serial publications. Papers are also delivered at residences. A fine stock of Artists' Materials is carried, also upwards of forty different styles of mouldings; and orders for every description of picture frames promptly filled at very reasonable prices. Patrons are assured prompt and polite attention, and all needful assistance will be cheerfully lent in the choosing of Books, or any other act in which the benefit of the firm's experience is desired.

James F. Rice, Dealer in Provisions, Fruits and Vegetables, 1600 Washington Street. The enterprise conducted by Mr. James F. Rice was founded over thirty years ago, and there is no Provision store at the South End that is better known, or that has a higher reputation, than that carried on by the gentleman mentioned. The premises occupied comprise one floor and a basement, of the dimensions of 20 x 45 feet, and contain a very large and varied stock of Provisions, Fruits and Vegetables. Mr. Rice is a native of Lincoln, Mass., and owing to his long and honorable business career, is one of the most widely known and esteemed men in the trade. His experience is of course of great value to him in directing the details of his establishment, and his customers know that his stock is sure to contain as fine a variety of the goods handled as the market will allow. Beef, Pork, Mutton, Lamb and Veal are always on hand, and Smoked and Salted Meats are also largely dealt in. Mr. Rice offers special inducements to those who appreciate Hams of fine and delicate flavor, for he handles the choicest of such goods and quotes very moderate prices on them. Foreign and Domestic Fruits and every kind of Vegetable in its season are also to be had at this store, and the employment of three polite and efficient assistants furnishes assurance that callers will be promptly served and orders delivered without delay.

Edward K. Smith, Pharmacist, 207 Warren Avenue, Corner Columbus Square. That there is a varying degree of responsibility attached to recommending different business enterprises, must be apparent to any one who will give the matter a moment's thought, for it is obvious that whereas a man might patronize a grocery store that had been unduly eulogized, without any special loss, except perhaps to his pocket, when it comes to the buying of Drugs and Medicines, confidence placed in an establishment that is unworthy of it, may result in sickness or something even more serious. Therefore it is only because we feel sure of our ground that we cordially commend to the patronage of our readers the enterprise conducted by Mr. Edward K. Smith at No. 207 Warren Avenue, corner of Columbus Square, for this gentleman carries on a retail Pharmacy at that point and gives particular attention to the compounding of physicians' prescriptions. Mr. Smith was born in North Adams, Mass., and has had an experience of fifteen years in his chosen business, although he has carried on his present establishment only since 1896. But that period of time, comparatively short as it is, has proved sufficient to assure the people in the vicinity that Mr. Smith is worthy of the most implicit confidence, both as regards his integrity and his professional skill, and the result has been the building up of a large and steadily growing trade. The premises occupied are of the dimensions of 20 x 35 feet and include one floor and a basement, employment being given to two courteous and efficient assistants. Family trade is made a specialty and prescriptions are put up with a celerity, neatness and accuracy only possible where the highest skill and every facility are combined. Prices are low and the quality of everything sold, is just as represented.

Chas. Atkinson, Manufacturer of fine Harnesses, and Riding Saddles, also, dealer in Whips, Robes, Blankets, &c., 609 Tremont Street, Boston. We would call attention to the enterprise of Mr. Charles Atkinson, Manufacturer of Fine Harnesses and Riding Saddles, whose store and shop is located at 609 Tremont street. This gentleman established this business in 1887, and has already met with much success. The premises occupied, are of the dimensions of 25 x 70 feet, and consist of a well arranged store with a shop in the rear. Skilled workmen are employed, and a large manufacturing and retail trade is transacted. Mr. Atkinson manufactures riding saddles, and fine harnesses of every description, and is prepared to fill orders at the shortest possible notice. He also carries one of the finest stocks of Harness, Whips, Robes, Blankets etc., in this vicinity, and at most reasonable prices. He also makes a specialty of repairing, washing and oiling harnesses in a neat and highly satisfactory manner. Mr. Atkinson is a native of Maine, well known throughout this section of the city as a gentleman of energy and ability. Well experienced in his business, and one with whom it is a pleasure to deal.

Olympian Cafe, W. H. Stevens, Proprietor. 511 Tremont Street and 6 Warren Avenue. A gentleman who has done much to prove that the best of food and the most prompt and polite service are not inconsistent with the maintaining of popular prices in a dining saloon is Mr. W. H. Stevens, the genial proprietor of the well-known Olympian Cafe located at No. 511 Tremont Street, and No. 6 Warren Avenue, under Odd Fellows Hall. This establishment is one of the most commodious in the city, having seating accommodations for one hundred and twenty guests, and this capacity is none too large at certain hours, for an immense amount of business is done and the trade is steadily increasing. It is open every day, the Sunday hours being from 8 a. m. to 8 p. m., and meals are furnished at any time during business hours, without delay and of fine quality. The Bill of Fare is sufficiently varied to permit of all tastes being suited and the prices are so graded that a quarter of a dollar will go nearly twice as far as a similar sum in many other eating saloons offering no better accommodations. The direction of so largely-patronized an undertaking is a matter of no small difficulty, but the system in operation is so perfect that everything in and about the establishment runs without a jar and prompt and polite attention is assured to all. An important department of the business is the trade in cigars, for Mr. Stevens is not a follower of the usual eating-house policy as regards the handling of these goods but on the contrary offers so large and so fine a selection at bottom prices that many purchase their cigars of him exclusively. Such celebrated and popular brands as the "U. & S.," "J. A.," "Spurs Deire.," "Number 7," and "Carl Upmann Boquets" are constantly on hand and are sold in any desired quantity at the lowest figures.

Amos E. Bates, Stationer and News Dealer, Circulating Library, and Laundry Agency, 633 Tremont Street. This popular Stationer and Newsdealer, although of but comparatively recent inception, has attained a position to be envied by many engaged in the same line. He occupies a store 18 x 35 feet in dimensions, located at 633 Tremont Street, which contains a fine stock of Books, also a complete line of Stationery Articles, etc. Mr. A. E. Bates, the proprietor, succeeded to this enterprise in 1885, and exhibits his taste and ability in the arrangement and selection of his stock, which in the periodical department includes the New York and Boston Papers, which are delivered at residences, Mr. Bates having one of the largest routes in this section of the city. Subscriptions are also received for all Daily, Weekly, Monthly and Foreign publications. In addition to the Stationery and News department is a fine circulating library is carried, containing 2,800 bound volumes, and 1,500 pamphlets. New books are added weekly. The store is attractive in all its appointments, and customers are treated in a polite and attentive manner, while the wants of the public are studied in every respect. Mr. Bates is agent for the Troy Laundry, and is a gentleman of rare business ability. He is a native of Boston, and eminently fair in all his dealings, and is well qualified to push his business to still greater usefulness.

John G. Benedict, Ph. G., Pharmacist, 154 Chandler Street and 91 Dartmouth Street. The ordinances adopted some time ago, requiring the registry of Pharmacists etc., were doubtless well-advised and a move in the right direction for, speaking broadly, it may be said that it cannot be made too difficult for incompetent persons to be allowed the handling, and more especially the dispensing, of Drugs and Medicines. That the United States has been strangely lax in the establishment of medical regulations, is a fact too notorious to call for proof, and indeed in case any of our readers should doubt it, let them compare the laws, or rather want of laws, of this nation with those in force in other civilized countries. But, however, we may be thankful for any protection, against imposture in this direction, and hence our municipal regulations are worthy of appreciation. Among our city druggists in whom the most implicit confidence may be placed, Mr. John G. Benedict is entitled to mention, and those who may favor this gentleman with their patronage at his establishment No. 154 Chandler Street cor. Dartmouth Street, may do so in the full assurance that their wants will be most carefully and skilfully attended to. Mr. Benedict is a native of Boston and inaugurated his present enterprise in 1885. He occupies one floor and a basement of the dimensions of 25 x 45 feet, and employing three competent assistants, is enabled to fill orders with celerity as well as accuracy. The assortment of Drugs, Medicines and Chemicals on hand is at all times complete in every department, and prescriptions are compounded without delay and at prices as low as the lowest.

J. E. Adams & Co. (E. A. Remick, Proprietor), Dealers in Coal and Wood, No. 784 Albany Street, between East Chester Park and Swett Street; Telephone No. 4502. The average citizen has given more care than ever to the selection of his coal supply since the beginning of the annoying shortage we have experienced here in Boston, in common with our sister cities; and there are very few. If indeed there are any, retailers that have made money during the past few months; for all the reputable concerns have supplied their customers practically at cost and looked to the future for the returns on the capital invested and labor done to which they are justly entitled. The establishment located at No. 784 Albany Street, between East Chester Park and Swett Street, was founded by Messrs. J. E. Adams & Co., over thirty years ago, and is still conducted under that firm name, although the present proprietor is Mr. E. A. Remick. This gentleman, who is a native of Boston, may be depended upon to fully maintain the ancient prestige of the concern, for he is very well acquainted with the coal trade in all its branches, and is determined to spare neither trouble nor expense in serving his customers in the best possible manner. The yard covers some 52,000 square feet of ground, and a heavy stock is carried of coal and wood of standard quality. Employment is given to sixteen competent assistants, and orders will be filled promptly, correctly, and at the very lowest rates that the state of the market will permit.

Hotel Johnson, 250 Shawmut Avenue, was erected and finished in the fall and spring of 1884 and 1885, by its present owner, J. F. Johnson, who had been located in the grocery business, nearly opposite, since 1870. This building is 54 feet front, by 61 in depth, five stories in height, its outward architecture is very pleasing and it adds another to the list of fine, substantial buildings which attract the attention of all in that section of the city. Inside it is finished in apartments and is nearer fire proof than almost any building at the South End; each floor is divided into three apartments, each separated from the other by a solid brick wall, while fire-proof paper is placed between the upper and under floors throughout the building. The apartments are finished in hard wood and frescoed. It is heated by an improved method called the "Hot Blast System", and a passenger elevator adds to the comfort of its occupants. On the first floor is located the large, light and commodious grocery store 28 feet front by 61 in depth, together with basement. This is occupied by the proprietor, Mr. J. F. Johnson, as a first class grocery store. Mr. Johnson was born at Rockport, Cape Ann, moving to Maine when very young; was reared on a farm with temperate habits. Coming to the city at the age of 18, a stranger, he found employment in a retail grocery store working three years as clerk, when he engaged in this business on his own account, June 18, 1870, at the corner of Milford St. and Shawmut Avenue. By close attention to business the store was soon too small to accommodate the increasing business when the owner was prevailed upon to enlarge it by extending it back through another building, thus giving increased facilities. This also proved inadequate to the growing trade and this new building was built, designed to contain a grocery store which would meet the growing requirements of the trade. Now after eighteen years successful experience in supplying the wants of the South End trade he feels grateful for patronage, and solicits a still wider field of distribution, believing his patrons want the best of goods, honest dealing, and prompt delivery of goods at the lowest cash price possible. Give him a trial.

Banks & Harriman, Dealers in Fresh and Salt Meats, and Manufacturers of the Original Corn Cob Ham; Fruit, Vegetables, Poultry and Game, Stalls 26 to 32 Washington Market. Washington Market is a big building, and contains a large number of business houses, but "there is room enough for all" in the building mentioned, and each house has its circle of patrons that prefers its methods to those of any other.

Well, those doing business with Messrs. Banks & Harriman, of Stalls 26 to 32 Washington Market, certainly have abundant reason to be satisfied with the treatment they receive, for this popular concern has built up its present very large trade by strict adherence to all promises, and by invariably supplying standard goods at low prices. This is a firm and enduring foundation on which to build, and as these business methods are employed today as much as ever they were, it follows that Messrs. Banks & Harriman have no reason to anticipate any falling off in their growing patronage. Fresh and Salt Meats, Fruits, Vegetables, Poultry and Game—such in a general way are the goods they handle, but little real idea of what their stock actually consists of is to be had without a personal inspection of the exceptionally varied and well-selected assortment which they offer. No special class of trade is entered to, for there are ample facilities at hand to supply goods suited to all tastes, and whether the most expensive or the cheapest cuts are wanted, this firm can supply them at bottom rates. Both members of the firm are natives of Boston, and employment is given to five assistants. In addition to their extensive trade in Fresh Meats, Provisions, Fruits and Vegetables, Messrs. Banks & Harriman have recently opened in the basement a large smoking establishment, fully equipped with every necessary facility for the business of smoking by the "Corn Cob Process," of which they are the only firm in Massachusetts having this patent right. Curing adds greatly to the flavor and wholesomeness of the Hams, and the extensive patronage this branch of their business has already received, gives evidence of its continued success. Every Ham, Bacon and Roasted Ham bearing the brand "Corn Cob," will be found unexcelled for flavor and general excellence. Choice hogs only are used, and every effort is made to keep the quality up to the highest standard of excellence.

W. J. Hurd, Dealer in Dry and Fancy Goods, 1241 Washington Street. There are not a few people who have a preference for being served with promptness and politeness when purchasing goods of any kind, and such people are very apt to fail to see the advantages of dealing at an immense establishment where there is so beautiful a "system" that while the customers are waiting for their goods so much time elapses that there is danger of their being out of style before they are received. To speak plainly, common sense people like common sense treatment, and will not tolerate being obliged to waste time, as is frequently the case in the larger stores. Therefore it is not surprising that such an establishment as that conducted by Mr. W. J. Hurd, of No. 1241 Washington Street, should receive cordial support, for in this store sensible business methods are adhered to, and all necessary transactions can be gone through with in a very short time. Mr. Hurd began operations in 1876, and soon built up a thriving trade, for he has always made it a point to carry a full stock and offer the same at bottom rates. The premises occupied are 20 x 60 feet in size, and comprise one floor and a basement. Dry and Fancy Goods of all descriptions are at hand to choose from, and the customer is not obliged to travel over several acres in order to reach a certain "department." The employees are well-informed and courteous, and as no misrepresentation is permitted at this store, callers may feel assured that all articles bought here will prove just as represented.

G. E. Lambert, Dealer in Choice Provisions, Produce, Fruit, Fish and Oysters, 761 Tremont Street. The great convenience, to say the least of it, of having relations with a dealer in Provisions, who not only carries the finest articles in stock, but who may be implicitly depended upon to supply the same when ordered, is not perhaps so apparent to those of small experience in housekeeping, as it is to those who have had a more extended opportunity to become conversant with the practices of some dealers in this respect; but at all events it must be obvious to all that a house which bears such a reputation as that enjoyed by the one conducted by Mr. G. E. Lambert, must be in the highest degree worthy of public appreciation and patronage. Mr. Lambert was born in Alfred, Maine, and founded the undertaking since carried on by him in 1880. One floor and a basement are occupied, of the dimensions of 20 x 85 feet, and as employment is afforded to six efficient and polite assistants, all orders are assured the most prompt and careful attention. A very large stock is carried at Choice Provisions of all descriptions, and special attention is paid to the handling of Canned Goods, Country Produce, Foreign and Domestic Fruit, etc. In the line of Fish and Oysters a brisk trade is carried on, and every precaution is taken to supply only such Fish and finely flavored articles of this kind as will fully maintain the high reputation held for excellence in this department. Prices are reasonable, and orders quickly and accurately delivered.

Joseph A. Hart, 597 Tremont Street, Fine Confectionery, Ice Cream, Soda. There are few residents in this part of the city who are not more or less familiar with the establishment of J. A. Hart which for the past two years has been prominently before the public as headquarters for Confectionery and Ice Cream. This House was founded by its present proprietor in 1886. The premises occupied for the transaction of this business are located at 597 Tremont Street and consists of one floor and basement each 22 x 70 feet in dimensions comprising a very attractive store with an Ice Cream parlor in the rear. The energies of this house are devoted to the retail trade in confectionery

of all kinds, and Ice Cream of which they handle only the finest grades. Employment is given to only thoroughly skilled and experienced assistants and all orders are promptly filled and Ice Cream delivered to all parts of the city week days and Sundays at forty cents per quart. In all departments of this business there is a marked orderly and systematic method for the proper and correct conduct of each operation of the work, thereby ensuring a uniformly first-class product. Orders by telephone promptly attended to. Mr. Hart is a native of Boston and is proficient in the confectionery business.

Forrest L. West, Dealer in Watches, Clocks, Jewelry, Spectacles and Eye-glasses, 522 Tremont Street. It is a mistake to suppose that it is always possible to make a saving in the purchasing of goods by buying them in town, for in not a few instances it will be found

that quite the contrary is the case, and that actually better bargains are obtainable south of Dover Street than are to be had the other side of that thoroughfare. But without entering into any argument on the subject, we may at least point out an establishment where the prices are uniformly low, the goods uniformly reliable, and the treatment accorded to callers uniformly courteous, and this store may be found at No. 522 Tremont Street, under the control of Mr. F. L. West, successor to George R. Lean. The enterprise was inaugurated in 1872, by Mr. C. P. Abbott, and passed into the hands of Mr. Lean in 1881. Mr. West has no small reason to congratulate himself on the manner in which the business has increased since passing into his possession. He occupies one floor of the dimensions of 14 x 35 feet, and carries an extremely varied and desirable stock of Watches, Clocks, Jewelry, Spectacles and Eye-glasses, which, as we have before stated, is offered at very low rates. Every facility is at hand for the doing of Fine Watch Repairing at the shortest possible notice and least expense, and the work done here is by no means to be confounded with that turned out at other establishments run by "Watchmakers" who evidently served their apprenticeship in a blacksmith shop. The Repairing of French and Old English Clocks is made a specialty, and every effort is made to combine satisfactory and durable results with low prices. We can heartily commend Mr. West's work, and do so without reserve.

H. H. ROBINSON,
GENERAL AGENT.
1689 WASHINGTON STREET,
BOSTON, MASS.

VINEYARDS & CELLARS

CORDELIA,

SOLANO CO.   CALIFORNIA.

When more "imported champagne" is consumed in this country than the entire champagne region produces, when chemist after chemist comes forward to declare as a result of his personal analysis that much of the stuff sold as foreign wine is simply an ingenious concoction of drugs and dyestuffs, *containing not one particle of grape-juice*, when expert after expert stakes his reputation on the assertion that this country can and does produce natural wines, equal to any to be found anywhere, it would seem as if the most confirmed admirer of "imported" articles would begin to think it time to at least investigate for himself. Despite all that has been said and written concerning California, few Eastern people have an adequate idea of the climate and agricultural resources of that wonderful State, and still fewer appreciate the difference that exists between the various parts of the country within her borders as regards its grape raising facilities. That a prejudice exists against California wine in some quarters, is unfortunately true, and it is to be regretted that the questionable practices carried on by certain houses handling this commodity, should have served to confirm the poor opinion of it that has been assiduously spread by those interested in so-called "Foreign" wines. The Cordelia Wine Co., of Cordelia, Solano county, California, has been established for 25 years, and during every month of that period has striven to so improve the grapes they raised, and their methods of cultivation as to enable them to produce a *pure wine* that would at least hold its own with the finest imported article. They have succeeded, and now offer to Boston patrons, through their general agent, Mr. H. H. Robinson, doing business at No. 1089 Washington st., under the Commonwealth Hotel, a complete assortment of the various brands of wine of which twenty-one kinds are handled, embracing all the varieties, which are offered at extremely low rates, considering the quality of the goods, and sold either by the bottle or in bulk, at wholesale or retail, and which hears on every bottle a sworn aintement, signed by the officers of the company, and setting forth the fact that *nothing but the pure juice of the grape* is contained therein. In order to familiarize the public with the many excellencies of these wines, Mr. Rob-

inson supplies them at retail as well as at wholesale, and invites those who desire to personally satisfy themselves that the goods are of fine flavor, as well as of undoubted purity to call and test their quality, carefully and thoroughly. A spacious store is occupied, of the dimensions of 35x90 feet, with basement for storage and a very large stock is carried, wholesale and retail orders being filled without delay. Mr. Robinson is a native of Boston, and employs three assistants. He is to be congratulated on the energy and skill he has displayed in extending his trade since beginning operations in 1887, and there can be no doubt but that Cordelia wine will soon hold the place in the New England market that its merits entitle it to. We would also call attention to the following facts:

This is the only house recievnig Wines in carload lots direct from the vineyard, and they can therefore vouch for the purity.

They own the land and raise their own grapes.

They make their own wine and sell no other.

The wines being always in their own hands, they can guarantee their purity.

No sugar or anything else added to the grape juice.

They have the finest cellars,the most improved machinery, and the best wine makers.

At great cost they imported cuttings from France, Germany and Spain, and now have vines in full bearing from these cuttings and have wine made from their product.

The wine made from these grapes is superior to any imported, as it is the first juice and the pomace thrown away.

This wine is thoroughly matured before being offered for sale.

This wine is simply grape juice, preserved by nature's own process of fermentation.

A sworn affidavit, signed by president, secretary and superintendent of the company hangs in their office, 1089 Washington street, under Commonwealth Hotel, and one hundred dollars reward will be paid if anything except pure grape juice is found in any of their wines. A copy of the affidavit will be on all bottles.

Ladies will please notice that this is simply a wine house with no bar, sample-rooms, cigars or loafers.

W. S. Folger & CO., Pharmacists; Justin Whitney & Co., 723 Tremont Street, Corner Concord Square. Of all the many pharmaceutical establishments located in the city of Boston, there are but few that can look back on a score of years of usefulness, and even among those that can do so, it is by no means all that have the reasons to rest satisfied with the record thus far made that are held by that conducted by Messrs. W. F. Folger & Co., at No. 723 Tremont Street, Corner of Concord Square. The establishment alluded to is par excellence a Family Drug Store. It bears practically the same relation to the ordinary city drug store that the "family physician" does to his brother professionals who have not attained that position; and, like him, while giving all needful and possible aid to strangers, it nevertheless finds its highest and most congenial field of usefulness in serving those among its customers who appeal to it in other than a strictly business way. There is a feeling of confidence experienced when dealing with this house, which, although hardly definable, is yet distinctly appreciable; and we are very happy to take this opportunity to state that this feeling is fully justified by the facts, for we know of no other pharmacy in the entire city, where more scrupulous, intelligent and unremitting care is exercised in the filling of orders, and more particularly in the compounding of physicians' prescriptions. The full supply of Drugs, Chemicals, etc., carried, permits all such commissions to be executed without delay, and it may be added that the prices are as low as at many similar establishments where no such precautions are observed. Mr. Whitney, who succeeded Mr. Folger several years ago, is a native of Westminster, Mass., and employs three thoroughly competent assistants.

L. H. Lanfair, Carpenter and builder, 97 Chapman Street, cor. Tremont. All kinds of Jobbing promptly attended to. But a comparatively small proportion of those who build houses for themselves, can spare the time to superintend the construction in person, and it is therefore of no small importance to engage the services of a Builder who may be trusted to carry out every detail as was agreed upon. Boston is fortunate in having within her borders many practical builders of high reputation, but among them all, there is not one more worthy of confidence than Mr. L. H. Lanfair, doing business on Chapman Street, near Tremont. This gentleman began operations in 1831, and is well known in the community, being a native of Boston. The premises occupied by him, measure 20 x 45 feet, and employment is given to a large number of competent assistants, this force being considerably increased at certain seasons. Mr. Lanfair has had an extensive experience in his line of business, and is in a position to render valuable assistance to those who wish to build a residence, but do not know just what they want. He will be found entirely willing to give any information in his power, and owing to his careful study of the subject, he is well prepared to offer suggestions that may save much useless expense. Jobbing orders are attended to without delay, and very low prices are quoted for first-class work.

Young's Home Made Bakery, 1491 Washington, Cor. Canton Streets. The contrast between the low, dingy and shabby appearing stores in which bakeries were generally conducted a few years ago, and such magnificent establishments as that carried on by Mr. C. L. Young at No. 1491 Washington Street, corner of Canton, is a most decided and significant one and shows that the public are beginning to demand first-class accommodations in every respect. The store occupied by Mr. Young is of the dimensions of 25 x 45 feet, is supplied with large plate-glass windows in which a portion of the stock is tastefully arranged and, taken all in all, is doubtless one of the most attractive bakeries in Boston. But beauty, although all very well in its way, goes for but little unless there are other good qualities to back it up, and Mr. Young's establishment, dainty as it is, would receive but little patronage were it not for the fact that the goods he offers are as appetizing and wholesome as the store in which they are sold is spacious and handsome. These goods comprise Bread, Cake and Pastry of all descriptions, and they are supplied fresh several times a day, so that their original virtues are not impaired by long keeping. Mr. Young is a native of Bethel, Maine, and began operations in this business in 1872, opening the present store in 1886. He is a member of the Odd Fellows, and several other organizations, and is a believer in energy being applied to any undertaking, no matter how firmly it may be established. As a consequence he is constantly trying to improve his service to the public and this course is appreciated by the rapidly growing number of his patrons. Employment is given to five efficient assistants and prompt attention is assured to every caller.

George F. Dow, Choice Provisions, Foreign and Domestic Fruits, Butter, Lard, Eggs, etc., Fish and Oysters, 1179 Washington Street, opposite Grand Opera House. Even when it is conceded that the field cultivated by Mr. Geo. F. Dow is a wide and promising one, it must be admitted that the development of that gentleman's business has been remarkably rapid and pronounced since its inception in 1875, and to those who are familiar with the methods employed at his establishment, the success attained by him will be hailed with no small gratification, for Mr. Dow has from the beginning manifested a desire to "do the fair thing," that has won for him many friends. The premises occupied comprise one floor and a basement, and measure 25 x 50 feet, employment being given to five experienced assistants. The store is located at No. 1179 Washington Street, opposite the Grand Opera House, and is occupied by a most extensive assortment of Fine Provisions, Foreign and Domestic Fruits, Butter, Lard, Eggs, etc., as well as a complete stock of Fresh Fish and Oysters. Mr. Dow gives special attention to the handling of Creamery Butter, and can furnish the finest goods in the market in this line. Fresh Country Eggs are also obtainable at his store at the lowest prices, and the supply of Fruits carried will be found to be full and desirable, while those who appreciate polite treatment and fair dealing will find additional reason for patronizing this store.

W. W. Newcomb, Dealer in Fresh and Salt Fish, Oysters, Clams & Lobsters, 52 & 53 Washington Market. It is a generally under-

stood fact, that much of the value of any given product is due to the manner in which it is handled preparatory to being sold, and particularly is this the case when food products are brought into the question. Of course, even in food-products there is no small variation as to the effects of improper handling and these effects are apt to be most clearly manifest where so perishable a commodity as fish is concerned. We all want our fish as fresh as possible, that is, if they are going to be fresh at all, and therefore we take pleasure in inviting our readers to learn of the advantages offered by Mr. W. W. Newcomb of Stalls Nos. 52 and 53 Washington Market, for at this establishment especial attention is given to the handling of Fresh Fish of all descriptions as well as of Oysters, Clams and Lobsters. Mr. Newcomb also sells Smoked and Pickled Fish of excellent quality, but, as we have before remarked, gives particular attention to the sale of Fresh Fish. He is a native of Wellfleet, and is a prominent member of various Fraternal Societies, being connected with the Knights of Pythias, Knights of Honor, Free Masons and the United Friends. Business was begun in 1877 and a large proportion of Mr. Newcomb's extensive trade is with those who have dealt with him for many years, as his business methods are such as will retain the patronage of those who can appreciate fair dealing and unswerving integrity. Orders will be called for and promptly delivered and every effort made to maintain the exceptionally high reputation now enjoyed.

C. G. Campbell, Painter and Glazier, Chapman Street, near Tremont. It is always good policy to keep a frame structure well painted, for paint is cheaper than wood, and an occasional renewal of a house's outer covering will add many years to the life of the edifice. Appearances also demand that this be done, and there is therefore no excuse for neglecting it, especially as the expense is comparatively small, and the effect so lasting. There are many good and reliable painters in this city, and it is not our purpose or our desire to draw invidious comparisons, but for all that we propose to call attention to such enterprises as deserve special mention, and hence take this opportunity to notice the establishment conducted by Mr. C. G. Campbell, on Chapman Street, near Tremont. This was opened in 1885, and Mr. Campbell has since shown himself to be a skillful and experienced painter and glazier, who gives prompt and painstaking attention to orders, and employs only reliable assistants. The premises utilized are of the dimensions of 20 x 35 feet, and every needful facility is at hand for the effectual and satisfactory filling of orders at the shortest possible notice. The stock used is of standard quality, and the lowest market rates are quoted.

John T. Powers, Grocer, 743 Tremont Street, and 107 Worcester Street, Dealer in Choice Wines and Family Supplies. It is very nearly thirty years since Mr. John T. Powers founded the business he now carries on and it is not too much to say that there is not a Grocer in the section of the city supplied by him that is better known or more generally esteemed. Mr. Powers was born in Brighton and inaugurated his present enterprise in 1861. He is a member of the Free Masons and has many friends in Boston and vicinity, some of whom became acquainted with him while he held the position of book-keeper just before starting in the grocery business at the Parker House, where he was employed for four years. The premises occupied are of the dimensions of 20 x 80 feet and comprise one floor and a basement, being located at No. 743 Tremont Street. Although fine staple and fancy groceries of all descriptions are handled, a specialty is made of the sale of Family Flour and all possible divergencies of taste are provided for in this line, all the approved brands of Southern, Western and Canadian Flour being dealt in. Fine Teas and Coffees are also given particular attention and full weight, low prices and uniformly superior goods combine to make this department a formidable rival to many houses which handle nothing but Teas and Coffees. Cocoa and Broma are also handled for the benefit of those preferring them for any reason and are offered at the lowest market rates. Butter in any desired quantity, Cheese both old and new and the finest Leaf Lard are also dealt in largely, and the stock of choice wines and family supplies on hand includes goods that are fully warranted to prove just as represented.

E. B. Crosby, Dealer in Beef, Mutton, Lamb, Veal, Butter and Country Produce, No. 137 Northampton Street. A well ordered and honorably conducted Market where families can be supplied, always promptly, with a class of goods that can be relied upon as fresh and first-class, is an important industry of a city. The one heading this sketch has been in existence since 1880, when it was established by its present proprietor, and since that date it has been conducted under the style of E. B. Crosby. His house has met the wants of the community to such a degree that its trade has rapidly increased and now does an extensive business. The trade of this Market requires the stock to be often replenished, so that it is constantly filled with a fresh and desirable assortment of provisions of all kinds, also Beef, Mutton, Lamb, Veal, etc., a specialty being made of Butter and Country Produce. This popular Market is located at 137 Northampton Street, and covers an area of 20 x 45 feet, with a cellar of the same size which is utilized for storage purposes. Mr. Crosby endeavors to meet the wants of all who desire first-class goods at fair prices. Mr. Crosby is a native of Boston. He enlisted in the Eleventh Massachusetts Regiment, Company H, and was actively engaged in twenty-two of the most noted battles which occurred during the late Rebellion, among which were the battles of Bull Run, Gettysburg, etc.

S. F. Coney, Cigars and Tobacco, 492 Tremont Street. One of the most amusing things failing to the notice of an observer of human nature, is the eagerness shown by certain zealous "reformers" to make everybody as miserable as themselves, and one of their favorite methods is to come out with alarming statistics regarding the use of tobacco. Forgetting that the average of human life has greatly increased since tobacco was introduced, forgetting that there are as many able and honest physicians that approve of tobacco-using as there are that oppose it, forgetting, in fact, everything against their pet theories and remembering everything favoring them, — they rant and roar and groan and shake their heads and predict dire disaster, and accomplish — what? Well, they make some people feel uncomfortable for a while, to be sure, but their exertions affect the use of tobacco about as much as a heavy ship holds down the waves — the smaller ripples may be interfered with, but the ocean moves the ship and not the ship the ocean. Good cigars and good tobacco, used in moderation, will hurt no one, and to get such goods, go to the store conducted by Mr. S. F. Coney at No. 492 Tremont Street. This gentleman began operations in 1885, and the excellence and moderate price of the articles sold by him have caused his trade to rapidly and steadily increase. One floor measuring 20 x 50 feet is occupied, and a fine assortment is carried of all the popular brands of Tobacco, both smoking and chewing, as well as one of the finest lines of Imported and Domestic Cigars to be found in this city. Some of the Cigars sold here for five cents will compare very favorably with those for which double that price is charged elsewhere, and all the goods are quoted at bottom rates.

The Blair Camera Co., Manufacturers of Photographic Apparatus, Factory & Warerooms, 471-475-477 Tremont Street. It seems a curious coincidence, that with the great revival of interest in out-door recreations that is now being manifested, there should occur a discovery in the line of photography, that permits of the bulky paraphernalia of the old process being dispensed with in favor of the "dry-plate" system of securing negatives, for by reason of this discovery and its application, out-door ramblers of all sorts, the canoeist, the bicyclist, the yachtsman, the oarsman, yes even the pedestrian, are able, not only to look upon the manifold beauties of nature themselves and for the time being, but also to secure for the entertainment of their friends an enduring record of any uncommon or beautiful scene that may be presented to them during their wanderings, a record that in after days will serve to recall many a happy hour. The Blair Camera Company, rank with the best-known manufacturers of Photographic Apparatus in the country, and the fame of the various appliances they produce, is by no means confined to New England but has extended to about every portion of the United States. The "Blair Lucidograph" has met with an immense sale, and it is stoutly maintained by not a few leading amateurs, that there is no portable Photographic apparatus manufactured, that can compare with it in effectiveness, reliability and lowness of price.

That it is an entirely practical arrangement needs no proof, for some of the finest negatives of waterfalls, boats and trains in motion and other difficult subjects that have ever been secured, are due to the Lucidograph and it is an established institution in the Photographic world. The Blair Camera Co. began operations in 1880, and its business has steadily increased, until now it requires the occupancy of five floors measuring 30 x 100 feet, and the employment of thirty efficient assistants to keep up with the demand. The factory and warerooms are at Nos. 471, 475 and 477 Tremont Street, where an exclusively wholesale business is done, the Lucidograph and other specialties of this concern being handled at retail by nearly all the first-class dealers. The President of the Company is Mr. D. L. Goff, and the Treasurer and Manager, Mr. T. H. Blair. Both of these gentlemen are well-known business men, and to their energy and push much of the success attained is due.

Cafe Waquoit, 249 Columbus Ave., Louis Frenkel. There is probably no business, if we except that of carrying on a hotel, in which the personality of the proprietor is more accurately reflected in the methods employed and the results attained than in that of conducting a Restaurant or Cafe. It is a singular, but none the less natural fact, that two-thirds of our city restaurants are well-nigh intolerable to people of good breeding, and without entering into a consideration of the reasons for this state of affairs, let us call the attention of our readers to an establishment that is all the more worthy of mention and of appreciation on account of the facts previously alluded to. We refer to the well-known "Cafe Waquoit" located at No. 249 Columbus Avenue and fully deserving the description given on its business card—"First-class Cafe for Ladies and Gentlemen." Its popular proprietor, Mr. Louis Frenkel, is a native of Germany and has an extremely large circle of friends in the community. He gives close personal attention to the direction of the Cafe and strives to treat his guests with liberality as well as with fairness, neglecting no opportunity to improve the character of the service rendered, and at all times supplying the best food the market affords, at reasonable rates. The premises utilized measure 25 x 65 feet and include one floor and a basement, there being seating capacity for sixty people. Although a specialty is made of Table Board, the business is not confined to this department, but includes the sale of choice ice-cream, cigars, etc. Mr. Frenkel's cream being celebrated for its delicate flavor and careful making. Everything in and about the establishment is orderly, neat and attractive and we can sincerely commend it to the patronage of our readers. Mr. Frenkel makes a specialty of a five course table d' hote dinner for 35 cents from 5 to 7.30 p. m.; breakfast and luncheon 25 cents each. These are a great convenience to the number of people having furnished rooms in this vicinity. Patrons number from six hundred to seven hundred and fifty per day.

Stephen Gale, Apothecary, Washington Street, Corner Chester Square. An establishment which is fortunately located, well managed and completely equipped, must of necessity enjoy a large share of the public patronage, and as the Apothecary store conducted by Mr. Stephen Gale at the corner of Washington Street and Chester Square, possesses all these advantages, it goes without saying that its proprietor has no reason to complain of lack of custom. Mr. Gale was born in Portland, Me., and became connected with the undertaking he now controls in 1880, having for many years previous been associated with one of the South End druggists. He has spared no pains to make the establishment a first-class city pharmacy in every sense of the word, and has striven especially hard to so systematize operations in the prescription department, that errors would be practically impossible. To secure this end, every modern facility for the handling, measuring, etc., of Drugs and Chemicals has been made use of, and the results attained are best seen in the hundreds of prescriptions filled annually without a mistake of any kind. It is therefore perfectly natural that this establishment should rate high in the confidence of the public, especially when it is noted that no exorbitant charges are made under any circumstances. The premises occupied comprise one floor and a basement, and are 20 x 70 feet in dimensions. Employment is afforded two experienced and careful assistants, and courteous and prompt attention is assured every caller. A fine line of Fancy Goods, Toilet Articles, etc., is offered for sale at prices worthy of careful comparison with those of many other concerns, and everything sold by Mr. Gale may be depended upon to prove as represented.

F. H. & W. F. Dowell, Dealers in Fine Groceries, No. 403 Columbus Avenue, Under Hotel Clifton. An establishment which may well be given prominent mention as an excellent example of a well-managed Grocery house is that of which Messrs. F. H. and W. F. Dowell are the proprietors, located at No. 403 Columbus Avenue, under Hotel Clifton. The proofs of the liberal and intelligent manner in which this enterprise is conducted are visible on every side in one form or another, but perhaps the most conclusive is that afforded by the exceptional development of the trade since business was begun in 1886. When the undertaking was founded, in the year above mentioned, there were, of course, many other concerns in the vicinity engaged in a similar line of business, and to have attained the success which has been granted Messrs. F. H. & W. F. Dowell in the face of such competition speaks volumes for the ability and enterprise of those having charge of operations. Both members of the firm are natives of Boston, and are perfectly acquainted with the demands of a high-class city trade. The premises occupied are of the dimensions of 30 x 100 feet, and include one floor and a basement. Five active and courteous assistants are employed, and the stock on hand comprises one of the most carefully selected assortments of Fine Groceries to be found in the city. Every effort is made to handle only such goods as are sure to give entire and uniform satisfaction,

and the system of delivery is such that orders are assured prompt and accurate treatment. The prices are as low as the lowest, quality considered, and no misrepresentation of goods is permitted or made.

Worcester County Creamery; Butter; Pure Creamy Milk Delivered in Glass Jars; Cheese and Fresh Eggs; 49 Berkeley Street, Parker Memorial Building; Branch Store, 503 Dudley Street. The constant complaints that were made, year in and year out, by the consumer of milk, butter and other dairy products, have finally borne fruit in the establishment of quite a number of enterprises having for their object the supplying of goods of this description against which no objection could reasonably be urged, and although it is notorious that some of these "Creameries" have much more cream in their name than they have in their products, still there are others which really do deal only in strictly pure and fresh articles, and among such is that known as the "Worcester County Creamery" located at No. 49 Berkeley Street, Parker Memorial Building, and having a branch store at No. 503 Dudley Street, Roxbury. Inaugurated by Mr. C. Brigham in 1830, this undertaking has been continued since 1883 by Mr. Geo. B. Bruce, who has manifested no little ability and determined perseverance in pushing it along to its present success in the face of an opposition, the nature of which those unfamiliar with the "inside" history of the city's milk supply have not the least idea of. But, however, he is in a position today to defy either calumny or dishonorable competition of any kind, and can confidently rely for support on the public he has served so faithfully. One floor and a basement are utilized, and a fine assortment of Butter (made fresh every day), Cheese, Eggs, etc., is always on hand. Pure Creamery Milk is delivered in Glass Jars, and both quantity and quality are guaranteed to prove as represented. The prices are very low, when the quality of the goods is considered, and the facilities at hand are such that customers are assured of prompt and polite attention.

W. W. Jones, Dealer in All Kinds of Fresh, Salt, and Smoked Fish, Clams and Oysters, 158 Northampton Street. All orders promptly attended to. Occupying a conspicuous position among the retail Fish Markets of this section of Boston, the establishment of Wm. W. Jones is worthy of more than a passing notice in this volume. This business was established in 1887, and has rapidly advanced in public favor. The premises occupied by this house for business purposes are located at No. 158 Northampton Street, and comprise a fine store, 20 x 25 feet in dimensions. The stock comprises all kinds of Fresh, Salt, and Smoked Fish, Clams, and Oysters. The prices will be found as reasonable as first-class goods can be sold. Orders will be promptly filled, and delivered free, to all parts of the city, and polite and attentive treatment will be accorded to all who visit this Market. Mr. Jones has built up a large trade and acquired the reputation of a careful conservative business man, and highly respected citizen.

S. F. Kittredge, dealer in Provisions, Fruit and Vegetables, Poultry, Game, Butter and Eggs, 280 Shawmut Avenue, (opposite Hanson street.) There is no commercial interest whatever, which comes nearer to the life and homes of all our citizens than that of the retail trade in Provisions, and it is a department in which are needed and exercised the most balanced judgment and thorough knowledge. That these are marked characteristics of the old established house of Mr. S. F. Kittredge is shown by the appreciative patronage which has met its enterprising and honorable endeavors. This business was established by its present proprietor, in Williams Market, in 1852, where he remained until removing to present location in 1887. The careful wisdom and foresight which have thus far marked all its transactions are lasting assurances of increasing progress and success in the near future. The premises occupied comprise one floor and basement, each 25 x 60 feet in dimensions, and are located at No. 280 Shawmut Avenue. Five assistants are constantly employed, and the stock carried consists of first-class Provisions, fresh Fruits and Vegetables, Poultry and Game, Butter and Eggs. Goods delivered free to any part of city or Highlands. The prices are exceptionally reasonable for the best goods, and prudent buyers will recognize after a short trial, that this is one of the houses with which it is both most economical, pleasant and profitable to deal. Mr. Kittredge is a native of N. H., and a thoroughly reliable and esteemed business man and citizen.

Galen Woodruff's Pharmacy, 500 Tremont Street, Corner Dover. An establishment which does a very large business, owing not only to its favorable location but also to the exceptionally high reputation which its proprietor has attained as a skillful and reliable dispensing chemist, is that conducted by Mr. Galen Woodruff at the corner of Tremont and Dover Streets. This enterprise had its inception in 1870, so that it has now been before the public nearly a score of years; and it is but simple justice to say that more convincing proofs of the entire trustworthiness of its management are perceptible with each added year. Mr. Woodruff is one of the leading practical pharmacists in the city. Recognizing the fact that no skill however great can accomplish satisfactory results while employing poor material, he makes it a point to keep a full and varied assortment of Drugs, etc., constantly on hand and is therefore prepared to undertake the compounding of physicians' prescriptions of any nature, with a guarantee that the ingredients used shall be the best that the market affords. Nothing is left to "luck" in the prescription department of this pharmacy and all that care and foresight can do to command accuracy is assured. Mr. Woodruff has able and courteous assistants in Messrs H. H. Dudley and C. C. Emerson who may be relied upon to zealously strive to accommodate every patron. The store is 20 x 35 feet in size, and a basement of similar dimensions is also utilized. Delicious Soda with Choice Fruit and Cream Syrups is dispensed here at five cents a glass, and the immense quantity sold shows that its quality and cheapness are fully appreciated.

Fox Brothers, Grocers, 685 and 687 Tremont Street. One of the very best examples of what a Metropolitan Grocery Store should be, with which we are familiar, is that afforded by the establishment of Messrs. Fox Brothers, at No. 685 Tremont Street, and we believe that it would be difficult for the most critical to suggest a needed improvement in the fitting up and management of the store under existing conditions. Neither pains nor expense is spared to make this establishment thoroughly attractive and "wholesome" looking, both within and without, and the result is seen in one of the neatest and handsomest Grocery Stores in the city. Fox Brothers began operations in 1865, as C. E. Fox & Co. (succeeded by the present firm); and thus having had very nearly a quarter of a century's experience, it is only natural that they should be perfectly conversant with their business in every detail. The premises occupied comprise one floor and a basement, their dimensions being 40 x 70 feet, and employment is afforded thirteen efficient assistants, who may be depended on to strive their utmost to show customers prompt and civil attention. The stock on hand is so large and varied that it would be idle to even attempt a full description of it, but it may be said to include all kinds of Groceries, both Staple and Fancy, and to be as remarkable for uniform merit as it is for variety. The very finest flavored Teas, Coffees and Spices are handled by this house, and those who are able to appreciate a good article in this line will find that their tastes may be fully suited here, as all grades, from the mildest to the strongest, are supplied at the lowest attainable rates. Canned Goods are also given particular attention, and some delicious relishes and condiments are also on hand.

A. Keller, Baker and Confectioner, and Ice Cream Parlor 639 Tremont Street. The bakery and confectionery business is one in which we are all necessarily interested, and its influence and practical importance are acknowledged by all. Mr. A. Keller of this city is widely recognized among first-class dealers in this line of business in this section of Boston, and everything made by him is always up to the highest standard of purity of material and excellence of cooking. This house was established in 1879 and has since that date been under the wise and popular management of its present proprietor. Mr. Keller now occupies a store and basement each covering an area of 20x60 feet, located at No. 639 Tremont Street, Employment is constantly furnished to four very capable assistants, and an extensive retail trade is transacted. His Bread, Cake, Pastries and Confectionery are unexcelled in point of purity, richness of flavor and fine preparations, and all his goods are in every way first-class. The house has a wide and honorable reputation for its liberal management and thorough reliability. Mr. Keller is a native of Boston, and is a highly esteemed and enterprising business man. In the rear of the store is a commodious Ice Cream saloon where all flavors are supplied. Orders for families, Church festivals, etc., receive prompt attention.

J. D. Knowlton, Pharmacist, Washington Street, corner Worcester. The Pharmacy carried on by Mr. J. D. Knowlton at the corner of Washington and Worcester Streets was founded in 1830 by Levi Tower jr. The firm became Tower & Co. in 1879, when Mr. Knowlton entered the firm. In 1884, Mr. Knowlton purchased of Mr. Tower his interest in the business, and has since conducted it alone. This store is one of the oldest-established Drug Stores at the South End, and, it may be added, is one of the most trustworthy as well. Mr. Knowlton is a native of Boston, and graduated at the Massachusetts College of Pharmacy in 1872. He is a member of the Odd Fellows. The reputation which the establishment conducted by him has attained since he took control, is best shown by the fact that many South End families make it a point to have all their prescriptions compounded here, and the wisdom of this course is manifest when we consider the many years that Mr. Knowlton has been engaged in this class of work and the freedom from errors of any kind that marks his record. Another point to be considered is that his stock of Drugs, Medicines, Chemicals, etc., is at all times maintained full and complete in every department, and that especial pains are taken to purchase only fresh and reliable goods. Then, again, the facilities for the weighing, etc., of the ingredients utilized cannot be improved upon, and although unnecessary delay is avoided, still speed is never sought at the expense of the proper care and attention. Mr. Knowlton employs four courteous assistants, and it is hardly necessary to say that these gentlemen will be found competent as well as affable. He deals extensively in Fine Toilet Articles, Soaps, Brushes, etc., and has a full supply of the standard Patent Medicines in stock. Prices are very reasonable, and the articles are warranted to prove as represented. Mr. Knowlton also manufactures

BAYOLINE

Bayoline Quinine Hair Tonic, a Preparation for Dressing the Hair, which has never been equalled. It excites the torpid glands to action, stimulates the secretions, opens the closed hair pores, and gives a vigorous and healthy action to the scalp. Has been used by thousands with perfect satisfaction in every case. Persons who are troubled with thin hair and falling out, will, by the use of Bayoline, soon see its beneficial effects, as by its tonic and stimulating properties, the hair glands will be filled with new life, and the hair will grow thick and strong, because it furnishes the lifegiving principle, which is essential to a healthy growth of the hair. It gives the hair that beautiful texture so much admired by all. It is wholly unlike the preparations of oil and alcohol, which destroy the hair by creating febrile affections of the scalp, but it is cooling and allays all unpleasant itching and irritations, which are brought on by an unhealthy state of the scalp. Bayoline will increase the growth of the hair; Bayoline is a delightful Dressing; Bayoline eradicates dandruff; Bayoline prevents the hair from falling out; Bayoline is not greasy or sticky; Bayoline is not an alcoholic wash; Bayoline gives new life to the hair; Bayoline keeps the head cool; Bayoline is the cleanest, best and most economical Hair Dressing now in use.

DEAR SIR: — It is with great satisfaction and pleasure that I give my opinion in regard to your Bayoline Quinine Hair Tonic. It has done wonders for me. I was troubled with thin layers of scurf around the roots of my hair, which would dry and scale off, itching almost incessantly, and was very annoying. The hairs seemed to have lost their proper nourishment and healthiness; would break off at unequal distances from the skin, leaving their rough ends twisted and matted into thick greyish and yellow crusts. On pulling out a hair and examining it, the root would be found thin, dry and starved in appearance. It was really alarming to see the amount of dandruff fall from my hair upon running my fingers through it. My hair was stiff and dry. I tried very many preparations recommended to me, but received no relief until I was induced to try your Bayoline, and the result is, that my hair and scalp are now in a perfectly healthy condition, free from dandruff, my hair has ceased to fall out, and is soft and pliable. I cheerfully recommend "Bayoline" to all who wish a healthy hair dressing. Yours, &c.

W. A. McCLELLAN.

DEAR SIR: — I wish you to know how much your Bayoline has done for me. I am seventy-two years old, and had lost nearly all my hair from sickness; was in a fair way to lose all of it, as nothing which I had tried did me any good. When I had nearly despaired of getting any relief, I purchased a bottle of Bayoline and began its use. Almost immediate relief was the result. My hair stopped falling out, and soon a new growth of hair started. I have now used four bottles, and I have nearly as thick a head of hair as I ever had. I am sure such an excellent preparation should be better known, and if this testimonial will aid you in any way to introduce it, you have my consent to use it in any way you may deem fit.

Respectfully yours,

J. P. THOMPSON.

I have used the Bayoline Quinine Hair Tonic in my family for a long time, and I can cheerfully and highly recommend it, not only for its cleansing qualities, but as a preventive of the falling off of the hair. Being acquainted with its composition, I unhesitatingly pronounce it free from any deleterious ingredients.

GEO. H. NICHOLS, M. D.

Price 50 Cents and $1.00 Per Bottle. For Sale everywhere by All Druggists.

Dentilavo, or Pearless Tooth Wash, a Preserver and Beautifier of the Teeth. A Toilet Luxury for twenty-five cents. Sample sent free. This elegant preparation, established by more than twenty years' experience, and numerous testimonials from dentists and others, is submitted to the public as a thoroughly satisfactory and perfectly safe Dentifrice. It is a highly saponaceous compound, that from its alkalinity neutralizes any acid that may be in the mouth, thus arresting and preventing decay.

J. D. KNOWLTON, Pharmacist,

Washington, Cor. Worcester St., Boston.

4

J. A. Bradford & Co., 588 Albany Street, Boston.

Considering the trials and tribulations that the citizens of Boston have experienced in keeping their stores of coal replenished during the past season, it may be safely assumed that more attention has been paid to the houses supplying this indispensable commodity, than was ever before the case. Everybody knows that our local dealers were not in any way responsible for the alarming scarcity and consequent high price of coal that caused inconvenience to so many families; but that on the contrary, not a few of them supplied their customers, and in many other ways showed that they were disposed to use every means in their power to accommodate the public at the least possible expense. One of the most liberal concerns to which attention was directed in this respect, is that of Messrs. J. A. Bradford & Co., doing business at No. 588 Albany Street, and their premises are all the better known to the general public, from the fact of their having been formerly occupied by the popular firm of Howard, Snelling & Co. Messrs. J. A. Bradford & Co. commenced operations in 1887, and their business has grown with steadiness and rapidity, the premises now utilized covering about three-fourths of an acre of ground, and employment being given to ten assistants. Being located on tide-water, the expense of handling the commodities dealt in is reduced to a minimum, and wood are quoted here at the very lowest market rates. The system of delivery is a most perfect one, and orders are therefore quickly and accurately filled. Having a large elevator they enjoy every convenience for loading and unloading.

J. A. Towle, Retail Dealer in Choice Teas, Coffees, Sugars, and the usual variety of Best Family Groceries, No. 16 East Dedham Street. It has always been the business man that was prompt to recognize and even anticipate the latest needs of the public, who has met with most abundant success; and this is as it should be, for enterprise and originality deserve being rewarded. This is true in all branches of trade, but particularly so in the Grocery business; for those engaged in this occupation are apt to be too conservative and unwilling to change their methods until obliged to do so by force of circumstances. No such charge, however, can be brought against Mr. J. A. Towle of No. 16 East Dedham Street, for although this gentleman has been engaged in the handling of Groceries for over a quarter of a century (having begun operations in 1860), he is not wedded to old customs by any means, but on the contrary is ever ready to make use of any method that will enable him to serve his customers more satisfactorily. He is a native of this city and a member of the Odd Fellows, and by reason of the exceptional experience he has had in his chosen business, he is able to buy and sell goods to the best possible advantage. One floor and a basement are occupied, measuring 40 x 50 feet, and stocked with a fine assortment of Choice Teas, Coffees, Sugars, and a full line of all the articles usually carried in a first-class city Grocery. Goods will be delivered free of charge, and with a promptness and accuracy that are highly gratifying to the purchaser. We need hardly say that Mr. Towle fully guarantees every article sold to prove just as represented, and his prices will be found as low as reliable goods can be sold.

M. J. Keane, Practical Plumber, 611 Tremont, opposite Odd Fellows' Hall. On two points — Ventilation and Drainage — the health of a community largely depends, and no person who has any regard for the physical well-being of his neighbors, his family or himself, should permit the drainage of his house to remain imperfect one instant longer than can be avoided. "Delays are dangerous" says the proverb and they are all the more dangerous when they afford opportunities for so subtle and deadly an agent as sewer-gas to get in its destructive work. Think of the feelings of a man who sees, perhaps, his wife or his daughter sinking into the grave from the effects of a disease which was brought on by defective drainage and which could have been avoided altogether had the proper measures been taken in time! The subject is too painful to dwell upon, but is worthy of earnest and honest consideration. There are many plumbers who give special attention to sanitary drainage, but we question if any of them are better fitted to undertake work of this kind with the assurance of satisfaction than is Mr. M. J. Keane whose place of business is at No. 514 Tremont Street, opposite Berkeley Street and Odd Fellows' Hall. Mr. Keane was born in Boston and inaugurated operations in the "Centennial Year," 1876. He has made a careful study of Ventilation, Drainage and such matters, and having had years of practical experience he is admirably fitted to accomplish the best results at the least expense. Mr. Keane gives personal attention to all orders of any importance, although he employs five skillful assistants, and it is largely due to this practice that his present and increasing business has been attained. Low rates are charged and commissions promptly executed.

Curtis & Pope, Lumber, Brick, Cement and Building Material, 774 Albany Street. The firm of Curtis & Pope stands so high among other houses engaged in the same line of business in this city, that no review of the lumber trade of Boston would be complete without mention of the establishment under their control. They began business in 1884, succeeding Mr. George Curtis, who had been identified with the enterprise for a number of years. The office and yard are located at No. 774 Albany Street, and some conception of the magnitude of the trade may be gained from the fact that the total plant covers an area of two acres of ground. This spacious yard is equipped with numerous large sheds and other buildings, and employment is afforded to seventy hands, both a wholesale and retail business being done. Lumber, Brick, Cement, and Building Material in general, are dealt in very extensively indeed, and the arrangements for the reception and shipping of goods are such as to reduce the expense of handling to a minimum—an advantage, the benefits of which are fully shared with customers. Carrying an immense stock, and having every convenience at hand for its economical transportation, this concern is naturally enabled to meet easily all competition, and maintain the leading position it now holds. Messrs. Curtis and Pope are both Bostonians by birth, and are too well known to our residents to render it necessary to give them further personal mention.

R. R. Merrill, Livery, Hack and Boarding Stable, Berkeley Street, Boston, Mass. The prominence which the leading newspapers of this city have been giving of late to the question of physical exercise, shows that the public is beginning to appreciate the value of this "road to health" but this prominence will by no means result in good unless it be borne in mind that the end to be gained by exercise is not supremacy in any special field of athletics, not the throwing of a weight a yard farther or the walking of a mile a few seconds quicker than somebody else, but the general improvement of the health of the individual. Taking this view of the subject, we see that there are many things not generally considered as exercise that may still be of equal if not greater value in bringing about the same results, and prominent, and in fact foremost, among these is driving. A good horse, a good road, good air and a good companion—there you have a combination that is enough to excite animation in the breast of a mummy and cause the blood in the veins of the most overworked business man to circulate with a briskness and vigor as delightful to him as it is novel. These conditions are by no means unattainable either, for Boston suburbs are noted for their fine roads and the air in the vicinity of the "Hub" is often surprisingly fresh and sweet, while as for the companion—but on the whole this part of the question is best answered by each individual for himself. There only remains the team, and this can surely be obtained by calling on Mr. B. R. Merrill on Berkeley Street, for this gentleman conducts one of the most completely equipped stables in town and has many speedy and safe horses and stylish and easy carriages to supply to customers. He occupies three floors and a basement, measuring 112 x 40 feet, and containing one hundred stalls and suitable carriage rooms, also vehicles of every description. Employment is given to fifteen skilled and reliable assistants, and carriages will be furnished at short notice, in any desired quantity for any public occasion. Hacks of the latest pattern and driven by experienced drivers are obtainable here, and horses will be taken to board at the lowest market rates and guaranteed kind and careful treatment.

Edwin T. Leach, Pharmacist, 655 Tremont, cor. West Brookline Street. Although it may seem to many as though there were an overplus of drug stores in this city, still the public is unquestionably all the better served thereby, and it must be remembered that in cases of emergency an instant of time is precious, and the few moments required to cover several blocks and return (should there be no store nearer at hand) may mean death to some victim of accident or disease. The druggist is very apt to be unappreciated in a community, but it would be very difficult to do without him, and his usefulness is none the less real because habit has caused it to be accepted as a matter of course, requiring no special notice. The store occupied by Mr. Edwin T. Leach, at No. 655 Tremont Street, corner of West Brookline Street, has been utilized as a pharmacy since 1863, and came under the control of the gentleman above mentioned in 1887. He is a native of Taunton, Mass., and admirably fitted for his present position as he is thoroughly conversant with both the theory and the practice of Pharmacy, having been upwards of eleven years with Melvin & Badger, and appreciates the grave responsibilities devolving upon one who makes choice of this profession. It is, therefore, only natural that he should have at hand all the most approved and delicate instruments and appliances called for by the most advanced scientific ideas, and that his two assistants should be not only courteous but well informed also. Prescriptions are compounded with exactness at all hours of the day or night, and continuous care and every effort is made to eliminate all sources of error.

August Dierkes, Hotel and Restaurant, Oysters, Wines and Liquors, Lager Beer of the best quality, 1482 and 1484 Washington Street. It is hardly probable that when Mr. August Dierkes opened the establishment he formerly occupied at the corner of Malden and Washington Street, that he had any idea of the prompt and decided success he was going to win, but it soon became plain that the public appreciated such liberal and intelligent management as he gave his enterprise, and his business constantly and rapidly increased, until, finally, he was obliged to remove to his present quarters, Nos. 1482 and 1484 Washington Street. Here Mr. Dierkes has at his disposal four floors containing thirty rooms, the premises being utilized as a first-class hotel. The street-floor is very handsomely and conveniently fitted up with large plate glass windows, etc., and is used as a restaurant and sample room, there being a seating capacity of thirty-six guests, and employment given to fifteen assistants. Oysters are served in every style at short notice, and an extensive variety of substantial food is always at hand for customers to choose from; and for a hungry man to get a "square meal," we know of no better place than right here. Foreign and Domestic Wines and Liquors are carried in stock at all times, and a Specialty is made of Lager Beer, which is to be had of the very best quality, and is freshly drawn from the wood. Mr. Dierkes is a native of Germany, and he fully deserves the patronage he receives, for he is ever anxious to use his patrons right and spares no pains to satisfy every reasonable customer.

E. V. R. Reed, Crayon Portrait Artist, 409 Tremont Street. Wonderful as are the strides that have been made in practical photography, of late years, it must still be considered as rather the means to the end than the end itself, and to make our meaning clearer let us explain that while photography is of the most signal service in assisting the landscape or portrait artist in attaining correctness of outline, etc., it falls short (as any mechanical means of necessity must) when the *spirit* of a scene or the *individual characteristics* of a sitter are to be portrayed. In proof of this, if proof be needed, compare the most artistic and finely finished photograph of a person, with a good crayon portrait of the same person,—such a portrait in short as may be obtained of Mr. E. V. R. Reed of No. 409 Tremont Street. You will then see that although the photograph is apparently without a flaw or imperfection, still there is something wanting, and it is precisely that something that is the essence of a good portrait—individuality. Holding up the photograph you might say "this looks like my friend," holding up the portrait you would say—"this *is* my friend."—and that is just the difference. Mr. Reed has followed his present profession since 1878 and has consequently the good effects of experience added to natural gifts. He devotes his entire attention to Crayon Portraits and, considering the high grade of his work, is extremely moderate in his charges. We will not attempt to describe what Mr. Reed can do, but will simply advise our readers to visit his studio and see for themselves.

Lamson Bros., successors to L. F. Broad, dealer in Provisions, Fruit and Vegetables, Poultry and Game, No. 811 Tremont Street. Nothing is more mortifying than to invite friends to dinner, only to find that the joint or poultry or game, or whatever may have been provided for the repast, is tough, stringy or anything but first-class in every way. It is an experience which, once gone through with, no one wants to repeat, at any cost, and there is but one way to guard against its repetition, and that is to deal only with an establishment that may be implicitly depended on, to supply goods that shall prove just as represented. It is difficult to find such a house, especially in the provision business, but still there are such, and one of the most deservedly popular, and entirely trustworthy of them, is that conducted by Lamson Bros., successors to Mr. L. F. Broad at No. 811 Tremont Street. This undertaking was founded in 1877 and soon gained a high degree of popularity, by reason of the uniform superiority of the goods handled and the low rates quoted in every department. One floor and a basement are utilized, measuring 20 x 80 foot, and five competent assistants are at hand, to give all customers prompt and courteous attention. Provisions, Fruit and Vegetables of all kinds in their seasons are supplied at bottom prices, and as fine an assortment of Poultry and Game as is to be found anywhere is carried at the proper time of year. Orders are accurately delivered, and full satisfaction guaranteed. Since succeeding to this business Messrs Lamson Bros. determined to adopt the plan of giving extra inducements to cash buyers, and by so doing they are enabled to offer the same quality of meats at a much lower price than if obliged to stand the loss arising from bad bills.

Philip Krim, Importer of Rhine Wines, warranted unadulterated, and dealer in Groceries and Foreign Produce, No. 103 Shawmut Avenue. We fancy that few who have resided in the vicinity of No. 103 Shawmut Avenue, for any length of time, are unfamiliar with the enterprise carried on by Mr. Philip Krim at the number given, for this establishment is one of the most popular of the kind in this city, and is more heavily patronized every year. Its proprietor is a native of Germany, and has a very large circle of friends and acquaintances in Boston, for he has prosecuted his present industry since 1871 and has been known for his liberal and enterprising business methods from the very first. The premises utilized are of the dimensions of 18 x 55 feet and contain as fine a stock of Rhine Wines, Groceries and Foreign Produce as can be found in the city. Mr. Krim is an Importer of Rhine Wines which he warrants to be unadulterated, and sells, wholesale and retail, at very low rates, quality considered. The Groceries offered by him will also be found to be of superior quality and the same may be said of every article in his stock, which includes Foreign Produce in general. Employment is given to two assistants, and one of the most popular features of the enterprise is the promptness with which all orders are attended to. Goods are delivered if desired, and courtesy and consideration are extended to all alike.

Henry S. Harris, Real Estate, Mortgages, and Insurance, 709 Tremont Street, and 72 Equitable Building. In the purchase or sale of real estate, or any of the thousand and one transactions connected with the handling of that form of property, the services of a competent, reliable and well-informed agent are often of the highest utility and value, and in the majority of cases will result in the saving of much more than they cost. Agents meriting the description given above, are not quite as plenty as they might be, but they are to be found, and one of the best of them known to us, is Mr. Henry S. Harris, who has an office at No. 709 Tremont Street, and another at No. 72 Equitable Building. Mr. Harris was born in Maine, removed to Boston in 1861, and commenced operations here in his present line of business in 1883. Anything concerning real estate, mortgages or insurance will receive prompt and careful attention, and money will be loaned on mortgages and collateral at moderate rates of interest. Real estate will be bought, sold or exchanged and also leased, special attention being given to the care of property and the collection of rents. Non-residents may safely and profitably give the care of their estates to Mr. Harris, for he is prepared to assume the active management of such trusts at any time, and to discharge the duties accruing thereto with fidelity and discretion. Fire, Marine and Accident Insurance is also given careful attention, and policies written in the best companies, Domestic or Foreign at the lowest rates. Renewals are looked out for with promptness and accuracy and the agency of the following standard companies is held: St. Paul Fire & Marine of St. Paul, Minn; Western Assurance Co. (Fire) of Toronto, Can.; Equitable Life Assurance Co. of New York; Mass. Mutual Accident Association, of Boston. Mr. Harris holds a commission as Justice of the Peace and may be found at 709 Tremont Street, from 8 to 10 A. M. also at 2 o'clock and 5 o'clock P. M. and at 72 Equitable Building from 10.30 to 12.30, where he will give all callers prompt and courteous attention.

W. C. Mayo, Fine Groceries, Teas, Coffees and Flour, 701 Tremont Street, Corner Springfield. It is by no means an easy task to find an establishment devoted to the sale of Groceries in which every preparation is made for catering to the finest trade, while at the same time the prices in every department are kept at the lowest prices consistent with the maintenance of the fine quality indispensable where trade of this description is to be supplied; but, nevertheless, there are such to be found, and none is more thoroughly worthy of a place among them than that conducted by Mr. W. C. Mayo at No. 701 Tremont Street, corner Springfield. This store has been utilized for the sale of groceries for a score of years, and has been under the management of Mr. Mayo since 1880. He is a native of East Boston, where he formerly conducted the same business, and a member of the Odd Fellows, and has shown himself to have a thorough understanding of the grocery business by the intelligent and successful management he has given his present enterprise. One floor and a basement are occupied, 25 x 80 feet in size, and all the goods usually handled in a first-class establishment of the kind are kept in stock, a specialty being made of Fine Teas, Coffees and Flour. Every article sold is fully warranted to prove as represented, and it it will be found that Mr. Mayo's prices compare very favorably with those asked by other dealers.

F. O. Anderson, Upholstery and Decorating, 31 Clarendon Street. That much of the upholstery work done nowadays is neither tasteful nor durable, is unfortunately but too true, and it is therefore important to exercise considerable care in the purchase of upholstered goods unless the buyer wishes to court imposition. Of course there are certain houses in this city whose word is as good as their bond, and whose articles may be accepted in the firm assurance that they will prove as represented but there are other concerns of quite the opposite character, and caution is consequently always in order. But of course the best upholstery will wear out eventually, and to ensure its being renewed in a thoroughly first-class manner, a call should be made on Mr. F. O. Anderson, at No. 31 Clarendon street for he makes a specialty of fine Upholstering and has every facility at hand to fill orders at short notice and in entirely satisfactory style. Mr. Anderson was born in Boston and established the enterprise he now conducts in 1870. The premises utilized comprise one floor measuring 20 x 60 feet, and employment is afforded to three skilled and reliable assistants. Upholstery materials of all descriptions are offered at the lowest market rates and entire dependence can be put on the uniformly superior quality of the articles on sale at this popular store. Orders for Upholstering or Decorating will secure instant attention, and personal care will be taken to see that they are filled satisfactorily.

Samuel Alexander, House and Sign Painter and Glazier, 458 Tremont Street. House-painting is one trade and sign-painting is another, and there are comparatively few painters in this city of whom it may be said, as it can of Mr. Samuel Alexander, doing business at No. 458 Tremont Street, that they can do equally good work in either. Mr. Alexander began operations in 1884, and has built up a patronage of extensive proportions by giving faithful attention to every order with which he has been favored, and by combining good work with moderate prices. He occupies one floor of the dimensions of 20 x 40 feet, and gives employment to four assistants, who are skilled and careful workmen and are able to "push things" when occasion requires haste. The handsome and elaborate signs now to be seen on every hand, show that our merchants are beginning to appreciate the advertising value of a striking and tasteful article of this kind, and nowadays, the business man who is satisfied to go along with a cheap and shabby sign over his door, is looked upon as being either old-fogyish or miserly — and poop s are not apt to patronize an establishment having such a reputation. Mr. Alexander can furnish Signs of any kind or dimensions desired, and he guarantees their durability as well as their beauty. His prices are low and his work is not to be beaten.

S. C. Johnson, Dealer in all kinds of Fish, Oysters, Clams, etc, 612 Tremont Street, Corner Canton Street. There is hardly a food-product so

dependent for excellence upon freshness as fish, and hence it follows that only such establishments as have the best of facilities for obtaining this commodity direct from the water can furnish their customers with perfectly satisfactory goods. In a large city like Boston it is difficult to make this "close connection" but still there are some few houses that are in a position to guarantee the perfect freshness of the fish they handle, and one of the most prominent and popular of these is that carried on by Mr. S. C. Johnson at No. 612 Tremont Street, corner of Canton. The market now conducted by this gentleman has been in operation for about a quarter of a century but has only been under his control since 1884. Mr. Johnson is a native of the beautiful town of Nahant, and like every other man hailing from that famous watering-place he knows a good fish when he sees it, a knowledge which has of course been greatly added to by the years of experience he has had in the handling of the "finny tribe." One floor and a basement are utilized, and all kinds of Fish, together with Oysters, Clams, etc., are kept in stock, two assistants being employed. A specialty is made of the opening of the oysters and clams handled, and customers are thus assured that they will be supplied only with fresh and appetizing articles. Prices are low and the service is prompt and polite.

Duffield & Davis, Beef, Lamb, Mutton, Poultry, Game, etc., Butter and Cheese a Specialty, Dover Market, No. 1 Dover Street. One of the most popular provision houses at the South End is that carried on by Messrs. Duffield & Davis at Dover market, No. 1 Dover Street and the reasons for this popularity are not hard to guess for no one can have dealings with the firm without being impressed by the uniform courtesy and consideration shown to customers and also by the very low rates at which goods are sold. It is, therefore, only natural that a very large business should have been already built up although operations were not begun until 1887, at which date the present firm succeeded Messrs. Larned and Mason. Mr. A. W. Duffield is a native of Boston and is connected with the Odd Fellows, Red Men and United Workmen, while Mr. Davis was born in Lexington and is a member of the Knights of Honor. The premises utilized are of the dimensions of 25 x 40 feet and include one floor and a basement, being fully stocked with a most extensive assortment of Meats, comprising Beef, Lamb, Mutton, Poultry, Game, etc. A Specialty is made of butter and cheese, and the productions of some of the most celebrated creameries in New England are handled, the best of goods being supplied at bottom prices. Employment is afforded to three efficient and polite assistants, and the means at hand for the prompt filling of orders are amply sufficient to meet every demand of the heavy trade carried on.

Herbert Neilson, Druggist, 1915 Washington Street. While it may be accepted as an undisputed fact that it is not at all pleasant to be sick, still that is no reason that any man should grumble and growl because he is so, for the only sensible course for him to pursue is to straightway set to work to get well again as soon as possible. Now this is not to be accomplished by unmanly repining, by any means, and as the poet sings, "There is a balm for every ill," why not go in person or send to some reliable Drug Store and try to get something to "suit your complaint." We won't say that Mr. Herbert Neilson has actually a "balm for every ill," as, with all due consideration for the poet, we don't believe that such has ever been discovered; but we will say, that at his finely equipped store at 1915 Washington Street, he has about as fine a stock of Drugs and Medicines as is found in the city. This enterprise was inaugurated by Mr. J. Henderson in 1858, and the present owner took possession about 1889 and soon gained the confidence of the public, who have found none but the freshest and purest materials used here, and that prompt and polite attention is assured to all. Mr. Neilson has resided in Boston for many years, and being a member of the Grand Army, is well known to many prominent people. He is well fitted for the position he has assumed, and maintains a close supervision over his establishment. One floor and basement are occupied. Special and most painstaking attention is paid the compounding of prescriptions, which are made up of the best materials and furnished at the most reasonable prices.

Mrs. E. S. Shedd, Dress Maker and Dealer in Dry and Fancy Goods, Small Wares, Stationery, Confectionery, etc.; Stamping of all kinds a Specialty; Instruction in Oil and Lustre Painting; No. 10 Union Park Street; Employment Agency for Select Help. The establishment conducted by Mrs. E. S. Shedd, at No. 10 Union Park Street, has gained a large patronage during the comparatively short time that it has been in operation, and its popularity is only what would naturally be expected by those who are aware of the many conveniences it affords to the public. The enterprise was inaugurated in 1885, and has been carried on under such liberal and intelligent methods, that its success was assured from the start. Mrs. Shedd is a dressmaker of large experience and educated taste, and offers her services to those who may need the assistance that only a skilled artist in this line can give. Her charges are very moderate, and satisfaction is assured to those employing her. Premises measuring 20 x 50 feet are occupied, and a carefully selected stock is carried, comprising Dry and Fancy Goods, Small Wares, Stationery, Confectionery, etc., which are offered at very low prices. A specialty is made of all kinds of Stamping, which is done at short notice and with uniform accuracy, and instruction is given in Oil and Lustre Painting. Mrs. Shedd maintains an employment agency for select help, in connection with her establishment, which is made frequent use of by ladies in the vicinity, and which has proved a great public convenience. This department is extremely well managed, and has gained a most enviable reputation.

C. W. Randall, Fine Millinery, 1091 Washington Street. Although South End establishments are not, as a general rule, supposed to vie with those carried on "in town" as regards the attractions shown and advantages offered, still there are a few that need fear no comparison of this kind; and prominent among these is that conducted at No. 1091 Washington Street by Mrs. C. W. Randall. This enterprise was inaugurated in 1882, and has steadily increased in favor and patronage, until at the present time many ladies make it a point to purchase all their millinery supplies at this store, having satisfied themselves by practical experience that no more satisfactory results were attainable elsewhere. A specialty is made of the finest custom trade. One floor and a basement are occupied, of the dimensions of 25 x 80 feet, and one of the most extensive, varied and complete stocks of millinery to be found in Boston is displayed. A prominent feature of the management, and one of the chief causes of its popularity, is the enterprise shown in obtaining the latest fashionable novelties at the earliest possible moment, and it should also be stated that such goods are not held at the exorbitant rates too generally charged under such circumstances. Attention is paid to the durability as well as to the appearance of the articles sold, and customers of the most refined taste will confirm our estimate of the intelligent discrimination shown in suiting the character and arrangement of the trimmings to the individual appearance of the purchaser.

C. H. Knox & Co., Painting and Decorating, 4 East Springfield Street. More than one house-owner has learned to his sorrow that it is important to close contracts only with reliable and responsible concerns if one is to feel sure of such agreements being carried out to the letter, and as not a few complaints have come to our ears respecting the manner in which certain firms violate the understandings they may reach with their patrons as regards the doing of house-painting, etc., we take this opportunity to call attention to a long-established and entirely reliable house engaged in Painting and Decorating and similar work; for we are perfectly sure that all orders the concern referred to may be entrusted with will be carried out in the same uniformly satisfactory and first-class manner that has characterized their efforts in the past. Mr. C. H. Knox started in 1840, and the present firm was formed in 1872, and have built up their present large trade by patient industry and equitable business methods. Mr. Knox was born in Maine, and is now one of the best-known gentlemen in his line of business in this city. The premises occupied are located at No. 4 East Springfield Street, and comprise one floor and a basement measuring 20 x 60 feet. An unusually complete stock of Paints, Oils and Varnishes, and other material necessary to the filling of the many orders received is carried, and employment is given to a force of from twenty-five to forty picked men — experienced, thorough, and conscientious workmen. Using the finest stock and employing the best skill, Mr. Knox can confidently guarantee satisfaction, and his prices are as reasonable as his work is acceptable.

Geo. F. Jowett, Wholesale and Retail Dealer in Beef, Pork, Mutton, Lamb, Veal, Salt Provisions of all kinds, Poultry and Game in season. Every Variety of Country Produce. Stalls 18 and 24 Washington Market, and Commonwealth Market, Eliot Square, Roxbury. Telephone No. 4527. Occupying a prominent position among the leading business enterprises that have been instrumental in giving Washington Market its present popularity, that conducted by Mr. Geo. F. Jowett deserves special mention, and, on the whole, might well be taken as a model of what such an establishment should be. There are a variety of reasons why it should be regarded so highly, and there is no occasion to mention them here in detail; but we may simply say that the management of the undertaking has been characterized by liberality as well as far-sightedness; and that the public has been taught to rely implicitly upon whatever representations Mr. Jowett or those in his employ may make. Stalls Nos. 18 and 20 are utilized, and all the available space is required for the accommodation of the stock carried, for both a wholesale and a retail business is done and an immense quantity of goods disposed of. The assortment of Meats on hand includes Beef, Pork, Mutton, Lamb and Veal, together with Salt provisions of all kinds, and Poultry and Game are also handled very extensively in their season. Every variety of Country Produce is also to be had here. Although the trade carried on is very large, the facilities for attending to it are ample, and there being five competent assistants employed, customers may depend upon prompt and polite service at all times. Orders by Telephone No. 4527 will be carefully filled and all goods are sold at the lowest rates consistent with their quality. Mr. Jowett is a native of Maine, and is a member of the Grand Army, having served in the First Maine Cavalry. He is also connected with both the Odd Fellows and the Royal Arcanum, and his present enterprise was inaugurated in 1883.

C. E. Baldwin & Co., Plumbers and Gas Fitters, 35 Clarendon Street, near Warren Avenue. The system of drainage and water-supply to be found in practically all city houses, requires careful attention and maintenance if the health of the occupants is to be preserved uninjured, and we may add that pains should also be taken to see that no leak or weakness exists in the gas or water pipes, and should any be found, some reliable concern should be called that makes a specialty of preventing and repairing damage by gas or water. Such an enterprise is that conducted by Messrs. C. E. Baldwin & Co., at No. 35 Clarendon Street, and orders left at this establishment will receive instant attention at the lowest rates. Business was first started in 1878, and a thriving trade has long since been built up, as the public have found that this firm do reliable and thorough work, and never charge exorbitant prices. Mr. Baldwin is a native of Boston, and resides at No. 50 Columbus Avenue, where orders will be received when more convenient to patrons. The store is 20 x 55 feet in size, and includes one floor and basement, a full stock of Plumbers' and Gas Fitters' materials being carried, and three assistants employed. Good work and low prices tell the story of this concern's success.

F. A. Barteaux, Pharmacist, 64-A Dover Street. Among the most popular pharmaceutical establishments to be found in this city, mention should be made of that carried on by Mr. F. A. Barteaux at No. 64-A Dover Street, for although this enterprise was only inaugurated in 1885 (it having been started by Mr. J. E. Phillips in that year), it has already attained an assured success and is, in fact, fully worthy of the confidence reposed in it by the public at large. The present proprietor has been in control since 1886, and to his watchful and discriminating care much of the present large trade is due, for he has neglected no means to satisfy his patrons and has taken advantage of every opportunity to protect and advance the interests of his customers as well as of himself. The premises occupied measure 20 x 50 feet and include one floor and a basement. A large and admirably selected stock is carried, and whether Drugs, Medicines, Chemicals or Toilet and Fancy Articles are wanted, the order may be filled here without delay and at very low rates. Mr. Barteaux is a native of St. John, N. B., and is a thoroughly skilled, practical pharmacist, having had twenty-four years' experience. Some of the special preparations put up by him have met with a very large sale, notably Barteaux's West End Cologne, which affords a delicate and yet lasting perfume and is sold at a very low price. Prescriptions are compounded at short notice and with a degree of care that assures avoidance of all mistakes, while the rates quoted in this department are especially low and satisfactory.

Horan Brothers, Cutlery, Hardware, Tools; manufacturers of Light Machinery, Locks, Bells; Brass Finishers, Metal Polishers; Edge Tools re-set; 1395 and 1397 Washington Street, opposite Cathedral. For nearly a score of years the establishment conducted by Horan Brothers at Nos. 1395 and 1397 Washington street has been before the public, and the firm can well afford to let the estimate of their ability rest upon the service extended to customers during that period. The firm is made up of Messrs. J. J. and P. H. Horan, both of whom are natives of this state and too well known to require further personal mention. The premises utilized comprise one floor and a basement and measure 25 x 70 feet, the manufacture of Light Machinery, Locks, etc., being extensively carried on, and employment given to eight skilled assistants. Brass Finishing, Metal Polishing and such work is done at short notice and in a superior manner, and Edge Tools are re-set and made practically as good as new. A very extensive stock is carried of Cutlery and Light Hardware in general, and Nails, Screws, Rivets, Tools and number of other commodities are offered for sale at the lowest market rates, in quantities to suit, both a wholesale and retail business being done. The repairing of Locks is given special attention and done expeditiously and cheaply, and keys will be fitted at short notice and warranted to work smoothly and well. One of the best-appointed light machine shops in this city is maintained, and models or other small mechanism can be made at low rates.

James Rough, Florist, 1559 Washington Street. The increasing use that is being made of flowers in society, is one of the most pronounced movements of the day, and it is evident the public have discovered that many sentiments can be expressed by the judicious employment of flowers, that would otherwise have to find imperfect utterance, or else be left entirely unsaid. A gift of flowers is always in good taste, and when any hesitation is felt as to whether a present would be appropriate or not, flowers may be given, with the assurance that no offence can possibly be taken. It is necessary of course to have such gifts selected and arranged in harmony with the spirit that prompts their sending, and in order to secure this result, it is well to patronize a florist who, from his experience and taste, is well qualified to be considered an authority on such matters. Such may truthfully be said of Mr. James Rough, doing business at No. 1559 Washington Street, near Newton Street, for this gentleman has been identified with his present enterprise since 1873, and has a reputation second to none for taste and reliability. The premises occupied comprise one floor and a basement, and the assortment of Plants and Cut Flowers carried, is always full and desirable. Floral Emblems of every kind are kept on hand and made to order at a few hours' notice, and whether the occasion be one of joy or sorrow, Mr. Rough can furnish an appropriate design, as elaborate as may be desired, and as low in price as circumstances will permit. The store has telephone connection, and orders will be acted upon as soon as received, and every effort made to please and satisfy every patron.

J. P. Johnson, Dealer in Beef, Pork, Lamb, Mutton, etc., also Poultry, Vegetables and Canned Goods; Choice Butter always on hand; 89 Shawmut avenue. The popularity of the establishment carried on by Mr. J. P. Johnson at No. 89 Shawmut Avenue, is unusual, but nevertheless, to those who are acquainted with the methods of management pursued, it is by no means remarkable. The enterprise was inaugurated in 1885, and the inducements held out to customers soon resulted in the establishment of a large trade, which has since steadily increased. The premises utilized measure 20 x 22 feet in dimensions and comprise one floor and a basement, the stock carried being a very varied and complete one, and selected especially with an eye to the demands of the best family trade. It includes Beef, Pork, Lamb, Mutton, Veal, etc., together with Poultry and Game in their seasons. Mr. Johnson makes a specialty of the sale of fine Creamery Butter, and always has a supply of the very choicest grade on hand. He offers it at prices as low as the market will permit, and fully guarantees its flavor, purity and general excellence. A fine assortment of Vegetables and Canned Goods is also carried in stock, and orders will be given immediate and careful attention. Employment is afforded to four competent assistants, and customers are assured civil treatment and positively fair dealing in every respect. Mr. Johnson is thoroughly acquainted with his business, and neglects no means to serve and satisfy his patrons.

A. Spear, Wholesale and Retail Dealer in Choice Provisions, Poultry & Game, Fish & Oysters, Fruit, Country Produce, &c., 100 & 102 Columbus Ave., Under Hotel Lafayette. Out of all the dealers in Provisions doing business in this city, there are few who have had the experience enjoyed by Mr. A. Spear, whose establishment is located at No. 100 Columbus ave. This gentleman began operations in 1862, and can consequently look back on over a quarter of a century during which he has been engaged in his present line of business. "Experience teaches" says the proverb, and it certainly has in Mr. Spear's case, for his thorough acquaintance with every detail of the provision trade is abundantly proved by the able manner in which he handles the immense business now done by him. One floor and a basement, measuring 20 x 60 feet, are occupied and a very large and varied stock is carried, comprising choice Provisions, Poultry and Game, Foreign and Domestic Fruit, Country Produce, Fish and Oysters, etc. Much of the great popularity enjoyed by this establishment is due to the absolute dependence that may be placed in the uniformly high quality of the goods handled, for Mr. Spear gives special attention to the handling of the finer cuts of meat, etc., and is at all times prepared to suit the most fastidious in this respect. He is a native of Maine, and is prominently identified with the leading Fraternal and Beneficial organizations of the country, such as the Odd Fellows, Knights of Pythias, Knights of Honor, Improved Order of Red men, Royal Society of Good Fellows, etc. As may be supposed, he has a very large circle of friends in the community, and is widely known as a representative citizen. Both a wholesale and retail business is done at his establishment, and employment is given to six courteous and efficient assistants.

P. Kyle, Modeler and Architectural Sculptor in Stone and Wood, No. 520 Albany Street. Nothing lends such an individuality to the exterior appearance of an edifice as skillfully sculptured designs, in either stone or wood, and in these days, when such attempts are made to construct every building of any pretension after a model of its own, the sculptor finds an extensive demand for his services. A gentleman who has met with great success in this field of action is Mr. P. Kyle of No. 520 Albany Street, and since he began operations here in 1884, he has executed many commissions in a style that has proved eminently satisfactory to his patrons and remunerative to himself, for it has resulted in the building up of a business that is at once extensive and select. Mr. Kyle brings to his chosen profession both natural fitness and a carefully acquired education. As a Modeler and Architectural Sculptor, he occupies a position of which he may well be proud, for he has proceeded on the assumption that "there is no royal road to art," and has gained whatever success has fallen to his lot by hard work and close application. Two floors are occupied. 25 x 40 feet in dimensions, and the employment of two efficient assistants enables Mr. Kyle to fill the many orders he receives with the greatest despatch consistent with the doing of the best work.

John Woodruff, Stationer, Bookseller and Dealer in Artists' Materials, 459 Tremont Street, Opp. Chapman. The establishment conducted by Mr. John Woodruff at No. 459 Tremont Street, is very popular in the vicinity, particularly among people of a literary turn of mind, for not only are the latest novels, and in fact books of all kinds, obtainable here at publisher's prices, but one of the best-selected Circulating Libraries in the city is maintained and is constantly being replenished with new and desirable works. Mr. Woodruff began operations at 453 Tremont Street in 1879, and removed to present quarters in 1884, and soon attracted to his store a very considerable degree of custom, for the inducements he offered were unmistakable, and his policy was, and is now for that matter, to give full value for money received in every instance. The premises in use are 20 x 40 feet in size and no available room is wasted, for the stock carried is a very large as well as varied one and includes Stationery, Artists' Materials and Fancy Goods in addition to the articles already mentioned. Mr. Woodruff keeps all of the leading weekly and monthly, Foreign and American publications on his news counter, and is prepared to receive annual subscriptions for the same at publishers' rates. His establishment is centrally located, being opposite Chapman Street, and although a large business is done, callers are assured prompt and courteous attention as ample assistance is at hand.

J. M. Waitt, Upholsterer, No. 520 Tremont Street. There are very few pieces of information more apt to be of use to the average householder than such as refer to where the services of a competent and responsible Upholsterer may be obtained, for Upholstery work enters so largely into the furnishing of our homes that it is of prime importance in the domestic economy. It very often happens that a chair or two, or more frequently a sofa belonging to a set, will be worn shabby as regards its upholstering, long before the other pieces in the set are worn at all. In such a case it is obvious that as long as this continues, the appearance of the whole set is spoiled, and just here it is seen how the truest economy can be subserved by having the injured article made to look as good as new, at a comparatively trifling expense. Mr. J. M. Waitt, of No. 520 Tremont Street, makes a specialty of the doing of work of this kind, and as for the manner in which he does it, there are hundreds of families at the South End and Highlands that can testify regarding his ability and taste, as he has carried on his present business in this city since 1871 and has gained a well-earned reputation for the best of work at moderate prices. He is a native of Gardiner, Me., and is one of the best-known business men in the section in which he is located. Two floors and a basement are occupied, measuring 14 x 75 feet, and there are six skilled assistants employed. All kinds of furniture, mattresses, window shades and draperies will be made to order, at the shortest possible notice, and furniture is repaired in the most skillful and durable manner. Carpets are made, cleaned and put down in thoroughly first-class style and satisfaction is confidently promised.

J. B. Colton, Apothecary, 766 Tremont Street, corner Springfield. An establishment which needs no commendation from us among those who have made adequate trial of its capabilities, is that conducted by Mr. J. B. Colton at No. 766 Tremont Street, but as this volume will be read by many who are in doubt as to where they may find a thoroughly reliable family drug store, we feel that the space devoted to a consideration of the advantages derivable from dealing at the establishment above mentioned is well utilized. Mr. Colton is a native of Springfield, Mass., and, by the way, it is worthy of mention as a curious coincidence that the store occupied by him is located at the corner of Springfield Street. He is a gentleman of long experience in his chosen business, as will be seen from the fact that he began operations over a quarter of a century ago, or in 1862. There are few similar establishments in this city carrying so carefully selected a stock of Drugs, Medicines and Chemicals, for Mr. Colton exercises great care in the ordering of those articles and spares no pains to ensure against furnishing anything that will fail to give satisfaction. In the compounding of physicians' prescriptions a high reputation has been won for promptness, skill and perfect accuracy, and patrons may feel positive that all possible precautions are taken against error in this most important department of the business.

St. Cloud Market and Grocery, E. G. Barnard, Proprietor, 561 Tremont Street. There are certain kinds of information that are always in request, and among these may be mentioned that pertaining to the purchase of Provisions, Groceries, etc., to the best advantage; for every householder wants to know where he may find goods suited to his taste at reasonable prices, and where he may depend upon receiving honorable treatment. In this connection, then, let us call attention to the St. Cloud Market located at No. 561 Tremont Street, for at this establishment the customer is assured of being served with strictly first class goods, and will find that all representations made are entirely warranted by the facts. This popular market was opened in 1885 by Mr. E. G. Barnard, who is a native of this city and well known throughout the Provision and Grocery trade. One floor and a basement are occupied, measuring 25 x 60 feet, and four assistants are at hand, who will be found prompt, obliging and well-informed. Mr. Barnard is at all times prepared to furnish the choicest Cuts of Meats of various descriptions at the lowest market rates, and a Full Line of Choice Family and Fancy Groceries, Canned Goods, etc. Another element in the building up of his large business, has been the celerity and accuracy with which orders are delivered. This store occupies a leading position among similar establishments all over the city, and deserves the most liberal patronage.

B. H. Butterfield, Mason & Builder, Office, 7 East Springfield Street. Among the various masons and builders doing business in this section of the city, there are none more worthy of patronage than Mr. B. H. Butterfield, whose office is at No. 7 East Springfield Street, for this gentleman is noted for the prompt and careful attention he gives the orders entrusted to him, and may at all times be relied upon to show regard for the interests of his customers as well as for those of himself. He is a native of Vermont, and inaugurated his present enterprise in 1874, so that neither experience nor ability is lacking in his case, and he may be considered as especially well prepared to undertake anything in his line of business and carry it out at the least possible expense consistent with durable, honest work. Mr. Butterfield is a licensed drain layer and gives personal attention to Kalsomining, whitening and jobbing in general, employing six very efficient assistants and warranting that all that skill and the use of the best materials can do to assure satisfaction shall be done in every instance. Orders by mail will be acted on as promptly as those given in person, and Mr. Butterfield will call and give estimates in cases where this is requested. His facilities for the carrying on of a general jobbing business are complete, and we feel that we can heartily commend this enterprise to our readers and all others interested.

G. H. Lougee & Co., Dealers in Dry Goods, Corsets, Hosiery, Gloves and Small Wares, 1837 Washington Street. Among the business enterprises in this section of the city, that are not only of considerable prominence already but are rapidly growing in size and importance, that carried on by Messrs. G. H. Lougee & Co. at No. 1837 Washington Street, deserves special mention. This undertaking was established and founded in 1844, yet already it has become an assured success and many residents of the vicinity purchase practically all of the Dry and Fancy Goods they may require at this store. One floor and a basement are occupied, of the dimensions of 22 x 75 feet, and employment is afforded four efficient assistants. The stock carried is a surprisingly large and varied one, and not the least attractive thing about it is the entire absence of any line of unsalable goods. Every dealer knows how hard it is to avoid an accumulation of such articles, and the firm under notice are to be congratulated on their success in so selecting goods and fixing the prices on the same that prompt and certain sale was the inevitable result. Among the articles most extensively handled, mention may be made of Ladies' and Children's Furnishings, for this department is given special attention and some very pronounced bargains are offered therein. It has long since been discovered by the public that the representations made at this establishment concerning goods may be safely depended upon, as Messrs. G. H. Lougee & Co. propose to dispose of articles on their merits and positively forbid any misrepresentation whatever, particular attention being paid to trade from children, who are waited on promptly, and every effort made to suit, of course making it a pleasant place for them to trade. Under such management, confidence and patronage are sure to increase rapidly and steadily, and it is gratifying to be able to make public record of a success so honestly won as that attained by this popular firm.

Martin J. McIntire. Druggist, 1401 Washington Street. The store occupied by Mr. Martin J. McIntire, at No. 1401 Washington Street, has long been identified with the handling of Drugs and Medicines, and was carried on for years before it came into the possession of Mr. Clarence E. McIntire in 1889, this gentleman being succeeded by the present proprietor five years later. The premises comprise one floor and a basement, and measure 25 x 60 feet, being well fitted up, and containing a skilfully selected stock of Drugs, Medicines, Chemicals, etc., as well as a fine assortment of Toilet articles, Fancy Goods, Cigars, etc. Mr. McIntire does a large business and puts his prices down to the lowest possible point, for he makes it a rule to constantly renew his stock, and so adopts means to "keep it moving," as the saying is. Employment is given to two competent and polite assistants, and especial pains is taken to accommodate those wishing prescriptions compounded, every facility being at hand to fill such orders without annoying delay, and no precaution neglected that is necessary to assure the proper safety to patrons. Mr. McIntire has built up a most thriving prescription trade, and has won the reputation of combining accuracy with low prices. His drugs are pure and carefully selected and not drawn from a stock injured by age or bad keeping. He also prepares the "Standard Extract of Sarsaparilla" and a "Vegetable Cough Syrup," which are unequaled for their intended purposes.

Frank P. Chaplin. Fine Boots, Shoes and Rubbers, 1307 Washington Street, Continental Block, Opposite Rollins Street. Since the gentleman whose card is printed above opened his present store in 1883, he has certainly been successful in building up a patronage of large proportions, and as this is by no means an easy thing to do, especially in the retail shoe business, it may be of interest to consider some of the methods adopted to secure this end. Mr. Chaplin occupies a handsome and commodious store, measuring 20 x 70 feet, and also utilizes a basement of similar dimensions. The store is located in Continental Block, No. 1307 Washington Street, opposite Rollins Street, and contains a stock of Ladies', Gentlemen's and Children's Boots and Shoes, that is well worthy of careful inspection. The goods offered are, in each and every case, warranted to prove as represented, and Mr. Chaplin not only stands ready to honor this guarantee, but will esteem it as a favor if any who think they have reason to complain will come to him and put the case before him. He maintains that one honestly dissatisfied customer may do his business more harm than a dozen sales can atone for, and hence claims no special credit for earnestly striving to satisfy every purchaser. Fine Goods are given especial prominence in this store, and ladies who appreciate artistic foot-wear should give Mr. Chaplin a call, as he can supply them with perfect-fitting and durable articles at the lowest market rates. Not a week passes but some special bargains are offered at this establishment, and although many of these are displayed in the show windows, others are not; so that the best way to do is to go inside and see for yourself.

A. W. Merrow, wholesale and Retail Dealers in Butter, Cheese, Eggs, Lard, Beans, &c., No. 1301 Washington Street. We often hear it said "I had rather have no butter at all than poor stuff," and it must be agreed that poor butter is about as mean and unsatisfactory an article of diet as we know of. Many people really do not know where good butter can be obtained, and, as a consequence, they trade first at this store and then at that, sometimes getting a good article but more often a poor one, and when the latter happens, transfer their trade to some other establishment, only to meet with the same experience. Now if they will place an order with Mr. A. W. Merrow, of No. 1301 Washington Street, they will most assuredly be supplied with fresh creamery butter of superior quality, and, what is more, they may always depend on getting the best of butter at this popular house, at all seasons and all times. And not only butter but country produce, such as Eggs, Cheese, Lard, Beans, etc. Mr. Merrow occupies one floor and a basement, of the dimensions of 20 x 50 feet, and does a brisk and growing business. He is a native of the Pine Tree State, and assumed possession of his present enterprise in 1887, it having been founded five years earlier by a Mr. Gladwin; later W. W. Freeman, who was in time succeeded by Cummins & Woodman. The assortment of goods carried is as large as it is carefully selected, and the employment of three efficient assistants, renders it an easy matter to give prompt attention to every caller and to fill all orders with dispatch and accuracy.

R. G. Morse & Co., Dealers in Coal, Wood, Bricks, Lime, Sand, Cement, Hair and Laths, 408 Albany Street; Branch Office, 1353 Washington Street. The establishment conducted by Messrs. R. G. Morse & Co., at No. 498 Albany Street (foot of Malden), may be said to be the pioneer of its kind in that portion of the city, for this was the first coal-yard opened on the street; and it is one of the most spacious in the entire city, affording accommodation for three large coal sheds, as well as storage facilities for Building Materials and 8000 barrels of Cement. The original firm was Cook & Rand, these gentlemen beginning business just thirty years ago, but in 1868 the present proprietors assumed control, and they have conducted operations ever since. Mr. Morse is a native of Maine, and is very widely known in Boston and vicinity. The commodities dealt in include Coal, Wood, Bricks, Lime, Plaster, Sand, Cement, Hair and Laths, employment being afforded to twenty assistants and an immense business done. Wood will be sawed and split by steam-power as required, and, having every improved facility to handle orders as soon as received, the firm is in a position to guarantee prompt and satisfactory service. An order box is maintained at No. 35 Hawley Street, and another at No. 164 Devonshire Street, and orders received through these or by mail will be given instant attention. A branch office is carried on at No. 1353 Washington Street, and any one wanting Coal, Wood, or Building Material, will find it to their advantage to place their order with this house, as its facilities are unsurpassed, and a sufficiently large stock is carried to meet all demands, while all goods are sold at bottom rates.

J. E. Freeman, dealer in all kinds of Fresh, Salt and Pickled Fish, Lobsters, Oysters, Clams, etc., 719 Tremont Street. Among the many advantages enjoyed by the residents of Boston over many not so fortunately situated, mention should be made of the cheapness and variety of the fish obtainable in that city, for Boston is well known as one of the greatest fish-markets in the world, and in no other city of equal size in the country are such opportunities afforded to the purchaser. This may, with truth, be called a great advantage, for fish forms one of the most economical, palatable and nutritious foods known to man, and as long as it is plentiful, there need be no fear of want and hunger. One of the very best known and most popular retail fish-markets within the limits of this city, is that of which Mr. J. E. Freeman is the proprietor, located at No. 719 Tremont Street; and it is not surprising that this gentleman should understand how to so conduct an establishment of the kind mentioned as to make it a favorite with the public, for he has been engaged in the business, for over a score of years, having begun operations in 1866. Mr. Freeman was born on Cape Cod, and has a large circle of friends in this community, where his straightforward business methods and careful attention to the wants of his patrons have caused him to be generally esteemed. One floor and a basement are occupied, measuring 20 x 80 feet, and a full assortment is carried of Fresh, Salt and Pickled Fish, Lobsters, Oysters and Clams. Employment is given to six assistants, and orders are assured prompt and accurate filling, while Mr. Freeman's prices are as low as the lowest for equally desirable goods.

L. K. Sweet, Dealer in Choice Provisions, Fruit, Vegetables, Poultry and Game in their season, also Fish, Oysters, Clams, etc., etc., 1496 Washington Street, corner E. Canton. A nicely appointed and largely patronized provision market, located at the South End, is that carried on by Mr. L. K. Sweet, at No. 1496 Washington Street. Mr. Sweet inaugurated his present enterprise in 1854, and the public have given evidence of their appreciation of his efforts to please them since the start. One floor is occupied, measuring 20 x 50 feet, and a superior assortment of goods is in stock, comprising provisions in general, foreign and domestic Fruits, Country Produce, Game, Poultry, etc. A prominent feature of this establishment is the promptness and courtesy with which customers are served, for employment is afforded to five efficient and polite assistants, and callers may be assured quick and intelligent attention, and also that the goods supplied them will prove just as represented. Beef, Mutton, Pork and Vegetables of all kinds in their seasons, supplied at bottom prices. All orders are delivered without annoying delay. Mr. Sweet also conducts a Provision Store for the season at Nantasket Beach, and keeps open as long as a customer remains at the beach. He has a first-class market in every respect. Having done all the buying for the Nantasket Market last season, and with long experience in buying provisions, is prepared to please all, in price and quality.

G. E. M. Confectionery Co., Geo. E. Martin, 1417 Washington Street. There is no danger of Bostonians suffering from a dearth of Confectionery or Ice Cream for there are many dealers in this city and the trade is in a prosperous condition; but there are some dealers who are also manufacturers, and it goes without saying that, other things being equal, these houses can offer more pronounced advantages to customers than if they were obliged to purchase the articles they handle, ready made. The "G. E. M." Confectionery Co., of No. 1417 Washington Street, succeeded Messrs. Green & Co., who established the business in 1884, and perhaps as good a reason as we can give for the large patronage that has since been accorded the company, is that hinted at in the announcement they make to the public, as follows: "We manufacture our Candies and Ice Cream and our goods can always be relied upon for 'absolute purity, as we make only the finest grades.'" One floor and a basement are occupied, of the dimensions of 20 x 45 feet, and the assortment of fine Confections shown is most complete and attractive. There is a sense of security in dealing with such a house that enhances the flavor of the goods obtained, and Mr. Geo. E. Martin, the proprietor, has no reason to complain of the support his enterprise receives, for a very large and growing business is done. An Ice Cream parlor is in the rear of the store, where choice flavors can be obtained by the plate, quart or gallon. Mr. Martin is a member of the Free Masons, and gives close personal attention to the carrying on of his establishment.

J. H. Nelson, 772 Tremont Street, Dealer in Stationery, Fancy Goods and Confectionery, Magazines, Periodicals, etc. An establishment which may well be called one of the "landmarks" of the South End is that conducted by Mr. J. H. Nelson at No. 772 Tremont Street, for this gentleman has occupied his present quarters for more than twenty-one years; and more than one old "Dwight School" boy, who now perhaps sports a heavy beard and supports a large family, can distinctly remember going to "Nelson's" to buy "slips," etc., when such articles were required for school use. And then Fourth of July goods, fire-crackers, torpedoes and all that fascinating family! How often has the writer fastened his nose against the glass, looking with longing eyes into attractive windows at the wealth of articles so loved by every boy, as the season approached for the celebration of the nation's birth. Were Mr. Nelson's fireworks brighter? Did his "crackers" make more of a resounding "bang" in those days than do any in these degenerate times? Perhaps so, or was it the eyes that were brighter and the ears that were keener to appreciate these effects? At all events, it may be safely said that all the goods handled by this gentleman, then, as now, were strictly to be depended on. And what a variety of goods there are! Stationery, Fancy Goods and Confectionery to begin with; then Magazines and Periodicals of all kinds, and, by the way, subscriptions are received for every publication at the very lowest rates. Mr. Nelson acts as agent for the well-known Philadelphia Ice Cream Company, and delivers Ice Cream promptly when ordered, and also acts in the same capacity for the Austin C. Wellington Coal Company, and is, therefore, prepared to guarantee the best quality of coal at standard rates. Goods are received for one of the best Laundries in the city, the wagon calling at the store twice daily; and an express leaves the store three times a day, by which goods may be sent to any part of the country at fair prices. Stratton & Storm's Cigars are sold, both by the box and at retail, and at prices as low as the lowest. Mr. Nelson is a native of Maine, and a member of the Odd Fellows. That he has many friends, not only including those he knows, but those who know him, goes without saying, and as an instance of this, the writer can recall how sorry he felt when an explosion and a fire caused Mr. Nelson considerable loss some years ago, although that gentleman has not the least acquaintance with him.

Stevens' Cafe, 1625 Washington Street. Among what may be called the "institutions" of the South End, mention should be made of "Stevens' Cafe" located at No. 1625 Washington Street, for this establishment is known to very many people, and in some respects has no equal in the city. It occupies premises of the dimensions of 20 x 80 feet, comprising one floor and a basement, and those who appreciate good food, neatly served amid pleasant surroundings, will thank us, after giving this Cafe a trial, for causing them to patronize it. Mr. Stevens is a native of Maine and has conducted the enterprise in question for several years. He employs five experienced assistants and places his prices at such low figures that everybody wonders "how he can do it." Table Board is furnished at the rate of $4.00 per week for ladies and $4.50 per week for gentlemen, twenty-one meal tickets being sold at those prices. It should be remembered that the food as well as the service is first-class and that great pains are taken to satisfy every guest. Mr. Stevens carries a fine assortment of confectionery and cigars, and conducts an ice-cream department that is much appreciated and largely patronized. Cream is sold by the pint, quart or gallon, and is warranted to be made of the best materials and to be of fine flavor.

H. G. Weston, Dealer in Stationery, Fancy Goods, Artists' Materials; Troy Laundry Agency; under Clarendon Hotel. We would call our readers' attention to the assortment carried by Mr. H. G. Weston at No. 523 Tremont Street, under the Clarendon Hotel, with the assurance that they will find it well worthy of inspection, for it includes a great variety of artists' materials of every description and of a uniformly high order of merit. Tube Colors, Plaques, Easels — in short, about everything desired by artists may be purchased here at prices that will compare favorably with those of any similar establishment in town; also, Art Novelties of choice designs a specialty. Stationery, in the latest fashionable novelties, etc., is also largely handled, and all the popular Periodicals are on sale, while a finely selected Circulating Library affords an opportunity for the latest novels of the day to be read at a nominal expense. Mr. Weston is agent for the Troy Laundry, and receives goods at the lowest rates, assuring prompt and regular delivery.

C. C. Ryder, Grocer, and Dealer in Foreign and Domestic Fruits, Cor. Tremont and Dartmouth Streets. An enterprise which will round out its fortieth year during the present season, is that of which Mr. C. C. Ryder is the proprietor, and which is carried on at the corner of Tremont and Dartmouth Streets. Established in 1848, this undertaking has grown with the city. Until today it enjoys to the highest degree the confidence and patronage of the community. Mr. Ryder was born in Chatham, Mass., and ranks with our best-known wholesale and retail grocers. He makes a specialty of the sale of Foreign and Domestic Fruits, and is prepared to furnish these in any desired quantity at the proper seasons. As agent for the "Pride of Key West" cigars he has been instrumental in widely extending the sale of this highly popular brand, and he reports an annually increasing demand for the same. One floor and a basement are occupied, of the dimensions of 25 x 45 feet and a very large stock of Staple and Fancy Groceries is on hand, comprising such goods as are required by the most fastidious trade, which are offered at the lowest market rates. The display of canned goods shown is especially fine, for it embraces the productions of the most reliable and celebrated manufacturers in this and foreign countries, and includes relishes and luxuries of every description. Employment is given to an adequate force of efficient and polite assistants, and all orders are delivered at short notice.

Mitton Bros., Dealers in Provisions and Poultry, Fruit, Vegetables and Canned Goods of all kinds, 1351 Washington Street. A conscientious desire to use customers right, and an exceptionally complete knowledge of every detail of the business, make up a combination that promises the best results, and we can assure our readers that in the case we have in mind (that of Mitton Brothers, carrying on operations at No. 1351 Washington Street) this promise is fully realized by the performance. The gentlemen we have named, began operations in 1881, and, on the whole, have little reason to complain of the reception their efforts to please the public have met with, for although they have worked hard, they have built up a large and growing trade and one that as yet shows no signs of having attained its full dimensions. The firm is made up of Messrs. G. A. and J. W. Mitton, both of whom were born in Fitchburg, Mass. One floor and a basement are occupied, of the dimensions of 25 x 30 feet, and employment is afforded five efficient and courteous assistants. Provisions, Poultry, Game in season, Fruits, Vegetables and Canned Goods of all descriptions are very largely handled, and a very popular feature of the business is the prompt and accurate delivery of orders, free of all charge. The most fastidious buyer will find meats, or other articles suited to his needs, at this establishment, for great care is shown in the selection of the stock carried, and special pains taken to cater to the best class of trade. Very low prices are quoted on all the commodities handled, and every article leaving the store is fully warranted to prove just exactly as represented.

Wadman's Stove Store, 21 Union Park Street, near Washington Street. The gain in convenience and the saving in labor attained by the use of a first-class cook-stove are generally appreciated, but what is not so often taken into consideration is the gain in economy as well. It is well within the bounds of truth to assert that from ten to thirty per cent. of the food cooked may be wasted in the process of cooking by reason of the imperfections of the oven in which it is placed, to say nothing of the difference in tastefulness and digestibility between food cooked as it should be, and food that has been slowly dried up or has not been thoroughly penetrated by the heat. It brings about a positive saving of money, time, fuel and temper to purchase a stove that will bake properly and that can be easily managed, and there is no better place in this city at which to procure such a stove, than the establishment conducted by Mr. J. C. Wadman at No. 21 Union Park Street, near Washington. This enterprise was formerly carried on at No. 1301 Washington Street, and was inaugurated over a quarter of a century ago. Its inception occurring in 1860. The present owner is a member of the Royal Arcanum, the United Fellowship and the Home Circle. Since assuming control, some ten years ago, he has made "Wadman's Stove Store" more popular than ever, and was never in a position to offer his customers more genuine advantages than at present. He is prepared to supply anything in the Stove or Furnace line at bottom rates, and we need hardly say that all goods coming from this store are sure to prove as represented. Every facility is at hand for the repairing of Stoves, Furnaces, etc., the filling of orders for Tin Roofing, Sheet Iron and Tin Plate work, etc., and commissions will be executed at short notice and at most reasonable rates.

Geo. H. White, Jobbing Mason, Whitening and Tinting, office, 6 1-2 East Springfield Street, residence, 53 Blue Hill Avenue. The work of the Mason holds a very high comparative position among that of the other trades, and it is but natural that it should do so, for Masonry is everywhere accepted as the type of solidity, and the skill of the architect would be of but little if any use were it not that the Mason stood ready to carry his plans into practical effect. The Jobbing Mason is one of the most useful members of a community, that is to say, if he is able and willing to do his work as it should be done; and a gentleman who bears a deservedly high reputation for the faithful manner in which all orders entrusted to him are executed, is Mr. Geo. H. White, whose place of business is at No. 6½ East Springfield Street, his residence being at No. 53 Blue Hill Avenue. Mr. White was born in this state, and inaugurated the enterprise mentioned in 1886. He is a member of the Odd Fellows, and is very well known throughout this vicinity. Nine men are employed by Mr. White, and no pains is spared to give that immediate and intelligent attention to orders that is so gratifying but so hard to obtain. Whitening and Tinting of every description are done, in addition to Mason work, and satisfaction is guaranteed, as every precaution is taken to avoid injury to furniture, etc., and only experienced and skilled hands are entrusted with the filling of such orders.

Walter G. Barnes, dealer in Teas, Coffees, Spices and choice Family Groceries, at lowest prices, 550 Shawmut Avenue, between Northampton and Camden streets. The popular house of Walter G. Barnes, has won a wide and merited recognition, as furnishing his patrons with the best and most reliable grocery goods, at most moderate rates. The careful attention to the smallest details of his stock, and the most rigid and thorough rejection of all inferior and adulterated goods, have obtained for his stock a valuable and honorable reputation, for purity and worth. The business was started in 1878, by its present manager. The store now occupied by him is well arranged, comprises one floor and basement, each 20 by 50 feet in dimensions, and is located at 550 Shawmut Avenue. The stock carried includes the finest grades of Teas, Coffees, Spices, and choice Family Groceries of every description, which are sold at the lowest market prices. Mr. Barnes is a native of Stoneham, well-known in social circles as well as commercial life, being a member of the Odd Fellows and Pilgrim Fathers.

Charles McLean, Boots, Shoes and Rubber Goods, 1815 Washington Street, corner Camden Street. It would not require a great while for even an absolute stranger in the Highlands to gain a pretty correct idea of the estimation in which the establishment carried on by Mr. Chas. McLean at 1815 Washington Street, is held. This store has been doing a large shoe trade for twenty or more years, and, if anything, has been more successful since Mr. McLean took hold of the business in 1887. One floor and basement are occupied, 25 x 60 feet in dimensions, and a competent assistant is always at hand to give courteous attention to all customers. Boots, Shoes and Rubbers of all grades and sizes are kept in large quantity, and at all prices. Fine Repairing, which is so hard to have executed to satisfaction nowadays, is made a specialty of. Mr. McLean, who is a native of Boston, understands the shoe trade thoroughly, and gives his business close attention. All those who will call at this establishment can see for themselves the honorable way in which all parts of the business are carried on.

Long & Keeler, Dealers in Beef, Pork, Lamb, Mutton, Veal, Poultry, etc.; also Fruits and Vegetables, 21 and 23 Washington Market. There are a good many Meat and Provision Dealers in Washington Market and its immediate vicinity, but there are also a good many people to supply throughout that section, and the generally prosperous condition of the enterprise alluded to shows that the field is by no means overcrowded. Messrs. Long and Keeler, who began operations at Nos. 21 and 23 Washington Market, in 1887, have reason to subscribe to the truth of this statement, for, recent as the establishment of their business is, they have already built up a trade which is one of the largest and most promising infants with which we are acquainted. Indeed, unless all present indications are very deceiving, the business of this house will before a great while rank with that of the most important establishments of the kind in the city; and this great success is entirely deserved, for the efforts made to please the public have been intelligent and continuous, and this policy is evidently to be adhered to in the future. Both members of the firm are connected with the United Friends, and the senior partner is a native of Nova Scotia, his associate having been born in Maine. Employment is afforded to three energetic and polite assistants, and the service will be found as first-class as the goods are reliable. Beef, Pork, Lamb, Mutton, Veal, Poultry, etc. are to be had of this house at the lowest market rates, and a fine and complete assortment of Fruits and Vegetables is also carried.

Peak Brothers, Funeral Directors, Warerooms, 1371 Washington Street. As there are few things more annoying, even distressing, than to have any mischance occur on the occasion of a funeral, it is useful to know of a concern that possesses such facilities and has had such wide experience as to render any accident practically impossible when they are given entire charge of the necessary arrangements. Such a concern is that of Peak Brothers, whose warerooms are located at No. 1371 Washington Street for the inception of this enterprise took place in 1840, it having been conducted by the present firm since 1876. One floor and a basement are occupied of the dimensions of 30 x 60 feet and a complete assortment of Caskets, Coffins and Funeral Goods in general is carried, comprising articles adapted to all tastes and purses and offered at extremely reasonable rates. The firm is made up of Mr. J. H. Peak and Mr. C. A. Peak, both these gentlemen being natives of Boston, and the former being a member of the Free Masons, while the latter is connected with the Odd Fellows. The firm is prepared to undertake the entire charge of Funerals, thus obviating the necessity of giving that personal attention to the numberless details attending the preparations for such ceremonies that is so unpleasant in time of grief. The utmost dignity and decorum will be maintained in cases where they have control of affairs and they may be depended upon to fully provide for every contingency that is liable to arise.

S. Webster & Co., Apothecaries, No. 63 Warren Avenue. Eighteen years of faithful and successful prosecution of a business enterprise affords satisfactory evidence that the person or persons holding such a record are entitled to the confidence and patronage of the community, and as this is just the length of time that the enterprise conducted by Mr. S. Webster & Co., at No. 63 Warren Avenue, has been before the public, it is only natural that it should be a very popular one, and receive the endorsement and support it so richly deserves. Mr. Webster is a native of Snco. Maine, and first began operations in his present business in 1870, and Mr. Griffin has been here for the past ten years. Both members have a vivid appreciation of the responsibilities attending a retail prescription pharmacy from the inception of the enterprise, and have therefore given that close and incessant attention to every detail of this department of this trade that has so often and favorably been remarked upon by those acquainted with it. As a result of this continuous caution, the establishment under notice holds a reputation second to none for reliability and conservatism, and its prescription trade is a large and steadily growing one. Messrs. S. Webster & Co. are also agents for the American Steam Laundry Co., for which goods are received every day. The Stock of Drugs, Medicines, etc. on hand, is complete and desirable in every feature, and there is also carried an Assortment of Fine Toilet Articles and Drug Store Goods in general that is worthy of careful inspection. The prices are very low, and three competent assistants are at hand to give prompt attention to customers.

F. G. Coughlan & Co., Manufacturers and Dealers in all kinds of Freestone and Marble, for Building purposes, Cor. Albany & Malden Streets. A stone-yard which, although of smaller dimensions than some, is still one of the best equipped in the city, is that conducted by Messrs. F. G. Coughlan & Co., successors to Crowley & Coughlan at the corner of Malden and Albany Streets, and the rapid but steady increase of patronage that has been accorded these gentlemen since they inaugurated their enterprise ten years ago, shows that their liberal business methods and the superior quality of the work produced are fully appreciated by the public at large. Mr. Coughlan the senior partner is a native of Boston and Mr. Carew the junior member is a Bostonian by birth, and they are extensively known here, not only in business circles but also socially as well. The premises occupied cover an area of about 2000 feet and employment is given to seven experienced and skilled assistants. The uses made of Freestone and Marble are so many and various that it is a matter of course that many firms should find employment in the handling and sale of these materials. Some very artistic work can be done in Freestone as well as in Marble, and a building into the construction of which these have largely entered, is sure to be both attractive and durable. Messrs. F. G. Coughlan & Co. are in a position to furnish their patrons with unusually fine work at moderate rates, and our readers who want anything in their line should give them an early call.

William Manning, Sexton and Funeral Undertaker, Dealer in Coffins and Caskets, 819 Albany Street. That Mr. William Manning is one of the best known Funeral Undertakers in the city, must be evident to all who are at all familiar with the magnitude of his business, for his long and varied experience is availed of by a very large circle of customers and his facilities, ample as they are, are not infrequently severely taxed to meet the heavy demands made upon them. Mr. Manning is a native of Boston and has carried on his present establishment for many years. It is located at No. 819 Albany Street, and is complete in every department, the premises occupied covering an acre of ground and a building 40 x 60 feet in size utilized, employment being given to nine officient assistants. Mr. Manning is Sexton and Funeral Undertaker of the Dorchester and Calvary cemeteries, and keeps constantly on hand an assortment of Coffins and Caskets of all sizes and kinds, as well as Grave clothes of various styles and qualities. Coffins and Caskets will be made to order when desired, and Coffin Plates engraved and Flowers, Wreaths and Crosses furnished. He is prepared to assume entire charge of Funerals and has a number of first class hearses and carriages under his control, which he will furnish at very moderate rates. Mr. Manning is very much respected and esteemed in the community, and is fully deserving of the good wishes so often bestowed upon him.

B. F. Washington, Merchant Tailor, 713 Tremont Street. The question of clothes is always one of interest, for the average man desires to present a neat and stylish appearance, and often goes beyond his means in trying to do so. Now there is no necessity for paying any such fancy prices for clothing as are demanded by certain "English" or "Art" Tailors, for, as a matter of fact, their work as a general thing is no better than that of some others who make no such pretensions and hardly charge half such high rates. If you doubt the correctness of our judgment in this matter, it is an easy thing to put it to the test; for we can point out an establishment where, although the lowest market rates are maintained, perfection in fit and workmanship is guaranteed. We refer to that of which Mr. B. F. Washington is the proprietor, located at No. 713 Tremont Street, and are confident that a trial will convince the most fastidious that this gentleman is not only a skillful tailor, but also that he employs only such assistants as will keep up the first-class reputation he enjoys in this line. Mr. Washington founded his present business in 1879, and his circle of patrons has constantly enlarged since that date. He is a native of Boston and a member of the Free Masons, being very well known about town. A store is utilized, measuring 20 x 25 feet, and a workshop is also occupied where a number are employed, and every facility is at hand for filling all orders in an eminently prompt and satisfactory manner. In addition to the making of garments to order, cleansing and repairing are also done in the neatest and most thorough manner, and at the lowest market rates.

C. A. Mumford, Watchmaker and Jeweler, Silver Ware, Watches, Clocks, Jewelry and Eye Glasses, 140 Dartmouth Street. It would be very hard to find a jewelry store in Boston in which more genuine advantages are offered to the purchaser, than is the case in that carried on by Mr. C. A. Mumford at No. 140 Dartmouth Street, and this statement is made with a full understanding of the fact that the stock here carried is small by comparison with those to be found in some of the great down-town establishments. Although Mr. Mumford's stock is rather small, it is extremely varied, as it contains very few duplicates, and hence affords much more latitude for choice than one unacquainted with it would suppose. Watches, Clocks, Jewelry, Eye Glasses, Musical Instruments, Japanese Goods, Silver Ware — these make up quite a list, as our readers can see, and it is worthy of mention that these articles are personally selected by Mr. Mumford with special reference to the requirements of his trade, and each and every one of them fully guaranteed to prove as represented. The proprietor of this establishment is a native of this city, and opened his present store in 1887, removing from 210 Tremont Street, where he had been situated for two years. One floor is utilized, of the dimensions of 20 x 45 feet, together with a basement of similar size, and employment is afforded to three assistants. Particular attention is paid to the Repairing of Watches, French Clocks, and Jewelry of all kinds, and those owning a watch whose vagaries have thus far proved uncontrollable should give Mr. Mumford's skill a trial, as he ranks with the most skillful watch repairers in the city and guarantees satisfaction to his patrons.

Thomas Ratigan, Practical Plumber, No. 770 Tremont Street. It is all very well to have correct theories, etc. as to how plumbing and such work should be done, but it is much better to be able to put these theories into practical operation. It should always be remembered that although book knowledge is admirable so far as it goes, still it can never take the place of that gained by practical observation and long continued experience. It is owing in no small degree to the public appreciation of these facts that the establishment of which Mr. Thomas Ratigan is the proprietor, situated on Tremont Street, No. 770, enjoys so large a share of patronage for it is generally known that orders left with this house will receive the benefit of both practical and theoretical knowledge. Mr. Ratigan senior founded the business alluded to in 1867. One floor and basement are occupied, of the dimensions of 20 x 35 feet, and employment is afforded six skilled assistants. The enterprise is now under the direct management of Mr. Thomas H. Ratigan, who has manifested marked ability in this position, and who may be confidently depended on to fully maintain the high reputation so long held by this popular house. Estimates are given for every description of sanitary Plumbing. All work is done in accordance with the latest rules of sanitary science and Repairing is given prompt and careful attention and personal supervision at the lowest rates.

St. James Stable, S. W. Spofford, Proprietor. Boarding, Baiting, Sale and Livery Stable, 1440 Washington Street, between Dedham and Malden Streets. No one, be he either native of or stranger to Boston, need lack for a day's wholesome and hearty amusement as long as our suburbs retain their present beauty and the roads their present excellence, for both are celebrated not only throughout the state but throughout all New England and the horseman or any body else who has blood in his veins, who can't find enjoyment in taking advantage of the opportunities thus offered, must be very hard to suit and is truly to be pitied. But beautiful scenery and smooth roads are of little practical use unless the means for enjoying them is at hand, and in this connection permit us to call our reader's attention to the advantages offered by the St. James Stable, of which Mr. S. W. Spofford is the proprietor, and which is located at No. 1440 Washington Street, between Dedham and Malden Streets. Mr. Spofford was born in Vermont, and he purchased the property mentioned in 1878. Thus he has been identified with it for just about ten years, and his business methods must consequently be thoroughly known by this time. That they are such as to meet the approval of the public is shown by the great popularity the establishment enjoys, and, indeed, to those who are acquainted with the accommodations furnished and the prices fixed on the same, this popularity is by no means wondered at. The premises in use comprise two floors measuring 85 x 70 feet and employment is given to fifteen competent assistants. There are eighty stalls and accommodations for 150 carriages in the stable, and horses will be boarded or baited at the lowest market rates and assured the best of food and care. Carriages either single or double, and good and speedy horses may be hired of Mr. Spofford at low prices, and those who are thinking of investing in horseflesh might do much worse than give this gentleman a call, as he generally has desirable animals for road use on hand, and often offers decided bargains to those desiring to buy.

Geo. A. Oakes, Grocer, 466 Tremont Street. Almost any person would hesitate a moment at least, if suddenly called upon to define the word "Groceries," for such an enormous variety of goods is included within this general title, that it must seem as if any short definition would fail to properly describe the meaning of it. A visit to any well-stocked city grocery store, will serve to show better than any words can the scope of the grocer's trade and a fine sample of a first-class establishment of this kind is to be seen at No. 466 Tremont Street, in the store occupied by Mr. Geo. A. Oakes. This gentleman is a native of Athol, Mass., and inaugurated the enterprise alluded to in 1885. The premises utilized are 25 x 60 feet in dimensions and very little of this large amount of space is unoccupied, for Mr. Oakes is a believer in carrying a stock sufficiently varied and sufficiently large to permit of all tastes being suited and all orders filled, and as his business is a large and growing one, he needs to have a heavy stock on hand in order

to carry this belief into practice. Employment is given to two efficient and polite assistants and orders are filled in the most careful and thorough manner, at the lowest rates that can be placed on first-class goods. No misrepresentation is permitted and patrons may consequently rely upon getting just what they pay for.

Wm. H. Boardman, Stair Builder. Estimates given and all orders promptly attended to. 300 Albany Street. This is not the place to enter into a discussion of the reason why stair-building is made a special branch of the carpenter's trade, but it may be briefly said that this industry is really quite distinct from any other, although it may be carried on in connection with general carpentering and building. What may be called the architectural possibilities of a stairway, are seldom realized in this country, where there is generally not enough space to spare in the buildings as designed, to give stairways the prominence that is their rightful due, but there have lately been noticed, very decided changes in this respect, and before long we may look for the trade of the stair-builder attaining the prominence it deserves. One of the most skillful to be found in this city, is Mr. W. H. Boardman, doing business at No. 300 Albany Street, and although he only began operations in 1886, he has already built up a large and growing trade. Mr. Boardman is a native of Boston and is very well known in the building industry. He occupies one floor measuring 40 x 80 feet, gives employment to six efficient assistants, and is prepared to fill all orders at the lowest attainable rates and in the most satisfactory manner. Estimates will be cheerfully given and any needful information courteously afforded on application.

W. H. Sheffield, Bell-Hanger and Locksmith, 482 Tremont Street. In almost any house, (and particularly where servants are employed) it adds much to the convenience of the occupants to have a well-arranged system of bells in operation, for by such means many an unnecessary step may be avoided and the various household operations greatly facilitated. The expense of putting in such a system is much less than most people imagine, and if a competent bell-hanger be entrusted with the work the result is sure to be satisfactory. We can assure our readers that they need feel no hesitation in placing orders of this kind with Mr. W. H. Sheffield, of No. 482 Tremont Street, for he has had a long and varied experience in bell-hanging, and stands ready to undertake the most extensive job in this line with a guarantee of satisfaction. Mr. Sheffield may also be entrusted with the repairing of locks, fitting of keys, etc., for he has given this branch of his business careful study and has every appliance and tool at hand that will enable him to carry it on to the best advantage. He will be found very moderate in his charges, and has sufficient assistance at his command to promise that all orders will be filled at short notice as well as in the uniformly first-class style for which he has been noted since he began operations in 1872.

5

J. B. Hunter & Co., Builders' Hardware, Carpenters' and Machinists' Tools, 1286 Washington Street. An attractive store, a more attractive stock and most attractive prices, is the summing up one might give of the establishment carried on by Messrs. J. B. Hunter & Co., at No. 1286 Washington Street, for this description is strictly justified by the facts, as will be agreed by all familiar with the enterprise in question. The firm alluded to founded this undertaking in 1884, and soon attained a gratifying amount of patronage which has steadily increased with the passage of years. The premises occupied comprise one floor and a basement and measure 25 x 65 feet. It is but rarely that so varied and complete a stock is to be found in a retail hardware store as is carried by this concern, for the assortment on hand includes Builders' Hardware, Carpenters' and Machinists' tools, and also a selection of general hardware embracing practically everything in this line. An order box is maintained at No. 104 Devonshire Street, and Telephone connection is had, thus making it easy to transmit orders from any part of the city. Employment is afforded four efficient assistants, and not the least popular feature of the establishment is the promptness and courtesy with which customers are waited on. It is the aim of those at the head of this enterprise to offer equal inducements to the down-town stores, and that this is done there can be no dispute whatever. The prices will be found to compare favorably with those of any similar house and no misrepresentation of goods is permitted. Mr. Hunter has supplied the trimming and hardware used in the construction of many of the principal buildings recently erected in Boston, among which are a number of School Houses, Engine House, Police Station, the new City Hospital etc.; also R. H. Stearns' new building and the elegant structure recently erected on the Back Bay for S. S. Pierce; also many fine private residences.

John J. Cuddihy, North River Blue Stone, Akron Sewer and Drain Pipe, 613 Albany Street. The policy now being adopted in the business district of this city of substituting flagstones for bricks for sidewalk purposes, is an extremely well-advised one, for the superiority of the former over the latter, specially where there is much travel, cannot be questioned. One of the heaviest dealers in North River flagging stone, etc., that can be found in Boston, is Mr. John J. Cuddihy, of No. 613 Albany Street; and although this gentleman has only conducted his present enterprise since 1876, he has gained a reputation of which he has every reason to be proud, for carrying a large and well-selected stock, offering it at bottom prices and filling every order given with promptness and accuracy. Mr. Cuddihy is a Bostonian by birth, and is very well known in business circles. The premises occupied by him are well-arranged, and there is carried, in addition to the stock of Flagging Stone, a full selection of Akron Sewer and Drain Pipe. We need say nothing concerning the merits of this pipe, for it is doubtless the best known in the market and has stood the severest tests of

practical service under all possible conditions. Mr. Cuddihy is able to supply it in quantities to suit, either at wholesale or retail, and those who have done business with him need not be told that his prices are as low as the lowest.

George E. Jaques, dealer in Provisions 601 Tremont Street, telephone No. 4081-3. The problem of how to feed such an enormous number of people as are contained within the limits of this city, is a most complex and interesting one and involves the handling of stupendous quantities of provisions in its practical carrying out. The magnitude of the interests involved is not generally appreciated, from the fact that we have all got in the way of taking things for granted as regards our food supply, and hardly bestow a thought upon the means by which our daily sustenance is brought to our doors. It is a vast subject and one well worthy of study, and as the only way to attain any adequate idea of it is to take it in detail let us consider for a moment the establishment conducted by Mr. Geo. E. Jaques, at No. 601 Tremont Street; for this gentleman is one of the largest dealers in Provisions in this portion of the city, and is one of the pioneers in the trade, having begun operations in 1801. He is a native of Tewksbury and is connected with both the Odd Fellows and the Royal Arcanum. Mr. Jaques' trade extends over a very considerable territory, for he has long held the reputation of handling only reliable and satisfactory goods and of supplying the same at fair and reasonable rates. His store occupies one floor and a basement, of the dimensions of 30 x 45 feet and the stock on hand is skilfully selected to meet the wants of the high class of patronage enjoyed. Six assistants are in attendance and orders by Telephone receive quick and accurate delivery.

M. A. Newton, Fancy Goods, and McCall's Bazaar Patterns, and Troy Laundry Agency, 709 Tremont Street. Among the best-known dry and fancy goods houses in this section of the city is that conducted by M. A. Newton and located at No. 709 Tremont Street. This establishment was founded by its present proprietor in 1880, who has met with marked success, being a lady of unusual business ability, besides paying strict attention to the wants of the public. The store is finely situated on one of the most prominent thoroughfares of the city, and is 20 by 75 ft. Orders received daily for Troy Laundry, and returned promptly. Miss Newton has recently added a full line of the celebrated McCall Bazaar Patterns, of which she will be pleased to furnish an illustrated catalogue on application. Attentive assistants are employed, who are ever ready to wait upon customers in an intelligent and courteous manner. The proprietor personally selects the entire stock, and being a lady of exceptionally fine taste, only the latest fashions and the choicest goods are to be found at this establishment. We advise all who have not already done so to patronize this store, and we feel assured they will be satisfied with both the selections and prices.

A. P. Gilson, Pharmacist, 630 Tremont Street. The South End being particularly a residential portion of the city, it is obvious that it presents a fine field for such business enterprises as cater expressly to family trade; and as drug stores are prominent among undertakings of this nature, it naturally follows that many of them are to be found in the section alluded to. One of the most popular and largely patronized of these is that of which Mr. A. P. Gilson is the proprietor, located at No. 630 Tremont Street, and as there is no effect without a cause, it may be well to touch upon the causes of this popularity. Mr. A. P. Gilson was born in New Hampshire, and began operations in his present field of usefulness in 1871. He utilizes one floor and a basement of the dimensions of 20 x 35 feet, and makes it a point to carry so full and complete an assortment of Drugs, Medicines and Chemicals as to assure the prompt and accurate filling of all orders for those articles which may be entrusted to him. Recognizing the fact that freshness and freedom from adulteration, exercise a most important influence upon the efficacy of drugs in general, he strives to guard against unwittingly handling any agents which are not susceptible of performing the duties, which under ordinary circumstances may be expected of them. To attain this end he deals only with such wholesalers as have a reputation for probity and reliability, and is, consequently, in a position to guarantee the excellence of the goods he sells. Prescriptions are promptly and carefully compounded, and very reasonable charges made. Mr. Gilson is also Proprietor of the WONDERFUL COUGH SYRUP, which relieves the worst cough in two minutes; cures with a few doses; recommended by physicians and nurses.

BOSTON, MASS., Oct 7th, 1880.

I have used Gilson's Cough Syrup for two years, whenever troubled by bronchial or pulmonary affections, and know it to be the best remedy I ever used. I cheerfully recommend it to others.

G. COLLINS, Chaplain U. S. A.

BOSTON, May 2, 1883.

My little boy, 7 years old, was given up by three of the best physicians in Boston, as just gone in consumption, and all that could be done was to make him comfortable while he lived. To quiet him I was induced to try "Gilson's Wonderful Cough Syrup," and to my great surprise and joy two 25c bottles cured him, and he is today perfectly well. I am happy to recommend it as a most wonderful medicine, and advise everybody not to be without it in the house.

MRS. MARY GANNON, 212 Columbus Av.

BOSTON, Nov. 22d, 1883.

Your Wonderful Cough Cure was first given me by a friend to try; since then I have purchased a bottle for my child who has been suffering with a bad cough, and is now entirely cured, and I would cheerfully recommend it to any one who may be in need and suffering with a cough. Respectfully yours,

H. B. HOPKINS, 61 Summer St.

☞ The above are only a few of the many testimonials received.

Price 25 cents, 50 cents and $1.00.

Mrs. E. F. Marble, Dealer in Bakers' Goods, Confectionery, Fruit, Soda, Choice Cigars, etc., 254 Columbus Avenue, Cor. Cazenove Street. A quite recently established but very popular enterprise is that conducted by Mrs. E. F. Marble, at No. 254 Columbus Avenue, corner of Cazenove Street; and we take especial pleasure in calling attention to it, from the fact that everything obtained at this store is sure to prove just as represented. Mrs. Marble begun operations in 1887, and has shown great ability in so managing the enterprise that its success was as immediate as it is pronounced. The premises occupied, comprise one floor and a basement, of the dimensions of 20 x 45 feet, and the large stock carried includes Baker's Goods, Confectionery made on the premises, Fruit, Soda, Choice Cigars and many other things too numerous to mention. It should also be stated that work is received here for one of the best Laundrys in the city, and collars, shirts, cuffs, etc., are laundered in the most satisfactory manner without injury or excessive wear. The line of confectionery offered to patrons is a varied and desirable one, and the goods composing it are made on the premises so that their freshness and delicacy of flavor are assured. Orders for either wholesale or retail custom receive prompt attention, and trade orders are filled at short notice. The cigars handled are also deserving of the appreciation of fastidious smokers, as they are carefully selected as regards strength and evenness of quality, and a really good article is sold at a very low price. Two competent assistants are employed, and callers promptly attended to.

J. B. Kempton, Dealer in Provisions, Fruit and Vegetables; Choice Butter and Eggs a Specialty; 765 Tremont Street, Corner Springfield. Although it may seem as if information regarding provision stores was hardly called for, there being so large a number of these establishments to be found throughout the city, still for this very reason we believe that the public will appreciate being told where there may be found a strictly reliable enterprise of this kind, as, unfortunately, all of them cannot truthfully be so described. We are confident that those who may favor Mr. J. B. Kempton with their patronage will have no occasion to regret having done so, for this gentleman carries on one of the best-equipped Provision Stores in this section, and proposes to do all in his power to fully satisfy his customers. The establishment in question is located at No. 765 Tremont Street, corner of Springfield, and comprises one floor and a basement of the dimensions of 18 x 35 feet. A very finely selected stock of Provisions, Fruit and Vegetables is constantly on hand, and customers are supplied at the lowest market rates with goods equal to any. Choice Butter and Eggs are made specialties, and Mr. Kempton has so arranged matters that he is assured a continuous and abundant supply of these articles directly from the producers. This will be appreciated by those who know the importance of having Butter and Eggs as fresh as possible, and, in fact, that it is already appreciated is proved by the large trade done in this department. Mr. Kempton was born in Boston, and is a member of the Odd Fellows.

F. S. Risteen & Co., 527 and 529 Tremont Street. , Without a doubt, the finest establishment of its kind in the section of the city where it is located is that conducted by Messrs. F. S. Risteen & Co., at Nos. 527 and 529 Tremont Street, under the Clarendon Hotel. It is really a model of what a high-grade Grocery House should be; for since the removal to its present quarters (which was consummated October 1, 1887) the greatly superior facilities enjoyed here enable patrons to receive an even more satisfactory service than before. The store now occupied is of the dimensions of 50 x 100 feet, and contains a stock of Fine Groceries, Wines, Fruits, etc., which for variety and excellence is unexcelled. Business was begun by this concern in 1868, at 1051 Washington Street, and at 585 Tremont Street, and the present very large and highly desirable trade has been honestly and laboriously built up by the employment of unremitting industry and honorable and liberal business methods for very nearly a full score of years. It is only by continued and painstaking effort that a reputation for entire reliability can be attained by any house, and that of F. S. Risteen & Co., assured as it is now, was only made by years of conscientious toil. Handling every description of Staple and Fancy Groceries, a Specialty is made of the Finest Creamery Butter, Factory Cheese, and Fresh Cape Eggs, as well as the various imported cheeses. Mr. Risteen has been a resident of Boston for thirty years, and is a prominent citizen in more respects than one. He is connected with the Free Masons, Royal Arcanum and Odd Fellows; also has been a member of both branches of the City Government, one of the Board of Assessors, has represented his District in the State Senate, and he has been, for the past ten years, a member of the Board of Directors for Public Institutions, and has an extremely large circle of friends who may congratulate him none the less on his business success, from the fact that it has been fairly and honestly won.

A. L. Marshall, Paper Hangings and Interior Decorations, Holland Shades made to order, 6 East Springfield Street. The enterprise conducted by Mr. A. L. Marshall at No. 6 East Springfield Street, was inaugurated in 1875 under the style of "Knox & Marshall," and passed into the sole possession of its present proprietor in 1878. Mr. Marshall is a native of Boston and has a very accurate idea of what is demanded by the best city trade. To the intelligence and liberality he has displayed in meeting this demand, the greater part of the exceptional success he has attained is due, and in his case at least it may be said, that hard and persistent work, and not "luck" at all, has won a victory. The premises utilized, measure 20 x 70 feet, and employment is given to ten efficient assistants. Mr. Marshall makes it a point to keep a sufficiently large and varied stock of the numerous materials required in his business, to allow him to fill all orders without delay, and he guarantees that the goods etc. used by him are strictly first-class in every particular and will be found most durable and satisfactory. The most convincing evidence that can be given of Mr. Marshall's competency and resources, is that afforded by the numerous commissions he has executed in the past and we have yet to hear a word of complaint from those who have taken advantage of the facilities he offers. To combine promptness with thoroughness and the use of the best stock and latest designs with reasonable rates, is a task of no small difficulty, and that Mr. Marshall has succeeded in doing it must be accepted as an undeniable fact. A large stock of American and Foreign Wall Paper is carried, also Holland Shades to order.

Charles B. Woolley, Wholesale and Retail Dealer in Beef, Pork, Mutton, Veal, and Poultry; Stalls, 25, 27, 29 and 31 Washington Market. If a sign should be hung out in front of the houses of all the families supplied with meats and provisions by Mr. Charles B. Woolley, it is probable that even that gentleman himself would be surprised at the showing made, for although he knows of course in a general way about what his business amounts to, still it is too large to be easily comprehended by the employment of the usual methods. Mr. Woolley is a native of N. H., and founded his present undertaking in 1870. His trade, although established now for nearly a score of years, is still rapidly growing, and indeed it would be surprising if it were not, for the more goods Mr. Woolley sells, the more pronounced are the inducements he is able to offer his customers, and he was never so well prepared as now to guarantee satisfaction to all who may make trial of the resources of his establishment. Stalls Nos. 25, 27, 29 and 31 Washington Market are occupied and an immense stock is carried, consisting of Beef, Pork, Mutton, Lamb, Veal and Poultry, together with Fruits both Foreign and Domestic and Vegetables of all kinds in their seasons. Both a wholesale and retail business is done, and the motto of the establishment is evidently "Reliable Goods at Bottom Prices." for this policy is adhered to at all times. Telephone connection is had, and orders, whether received in this way or any other, are assured prompt and careful attention. Employment is afforded to eight efficient and courteous assistants and the large patronage enjoyed can thus be easily and satisfactorily handled.

E. T. Lamb, Dealer in Furniture, Carpets, Ranges, Stoves, and General House Furnishing Goods, 1375 Washington Street, cor. of Union Park Boston. No intelligent person needs to be told that there have been decided reductions made in the prices of House-Furnishing Goods of late years, for the fact is so plain as to be self-evident. This condition of things has been brought about by a variety of causes which it is not necessary to consider here, prominent among which is the competition that has arisen between rival dealers. The establishment conducted by Mr. E. T. Lamb, at No. 1375 Washington Street, corner of Union Park, has repeatedly proved its ability to hold its own as long as legitimate methods are employed, and certainly was never better prepared than it is to-day, to meet all demands upon its resources by those who desire fashionable and durable household goods at a fair price. Mr. Lamb started his present business in 1890, and has built up a large and growing trade. He is a member of the Odd Fellows and also of the Free Masons, and is well and favorably known in trade-circles as a careful and enterprising buyer. The premises utilized, comprise one floor and a basement, measuring 30 x 70 feet, and a store-house of the dimensions of 30 x 50 feet, there being employment given to six competent assistants, a fine line of Furniture, Carpets, Ranges, Stoves and other Household necessities is carried in stock at all times, and it would be useless to attempt to describe an assortment that is at once so varied and so complete. Callers are given polite and cheerful attention, and Mr. Lamb makes it a rule to instruct his salesmen to show equal consideration to all who visit his establishment. It is not regarded as a hardship to be asked to show goods by any means, and the utmost facilities are afforded those wishing to ascertain the advantages Mr. Lamb has to offer. Upholstering and Repairing are done at short notice and at prices as low as the lowest.

Sargent's Steam Laundry, and Dye House 1862 to 1868 Washington Street. Notwithstanding that Public Laundries are so numerous in this city at the present day, it is not a great many years since they were few and far between, and in fact by far the larger portion of them have been established since 1880. It is not our purpose to present arguments in favor of these enterprises, for the people know of what great convenience they are, or else there would never have been so many of them started. But their merits vary. Some can be given unreserved commendation, while others are quite unworthy of patronage for reasons that it is not necessary to mention here in detail. But we may say (and our verdict has long since been confirmed by the public) that Sargents' Steam Laundry and Dye House, located at Nos. 1862 to 1868 Washington Street, is an establishment that is managed in a thoroughly straightforward and honorable fashion, and the uniform excellence of its work really leaves very little to be desired. Mr. Sargent became identified with this enterprise in 1881, and under his direction it has developed and extended with a rapidity as steady as it is surprising. Those who have been subjected to the annoyance of frequently not having their laundry work delivered when it was promised, will appreciate the advantages of patronizing the establishment in question, when we say that this is a very unusual occurrence indeed with Mr. Sargent, who has the business so admirably systematized and employs so large a corps of assistants together with the latest improved appliances, that he is enabled to turn out an immense amount of work at short notice and to keep his promises to the letter. Goods are collected free of charge at all the railroad, steamboat and express offices, as well as at residences or stores, and will be delivered free also. The charges made are as low as the lowest, and the quality of the work speaks for itself. No injurious chemicals are used, and satisfaction is confidently guaranteed.

J. C. Russell, Dealer in Groceries, Provisions and Fruit, 1724 Washington Street, Corner Springfield. One of the most widely known of our South End business men is Mr. J. C. Russell, whose establishment is located at No. 1724 Washington Street, and this gentleman is as popular as he is well known, for his honorable and enterprising business methods have combined with his social qualities to give him the prominence he now enjoys. Mr. Russell was formerly in business at Wollaston, Mass., and was Postmaster at that place for six years. He belongs to many of the best known Fraternal societies, among which may be mentioned the Free Masons, Odd Fellows, United Workmen, Knights of Honor and the Grand Army, and as a Member of Company B. Twelfth New Hampshire Volunteers he was "on hand" at Fredericksburgh, Cold Harbor, Chancellorsville and other famous engagements. One floor and a basement are occupied, of the dimensions of 25 x 125 feet, and an immense stock is carried, comprising Choice Staple and Fancy Groceries, Provisions, Fruit, etc., while employment is afforded to four competent and polite assistants. The goods handled by Mr. Russell will be found uniformly reliable and desirable in every respect, and are offered at prices that no one can reasonably object to. Operations were begun in 1890, and the rapid growth of the business since that date would seem to indicate that the public appreciates the advantages to be gained by patronizing this establishment. Orders are very promptly delivered, and every caller may depend upon receiving the uniform courtesy and consideration that Mr. Russell believes to be the due of all customers.

Hentz & Bennet, House-painting, East Springfield Street. Economy is an excellent thing in its way; but there is a decided difference between true and false economy, and care should be taken lest in seeking one the other should be fallen into. For instance, it used to be the custom to allow buildings to remain unpainted to save the expense of painting them; but it has been discovered by experience that such a course, far from saving money, actually wasted it, as the elements beating on the bare boards soon reduced them to decay and uselessness. It therefore follows that no frame structure should be permitted to be exposed, wholly or in part, without the protection afforded by paint, and considerations of economy as well as of pride should induce every house-owner to see that his buildings are thoroughly covered with this useful material. It will not require frequent renewing if applied by skillful hands, and as good a concern as can be found to attend to work of this kind, is that of Hentz & Bennet, doing business on East Springfield Street, up stairs. This firm commenced operations in 1885, and have gained the confidence and patronage of the public by the use of first-class stock and the prompt and careful filling of all orders. One floor is occupied, of the dimensions of 29 x 90 feet, and a sufficient force of competent workmen is employed to assure that all commissions shall be executed in a manner that leaves nothing to be desired. Orders by mail will be acted upon without delay, and the lowest prices are charged that are consistent with fine material and skilled labor.

J. H. Healey & Co., Boarding, Hack, and Livery Stable, 26 and 28 East Concord Street. No man who deserves to own a good horse, will board him at an establishment where he is not assured the best of care and atten-

dance, and every horseowner should make it a point to see that his animal receives all that is due him, in this line. We know that most residents of the city that own horses, have no time to personally investigate the various stables that announce they are prepared to undertake the boarding and care of these animals, but they can at least patronize only such establishments as have a high reputation for reliability and honorable business methods, and one of the very best of these is that conducted by Messrs. J. H. Healey & Co., at Nos. 26 and 28 East Concord Street. A public stable has been maintained here for over a score of years, but since the present concern assumed possession in 1884, a great increase in business and popularity has been noticeable. Well, this is not to be wondered at, for Mr. Healey is an experienced and able Stable man and believes in furnishing the very best accommodations at all times and at the lowest prices consistent with the maintenance of the high standard of merit he is determined to reach. He is a native of Boston, and is connected with the Odd Fellows and also with the Grand Army, having served in the Department of the Gulf during the Rebellion as a member of Co., A, 42d Massachusetts. Four floors are utilized and ten hands employed, there being a very extensive Hack and Livery business done. In addition to the Boarding facilities furnished, carriages will be supplied for Weddings, Parties, Funerals, and conveyances to the Depots, etc., all orders being given prompt and careful attention, and teams being at hand sharp on the hour promised. Some good horses are available for Livery use, and no lover of driving, will regret favoring this popular concern with an order.

E. Thompson, Furniture, Stoves, &c., 1883 Washington Street, directly opposite Washington Market. Well known among houses of a similar kind, is that of Mr. E. Thompson at No. 1883 Washington Street. Mr. Thompson is a native of Glasgow, Scotland, and a member of the order of Free Masons. He began operations here in 1873, and his success has been all that could be desired. The premises occupied are four floors, 25 x 120 feet in dimensions, and are stocked with a well-selected variety of Furniture and General Household Goods of all the latest styles. Mr. Thompson's qualifications are such as to enable him to give the best advantages to his customers. All goods are sold at the lowest prices to be found in this city, and are all as represented. His stock comprises full lines of parlor, chamber and household furniture generally, and a very select and complete

assortment of latest styles and designs in Spring Beds, Mattresses, Mirrors, Clocks, Wringers, and a thousand and one articles and specialties in house-furnishing goods. He supplies merchandise of superior quality at lowest prices, and delivers goods free of expense to all, guaranteeing satisfaction in every particular.

B. F. Colcord & Co., Carpenters and Builders, 477 A Tremont Street. Although the importance of employing a good Architect to draw up the necessary plans, etc., when one determines to build, can scarcely be overestimated, still there should be at least an equal amount of care displayed in the choice of a builder to put the same into practical operation, and it is just here that we are able to offer our readers useful information, for it is a fact that will be cheerfully testified to by all who have dealings with the firm in question, that Messrs B. F. Colcord & Co. are among the most skillful and reliable builders in this city. The enterprise they conduct was inaugurated in 1860, and the public was not slow to perceive the advantages they had to offer, and the faithful and satisfactory manner in which every promise made was cheerfully carried out. Under these circumstances, it is but natural that the business of this firm should now have reached very large proportions, and, in point of fact, it now ranks with the most extensive in Boston. The premises occupied are located at No. 477 A Tremont Street, and comprise two floors, measuring 25 x 70 feet. A force of twenty assistants is employed, and not only building but repairing of all kinds will receive prompt attention. The men employed are experienced and careful, and as every facility is at hand to work with, the quality of what is done is of the best, and durability as well as beauty provided for.

J. Smith & Son, Dealers in All Kinds of Fresh, Pickled and Smoked Fish, 470 Tremont Street, near Dover. Although the firm of J. Smith & Son have only been established in their present quarters since 1884, they are by no means inexperienced in the business or unknown in the vicinity, for Mr. Smith has carried on operations at the South End for a quarter of a century, and what he don't know about fish is not worth knowing. This knowledge is availed of freely by customers, and the public have learned that they may depend upon getting fresh fish at this store at all times during business hours and at the lowest market rates. One floor and a basement are occupied, measuring 2½ x 90 feet, and all kinds of Fresh, Pickled and Smoked Fish are kept in stock, together with Oysters, Lobsters, Scallops, Quahaugs and South Shore Clams. The store is located at No. 470 Tremont Street, near Dover, and as employment is given to five competent assistants, customers are assured the most prompt and polite attention. A specialty is made of Cape Cod Oysters, which are kept constantly in stock, and all the goods coming from this store are fully warranted to prove just as represented in every respect. The business done is very large and is steadily increasing, as the customers are not only well enough satisfied to come again themselves, but feel as though they must bring their friends also.

Harvey Blunt, Confectioner and Caterer, No. 715 Tremont Street, between Rutland and Concord Squares. That the Caterer is a necessity in every city is a fact that needs no demonstration, for his usefulness has long since been proved, and there is not a supper or a ball given of any importance but what his services are called into requisition. That some should be more reliable than others is perfectly natural, and in accordance with observations made in every line of trade and as perfect reliability is one of the chief virtues in a caterer we take great pleasure in commending to the favorable notice of our readers the establishment conducted by Mr. Harvey Blunt at 715 Tremont Street, between Rutland and Concord Squares, for this gentleman has so abundantly proved himself fitted to be assigned a leading position in his profession during the score of years that he has been engaged in it that those securing his services have reason to congratulate themselves on the fact that success in his departments at least is assured, and that nothing will be left undone that his wide and varied experience can suggest. Mr. Blunt is a member of the Free Masons, Odd Fellows, Royal Arcanum and Knights of Honor. He inaugurated his present enterprise in 1867, and has reached the prominent position now accorded him by dint of energy, ability and perseverance. The premises utilized comprise four floors and a basement of the dimensions of 20x90 feet, and employment is afforded to 10 assistants. Having every facility at hand, Mr. Blunt is prepared to furnish silver ware, china, etc., for formal or social occasions as well as supply collations of any desired cost, and he also provides for the presence of an adequate number of well-trained waiters, etc. He is an extensive dealer in the finest Confectionery, Ice Cream, etc., and makes Wedding Cake to order, either plain or elaborately and beautifully ornamented, at the lowest rates for the very best goods. One of the chief causes of Mr. Blunt's popularity as a furnishing caterer is found in the strictness with which he adheres to all agreements entered into, and this integrity alone should assure him the patronage of all who can appreciate business honor.

Union Park Cigar Store, S. Friedlander, Sole Manufacturer of the "New England" ten cent cigar and Dealer in Tobacco, Pipes, Snuff, and Smokers' Articles, 1878 Washington Street. A business that has been conducted by its present proprietor for more than ten years and successfully given evidence of the intelligent management and honorable methods that have been manifested in it, is the record of the business carried on by Mr. S. Friedlander at 1878 Washington Street Manufacturer of and wholesale and retail dealer in fine cigars, also a large and reliable stock of pipes, snuff and all articles used by smokers. Mr. Friedlander occupies one floor 20x60 feet in dimensions and keeps constantly employed nine competent men. Mr. Friedlander is a German by birth but is well known in Boston as a practical energetic and honorable man, and his long experience enables him to offer decided advantages to his customers. Cigars of fine flavor, both domestic and imported, may be had here, and in the way of Tobacco all the standard brands are represented.

Henry W. Tombs, Plumber, Sanitary Drainage and Ventilation, No. 717 Tremont Street; Residence over Store. The South End and the Back Bay are very desirable places of residence in many respects, but, nevertheless, it is undeniable that those living within this territory should take special care to see that the drainage, etc., of their houses is in perfect condition, as owing to the uniformly level character of the districts mentioned, and other facts unnecessary to mention here in detail, defective drainage, dangerous anywhere and under all circumstances, is doubly dangerous when occuring within the limits indicated. There need be no necessity for putting up with anything wrong in the line of drainage and plumbing for a single day, as there is more than one competent concern at the South End that makes a specialty of remedying such defects, and as desirable an establishment to patronize, when any work of this kind is to be done, as we know of in the entire city, is that carried on by Mr. Henry W. Tombs at No. 717 Tremont Street. Business was begun by this gentleman in 1880, and the superior and thorough character of the work done, the faithfulness with which all agreements, contracts, etc., were carried out, and the equitable prices asked in every instance have combined to build up a large and still growing trade. Mr. Tombs was born in Boston, and is well known here, having spent twenty years in the plumbing business. He makes a specialty of Sanitary Drainage and Ventilation, and gives particular attention to House Drainage and Water Service. Residing directly over his store, orders may be left outside of business hours, and as eight to ten competent assistants are employed, work can be "rushed through" at very short notice when necessary. Gas-fitting is also done with neatness and despatch, and at low rates for reliable service.

G. F. Davis, Grocer, Teas, Coffee, Spices, Flour, &c. Choice Butter a Specialty. 393 Shawmut Ave. The handling of Groceries is one of the most important branches of business carried on in any city. All corners of the earth are brought under contribution to furnish their products, and the facilities for their distribution to customers offered by the merchants engaged in the trade, are annually becoming more extensive. Among the old and well known houses engaged in this department of commerce in Boston, is that of Mr. G. F. Davis, which was founded in 1872. The premises occupied for the transaction of this retail business consist of a store and basement each 25x60 feet in dimensions located at 393 Shawmut Avenue which are fitted up with special reference to the requirements of the business. The stock of goods carried here is large, and well-selected, embracing everything in the Grocery line, Teas, Coffees, Spices, Flour, etc., choice Butter being made a specialty. Experienced assistants are employed and the entire management of the business is under the direct personal supervision of the proprietor. Mr. Davis is a native of Massachusetts and a well known citizen of this community, having had a successful business career in Boston, for the past sixteen years.

H. D. Smith, Hack, Boarding and Livery Stable, Cor. Northampton & Wash'n Streets.

Boston is attracting more and more attention every year as a desirable city in which to live, and not the least among its many attractions to the pleasure-seeker is that afforded by the many excellent Livery Stables to be found within its limits. Of course there are some establishments of this kind, even in Boston, that are by no means "excellent," but still there are enough good ones if you know where to find them and one of the best of these is that of which Mr. H. D. Smith is the proprietor, located at the corner of Northampton and Washington Streets. If this gentleman don't thoroughly understand how to carry on an establishment of this kind, it is certainly not from lack of experience for he began operations in 1851 and has been in present place twelve years, he has thus served the public for over a quarter of a century. There are occupied three floors, measuring 60x123 feet and affording accommodation for fifty Stalls and seventy-five Carriages, employment being given to six competent assistants. Hacks will be furnished for any occasion such as Weddings, Funerals, Balls etc., at very reasonable prices and patrons are assured of being supplied with an easy riding vehicle, in thorough order and neat and stylish in appearance. The drivers are men thoroughly acquainted with the city and its environs and will be found careful, accommodating and courteous under all circumstances, as Mr. Smith insists on his patrons being treated with uniform respect and will retain no man in his employ who is remiss in this particular. Light carriages and good horses may be hired at bottom rates and the luxury of a drive over Boston's good roads enjoyed under the most favorable conditions. Large barges and sleighs and careful drivers are furnished to parties for all occasions at very reasonable rates.

James O. Gray, Brewers' Agent and Bottler of Niagara Falls Lager Beer, Gray's Cincinnati Lager Beer, Greenway's India Pale Ale and Sparkling Spray Lager, 302 Tremont Street. It is not our purpose, and indeed it is not within the province of this book, to enter into an elaborate argument to prove the harmlessness and even the positive value of a pure lager beer or ale, and in fact we do not consider such argument necessary at this day, for it has been repeatedly announced by leading physicians that pure malt stimulants of the kind mentioned are efficacious, not only in stimulating the weak and nervous, but in so building up the constitution as to enable it to defy all ordinary diseases when reasonable care is exercised. This statement, we say, has been frequently made in one form or another, and this being the case, the only remaining question is, "Where can such a pure malt stimulant be found?" A call on Mr. James O. Gray at No. 492 Tremont Street, and a trial of what he has to offer will answer this question better than we can do it. Mr. Gray is the selling agent for the Niagara Falls Brewing Company's Lager Beer, which he can supply by the barrel or case, and is also agent for Greenway's India Pale Ale, besides handling Gray's celebrated Cincinnati Lager Beer. It will be seen that he deals in two kinds of Lager Beer, and for the benefit of those who are unacquainted with the peculiar characteristics of each, we would say, that while both are perfectly pure articles, made of the best materials and very carefully compounded, there is a decided difference in their flavor, due to certain peculiarities of manufacture which we have not space to mention here in detail. Some will prefer one and some the other, but no matter which is used, the consumer may feel assured that he is being supplied with an article that, in its special line, has no superior in the market. Greenway's India Pale Ale has been before the public for some years now, and may safely depend on its reputation for its continued popularity. It has been analyzed by some of the most eminent chemists in the country, and their reports agree with those given by the senses when the ale is drunk — "absolute purity, sparkling life, delicious flavor." Mr. Gray supplies families with the goods he handles at very reasonable rates, and gives all orders prompt attention. He does both a wholesale and a retail business, and employs fifteen assistants.

W. J. McPherson, Decorative Stained Glass, etc., 440 Tremont St. The merited reputation of Boston as a literary and artistic centre is too widespread to require comment here, but many of our readers may not be aware to what an extent, in the field of decorative art, she has moulded opinion, cultivated taste and inspired feelings of refinement throughout the country, by the works which have been produced in her midst. It is the superior excellence and high artistic quality of her work which has gained for her the reputation she enjoys, and won for her the leading position she occupies to day among other cities. Of late years the development of decoration has been very rapid, owing to the great increase of wealth in the community, and the attendant desire for better things than heretofore existed, and the growth and progress have been such as to seem to leave no limit to the extent to which decorative features might be carried in point of richness and elegance. To the interior treatment and furnishing of residences more attention is paid to day than was ever before dreamed of, and the minutest details are often carefully studied in order to combine utility with artistic effect. The most prominent house in Boston in the field of decoration, and one whose reputation is well known throughout the country, is that of W. J. McPherson, 440 Tremont street, which has occupied the leading position ever since its establishment in 1845. In a building, the very quaintness of which would attract observation, are installed two large but quite distinct industries, one pertaining to decoration and painting in all its branches, the other to the manufacture of stained glass windows. The Art Rooms on the first floor are most attractive, and would well repay a visit, for here are exhibited choice bits of decoration, beautiful samples of artistic glass, cartoons of notable productions, and objets d'art for the embellishment of interiors. A corps of talented artists and skilled workmen is constantly employed to meet the different requirements of the work, whether of a domestic or ecclesiastical character. Careful attention is paid to work of the simplest kind, that it may be harmonious in coloring though no elaboration is attempted, and everything is done in the most thorough manner. For decorations of an elaborate nature, whether for residences or churches, original compositions are made and executed in the highest style of the art, and for carrying out works of magnitude, Mr. McPherson's facilities are unequalled, the numerous buildings throughout the country, of a public or quasi-public character, being conspicuous examples of the taste and skill displayed with great success in the treatment of large surfaces. In the Stained Glass department are produced decorative windows of all qualities, from those of the simplest design and low cost, to the most elaborate ornament or expensive figure work. Memorial windows are made a specialty and executed in the most artistic manner, appropriateness of selection in the matter of subjects being carefully observed, and the treatment of the figures portrayed based on a thorough knowledge of church requirements. Staircase windows are made prominent and attractive features in the decoration of private residences, and heraldic windows are executed with every regard for accuracy of detail and correct coloring. Mr. McPherson is always pleased, upon application, to prepare and submit designs for work of all kinds, in connection with decoration and glass, and furnish estimates as to cost, and communication with him cannot fail to be of advantage to one who desires to obtain work unique in character and possessing beauty of form, harmony of color and artistic worth.

M. E. Osgood, Books, Stationery, Periodicals and dealer in Small Wares, No. 470 Shawmut avenue, Boston. This popular Stationer and News Dealer, although established as recently as 1880, has attained a position to be envied by many engaged in the same line. A store covering an area of 18 x 35 feet is occupied, located at No. 470 Shawmut avenue, which contains a fine assortment of goods usually handled in this line of trade, including Stationery of all kinds, Small Wares and a general News Stand, where may be found all the daily papers, also periodicals, magazines, etc. The retail trade extends throughout this vicinity, and is rapidly increasing. The proprietor exhibits taste in the arrangement of his stock, and the store is attractive in all its appointments. Every customer is treated in a polite and attentive manner, and the proprietor studies to meet the wants of the public in every respect, and is eminently fair in all dealings and well qualified to push his business to still greater usefulness and importance.

F. P. Haskard, Dealer in Fish and Oysters, 711 Tremont Street. The philosophical Mr. Weller's exclamation — "Weal Pie is werry good, provided you know the lady wot makes it" might be with equal truth applied to fish with some slight alteration, for " Fresh Fish are werry good, provided you know that they came from the right place." Being a sea-coast city, it is of course natural that Boston should consume an enormous quantity of food, in the way of Fish, Meat, Vegetables, Fruit — these depend for their goodness upon their freshness, to a greater or less degree, but none of them one half so much so, as does fish. The difference between fish freshly caught, and fish that is just inside the line of badness is so great, as regards both palatableness and healthfulness, that the importance of having it delivered as quickly as possible to the consumer, can hardly be overestimated, and it is therefore with pleasure, that we recommend the establishment conducted by F. P. Haskard, successor to Chas. H. McGowan, at No. 711 Tremont Street, for this gentleman deals in Fish and Oysters very largely, and makes a specialty of supplying these toothsome articles fresh from either the salt or the fresh water, as the case may be. Game, Fish and Fancy Oysters are given particular attention, and are handled by Mr. Haskard at the lowest market rates, and carried in seasonable variety. The premises in use, measure 20 x 40 feet, and comprise one floor. Employment is given to two competent assistants, and every effort is made to make each customer a permanent one. Mr. Haskard was born in N. J., and began operations in 1888, and abundantly deserves his success.

Richard Addison, Provisions and Fruits, No. 212 Shawmut Avenue, corner Dover Street. A gentleman who has carried on his present business for very nearly a score of years and who has added to his reputation for enterprise and fair dealing with every year that he has served the public, certainly deserves prominent mention in these columns and we therefore take pleasure in alluding to the enterprise conducted by Mr. Richard Addison at No. 212 Shawmut Avenue, for it is he who has made the honorable record before spoken of. He was born in this city and opened his present store in 1869, and is a member of the Odd Fellows, and also of the Knights of Honor. The premises utilized measure 20 x 20 feet and comprise one floor and a basement, employment being afforded to four efficient assistants. The stock of Provisions carried by Mr. Addison is complete in every detail and includes meats of various kinds, such as Beef, Pork, Lamb, Mutton, Veal, etc., together with Hams, Shoulders, Smoked Beef and other preserved meats. Vegetables of all descriptions are also on hand in their seasons, and a specialty is made of the handling of Foreign and Domestic fruit, this being received direct from the producers and placed on sale fresh and tempting at the lowest market rates. Mr. Addison's prices in every department are as low as the lowest (quality considered) and orders are promptly and accurately filled.

Creamery & Bakery, Butter, Cheese, Eggs, Cream, Milk & Buttermilk, Bread, Cake, Pies &c, Fresh Daily. J. B. Whitney Jr. 424 & 776 Tremont Street and 744 Harrison Avenue. In each different kind of business there will be found firms whose goods have a very high reputation, which fact is no doubt due to the high standing of the house and the very careful attention that is paid to procuring the best stock. These remarks are applicable to the house of J. B. Whitney jr., located at No. 424 Tremont street who established only since 1883 has already acquired a wide-spread reputation for the manufacturing of fine Bread, Cake, Pies, etc., which are made fresh daily. The premises occupied for the retail business purposes, consist of one floor and basement each 25 by 18 feet in dimensions. This store is very attractive in appearance and great taste is displayed in the arrangement of goods. In addition to the manufacturing and sale of Bread, Cake, Pies, etc., Mr. Whitney deals extensively in Butter, Cheese, Eggs, Cream, Milk and Buttermilk, which are warranted pure and unadulterated. These articles are sold at his branch stores 776 Tremont Street and 744 Harrison Avenue. He has at 424 Tremont Street a large bakery where eight skilled hands are constantly employed and everything purchased at the Creamery & Bakeries of Mr. Whitney will be found fresh and of first-class quality. Mr. Whitney is a native of Boston and a prominent Odd Fellow. The community at large are so familiar with the superiority of the goods sold, as to require no further comment, at our hands and the high standard of the proprietor is such as to entitle him to the respect with which he is regarded. He makes a specialty of old fashioned Steamed Brown Bread Saturday evening and Sunday morning. Saloons and Stores supplied. Home-Made Bread, Cake and Pastry. Cooked Meats sold by the pound, comprising Boiled Ham, Boiled Tongue, Roast Beef, Roast Pork, Chickens, Turkeys, &c., cooked to order.

Chas. F. Toothaker, Dealer in Meats, Vegetables and Fruit, Butter, Eggs, Beans, Lard, Hams, etc., No. 632 Shawmut Avenue, Opposite Sawyer Street. The commercial advantages of Boston have brought men of enterprise and capital to establish themselves in our midst, and nearly every branch of industry is carried on here vigorously. Mr. Chas. F. Toothaker is among the leading dealers in Choice Meats and Provisions. This gentleman began business here in 1887, and has conducted it upon such liberal and just principles that a large and increasing trade has grown up, and today he holds an enviable position in the Meat and Provision trade of this section of the city. He has ample accommodations, the premises occupied consisting of a store and basement, each 18 x 40 feet in dimensions, located at No. 632 Shawmut Avenue, where will be found a choice selection of Meats of all kinds, Vegetables and Fruits in great variety in their seasons, also Butter, Eggs, Beans, Lard, Hams, etc. Mr. Toothaker has secured the valuable services of Mr. Charles Jones, who was formerly with Mr. F. J. Herthel jr., as manager of his business, and we would advise all who desire to obtain first-class goods in the above named lines of food supplies, to give this establishment a call, as its proprietor and manager insure satisfaction to all patrons.

Clarendon Hotel, Tremont Street, Near Berkeley, Boston, Mass., F. S. Risteen, Proprietor. For its size and population, Boston is probably as well supplied with hotels as any city in the United States, and not only is their quantity sufficient, but their quality is as a rule considerably above the average. Some of these hotels are intended for the accommodation of families, as well as transient guests, and among such, a leading position is held by that known as the "Clarendon," located at 517 to 529 Tremont Street. It would be difficult to improve on the situation of this house, for the special service for which it was built, as it is at once central and quiet, and combines healthful surroundings with nearness to the center of the city. The building, which has a front on Tremont Street of 118 feet, contains five floors, and one hundred rooms are utilized altogether for transient and permanent guests, employment being given to upwards of fifty assistants. That these latter are perfectly conversant with their duties and are under the management of an experienced and able head, is evident to any one noticing the unusual smoothness and regularity with which the affairs of the hotel are conducted, and those enjoying the hospitality of the "Clarendon" are very apt to draw unfavorable but unavoidable comparisons, when business or pleasure takes them elsewhere for a season. The proprietor of this well-managed hostelry is F. S. Risteen, who also runs a hotel at Hingham during the heated term, which contains one hundred and fifty rooms. The "Clarendon" is supplied with a well equipped Billiard-hall, and all the modern conveniences are at the disposal of guests. Mr. Daniel W. Stevens, who has so long been head clerk at this house, is still to be found here.

Battle of Bunker Hill Cyclorama. Frank Prescott, General Manager, Tremont Street. The many people from the West, and elsewhere, who visit Boston on account of its being located on historic ground, and who recall to mind the thrilling scenes previous to and during the progress of the Revolution, as they call at the "Old State House" and look down upon the spot where the "Boston Massacre" occurred, will now have an additional incentive to make a patriotic pilgrimage to the Hub; for the recently completed Cyclorama of the Battle of Bunker Hill is not only worthy, considered merely as a work of art, of traveling many miles to see, but every means have been taken advantage of by Monsieur L. Kowalsky and the artists associated with him in this grand work to secure historical correctness in every detail represented on the twenty thousand square feet of canvas, and so successful have these efforts been that it may be accepted as a positive fact that the spectators see the country around Boston just as it actually was on the morning of the eventful Seventeenth of June, 1775. So conservative a newspaper as the Boston Daily Advertiser has remarked that this Cyclorama should be continuously maintained here as an object-lesson in history more valuable than pages of wordy description. Entering the imposing brick building with its picturesque, rough-stone front, the spectator passes through corridors hung with spirited paintings of Revolutionary events and comes out on the summit of "Breed's Hill," as it was called previous to the battle, but since known as "Bunker Hill" the world over. Round about is the redoubt erected by the patriots, and within the enclosure formed by it are to be seen the men who had resolved to risk all, rather than endure the galling yoke of British tyranny. Every face is a study; every form has meaning in each curve and posture. Here we see a British officer about to plunge his sword into the breast of his disabled adversary; there stands a defender of the redoubt discharging a huge pistol in the very face of a red-coated soldier who is just thrusting his bayonet into the body of an unarmed American; a deadly hand-to-hand combat of intense fierceness is raging in one corner of the works, and men grasp each other by the throat, struggling upon the ground, and fight on, unconscious and unmindful of the pelting lead that fills the air above their heads. The smoke of burning Charlestown hangs like a pall to seaward, and sharply relieved against the lurid glare of the flames, stands the steeple of the church which established the first Sunday-school in New England. The British men-of-war drop slowly down the stream, keeping a constant fire on the doomed town from which the inhabitants are fleeing as best they can; and from some of the houses as yet spared by the flames, sharpshooters are pouring a scathing fire into the rear of the British lines. But it is impossible to convey an adequate idea of the scenes presented, and the most we can hope to do, is to so stimulate the interest of our readers as to cause them to visit the Cyclorama themselves. No one with a spark of patriotic spirit can view the scene unmoved, and those who wish their children to feel a live interest in American history, will find that a few visits to this stirring representation will do more toward accomplishing that end than the perusal of volumes of description, however ably written. This Cyclorama was opened to the public in February, 1888, and thousands of people have already given it their cordial endorsement. In connection with the Battle of Bunker Hill is exhibited the Diorama of the "Boston Tea Party." This scene is presented in a subdued light, and after leaving the more brilliantly illuminated Cyclorama, one must wait some little time before his eyes will reveal to him the details of the "Tea Party." But the wait is well repaid. There, alongside the wharf is the ship containing the obnoxious ten, and on its deck is a swarm of fantastic figures in nondescript Indian costume. A number of spectators are to be seen in the vicinity, and the illusive moonlight reveals the dark waters of the harbor, covered with the chests from the ship's hold. The effect is wonderfully well managed, and there is a fascination about the scene that makes one hate to leave it in order to examine the curious collection of arms and prints of the Revolutionary period with which an adjoining apartment is filled. The Battle of Bunker Hill may be seen to equal advantage night or day, for the building is illuminated by electricity, and every feature is distinctly brought out. The General Manager, Mr. Frank Prescott, spares no pains to make a visit to the Cyclorama pleasant and profitable, and ladies without escort may feel assured that no annoyance will attend a call at this popular resort.

Nicholas M. Williams, Catholic Bookseller and Stationer; also Undertaking and Caskets; 1386 Washington Street, near the Cathedral. The gentleman whose card heads this article is well known as one of the largest dealers in Catholic Books in the State, and his establishment is a favorite resort with those seeking works explanatory of, or otherwise devoted to the propagation of the doctrines of the Catholic religion. The enterprise was inaugurated in 1863, and has met with pronounced success, a success which we may take this opportunity to say is well deserved, for Mr. Williams has spared no pains to satisfy his customers to the utmost of his ability, and has made it a point to see that all callers at his store should receive prompt and uniformly courteous attention. A fine assortment of Stationery is also shown, in addition to the books mentioned, and it is sufficiently varied to allow of all tastes being suited. Mr. Williams is a prominent member of the Foresters, being also widely known in connection with his position as sexton of the Cathedral. An important department of his business is that devoted to Funeral Undertaking, this branch being added in 1881. Caskets, Coffins, and everything called for in the performance of the rites of burial are supplied by Mr. Williams, and he strives to make his charges as low as possible. His prolonged and varied experience and the extent of his business, enable him to furnish everything in the Undertaking line at very reasonable rates indeed, and one advantage gained by dealing with him is the certainty that everything coming from his establishment will prove precisely as represented.

Miller & Fiske, Manufacturers of Harnesses and Saddles, Collars, Halters, &c. also Dealers in Horse Clothing, Whips, Brushes, &c., 227 Dorchester Avenue, South Boston, and 1274 Washington Street, Boston. It is very poor policy to buy a valuable horse and then allow him to work under the disadvantages unavoidable when a poorly designed or bad fitting harness is used. In the first place the animal is apt to injure himself, and then again he cannot pull so hard or travel so fast under such circumstances as he could under more favorable conditions. This is no mere theory of our own, but is asserted by the most eminent veterinary surgeons as well as confirmed by practical experience every day. A harness being of so much importance, it follows that too much care cannot be used in the selection of it, and in this connection we would direct the reader's attention to the stock of such goods shown by Messrs. Miller & Fiske at No. 1274 Washington Street, Boston, and also at No. 227 Dorchester Avenue, South Boston. This firm manufacture the harnesses they sell and hence are in a position to know just exactly what they are. A large business is done and the trade is steadily and rapidly increasing, for every article sold is guaranteed to prove as represented, and no lower prices are to be got anywhere on equally good stock. The Washington Street store is 20x80 feet in size. Five assistants are employed and Harnesses, Collars, Halters, etc., offered in great variety, being made to order when desired. Horse Clothing, Whips, Brushes, etc., are also largely handled and second hand harnesses are bought and sold. Particular attention is given to repairing, the most difficult job being undertaken at short notice, and satisfaction is confidently promised, as every facility is at hand to turn out such work in a thoroughly first-class style. Neatness and durability are both looked out for, and no fancy prices are charged under any circumstances.

S. E. Wilson & Co., Fine Groceries, corner Washington and Worcester Sts. There has been a most remarkable and striking change in the methods of carrying on a first-class city grocery store, within the past ten or fifteen years and the result is that a properly managed establishment of this kind is now one of the most attractive places imaginable, especially to those who are fond of the "good things" of life. Pay a visit for instance to the spacious premises occupied by Messrs S. E. Wilson & Co., at the corner of Washington and Worcester Streets, and examine the heavy and varied stock constantly carried by this popular firm. It is displayed to most excellent advantage and contains an unusually large proportion of fine imported articles, such as Cross and Blackwell's Pickles, Jams, etc., Pure Olive Oil, "P. and C." Sardines, choice Italian Maccaroni, Olives etc., together with a large and skillfully selected line of Condiments and Table Relishes such as have received the approval of the most competent connoisseurs. In the single item of Canned Goods, a large enough stock is carried to supply half a dozen ordinary grocery stores and this stock is made up, not of the cheap and worthless productions with which the market is flooded, but of the productions of the best Packers, whose goods form the accepted standard of merit in articles of this description. Fruits, Vegetables, Meats etc., can thus be enjoyed at any season and under any circumstances, and Picnic Parties, or Beach residents would do well to obtain their supplies at this store, for the goods are as reasonable in price as they are excellent in quality. But to go on and describe the stock in detail would exhaust our available space many times over, so we will content ourselves with calling attention to the exceptionally fine Teas and Coffees offered by Messrs. S. E. Wilson & Co., and trust that our readers will give the firm a call and thus learn for themselves the many advantages extended to customers.

CYCLORAMA OF THE BATTLE. OF GETTYSBURG.

BOSTON CYCLORAMA CO., PROPRIETORS.

A. T. DONNELLE, Proprietor,   541 TREMONT STREET.

Cyclorama of the Battle of Gettysburg, Boston Cyclorama Co., Proprietors; A. J. Donnelle, Manager; 541 Tremont Street. It is difficult at this late day to write anything new concerning the magnificent Cyclorama of the Battle of Gettysburg, exhibited by the Boston Cyclorama Co. In the massive and costly brick building located at No. 541 Tremont Street, for the reason that, since this painting was submitted to the press and the public in December, 1884. the dictionary has fairly been exhausted, searching for laudatory adjectives to apply to it. We recall no instance in which the verdict of newspapers of all kinds, men of all professions, and, in short, everybody and everything interested, has been so clearly unanimous, and we can truthfully state that not a single person of the many individuals asked concerning this masterpiece of the great French artist. has failed to declare that not only was it "worth the price of admission," but that after spending hours in studying it, one can return again and again with renewed pleasure and profit. To one visiting the Cyclorama for the first time, the effect, especially if it be during business hours, when the rush and roar of a great city fill the streets, is quite indescribable. You step, from Tremont Street, through a winding passage and up a few stairs, emerge on what is apparently a rounded eminence, and with the swiftness of thought are transported to the beautiful field of Gettysburg and back through a quarter of a century of American history to the morning of July 3d, 1863. You look about you, and you see — what? You behold a scene that cannot be taken in, in every detail, for hours. It is quite beyond description on paper; but imagine two bodies of men, numbering thousands on thousands facing each other after being excited nearly to madness by two days'

bloody fighting. Imagine that, shortly before your arrival, a tremendous artillery duel had been in progress. continuing for hours, filling the air with ponderous missiles whose destructive effects are to be seen close at hand in the shattered remnants of Battery B, that was posted on the very spot where you stand, and imagine that the slacking of the Union fire was the signal for the desperate charge now being made by Pickett's Division from the friendly shelter of the woods, across the fields. on the key of the position held by the Northern forces. All is vigor, stir, and turmoil! Batteries dash hither and thither, staff officers ride at full gallop in every direction—not a figure on the mighty canvas but what is replete with life or else yet more effective in death; and no orator in the world could so impress the people with a due sense of what war really is, as a silent inspection of this painted surface can do. The foreground is taken up with real objects — cannon, shells, guns, swords, grass, etc., but where what may be called "nature" ends and art begins, is by no means evident. Regretfully leaving the Cyclorama, a visit is paid to the Diorama, "The Uprising of the North;" and here, too, one may tarry long and thoughtfully. As a typical representation of what influences nerved the arms of those who fought, that "this nation might not perish from the earth," the Diorama is as great in its way as is the more extensive painting, and no believer in a republican form of government can study it without renewed hope and more steadfast courage. The Boston Cyclorama Co. was incorporated April 1st, 1885, with a capital of $300,000. The president is G. W. W. Dove; treasurer and manager, A. J. Donnelle; directors, G. W. W. Dove, Paul West, Jas. W. Smith, E. Herbert Ingalls, Dr. C. M. Newell, Chas. F. Perry, and A. J. Donnelle.

W. C. Tannatt, Dealer in Hats, Caps, Trunks and Gent's Furnishing Goods, 1840 Washington Street. Also dealer in *Dry Goods* at No. 1843 Washington Street. This mention of the more prominent business men of this city would be decidedly incomplete unless it included the name of Mr. W. C. Tannatt, for this gentleman conducts two different establishments and gives close personal attention to both of them. The public have long since discovered that they are good places to visit, both as regards the purchase of reliable goods and the obtaining of the lowest market rates and on this account a very large and growing patronage is enjoyed by both of the stores mentioned. They are numbered 1843 and 1840 Washington Street, respectively and at the first-named address is carried a fine assortment of Dry and Fancy Goods, embracing the latest novelties in these lines as well as a complete stock of staple products such as blankets, sheeting, etc. Mr. Tannatt is a native of Springfield, Mass., and begun operations in 1880. The store is 40x100 feet in size and employment is given to four competent assistants. South End ladies will find it to their advantage to give Mr. Tannatt a call rather than to go in town to make their purchases, for aside from the time and trouble expended in trading at the large down-town houses, their goods are by no means so uniformly reliable as those supplied by Mr. Tannatt while in case any exchange should be desired, it is much easier to make it at his store, than to spend the better part of a day, going through the red tape necessary in making exchanges at the larger establishments. A Laundry Agency is held by Mr. Tannatt and work will be done at bottom prices and in first-class style. At No. 1840 Washington Street, a store measuring 20x50 feet is utilized and employment afforded to two efficient clerks. Hats Caps, Trunks and Gent's Furnishing Goods in general are displayed here in all the latest styles and young men will find the nobbiest patterns in hats, neck trimmings etc., offered at very reasonable figures. Hats of all kinds are carried in stock and whether it be in warm weather when straw goods are found most comfortable or during a "blizzard" when fur hats are at a premium, Mr. Tannatt will be found equal to the emergency and able to furnish reasonable head gear at bottom rates.

S. C. Smith, Creamery and Grocery, Corner Shawmut Avenue and Windsor Street; also 46 Stamford Street. The Grocery and Creamery business, above almost all others, increases in importance as the country grows older and more thickly settled, but the degree of perfection which it attains is due to the energy of individuals who have been for years connected with the business, and who have developed a fitness and capacity for it gained from long experience. Such a one is that conducted by Mr. S. C. Smith at No. 677 Shawmut Avenue. This branch house was established in 1887, and since its inception it has been an active, enterprising concern, and an honorable competitor for legitimate business. Here will be found constantly, all the products of a dairy farm, such as Fine Creamery Butter, made fresh every day,

Sweet Cream, Butter, Milk and Skimmed Milk, also Fancy Groceries of every description, which are sold at the lowest prices. The celebrated Oriental Condensed Coffee is kept on hand and served by the cup. The business conducted by Mr. Smith is exclusively retail, and of such magnitude as to require two stores, one located at the corner of Shawmut Avenue and Windsor Street, which comprises one floor and a basement 20 x 83 feet in dimensions, and the other at 46 Stamford Street, consisting of a store and basement 20 x 50 feet. The services of five experienced assistants are required in the several departments, and the entire business is under the direct personal supervision of the proprietor. Mr. Smith is a Maine man by birth, a gentleman of experience and practical knowledge of his business, and is well known and esteemed in this community.

Mrs. E. M. Mulliken, Dry Goods, Small Wares, Choice Cigars, Confectionery, Periodicals &c., Agents for Troy Laundry, 73 West Brookline Street, corner Shawmut Avenue. Nothing so much conduces to the advancement and prosperity of a locality as the formation of attractive places of business, and among others we wish to call the attention of our readers to the house of Mrs. E. M. Mulliken, dealer in Dry Goods, Small Wares, Choice Cigars, Confectionery, Toys, Periodicals, etc. This establishment was started 14 years ago, but the present proprietor assumed control in 1887. The premises utilized for the transaction of this retail trade are located at 73 West Brookline St., corner of Shawmut Ave. In addition to the retail trade in the above named articles Mrs. Mulliken is agent for the Troy Laundry and everything in this line of business is satisfactorily conducted. Mrs. Mulliken is a native of Cape Cod, and we may say to our readers interested, that it will be to their interest to visit her store and inspect her stock before purchasing elsewhere.

P. T. Conlan, Architectural Wood Carver, 3 Bristol Street, cor. Harrison Ave., Estimates on Plans, etc. The work of the wood-carver is fairly entitled to rank among the fine-arts, for it requires talents of no common order to attain distinction in this field of effort, and there is ever an active demand for the productions of those who are true artists in this line. The term "wood-carving," is a very indefinite one and its scope is so great that it includes all working in wood, from the carving of an ornamental piece of furniture to the production of a symbolic figure of heroic proportions. We have more than one wood carver, of reputation in this city, but prominent among them is Mr. P. T. Conlan of No. 3 Bristol Street, for although this gentleman has only been before the public since 1877, he has clearly proved his right to be granted a position among the leaders in his art. The premises occupied, are of the dimensions of 20x30 feet and the facilities at hand are such that all commissions can be promptly and satisfactorily executed, employment being given to from twelve to twenty skilled assistants. Mr. Conlan is a native of Boston and has a large circle of friends in this city and vicinity.

Horace Draper's Livery, Boarding and Riding Academy, 91 West Dedham Street, Boston. It is now just a score of years since the establishment known as "Draper & Hall's" was founded, and it is safe to say that there are very few people in the city who have not heard of this enterprise in one way or another. No one at all interested in riding or driving can have remained in ignorance of it, for it is without a doubt the foremost establishment of the kind in Boston, and has done more to render accessible the healthful delights of "the road" to the best class of people than any similar enterprise with which we are acquainted. The present popularity of horseback riding in this city and vicinity is due, in no small degree, to the example and enthusiasm of those who have mastered the art in the finely equipped riding school connected with these stables; and in this connection we would say, that those who wish to acquire an accomplishment no less healthful than fashionable, and as enjoyable as it is healthful, should most certainly avail themselves of the advantages here presented, as careful and experienced instructors, a spacious track 90 feet square, and specially trained horses, all combine to make learning a pleasure, and not a task. The management of this school is most admirable, and every care is taken to exclude people in any way objectionable, references being required from strangers, and every needful precaution taken. Special hours are assigned for tuition to the different sexes, ladies being taught from 9 to 12 A.M. and 2 to 4 P.M., and gentlemen from 7 to 9 A.M. and 4 to 6 P.M., and no gentlemen are admitted during the hours appropriated for ladies. Exercise rides for ladies and gentlemen are taken between 12 and 2 P.M. and 7 and 9 P.M., and music is furnished Tuesday and Saturday evenings from 8 to 10 o'clock. The terms for tuition are very reasonable, and road lessons are given if desired. Horses will be boarded for six dollars per week, the use of the school being included, and will be carefully trained to saddle for ladies' or gentlemen's use, thoroughly and expeditiously. The Boarding Stables contain accommodations for over three hundred horses, the stalls being of extra width, on the second floor of the building, which is light, airy and perfectly ventilated. Stylish Teams of every description will be rented by the day, week, month or season at moderate rates, and in response to order by Telephone or otherwise, will be sent whenever desired. Employment is afforded to twenty-five assistants, and no pains are spared to give patrons the perfect satisfaction they have been taught by experience to expect from this popular house. We have thus far referred to the concern as "Draper & Hall," but in point of fact, this is incorrect, as Mr. Horace Draper is now sole proprietor and has been for about a year. He is a native of Dedham, but resides in this city where he is very extensively known. Since assuming sole charge of the enterprise, he has endeavored to even improve on its former high record, and is by no means content to prosper under a reputation gained in the past, but constantly strives to gain fresh laurels for the future.

Henry Scales, Upholsterer, 47 West Canton Street. An establishment which richly deserves a prominent mention in this volume, by reason of the enterprise exhibited in every department and the honorable, yet pushing business methods, employed, is that conducted by Mr. Henry Scales, Upholsterer and Furniture repairer, at No. 47 West Canton Street. This enterprise was inaugurated in 1869, and has since been pushed with an ability and vigor that demanded and has achieved success. Mr. Scales is a native of England and has many friends in this city, being a member of the Knights of Honor and a popular business man. The premises utilized for business purposes comprise three floors each covering an area of 20x60 feet, and there is carried therein a stock of goods that it would be hard to duplicate both as regards variety and general desirability in this section. Among the articles it comprises may be mentioned Hair, Husk, and Excelsior Mattresses, Window Shades, Wire Screens, Italian Awnings, Brass, Nickel, Ebony, Walnut, Ash and Mahogany Poles and rings for Drapery, Spring and other curtain fixtures, Tassels, Cords, etc., Shades and Laces cleansed and made to hang and run as good as new. Also furniture repaired and re-upholstered and Carpets taken up cleaned and relaid, new carpets cut, made and put down. Experienced assistants are employed and orders received by mail or otherwise are promptly attended to. We would recommend the residents in this section of Boston, to give this establishment a trial when anything is needed by them.

Geo. A. Berry, Dealer in Provisions of all kinds, Fruits and Game in their season, 274 Shawmut Avenue, between Hanson and Milford Streets. History has shown (and common sense supports the showing), that the welfare and the character of a people are largely dependent upon the food they eat, and that although gluttony is of course to be avoided, the nation that consumes the most hearty and nutritious food, will prove stronger, both mentally and physically, than the people who from necessity or choice are more stinted in their diet. Some ingenious gentlemen argued that man should not eat meat, and "point with pride" to certain individuals who by careful observation of the laws of health, and a strong constitution, have attained an advanced age on a strictly vegetable diet. But for every one such person, there are hundreds who have reached as great an age and eaten meat whenever they were so disposed, so that it is difficult to see what is proved by the "shining example" mentioned. Be sure that the quality of your meats and other provisions is good, that they are cooked properly and are appetizing to the taste, and, other things being equally favorable, your health will take care of itself in a most satisfactory fashion. Of course to be sure of obtaining reliable goods you must deal with a reliable house, but such houses can be found without a very prolonged search, and prominent among them, is the establishment conducted by Mr. Geo. A. Berry, at No. 274 Shawmut Avenue, between Hanson and Milford Streets. This gentleman carries a fine stock of Provisions of every description, including Poultry and Game in their seasons, and caters to the most fastidious trade by handling none but standard articles, and fully guaranteeing everything sold to prove as represented. Moderate prices are quoted in every department, and orders are filled without delay in a careful and painstaking manner.

C. H. Stone & Co., Dealer in Family Groceries, Fine Teas, etc., 591 Shawmut Avenue, Corner Lenox Street. As a source of food supplies of all kinds, the city of Boston will be seen through these pages to possess advantages equal, if not superior, to many other large cities in the United States. Among the numerous houses engaged in this line, we note that of C. H. Stone & Co., which is located at 591 Shawmut Avenue, corner of Lenox Street, and which was established in 1887 by the present enterprising manager, and has become well and favorably known throughout this section of the city for the fine quality of its goods, as well as the reasonable prices maintained. The store, which is 25 by 60 feet in dimensions, is admirably arranged for the display of goods dealt in, being finely and fully stocked with a carefully selected line of Choice Family Groceries, Teas, Coffees, etc. Three efficient assistants are employed to wait upon customers, and all orders are carefully and promptly filled. Mr. Stone is a native of Vermont. We can commend his house to the attention of our readers, believing, as we do, that his facilities, goods and terms are sure to be found desirable and highly satisfactory, and knowing him to be an honorable and liberal gentleman in all business transactions.

H. S. Litchfield, Dealer in Fresh, Smoked and Pickled Fish, Lobsters, Oysters, Clams, &c. Pure Cod-Liver Oil, removed to 274 Shawmut Avenue, between Hanson and Milford Streets. All orders promptly attended to. The advantages of living in a great city like Boston, are even more pronounced in some respects than would be supposed possible at first thought, and in this connection, mention should be made of the comparative ease with which the city purchaser can obtain certain articles of food in fresh and first-class condition. Experience has shown that going into the country in summer with the idea of getting fresh vegetables, etc. is a very mistaken thing to do in most cases, for the finest vegetables and other country produce are shipped to the highest market — or in other words — to Boston. The same thing is true regarding fish, and it is a standing joke among those who "know the ropes," at some of the suburban beaches, to see how new-comers enjoy the fish they are served with there "right from the sea, you know," the fact being that they are supplied with fish, as with groceries and meats, direct from the Boston Markets. Freshness is certainly of the first importance where fish are concerned, and it is easy to obtain perfectly fresh fish by patronizing such an establishment as that carried on by Mr. H. S. Litchfield at No. 274 Shawmut Avenue between Hanson and Milford Streets. Mr. Litchfield has made arrangements that enable him to carry a fine assortment of all kinds of Fish, freshly caught and in first-class condition, and despite the uniform excellence of his goods, his prices are as low as the lowest at all times. Smoked and Pickled Fish are also extensively dealt in, together with Lobsters, Oysters, Clams etc., and particular attention is called to the strictly pure Cod Liver Oil obtainable at this establishment. Orders are given prompt attention, and polite treatment is assured to every caller.

D. J. Hickle, Baker. No. 52 West Canton Street. Bread is the "Staff of Life," and a fine display of Bread and Cake is made in the windows of the first-class bakeries, which will be found in almost every well regulated community. Among the attractive establishments of this kind located in this section of Boston, is that conducted by Mr. D. J. Hickle, at No. 52 West Canton street. At this Bakery can always be found fresh, every day, a full assortment of choice Bread, Cake, Plain, Frosted and Fruit Cake; also a large variety of small Cakes, comprising Jumbles, Cookies, Gingerbread, etc. Mr. Hickle established his bakery in 1884, and occupies premises covering an area of 18 x 25 foot, where he conducts a fine retail trade among the best families in this section of the city. He devotes his personal supervision to all branches of the business, and merits his already achieved success. Mr. Hickle is a native of Boston, and by his strictly conscientious and upright dealings has won the esteem of a large circle of friends, both in social and business life. Baked Beans every Wednesday, Thursday, and Saturday nights; Brownbread Sunday mornings. We commend his establishment to all desiring first-class goods in his line at very reasonable prices.

The Reece Button Hole Machine Co., Manufacturers of the Reece Button Hole Machine; Office and Factory, 458 to 462 Harrison Avenue. The invention and introduction of the Reece Button Hole Machine marked a new era in the making of machine button-holes in all kinds of fabrics, and its success through six or seven years of practical use, under all circumstances, proves it to be, as claimed by its manufacturers, "the *first* and *only* button-hole machine constructed upon *true principles.*" Mr. John Reece, its inventor, and the president of the Reece Button Hole Machine Co., is a native of Maine, under whose laws the company is incorporated. The main office and the factory are located at Nos. 458 to 462 Harrison Avenue, where three floors, of the dimensions of 40 x 100 feet, are occupied, and power is supplied by a 400 horse-power engine, seventy-five hands being employed. Branch offices are maintained at Lynn, Haverhill, New York City, Philadelphia, Chicago, St. Louis, Cincinnati and Rochester, N.Y., and the system employed is so perfect, that all orders can be filled without delay. The machine was awarded a gold medal in 1884, and was also awarded a gold medal in 1887 for improvements, by the Massachusetts Charitable Mechanic Association, and it has never failed to demonstrate its superiority during years of practical use. The fabric which is being stitched remains motionless during the entire operation. The stopping and starting of the stitching mechanism at the commencement and finish of the button-hole are entirely automatic, the needle *always* stopping out of the fabric. The button-holes are cut automatically, the labor of the operator is about one-third of the amount required by any other method, and the stitching mechanism is actuated by a *simple* crank *movement*, enabling a high speed to be attained with but little wear or noise. A complete button-hole stitch is made at each stroke of the needle bar, and thus, when run at the same speed, this machine will produce double the number of stitches of any other clamp machine in the market. It runs equally well on all kinds of fabrics, either with silk or cotton thread. It makes a button-hole, that for quality and durability is unsurpassed either by hand or machine work, and owing to its simplicity and easy, direct action, the machine can be kept in repair at about one-half the expense of any other button-hole machine known. On boots and shoes from twenty to forty cents per case can be saved on worked button-holes by the use of the Reece Button Hole Machine, and a single operator can make from 4,500 to 5,000 button-holes per day. The company leases machines

on liberal terms, and no manufacturer of any goods requiring button-holes can afford to throw away the advantages gained by the use of this machine.

J. F. McDowell, Livery, Hack, Boarding & Sales Stable, 576 Shawmut Avenue. One of the best appointed Livery, Boarding, and Sale Stables, in this city is that conducted by Mr. J. F. McDowell at No. 576 Shawmut Avenue. It occupies an eligible location and the stable covers an area of 85x45 feet, with an additional carriage house, which are conveniently arranged in all their departments. These stables are supplied with thirty-five stalls, and fifty carriages, and customers can be supplied with first class driving horses, with carriages, by the hour or day. Mr. McDowell has thoroughly repaired, ventilated and lighted, his stables and is prepared to give first-class accommodations for boarding horses. They will receive the best of feed and every attention for their comfortable condition and health. A specialty is made in boarding gentlemen's private driving horses. Mr. McDowell established this business in 1886, and has met with an extensive patronage. He employs five skilled and experienced assistants, and satisfaction is guaranteed to all having business dealings with him. Parties visiting the city by private conveyance will find no better or more trustworthy hands in which to leave the care of their animals. Mr. McDowell is a native of Worcester Mass. and a member of the Odd Fellows and is highly esteemed throughout this community. He is an experienced and competent horseman in every respect and thoroughly understands the proper care of stock, and our many readers will find this establishment as desirable as any other in the city.

Lawrence Cunningham, Plumber and Gas Fitter, 570 Shawmut Avenue; Residence 170 Blue Hill Avenue. Among the many complete establishments in this city, where the most thorough work is performed, is that of Lawrence Cunningham, Practical Plumber and Gas Fitter, whose place of business is located at 570 Shawmut Avenue. The premises comprise a store 18 by 20 feet in size, and contain the most approved and modern tools and supplies for the prosecution of the business. He employs only skilled workmen, realizing the fact that good help does good work. Special attention is paid to the ventilation of dwellings and sanitary plumbing. Mr. Cunningham, who is a practical and thorough master of every detail of his line of business, superintends all work personally. He founded his business here in 1883, and has from the first met with unusual success. He carries a full and complete line of plumbing and gas fitting materials, which enables him at all times, with the assistance of his competent workmen, to execute the most complicated and difficult work at short notice. Orders by Mail or Telephone are promptly attended to, his Telephone connection being No. 4465-3. Mr. Cunningham is a native of Boston, and resides at No. 170 Blue Hill Avenue, where orders may be left at any hour, day or night. He keeps all his contracts to the letter, and as a fair and honorable business man has no superior in the city.

W. N. Reed, Men's Furnisher, Shirt Maker, and Laundryman, 1099 Washington Street, Troy, New York Laundry, Commonwealth Hair Dressing Rooms, also Trunks Made and Repaired. Many people are apt to wonderingly remark at the smooth and trim appearance presented by certain gentlemen whom they may chance to notice, and bother their heads over the problem of why they cannot get clothes that will fit them equally well, when they patronize the best tailors, and in short spare neither trouble nor money to ensure their garments looking as well as anybody's. Now there is no reason why a man who is not deformed should not be able to obtain perfect fitting clothing, and in the majority of instances where there is a failure to do so, it is not the fault of the tailor or the customer's figure, but rather of the undergarments that are worn. This view of the case is not taken by many we are aware, but nevertheless we are convinced that were more care exercised in the selection of what clothing is worn next the skin, there would be much fewer complaints of ill-fitting over garments. In this connection let us call attention to the establishment conducted by Mr. W. N. Reed, at No. 1699 Washington Street, for this gentleman is prepared to furnish underwear, business and dress shirts that shall be perfect fitting in every respect, and having had an experience of over twenty-five years in the business, it is presumed that he is able to do so if anybody is. Mr. Reed was born in Boston. He occupies premises 20 x 80 feet in size, and carries a beautiful stock of Men's Furnishing Goods in general, comprising the latest London patterns and complete in every detail. His facilities for making fine shirts to order are of the very best, and a large patronage is enjoyed in this line alone. Mr. Reed is interested in the Commonwealth Hair Dressing Rooms, and receives orders for the Troy, New York Laundry, guaranteeing the finest work attainable, and having in operation so accurate and well considered a system of delivery that mistakes are almost impossible. Employment is afforded to five efficient assistants, and those who appreciate fair dealing and gentlemanly treatment, will thank us for calling their attention to the advantages offered by Mr. Reed. In addition to his large trade in Gent's Furnishing Goods Mr. Reed also makes and repairs Trunks of all kinds to order. This is a great convenience to people in this vicinity, who thus save their expressage down town for repairs. Sample trunks are also made to order, and among his customers are some of the leading wholesale houses in the city.

Charles H. Chase, Meats, Fruits, Canned Goods and Vegetables; Vermont Butter a specialty; 382 Shawmut Avenue. Among the many houses in Boston that have for several years carried a superior grade of Meats and Provisions, that of Charles H. Chase, located at 383 Shawmut Avenue, deserves special mention. This establishment was founded by Mr. H. Lovesy in 1883, who was succeeded in 1885 by the present proprietor, Mr. Chase. This gentleman has by energy and perseverance attained the position he now occupies among the business men of Boston. His premises consist of a store and basement, each 20 x 15 feet in dimensions, and all necessary facilities for carrying on the business are at hand. Five courteous and obliging assistants are employed, while the stock comprises all kinds of Meats, Fruits, Canned Goods and Vegetables, Mr. Chase's facilities for furnishing choice goods being equal to any house to this line of trade. He is an energetic gentleman of large practical experience in his business, and well deserves the wide-spread reputation and success he has attained. The residents of this section of the city will find this an establishment well worthy their attention and patronage.

C. H. Chappell, Boarding, Livery and Sale Stable, 70 and 81 Northampton Street. W. P. Harrington, Manager. It is hard to determine when the drives to be had through Boston's suburbs are most enjoyable—in the spring when a delightful warmth and freshness are in the air, in the summer when the leafy avenues afford grateful shade, and the motion of the carriage produces a cooling breeze, in the fall when there is a crispness and sparkle in the atmosphere which is so exhilarating as wine, or in the winter when the light cutter is whirled along at a railway speed over the smooth, white snow—all four seasons have their special delights and each in its turn seems incapable of improvement. But the first essential under all circumstances to enjoyment on the road is a good horse, and next to this comes a stylish and comfortable vehicle, and as most of us have to depend upon hired teams for our driving facilities, it is important to know just where such desirable accommodations are to be obtained. Well, no mistake will be made if the establishment conducted by Mr. C. H. Chappell, at No. 81 Northampton Street be patronized, for this gentleman holds at the disposal of his customers some of the most satisfactory turnouts to be had in the city, and what is more, he is prepared to let them at very reasonable rates.

Mr. Chappel was born in Rhode Island, and inaugurated the enterprise with which he is now connected in 1887. When he began operations, he did so with the idea that there was an opening for a livery stable where first-class accommodations were combined with popular prices, and the hearty and increasing patronage and support extended to him, shows that he was perfectly justified in this assumption. Five doors are occupied and five assistants employed, all orders being filled with despatch.

Mrs. T. M. Mendum, Fancy Goods and Stationery, Circulating Library, Demorest Patterns, Troy Laundry Agency, etc., 607 Tremont Street. Every branch of business has a number of firms that have excelled therein and are thoroughly representative. Among the most successful and enterprising retail dealers in Fancy Goods and Stationery in this section of Boston is Mrs. T. M. Mendum, whose well-known establishment embraces the store No. 607 Tremont street. Mrs. Mendum established her business in 1860, rising by degrees to the enviable position she now occupies, by hard, persistent work, courteous demeanor to all her patrons whether rich or poor, and by unfailing integrity in all her transactions. She employs two assistants and keeps constantly on hand a well assorted stock of everything usually included in this particular line of business. She has a well selected Circulating Library, also has an agency for Troy (N. Y.) Laundry, and Demorest Patterns. Her facilities for obtaining goods at first hands and at the lowest possible figures are well-known and recognized, and her experience leads her to anticipate and meet the wants of the public in a prompt and satisfactory manner, a self-evident fact, judging from the large number of patrons who are to be seen in her store at almost any time during the day

Sturdivant Brothers, Grocers, No. 686 Harrison Avenue. An establishment that has proved very popular in the neighborhood where it is located, is that conducted by Sturdivant Brothers at No. 686 Harrison Avenue, and but a comparatively small amount of investigation is required to ascertain the cause of this popularity. Everybody likes to be sure of getting the worth of their money when they make purchases, everybody likes to know that the groceries they are consuming are as pure and fresh as the market affords, and everybody likes to receive prompt attention and civil treatment when they have occasion to visit a store and give an order. Now when we say that all these desirable things are to be secured by dealing with Sturdivant Brothers, we think that no further explanation is needed of the popularity of the undertaking they control. Business was begun in 1882, and the sales have showed a steady increase ever since. The assortment of goods shown includes Staple and Fancy Groceries in great profusion and of standard excellence. The prices quoted are at all times as low as the market will permit and employment is given to two efficient assistants, who spare no pains to extend satisfactory service to the public. The system in force for the delivery of orders is very complete.

S. C. Hopkins, Wholesale and Retail Dealer in Fresh, Smoked & Pickled Fish, also Cod Liver Oil. Established 1853. Monument and Cotuit Oysters, Lobsters, Clams, etc., 559 Tremont & 4 Montgomery Streets, Boston. Orders called for and delivered.

The oldest and among the most reliable houses in its line in Boston is the well-known business conducted by Mr. S. C. Hopkins. It dates its history back as far as 1853. For the past thirteen years Mr. Hopkins has had the sole control and interest of the business, which he has managed and increased in an enterprising and honorable manner, thoroughly keeping with the established reputation of a first-class house, and the requirements of the trade. The premises utilized by Mr. Hopkins are located at 559 Tremont street, and comprise a store and basement each 20 x 45 feet in dimensions, where an extensive wholesale and retail trade is transacted in Fresh, Smoked and Pickled Fish, Monument and Cotuit Oysters, Lobsters, Clams etc. The extensive trade requires the employment of three capable assistants, and orders are called for and delivered promptly. Mr. Hopkins is a native of Truro, Mass. Both wholesale and retail customers will here find rare advantages and bargains in the line of the products of the sea, which make it advisable and profitable for them to trade with this house.

Stephen Murphy, Carpenter and Builder, 481 Tremont Street up stairs. Among the many carpenters and builders doing business in this city, mention should be made of Mr. Stephen Murphy, located at No. 481 Tremont Street, up stairs, for the shop of which this gentleman is proprietor has a well-deserved reputation for turning out good work and the business done is a large and growing one. Mr. Murphy inaugurated the enterprise with which he is now identified in 1881 and has filled many commissions of importance since that time. The premises in use measure 25x50 feet and employment is ordinarily given to fifteen efficient and skilled workmen. Jobbing orders are given special attention, and it is safe to assert that all who may favor Mr. Murphy with their patronage in this department, will have no reason to regret doing so. Contracting for Buildings and every description of mechanic's work done, estimates cheerfully furnished for the erection or remodelling of Buildings etc. His facilities are of the best and his experience enables him to undertake repairing with the certainty of giving complete satisfaction. As a builder also, Mr. Murphy has made a record of which he has no reason to be ashamed, and we can assure our readers that he may be depended upon to carry out whatever plans may be submitted to him, faithfully and well, and also that he will give whatever counsel his practical experience may suggest to advance his customers' interests.

E. Moulton, Dealer in Groceries & Provisions, No. 647 Tremont Street. Among the most active, enterprising and successful of our So. End business men, is Mr. E. Moulton doing business at No 647 Tremont Street. This gentleman is engaged as a dealer in Groceries and Provisions and holds a very high position in the city in his line of business. The establishment he carries on was founded by him in 1872 having been for four years previous on Washington Street. The business has steadily increased from year to year and is retail in character, a very large stock being carried. The premises utilized comprise a store and basement each 20 x 90 in size, and employment is given to five experienced assistants. Owing to the long continuance, and high reputation of this house, the proprietor is enabled to secure his goods at the very lowest market prices, and is consequently in a position to furnish his customers with standard articles on most reasonable terms. Everything sold is warranted of the best quality and guaranteed to prove as represented, a full line of Fancy Groceries also Wines, Liquors and Beer for Family trade; and no doubt it is to this strict integrity, which has characterized all the business operations that this house largely owes its success. Mr. E. Moulton is a native of the State of Maine. He is a member of the Knights of Honor and G. A. R. and a gentleman of capability and energy and thoroughly experienced in all the details of his business.

C. A. Siegemund, Pharmacist. Corner Newton and Washington Streets. It is not to be denied that the location of the Pharmacy conducted by Mr. C. A. Siegemund, at the corner of Washington and Newton Streets, is a fine one in many respects, and no one who has visited the establishment will question our statement, that its interior appointments are in keeping with its prominent situation and exterior appearance. Mr. Siegemund has been successful in largely extending the magnitude of the patronage year by year. Those at all acquainted with the present owner and his business methods need not be told that this success has been brought about by purely legitimate means, and that so far from being satisfied with the record already made, Mr. Siegemund is constantly trying to add to his resources and to increase his capabilities of serving the public to the best advantage. An assortment of Drugs, Medicines and Chemicals selected with the greatest care, and obtained from the most reliable sources, is always on hand, complete in every department and maintained in first-class condition, and the compounding of Physicians' prescriptions is given special attention, no precautious being neglected that science and experience can suggest. A liberal patronage is accorded this establishment in the particular line alluded to, for the care and skill that are manifested in filling such orders, cannot fail to inspire confidence and win appreciation, while the charges made are reasonable and correspondingly popular. A beautiful selection of Toilet Articles, Fancy Goods, etc., is also a strong attraction to the public, and the assortment of choice Foreign and Domestic Cigars in stock is worthy the attention of every discriminating smoker. Mr. Siegemund also prepares the following well known articles which have an extensive sale: Siegemund's Quinine Hair Tonic, an elegant toilet preparation for preserving, restoring and beautifying the hair, rendering it soft, glossy and beautiful, stimulating and promoting its growth; removes dandruff, prevents baldness and gray hair, curing all diseases of the scalp, and producing a healthy reaction of the torpid glands. A perfect hair dressing free from all irritating matter. It softens the hair when hard and dry; it acts upon the roots; it keeps the scalp in a healthy condition. Siegemund's Cherry Cough Balsam, for coughs, colds, whooping cough, croup, influenza, bleeding at the lungs, etc. Siegemund's Coca Wine is made from fresh coca leaves, and a superior quality of wine. It is prepared with great care, and is a valuable Tonic for children, elderly people and convalescents; also, for public speakers, singers and actors. It will be found a valuable Tonic for the vocal cords, and as an anodyne for allaying nervous fright without any perceptible after effect.

Carter, Dinsmore & Co., Inks, 162 to 172 Columbus Avenue, Boston. To many people, ink is ink, and never a thought is bestowed on the process by which it is manufactured, or even whether it is an animal, vegetable or mineral product. But to bookkeepers and others who have occasion to use it daily for a variety of purposes it soon becomes evident that there is as much difference in inks as there is in people, and that while some "make an impression" at once and give signs of having "come to stay", others barely stain the paper, or else are so heavy and thick as to be as incapable of recording an idea as they are of receiving one. This being the case, we have determined to earn the gratitude of our readers by giving a few simple but infallible directions showing how to get an ink that will suit you. For copying and for general use, buy Carter's Combined Writing and Copying Inks. For bookkeeping and fine writing, buy Carter's "Black" Fluid. For marking any fabric with a common pen, buy Carter's Indelible Ink, and finally if you have a good thing and want to "stick" to it, or if you want to stick anything so it will stay, buy and use Carter's Mucilage, the "great stickist". The form of this advice is not original with us, but the spirit of it meets with our cordial endorsement, and we have no hesitation in saying that in our opinion (and that of thousands of others) Carter's Inks and Mucilage are the best in the world. Well, they ought to be. Messrs. Carter, Dinsmore & Co. occupy the largest and best equipped writing ink factory on the globe. They employ practical chemists of the highest skill, who do nothing but test the ingredients entering into the composition of the firm's products, and strive to improve the goods now made and originate new ones. This is cause of the evenness of excellence so noticeable in the inks made here, and of the sameness of shade which enables a bookkeeper to use one bottle of ink after the other, and be sure that his books will present a uniform appearance as long as he writes with the same brand of ink. Carter, Dinsmore & Co., have received the highest awards wherever they exhibited for the past twenty years, and regarding the ability of their products to stand variations of climate it only needs be said that these awards have been given in all parts of the world from Montreal to Australia, and from St. Louis to Paris. The present firm is constituted of Messrs. J. W. Carter and J. H. Child, both natives of this city. These gentlemen are well known in the community, and the more prominent features of their careers are familiar to the public. "Carter's Inks" have a world-wide reputation, and their sale is as large as superior merit and persistent and intelligent advertising can make it.

Daniel Wood, Boarding Stable, 107 and 109 W. Brookline Street. The increase in the population and constant growth of the city must have its legitimate effect upon the general business interests, and in connection with a comprehensive display of the business institutions of Boston, it affords us no little pleasure to notice the establishment of Mr. Daniel Wood, located at Nos. 107 and 109 West Brookline Street. This popular stable was started in 1860, by its present proprietor. The premises located as above are eligible to all parts of the city, well lighted and airy; they cover an area of 40x90 feet, and comprise five floors, having accommodations for seventy-two horses and eighty carriages, making it a most desirable stable for those having horses to board. They receive the best feed and every attention to their comfort, and condition and health. Thirteen experienced hands are employed in the various departments, and perfect satisfaction is guaranteed to all who entrust the care of their horses to this establishment. Mr. Wood is an experienced horseman in every respect, and thoroughly understands the proper care of stock. His prices are very reasonable, and our readers will find his establishment first-class in every respect. Mr. Wood is a native of Ware, N. H. Though a business man in the fullest sense of the term, his genial disposition has made his establishment popular in this section of Boston.

F. N. Dunbar, Home Bakery and Confectionery, 514 Shawmut Avenue, corner Springfield Street. The establishment popularly known as the Home Bakery was founded in 1885 by its present proprietor, Mr. F. N. Dunbar, who from the first has been very successful in building up a substantial trade, throughout the neighborhood, in bread, cake, pastry, and confectionery. This well known bakery is located at No. 514 Shawmut Avenue, corner of Springfield Street, and consists of a store and basement, each covering an area of 18 x 45 feet, which are equipped with every necessary requisite for the successful prosecution of its retail and manufacturing business. Mr. Dunbar carries a fine stock in all branches of his business. Two experienced assistants are employed, and customers can be supplied at short notice with anything in his line of manufacture, and satisfaction is guaranteed as to both quality and price. Mr. Dunbar is a native of Milford, N. H., and has a high reputation and standing in this community, and his store is largely patronized by families in this section of the city, who appreciate first-class bread, cake, pastry and confectionery.

Stevenson & Co., Dealers in Choice Family and Fancy Groceries, Corner Washington and Dover Streets. There is no community of equal size in this country in which the grocery trade has reached larger proportions than it has here in Boston, and among the most prominent and popular enterprises of this kind carried on in the Hub, is that conducted by Messrs. Stevenson & Co., at No. 1135 Washington Street, cor. Dover. The premises occupied comprise a storehouse, three floors and a basement, and a store measuring 25x80 feet in dimensions, the stock on hand being complete in every department, but particularly so in that devoted to the sale of Fancy Groceries, of which an assortment is carried that for comprehensiveness and desirability it would be very hard to equal. Mr. Stevenson is a native of Chelsea, and a member of the Free Masons, and is well known in trade circles as an energetic and capable business man. He is in a position to offer exceptional advantages in the line of Fine Family Flour, for he handles this commodity very extensively, and enjoys the most favorable relations with producers. Both a wholesale and retail business is done and employment afforded to competent and polite assistants. The choicer articles of a grocer's stock such as Tea, Coffee. Spices, Condiments, Relishes, etc., are dealt in very largely, and the quality will be found to be far superior to the average, as the concern gives particular attention to the selection of such goods and strives to fully maintain the high standard that was long since established. Customers are assured prompt attention, and orders are carefully and accurately delivered.

Rock & Forrest, Manufacturers of Copper, Galvanized Iron and Zinc Architectural Work, Patent Skylights and Ventilators, 436 Harrison Avenue. Copper is much more generally used than it was a few years ago, for it has been reduced greatly in price, and articles made from it can consequently be sold in competition with those made of other materials. The advantages of copper are many and important, but chief among them are the ease with which it can be worked and the entire absence of any tendency to rust or decay in any way. Messrs. Rock & Forrest, of No. 436 Harrison Avenue, are very extensively engaged in the manufacture of Copper and Galvanized Iron goods, and since beginning operations in 1880, they have built up a business of which they may well be proud. Their productions have become generally known to builders and others for their careful and durable construction, and so ample are the manufacturing facilities at the disposal of this firm that they are able to combine conscientious and thorough work with a price as low as the lowest. The premises occupied are of the dimensions of 25 x 40 feet, and there are ten competent assistants employed. Cornices, Gutters, Conductors, Skylights and Architectural work of all kinds are manufactured at short notice and in a uniformly superior manner, and both material and workmanship are such as to assure satisfaction to every patron. Messrs. Rock & Morin began operations in 1880. Mr. Rock purchased Mr. Morin's interest March 7, '85, and Mr. A. W. Forrest entering the firm it became Rock & Forrest.

Charles A. Adams, Groceries and Provisions, 55 Berkeley Street, Parker Memorial Building. Many householders prefer placing their orders with such firms as can supply them with about all that is needed in the way of food, for they have discovered that not only does such a course save trouble, but that in many instances it saves expense also. Therefore, we feel sure that not a few of our readers will be pleased to learn of an establishment that is well prepared to furnish them with the best of Groceries and Provisions, especially when we add that the prices quoted by those having it in charge are in the highest degree reasonable and just. We refer to the enterprise carried on by Mr. Charles A. Adams, at No. 55 Berkeley Street, and the exceptional success which this gentleman has met with since beginning operations in 1886, shows that the many advantages he has to offer are such as will win appreciation. He is a native of this city and is very well known here, particularly in the Grocery and Provision trade, where he is recognized as an enterprising merchant, and as a man who believes in the use of honorable methods to carry on an honorable business. The store utilized by Mr. Adams is of the dimensions of 25 x 65 feet, and includes a basement of similar proportions. The assortment of goods offered to choose from is so thoroughly complete that all tastes can be satisfied; and the presence of five efficient and polite assistants permits quick and courteous attention to be paid to all.

Model Bakery, No. 313 Shawmut Avenue, Boston, Patch & Clark, Proprietors, also agent for Boston Hotel and Steamboat Laundry. The mercantile history of Boston furnishes few more brilliant examples of what unusual business talent, united with the most honorable dealings, can accomplish within a short time, in the way of building up an immense trade, and establishing a widespread reputation, than is presented by Patch & Clark, proprietors of the Model Bakery, located at 313 Shawmut Avenue. The Bread is made of the best quality of flour which is bought in large quantities. This business was established several years ago, the present proprietor assuming control in 1888, and the trade and reputation of this house has continued to increase month by month, until now it is one of the largest Bakeries in this section, and the only one where pies are made by steam. The floor space covers an area of over 2,000 square feet, and the capacity for Pies alone is very large. Teams deliver to all parts of the city and suburbs. The extensive wholesale and retail trade requires the services of fourteen assistants, and the products of this establishment are well known throughout the city.

John H. May, Boarding, Baiting, Livery and Sale Stable, Tremont Stables, 439 and 441 Tremont Street, corner Appleton Street. Some of our readers have horses that they would like to board at some reliable stable where they would have the best of accommodations, food and attendance at moderate prices. Others may

wish to know of a stable where they may bait their animals, and some may wish to hire or to purchase a horse suited to their needs. To all such we would say "go to the Tremont Stables, Nos. 439 and 441 Tremont Street, and see what Mr. John H. May can do for you, for if he can't suit you, the chances are that nobody can." The Tremont Stables were formerly conducted by Messrs. May & Goodridge, but for some time past have been under the sole control of their present proprietor. They occupy four floors and a basement, of the dimensions of 80 x 133 feet, and contain 150 stalls and accommodations for about 100 horses. We would mention in particular the perfect *ventilation* and *light*. Stable being situated on a corner lot with no building to obstruct the light or air, it is thus very healthy and desirable. There are also particular accommodations for ladies. Patrons will find a pleasant room fitted up exclusively for ladies, with all the modern conveniences. Employment is afforded to twenty five assistants, and orders by mail or telephone, number 4229, will receive prompt and satisfactory attention. Mr. May can furnish speedy and stylish turnouts to those who want to drive through our beautiful suburbs, or he can supply ladies with teams especially suited to their needs, the carriages being easy-riding and convenient, and the horses kind and fearless but good, fast roadsters. To those wishing to buy or exchange a horse Mr. May offers special inducements, for he carries a fine assortment of Maine bred horses and fully guarantees every horse to prove strictly as represented, a fact that will be appreciated by those who don't "know it all." If people were to deal exclusively with such reliable dealers as Mr. May, there would soon be an end to fraud in horse trading.

Chace & Co., Bakery, Confectionery and Billiard Hall, 245 Columbus Avenue, under Hotel Waqcolt, Boston. One of the most enterprising versatile business men with whom we have met in the preparation of this volume is Mr. Albert F. Chace, of the firm of Chace & Co., doing business on Columbus Avenue. This gentleman is a native of New Bedford, Mass.,

and prior to engaging in his present undertaking was concerned in the manufacture of the "Chace Gas Governor and Carbonetter." This appliance was designed to so regulate the pressure in the pipes that gas could be burned to the best possible advantage as regards economy and perfection of combustion, and that it fully answered the purpose for which it was intended; those who have given it a practical trial can and will cheerfully testify. Mr. Chace utilizes one floor and a basement in the carrying on of his present business. A finely equipped Billiard and Pool Room is maintained, there being six Billiard and three Pool Tables on the premises, and every facility usually found in an establishment where the finest trade is catered to. Gentlemen fond of a quiet game in a place free from the objectionable surroundings too often associated with Billiards or Pool, would do well to give Mr. Chace a call, as the conveniences he has to offer are of the most satisfying description, and perfect order and decorum are maintained in his establishment. Employment is afforded to four efficient assistants, and customers are assured courteous attention.

George E. Rollins, Grocer, 714 Harrison Avenue. Although we sometimes hear it said that "all grocery stores are alike." a little thought will bring to mind the fact that those who make this assertion, are either people who have had no experience in the purchase of groceries, or else are individuals whose powers of judgment are, to say the least—limited. No person of ordinary intelligence can have much to do with the various classes of grocery stores to be found in this city, without discovering that there is a very wide and distinct difference between them, and if any one wants an example of an establishment that is clearly entitled to be placed in the first class, let him direct his attention to the enterprise conducted by Mr. George E. Rollins, at No. 714 Harrison Avenue. This undertaking was founded in 1881, and at once met with popular favor, a favor which has been steadily added to from that time to this. Mr. Rollins is a native of Boston, and has a very intimate acquaintance with the various branches of the business he conducts. He makes it a point to secure his supplies only of the most reliable and reputable houses, and can consequently vouch for everything he sells proving precisely as represented. One door

and a basement are utilized, their dimensions being 20 x 50 feet, and employment is given to three polite and efficient assistants. Fine Groceries of all kinds are to be had here at prices that will stand the severest comparison with those of other dealers, and orders are assured quick and accurate delivery.

J. J. Delaney & Co., Monumental Works, Westerly, Scotch, and all kinds of American & Foreign Granites, Italian Marble, Statuary, Free Stone, Wyoming Valley & Flag Stone. 510½ & 518 Tremont Street. Formerly Carew's established 1843, Boston, Mass.

The monumental works of Messrs. J. J. Delaney & Co., located at Nos. 510½ to 518 Tremont Street, are among the best known in the entire state and turn out stone work which for beauty of design and perfection of execution excites favorable and even enthusiastic comment from the most fastidious critics. The art of stone cutting has reached such a high point of excellence that to say that a certain firm does work equal to the best is to give it unqualified and unreserved indorsement, but this is just what may truthfully and reasonably be said of the one before alluded to and those placing orders with Messrs. J. J. Delaney & Co. are assured of having them filled in a thoroughly artistic and satisfactory manner. The enterprise conducted by this house was inaugurated in 1843 by Mr. Joseph Carew who was succeeded by the present firm in 1878. Mr. Delaney is a native of Cambridge and is known as one of the foremost contractors in New England. He is prepared to furnish estimates at short notice on the probable cost of building stone in quantities to suit and conducts extensive granite yards at Quincy, dealing in Quincy, Westerly, Scotch and all kinds of American and Foreign Granites, Italian marble, Statuary, Free Stone, Wyoming Valley and Flag Stone are also largely handled and can be furnished at the lowest market rates at all times. An immense business is done, particularly in monumental work, and we cannot too strongly urge such of our readers as may desire anything of this kind, to give his house a call as very superior and exceptional inducements are offered.

C. C. Howland, Dealer in Choice Family Groceries, Provisions and Flour, 648, 650 and 652 Shawmut Avenue, Corner of Arnold Street. Among the old business houses of this city, which may well be called the corner-stones upon which her commercial greatness has been reared, and to whose honorable record and enterprising management and business methods, the extensive grocery and provision trade of Boston is largely due, an important position must be accorded to the house of Mr. C. C. Howland. The foundation of this extensive and prosperous establishment was laid in 1865 by Mr. C. C. Howland, who has successfully continued the business. The store utilized by him is of the dimensions of 100 x 50 feet, with basements, located at Nos. 648, 650 and 652 Shawmut Avenue, corner of Arnold Street, where will be found an extensive stock of Choice Family Groceries, Provisions, Poultry, Game, Meats, Vegetables and Fruits in their season, and the best brands of flour. The extensive retail trade of this house requires the services of seven competent assistants, and all orders are promptly attended to, and goods delivered to all parts of the city. The reputation of this house for enterprise and liberality is not excelled by any contemporaneous concern here or elsewhere, while the facilities at command of the proprietor make it one of the most desirable houses of its kind in the city with which to establish pleasant and profitable relations.

Mrs. M. L. McDonald, Grocery and Bakery, 587 Shawmut Avenue. Among the important lines of business for which Boston has become renowned, that of the Grocery and Bakery industry is entitled to a prominent position. The fine quality offered at Boston is generally recognized in the trade. Among those houses devoted to the above named line of trade which have been recently established is that conducted by Mrs. M. L. McDonald, which was started in 1880, by its present proprietress. The premises utilized are 20 x 40 feet in dimensions, and are located at No. 587 Shawmut avenue. The energies of this house are devoted to the retail trade in Groceries, and Bread, Cake, Pies, etc. The stock embraces a first-class line of staple and family Groceries, Teas, Coffees, Sugar, etc., Also all the productions of the Baker which are received fresh daily. Mrs. McDonald is a native of Boston, and practically familiar with all the details of her business, and is in every way a thorough and skillful business manager, and we commend her enterprise to all in this section of the city, who desire first-class goods in her line and courteous treatment.

M. M. Lithbridge, dealer in Fancy Goods, 721 Tremont Street. Among the first-class retail Fancy Goods establishments in the city, that of M. M. Lithbridge is deserving of prominent notice in this work. This store was occupied by its present proprietor in 1887, who has been on Tremont Street four years, the premises utilized are well located at No. 721 Tremont Street, and comprise a store and basement 18 x 75 feet in dimensions, which are plentifully stocked with all the novelties as well as the staples in this line of business. The proprietor exhibits refined taste and excellent judgment in the selection and assortment of goods of every description, and the latest novelties will always be found at this establishment. The services of two capable assistants are constantly required, and in addition to the retail trade in fancy goods, Miss Lithbridge is agent for the Cambridge Laundry. This lady is a native of Boston, and it is with pleasure that we refer to the honorable business career of this house, and the success it has attained as we believe our readers will be both interested and profited by such information.

Wm. H. Gleason, Dealer in Provisions, Game in season, Fruits, etc., 512 Shawmut Avenue, Corner of Springfield Street. It is pleasant in compiling these chronicles of Boston business houses, to make mention of certain ones, which, by reason of their long establishment, have become so thoroughly identified with the city's progress as to almost seem like public and not private enterprises. Such an establishment is that conducted by Mr. Wm. H. Gleason at No. 512 Shawmut Avenue. The inception of this business was in 1843, the present location since 1865, and it has been successfully conducted since that date by its present proprietor. The premises occupied consist of a store and basement, each 20 x 55 feet in dimensions, and are well stocked with a choice assortment of Provisions of all kinds, also Fruits and Game in their seasons. The extensive retail trade requires the services of five assistants, and the entire details of the business are most ably and systematically managed. Mr. Gleason is a native of Hanover, N. H. He is one of the most highly esteemed and well known of our older business men, and his career furnishes in many respects a worthy example for young men to follow.

J. B. Woodbridge, Dealer in Choice Family Groceries, Fine Grades of Butter and Teas, 118 West Canton Street, near Tremont. In the preparation of the history of a city, its establishments and noteworthy enterprises, we naturally come in contact with those useful avocations which conduce so much to the convenience of the public and which are, in a measure indispensable in a community. Located at No. 118 West Canton Street can be found one of those enterprises of which we speak. This house was established in 1880 by Mr. J. B. Woodbridge, dealer in fine Staple and Fancy Groceries, also the best grades in Butter and Teas. The premises occupied for the transaction of this flourishing retail store consist of a store and basement, each of the dimensions of 20 x 40 feet, which are well stocked with a choice selection of the above named line of goods. Consumers wishing goods in this line will find this a pleasant place, and its management courteous to deal with. Mr. Woodbridge is well and favorably known in this community, being a native of Boston. In conclusion, we may say that Mr. Woodbridge has established a wide-spread reputation for reliability and honorable business management.

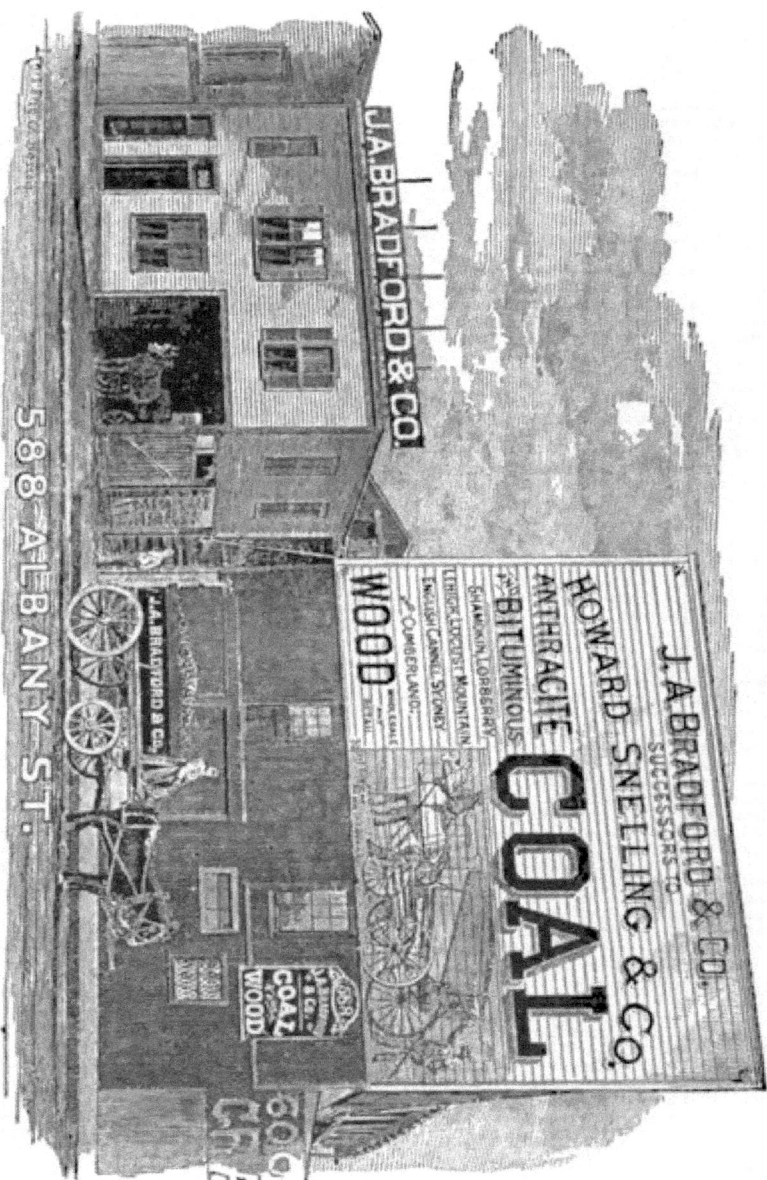

J.A. BRADFORD & CO.

588 ALBANY ST.

(See notice on page 50.)

J. A. BRADFORD & CO.
SUCCESSORS TO
HOWARD, SNELLING & CO.
ANTHRACITE COAL
AND BITUMINOUS
SHAMOKIN LORBERRY
LEHIGH LYKCOLT MOUNTAIN
ENGLISH CANNEL SYDNEY
CUMBERLAND
WOOD

New England
CONSERVATORY OF MUSIC
Franklin Square Boston

The New England Conservatory of Music. Among the attractions of Boston is this interesting and famous institution, which now attracts a larger attendance of students than any other in the country, though it may be said that some of its pupils remain for shorter periods than the students in colleges and universities remain. During the year ending in June, 1887, the number of pupils registered was 2252. The aim of this unique institution is to furnish, not musical instruction alone, but a complete education in all essential lines of culture. Besides its schools for the Piano-forte, Organ, Formation and Cultivation of Voice, Lyric Art and Opera, Violin Orchestral and Band Instruments and Conducting, Harmony, Composition, Theory and Orchestration, Church Music, Oratorio and Chorus Practice, Sight Singing and Vocal Music for Public Schools, Tuning Pianos and Organs, it also has a "School for General Literature and Languages" Ancient and Modern. A School of Elocution and Dramatic Art. A School of Fine Arts and a School of Physical Culture. Its good body of instructors, numbering about one hundred, are the ablest that can be found in America or Europe. It is therefore now needless for an American to go abroad to complete a course of musical study. Every advantage and facility is here, and some features which cannot be found in Europe. This is the only institu-tion in the world which furnishes pipe and pedal organs for the practice of the students. Of these it already has fourteen. The building is the largest and finest in the world devoted to this style of education. A vast structure, seven stories in height, lighted by electricity and heated by steam, situated upon one of Boston's most famous squares and in the heart of the city near to the museums, libraries, great churches, and every attraction the city affords. This structure, besides its large number of class rooms, halls, studios, parlors, etc., has elegant accommodations for 400 lady pupils who are cared for as they would be at home. Gratuitously furnished to its students is the most extraordinary and abundant provision of recitals, lectures, and addresses. On the average perhaps a dozen per week of the finest literary and musical performances are freely given to the students of this institution. In ad-dition to these regular benefactions, from time to time the great lights in the musical and literary world visit this vast concourse of students and kindly encourage them by the ex-hibition of their powers. Among the great musicians who have recently delighted the students may be named Fursch Madi, Hasbreetu, Ous Du Ohs, Maud Powell, McGuckin, Hoff-man, the boy pianist, and Carrino. Of eminent authors and lecturers, H. Butterworth, E. E. Hale, A. D. Mayo, W. J. Rolfe, and others. The demand for the graduates of this institution for service in colleges and schools is twice as great as the supply and this fact is very attractive to those who aim at success in life. This institution, while it belongs to the public and is in the hands of its fifty trustees, has still the advantage of the same wise management and direction which has brought it to its present colossal dimensions, and obviously has before it a career of unparalleled usefulness and development. The great concourse of students has made it possible to offer these advantages to the students for a payment astonishingly small. No where else can so much be had for so little. While the institution is not sectarian its aim is distinctly and definitely Christian and its resident pupils are under influences elevating and ennobling.

F. A. Langley & Co., Dealers in Coal and Wood, Hard and Soft Wood, 600 Shawmut Avenue. The enterprise carried on under the firm name of F. A. Langley & Co., at No. 600 Shawmut Avenue, will attain its "majority" during the current year as it was established in 1867. The past twenty-one years have brought about many changes in commercial methods, but there is still a demand for enterprise, knowledge and integrity in the successful carrying on of a business, and as long as these qualities ensure patronage, there need be no fear that the undertaking to which we have alluded will lack support and appreciation. Messrs. F. A. Langley & Co., occupy premises comprising about an acre of yard room, etc., and always carry a full supply of Coal and Wood, in which they deal very extensively, both at wholesale and retail. They are prepared to deliver the best quality of Red and White Ash Coal at wharf prices, and to furnish families with Hard or Soft Wood, sawed and split by steam to the dimensions desired. The lowest market rates are quoted on this wood as well as on the coal handled, and orders will be received for wood in quantities to suit, either by the cord, foot, box or bundle. Mr. Langley has many friends in this city and is a popular member of the Grand Army. During the great Rebellion he served in the Navy, under the command of Commodore Farragut, and participated in some of the most decisive and important engagements that took place, among which may be mentioned those occurring at Baton Rouge, Port Hudson, Red River, etc. The firm of which he is a member do a large business and rank with our most reliable city houses.

E. J. Yerxa & Co., South End Branch Tea & Grocery House, 2037 Washington Street. Yerxa is an uncommon name in most localities, but it is one which the residents of Boston and vicinity are extremely familiar with, as it has been prominently identified with the wholesale and retail Grocery business in this city for many years. It is with the South End Branch Tea & Grocery House conducted by Messrs. E. J. Yerxa & Co., at No. 2037 Washington Street, that the present article has to deal and it can be commenced in no better way than by stating that the well-established reputation of the name to which reference has been made, has been raised higher than ever by the methods practised in this establishment since its doors

were first opened to the public in 1880. One floor and a basement are occupied measuring 25 x 60 feet, and an extremely large and skilfully selected stock of Teas, Coffees, and Staple and Fancy Groceries is always open for inspection, and enables the firm to satisfy all tastes and fill every order without delay. In the line of Teas and Coffees special efforts are made, and the very finest and choicest brands are offered at prices that will bear comparison with those quoted at many other houses on far inferior articles. Spices also, of perfect purity and uniform strength, are dealt in very extensively, and the assortment of Table Condiments and Luxuries, Canned Goods, Preserved Fruits, Vegetables, etc., is a large and complete one, the most celebrated and popular packers being represented. Flour, Sugar and other staple goods are offered at the lowest market prices, and as employment is given to five assistants, customers are assured of prompt, polite service, while the arrangements for the quick and accurate delivery of orders are complete and satisfactory.

Smith Brothers, 1207 to 1219 Washington Street. Manufacturers and Dealers in Furniture of all kinds, Crockery, Glass and Silver Ware, Carpets, Ranges, etc. Furniture neatly Re-

BOSTON MANTEL BED, DRAPED.

BOSTON MANTEL BED, WITHOUT DRAPERY.

paired and Upholstered. There may be, as social Philosophers say there are, certain tendancies in operation at the present day that render marriage less desirable than it otherwise would be, but on the other hand there are also circumstances that make the establishment of a home a comparatively easy thing, and among these may be mentioned the inducements held out in the line of housekeeping goods, etc. Among the many houses handling these articles, we would like to call attention to that of Smith Brothers, doing business at Nos. 1207 to 1219 Washington Street, for since this enterprise was inaugurated in 1865, it has grown to very large proportions, and the firm are now able to meet all honorable competition and supply standard goods at prices as low as the lowest. They occupy premises comprising three floors and a basement, and measuring 40 x 70 feet, and carry a stock that our space will not permit us to describe in detail, but which includes everything in the line of House Furnishing Goods and especially complete as regards the selection of Furniture offered. Messrs. Smith Brothers are manufacturers of, as well as dealers in, furniture of all kinds, and the variety of styles which they show, as well as the bottom prices they quote, are quite sufficient explanation of the immense business they do in this line. This house (as all its old customers will cheerfully testify) does not get up goods simply "to sell," but on the contrary makes it a rule to furnish a durable as well as an attractive article. In no other way could a business such as theirs have been built up, for their patronage, although of course made up largely of new customers, is still drawn in a great degree from those who have dealt with this house for years. We cannot too strongly emphasize the fact that Household Supplies of nearly every variety are handled at this establishment, and whether you want Furniture, Carpets, Oil-cloth, Matting, Ranges, Stoves, Crockery, Glass, Silver or Tin-Ware, you can place your order with Smith Brothers, and rest assured that you will do at least as well as though you tramped all over the city and dealt with some house of which you knew nothing. A specialty is made of the Repairing and Upholstering of Furniture, and all orders are given careful and prompt attention and accurate delivery.

Charles H. Bell, Painter and Glazier, 477 Tremont Street. Nearly every man of middle age has tried at one time or the other to do some painting "on his own hook," and if he had no previous experience, the chances are that when he got through with his first attempt he had more respect for a professional painter than he ever had before. Painting looks very easy, and in one sense of the word it is easy, for anybody can dip a brush into a paint pot and plaster the paint on a wall or other smooth surface, but it is not everybody that can put on just enough paint and that can distribute it as evenly as it must be distributed if the final result is to be at all satisfactory. Therefore, we say it always pays to employ a good painter, and as some of our readers may not know just where to find such, we take pleasure in calling their attention to the paint-shop carried on by Mr. Charles H. Bell, at No. 477 Tremont Street, up stairs, for

this gentleman has conducted the shop in question since 1834, and has proved himself equal to all demands, and able to do the very best of work at bottom prices. He makes a specialty of matching any shade desired in painting buildings. One floor is occupied, 20 x 30 feet in size, and a full assortment of paints and every needful facility is carried at all times. Employment is given to from fifteen to twenty-five assistants, and all orders will be filled at the shortest possible notice.

W. H. Clement, Dealer in Choice Provisions, Poultry and Game, Vegetables, Domestic and Foreign Fruits, Appleton Market, 402 Tremont Street. If all provision stores were conducted on the same principles as that carried on by Mr. W. H. Clement, at No. 402 Tremont Street, the objectionable features of

marketing would be entirely removed, and every lady might order the supplies she required in person, without incurring any annoyance or having to go amongst uncleanly surroundings. But as all such stores are not conducted in this fashion, unfortunately, the least we can do is to call attention to those that are, and prominent among them is the one that forms the subject of this article. Mr. Clement opened the establishment to which we have reference in 1845, and occupies one floor and a basement, their dimensions being 25 x 60 feet. He employs four efficient and courteous assistants, and offers to every customer prompt and polite attention. The stock on hand is a very large one, and is as varied as it is large, for it comprises Choice Provisions of all descriptions, Poultry and Game of every kind in its season, Vegetables in great profusion, and Domestic and Foreign Fruits of first class quality. This store is also known as the Appleton Market, and is, as may well be imagined, extremely popular and well patronized. Orders are very promptly delivered and all goods are warranted to prove as represented. Mr. Clement was in Faneuil Hall Market for fifteen years. Is a member of the Odd Fellows and A. O. U. W.

J. H. McCafferty & Son, Brass Founders, Brass, Bronze and Composition Castings, Bronze Tablets and Memorial Work. Dealers in Solder, Babbitt's and other metals, 147 Columbus Avenue. But very few people, outside of those more or less directly interested in the subject, have any idea of the difficulties involved in making fine castings of metal, for 999 out of 1000 think that all it is necessary to do is to "make a mould of something or other, and pour the molten metal into it." Just so. All the sculptor has to do is to take a square block of marble and knock the superfluous material out of the way, but still we are not all sculptors, and even some of those who profess to be have evidently made a mistake in their vocation. But in spite of the variety of really fine metallic castings, we have a concern here in Boston that has a most enviable reputation for the production of high grade and artistic work in this line, and it may be said that few houses in the country are capable of turning out articles of a more high and even order of merit. We refer to the firm of Messrs. J. H. McCafferty & Son, doing business at No. 147 Columbus Avenue, where premises are occupied of the dimensions of 50 x 80 feet, and where Brass, Bronze and Composition Castings, Bronze Tablets and Memorial Work are produced in large quantities, employment being afforded to twenty-one skilled assistants. Business was inaugurated in 1886, and a large trade has already been built up, as the merits of the work done were too obvious to escape recognition, and the facilities at hand allow of the lowest market rates being quoted. Both partners are thoroughly conversant with the innermost details of the business under their control, and take every precaution to see that the high standard they have adopted for their productions shall be rigidly adhered to. Estimates will be furnished if desired, and Solder, Babbitt's and other metals are on sale at prices as low as the lowest.

William H. Fairfield, Registered Pharmacist, Nos. 621 and 623 Shawmut Avenue, Boston. One often hears it stated in conversation that those attributes which fit a man for success, in business, are apparently incompatible with those which cause one to win distinction in scientific pursuits, and perhaps broadly speaking that may be the case, but like all rules it has its exceptions, for more than one individual who has unequivocally succeeded in business has also proved his eminent fitness to follow the paths of science. A case in point is that afforded by the career of Mr. William H. Fairfield, who carries on business at Nos. 621 and 623 Shawmut Ave., for as the high position he holds among contemporary Registered Pharmacists is a proof of his scientific capabilities, so is the large patronage his establishment receives, convincing evidence, of his business tact. Operations were begun by him in 1881, and although the field was quite well occupied in which he selected to labor, still quite a large and growing trade was soon established. Mr. Fairfield is a native of Boston, and has many friends in this community. He is a member of the Odd Fellows. His store is 25x18 feet in size a basement of the same dimensions being utilized for storage and other purposes. Capable assistants are employed and customers are invariably served with care and politeness. The stock carried comprises among other things a fine line of toilet requisites of various kinds, which are offered at very low rates. The assortment of drugs, medicines and chemicals is extensive and made up of fresh, pure goods, whose strength and virtue may be confidently relied upon. Prescriptions are compounded with care and dispatch at all hours and no exorbitant prices are demanded. Sole N. E. agent for the celebrated Female Regulative Pills which are safe, certain and effective. A full line of choice cigars and pure confectionery is carried which is sold at popular prices. Owing to his large and increasing trade in Soda, Mr. Fairfield has just purchased an elegant Soda Fountain from which to draw delicious soda with fruit syrup and genuine Oak Grove Farm

Cream. This is sold at only 5 cents per glass and is not excelled in this section.

Reed's Block. This immense building was erected by Mr. Eliot D. Mayo in 1880 and 1881. It consists of a block of nine buildings, running from Albany Street to Harrison Avenue, the total length being 650 feet. The width is only 50 ft. giving ample light even in the center of the rooms. Two large, horizontal engines supply power to run the elevators, of which there are eight in the block, and also the various machines used by the several tenants. Two large fans keep a continuous current of hot air pouring into the forty rooms during the winter season making the temperature about sixty to seventy degrees even in the coldest weather. This system also has the merit of heating the rooms uniformly throughout. Four large boilers supply the steam for the engines, and also the glue heaters, jacket kettles, cauldboxes, lumber drying kilns, etc. The building was expressly erected for general manufacturing and is as complete in its details as is desirable. Shafting is provided in every room and there are 3000 to 4000 feet of "main line" kept in motion constantly. The rooms vary in size from 8000 to 5100 feet floor space and are all light and airy. The reputation of the "Block" for square dealing and reliable Steam Power is something more than local, and there are seldom more than two or three un-

cant rooms at any one time. The enterprise of the proprietor has been seconded by his able assistant Mr. R. G. Morris, and the engineer Mr. E. E. Ordell, who have largely contributed to make "Reed's Block" the success that it is today.

Woodberry & Harris, Church Organ Manufactory. Of all musical instruments ever designed by the ingenuity of man, the church organ is the grandest and the most magnificent and its capabilities are so wonderfully varied, that the whole gamut of expression from the faintest whisperings of entreaty to the awesome thunderings of command, find in this instrument an adequate and unapproachable interpreter. Of course to attain the best results it is necessary to have perfect mechanism, mechanism that will respond to the slightest touch of the player and combine the utmost delicacy with great durability, and it is just here that the superiority of one organ builder over another is most plainly manifest, and the true touchstone of merit is to be found. Messrs. Woodberry & Harris have been associated together in this branch of industry since 1885, but they have already gained an enviable reputation and proved their right to challenge comparison with the finest builders in the country. Especial attention is given to Tuning and Repairing, and in the latter, which is no doubt the most difficult branch of the organ industry a particularly high record has been made. Among the more important commissions in this line executed by this firm, may be mentioned the practical rebuilding of the magnificent instrument used in Warren Avenue Baptist church, and those who were present at the concert given to commemorate the completion of these repairs, will agree with us in saying that Messrs. Woodberry & Harris have reason to be proud of their work. They occupy two floors of the dimensions of 40 x 80 feet, at No. 390 Albany Street, and give employment to fifteen assistants. All orders will be attended to promptly and carefully and at very moderate rates. The firm is made up of Messrs. Jesse Woodberry and Chas. T. Harris, the former a native of England, and the latter of this city. The senior partner is a gentleman of very wide experience in organ building and repairing, and is well associated with Mr. Harris, who is a most enterprising business man, and neglects no means to improve the efficiency of the service offered to the public. From a New Hampshire paper we take the following: "Hudson's New Organ. During the past winter extensive changes have been made in the Baptist church in Hudson, and on Wednesday even-

ing, April 25, a large company gathered to view the new interior and hear the organ which had just been presented to the church by Dr. D. O. Smith. The new organ, however, is the special attraction. It was made by the firm of Woodberry & Harris of Boston, and is pronounced by competent critics to be the best instrument ever turned out by this reliable firm. In purity of tone it certainly cannot be surpassed, and it has, besides, certain swell effects rarely obtained in an organ of this size. Many expressions of approval were heard after the recital, and all seemed of the opinion that the new organ is most excellently adapted to the auditorium, and that one might search among many more pretentious instruments without finding its equal."

R. F. Clark & Co., Dealers in Provisions, Poultry, Game, Fresh Fish, Oysters, Clams, Fruit, Vegetables, etc. Also N. E. Agents for Robe & Bros' Imperial Hams and "The Bonanza" Boneless Meat, 15 Worcester Street. We know of no more worthy example of the reliable and representative houses of Boston than the popular establishment conducted by R. T. Clark & Co. This store was opened May 27th, 1885, by the present proprietors and the management was placed in the hands of his nephew, Mr. Geo. N. Smith, who had enjoyed ten years' previous experience in the same line in Lawrence and was amply qualified to conduct the business in all its branches. Mr. Clark is employed by one of the largest Belting companies in the United States and is thus necessarily absent most of the time. The store occupied is 80x20 ft in size and is one of the handsomest and most conveniently arranged in the city. There are eighty running feet of marble slabs, extending on two sides of the store, while in the center is a "vegetable fountain" which was designed by Mr. Clark and is the only one of the kind in existence. It consists of a spray of water rising some four feet above a marble slab on which is displayed a tempting array of fresh and early vegetables. There are also a number of glass shelves on which the water falls and as these are also filled with vegetables they are kept cool and fresh; a fact which his large number of patrons fully appreciate. Mr. Clark makes a specialty of supplying his customers with the heaviest Chicago Stall-fed beef ensuring thick, juicy steaks and tender roasts. This firm has the N. E. Agency for Robe &

Bros' Imperial Hams and Bonanza Shonklers which are sold both at wholesale and retail. These Hams are the best Sugar Cured, Boneless and Cooked, ready for the table. Will retain its natural Moisture, Flavor and Sweetness in any climate for years. Will be found indispensable in Hotels, Restaurants, etc. The Bonanza is a superior article of Boneless Meat, used as Ham or Breakfast Bacon, and cheaper than either. The low prices and the fine assortment of goods carried have given this house the large trade it enjoys. Goods may be ordered by telephone 4454 and receive prompt attention. This is also a telephone pay station. Mr. Clark is a native of New Hampshire, and is an active business man. He is a member of the Masons, K. of H. and G. A. R. He was captain of Co. A, 3d New Hampshire Regiment and was in active service in almost all the engagements in the late Rebellion.

Mr. Clark also sells the Crystal Mineral Water from the Old Original Indian Kibby Spring of Stoneham, Mass., R. B. Chapman, proprietor. The medicinal qualities of this Spring have been known for many years. It was formerly known as "The Old Kibby Spring." I have some water from the Spring which I have kept seven years, and it is perfectly sweet. I have more than five hundred customers in Stoneham who use this water daily, which shows its merits are known in its own town. It has been known to cure many cases of Kidney and Liver Complaint, etc. Allow me to call your attention to the Crystal Mineral Spring Water of Stoneham, which is delivered in Boston only by R. F. Clark & Co., Boston Agents.

Mexican Rheumatic Cure, The Formula for "The Mexican Rheumatic Cure" was obtained by me from a Spaniard at Minatitlan, Mexico, and I am the only person using it in the United States. When I commenced using this medicine, I had been entirely helpless for seven months. I could not raise my feet from the floor, or lift my hands to my shoulders. My fingers were all drawn to the palms of my hands, and my sufferings were intense. I tried any and everything prescribed by the best physicians within my call, or recommended by anyone else, both in internal and external treatment, but all to no purpose. In ten days after I commenced to take "The Mexican Rheumatic Cure" I walked four miles, and in twenty days I contracted for and built a vessel, and resumed my usual avocation, since which time I have entered and passed the four zones of the earth repeatedly, and have been entirely free from Rheumatism in any form whatever. Go and ask them what they think of The Mexican Rheumatic Cure, which is prepared only by Gilman M. Ryder, No. 355 Shawmut Avenue, Boston. Circular with other testimonials mailed on application.

BOSTON, May 19th 1884.

For about thirty years I have been a great sufferer from Rheumatism, and almost helpless for a long time. In fact, I could not rise from a chair without help, or walk a step, or use my hands so as to dress myself. My ankles and wrists were so stiff they would not bend, and all of my fingers were drawn inward to the palms of my hands, so that I could not open

them in the least. In September, 1883, I by accident, heard that Capt. G. M. Ryder had an almost infallible cure for Rheumatism. I sent for a bottle, and after taking the medicine about a week all the pain left me. After taking two bottles I was cured, and have had no trouble since. I would also mention that, at the time I commenced taking this medicine, my hands were very rough, and covered with dry scales from Salt Rheum. They soon became soft and smooth, and continue so. I have gladly recommended this medicine to friends who are suffering from Rheumatism, and in many instances they have been cured by its use. No words of mine can speak more for the praise of the medicine than it truthfully deserves. I will gladly give a more detailed statement of the great benefit I have received from this Rheumatic Cure to any one who will call on me.

MRS. A. H. SPARROW,
42 Edgeworth Street, Highlands.

Style of Sizes 1 to 3 inclusive.
Suitable for running Coffee Mills, Job Printing Presses, Ice Cream Freezers, and all small machinery requiring One Horse Power.

The Chandler & Silver Hydraulic Engine.

This is a Piston Engine very simple in construction, and so arranged that those parts in motion which receive the reaction of force have but little movement, consequently but little wear and friction.

It has no dead center and but one valve, which is moved by the same motion which propels the fly-wheel without gear or slides. Instead of four valves to one cylinder, as is usual in Water Engines, the Chandler & Silver Engine contains but one simple valve which answers for port and exhaust for five cylinders, thus avoiding the friction of extra valve connections.

The water has a direct passage from the pipe to each cylinder, saving the power usually applied to force water through crooked passages. The exhaust is as free as the port, no obstruction whatever.

One half of the cylinders take water at the same time,—one is increasing while the other is diminishing, one is using the most when the other is the least. This prevents a change in the speed of the water, thereby avoiding that pounding so common to Hydraulic Engines.

We mention below some of the advantages of our Engines for any purpose where a power of from one to fifteen Horse Power is required.

FIRST. It is compact in form, occupies but little space, and has no springs or delicate working parts to get out of order, and may be run many years without any expense for repairs.

SECOND. It makes no dirt, causes no extra insurance, throws out neither heat or smell, requires no engineer or attendance other than occasional oiling, and is always ready for use at any moment.

THIRD. It uses from thirty to fifty per cent less water than any other Motor, for the reason that its construction is such *that it is impossible for one drop of water to pass through without doing its share of the work to be done*, and therefore is the most economical Motor that is made.

FOURTH. The consumption of water is still further reduced by the AUTOMATIC VARIABLE STROKE, an adjustment *to be found in no other Motor*, which instantly decreases the thrust of the pistons, and reduces the flow of water when there is less demand for power, or less work to be done.

All Engines sold by us are guaranteed to give satisfaction. Catalogues and price lists furnished on application.

Chandler Water Motor Co., office and salesroom 1321 Washington Street, Factory 132 Oliver Street, Boston.

A. M. Gardner, Jobber and Retailer of Hardware and Cutlery, 1321 Washington and 33 Waltham Streets. A store that has come to be known during the past eighteen years as a most desirable place at which to purchase anything in the line of fine Builders' Mechanical Tools, Hardware and Specialties, is that conducted by Mr. A. M. Gardner at No. 1321 Washington and No. 33 Waltham Streets, and it is not surprising that a very large business has been built up, for the advantages held out to customers are too manifest to be passed over, and when once dealings are begun with this house they are generally continued. Mr. Gardner began the business in 1860, with less than $1,000 capital. His store at that time was small and the stock carried was, although carefully selected, quite limited in comparison with the immense assortment of goods now handled. In 1871 a partnership was formed with Mr. M. A. Chandler which continued until 1887, when Mr. Chandler retired, and the business passed under the sole ownership and control of Mr. A. M. Gardner. The stock at present is one of the most extensive and complete in New England. Not only a first class line of Builders' Hardware is carried, but this house handles certain specialties in the hardware line not usually carried; in fact, it is a common expression among builders and mechanics, "If not to be found at Gardner's it is useless to look elsewhere for it." This business, by careful attention to the wants of the trade and low prices, has grown to immense proportions, second to none in Boston, goods being shipped to every section of the United States. The stock carried is one of the most extensive and comprises over *ten thousand* different articles. The premises occupied are two large stores and basements, employment being given to seventeen efficient assistants and both a jobbers' and retailers' trade carried on. Mr. Gardner is in a position to sell goods at the lowest market price, and the uniform reliability of the articles coming from his store has been often commented upon and is fully appreciated. A most complete and beautiful assortment of Cutlery is also offered to choose from, and goods of Foreign as well as of Domestic manufacture are always in stock. The store has telephone connection and prompt and careful attention will be given every order.

J. W. Hanlon, Harness Manufacturer, and Dealer in English Harnesses, Saddles, Bridles, etc., No. 770 Albany Street, corner Chester Park. When one stops to think that the only connection between the horse and the carriage

is the harness which is worn, and that on the strength of that harness depends the safety of the occupants of the vehicle, while on the fit and general arrangement of it depend the comfort and much of the speed of the horse, it will be seen that it is worth while to use a little care and common sense at least in buying a harness. The good old rule of purchasing of a manufacturer whenever possible, should be followed in this case at all events, for no matter who the dealer is he cannot be as sure of the quality of the goods he handles as is the man who made them. Mr. J. W. Hanlon, of No. 770 Albany Street, opposite East Chester Park, has carried on his present enterprise since 1874, and is known to many prominent horsemen as one of the most skillful and reliable harness makers in the city. The premises utilized measure 40 x 20 feet, and employment is afforded to four experienced and careful assistants. No one who is a good judge of harness and leather, can examine Mr. Hanlon's stock without being impressed with its uniform excellence, and the same good points are observable in the work done to order, which is furnished at the lowest market rates consistent with the use of the best material.

GLIMPSES OF THE BACK BAY.

By WM. HALE BECKFORD.

When the sturdy band of Puritans whom John Winthrop led took their first lingering survey of "Mushauwomuk," in 1630, from what is now Beacon Hill, they little thought that the long, low, marshy tract running off toward the south-west, along the shore of the Charles, would become the most beautiful part of the world's "Hub"; and to imagine spacious avenues and palatial residences arising from the territory of the river itself (as their energetic descendants followed the example of the ancient Romans and Venetians in usurping the sea's domain), would have been far beyond the power of their wildest dreams. And while the nascent city, through all the wars and stirring changes of the colonial period, the fierce controversies and ensanguined uprisings of the revolutionary time, and the period of internal development, up to the middle of the present century, was steadily rising to its present pre-eminence, the faintest conception of the possibility or utility of creating a new Boston amid the mud and shifting tides of the "Back-bay," does not seem to have ever dawned upon the inner consciousness of a solitary Bostonian. If such a brilliant intellectual event ever transpired, the modest discoverer succeeded marvelously well in keeping it a secret from the patent-office and the world at large. But about the middle of the present century, in the evolution of Boston, "a change came o'er the spirit" of the place, and a few rare minds followed out a line of investigations of vaster importance to the city's well-being, than any that had been made since the stern-lit eyes of its heroic defenders, glancing along the muzzles of their flint-locks, saw the broad backs of the red-coats gleaming and dancing in that extempore foot-race which immortalized the 17th of June, 1775.

Among the earliest in directing public attention to this district, and the most energetic in its development, was Mr. Norman C. Munson, whose name will not rank far from the first among those to whom Boston owes most of its growth and power. As is always the case when a novel project is proposed, the first attempts to have the commonwealth superintend the transformation of these useless flats into valuable property, met with the most strenuous opposition from those narrow-minded obstructionists from whom even Boston is not entirely free. But the inevitable movement went steadily forward, and about 1852 began to take definite shape. The commonwealth, to which the flats belonged, assigned the contract for filling them in to Mr. N. C. Munson, and doubt rapidly passed into surprised delight and admiring applause, as the people opened their eyes to the fact that a "*new*" Boston was coming into existence. The first contract resulted in the reclaiming with the best of real estate, over a million square feet of land, for which Mr. Munson received in payment two hundred and sixty thousand square feet of the ground he had, so to speak, made; and for subsequent contracts which have changed what was formerly the narrowest part of Boston into the widest, he has received about the value of $7,000,000. The whole cost to the commonwealth has been less than $1,750,000, and the receipts from the sale of the lands have exceeded $4,025,000; a round two hundred thousand acres yet remain to be disposed of, and the full fruition of this great movement will only be realized by distant generations.

The old families of Boston, unlike the Roman patricians, who built only on the hills of the city, have displayed their usual originality and enterprise in the manner with which they have improved this manufactured land, and made out of it one of the most beautiful city districts in the world. The stately magnificence of Commonwealth Avenue, in its successful blending of nature and art, and in its architectural effects, has no equal in this country, and in many respects is not unworthy of comparison with the noted avenues of Europe, though of necessity it still lacks, and must for centuries, the mellowed and harmonious grace which only comes with age and traditional glory. Commonwealth Avenue has a width of two hundred and forty feet across and is over a mile and a half in length. Through its center, for the whole distance, runs a beautiful park with double rows of shade trees, making a delightful promenade. On each side of the park are wide driveways, and the sidewalks are also of unusual breadth. Near the beginning of the avenues, opposite the Public Garden, stands the statue of Alexander Hamilton, the first erected on the avenue. It was presented to the city, in 1865, by Mr. Thomas Lee, and was sculptured by Dr. Rimmer, — said to have been the first in this country made of granite. It is inscribed: "Alexander Hamilton, born in the Island of Nevis, West Indies, 11 January, 1757, died in New York, 12 July, 1804,— Orator, Writer, Soldier, Jurist, Financier. Although his particular province was the Treasury, his genius pervaded the whole administration of Washington." Some distance further up the avenue stands the statue of John Glover, presented to the city by Benjamin Tyler Reed in 1875. Martin Milmore was the artist, and the form of the old revolutionary soldier is admirably reproduced. The statue is of bronze, and the effect of the pose, the old Continental uniform, and the sword and cannon is very striking. The inscription reads as follows: "John Glover, of Marblehead,— a Soldier of the Revolution. He commanded a regiment of one thousand men, raised in that town, known as the Maine regiment, and enlisted to serve through the war; he joined the camp at Cambridge, June 22, 1775, and rendered distinguished service in transporting the army from Brooklyn to New York, August 28, 1776, and across the Delaware, Dec. 25, 1776. He was appointed by the Continental Congress a Brigadier-General, Feb. 21, 1777. By his courage, energy, military talents and patriotism, he secured the confidence of Washington, and the gratitude of his country. Born November 5,

1782, died at Marblehead, January 80, 1797." The architectural grandeur of Commonwealth Avenue, and of all the neighboring avenues in the Back Bay, well deserves the great pride which all Bostonians take in it. The celebrated architect, Richardson, and several home artists, have here displayed their finest conceptions and work. The results are unequalled in this country, and can stand comparison with European cities.

The system of cross streets in this district is a fine example of the originality and resource of the Boston mind. Beginning with Arlington street which faces the Public Garden, the streets crossing Commonwealth Avenue are named Berkeley, Clarendon, Dartmouth, Exeter, Fairfield, Gloucester, Hereford, etc. Thus the alphabet is followed in a more artistic and characteristic manner than is customary in most cities. The street names are also alternately trisyllabic and dissyllabic.

Among the most prominent buildings in Commonwealth Avenue are the Hotel Vendome and the Brattle Square Church.

The Brattle Square Church, on the corner of Commonwealth Avenue and Clarendon street, presents a most attractive aspect, its principal feature being the tower, which

with its tapering yet substantial beauty is one of the best known features of the Back Bay. It is modeled on the Italian style. On the four corners, near the top, are carved figures of angels, after the Renaissance. The whole exterior of the body of the church is a great architectural triumph, but the interior, though also very beautiful, proved of poor acoustic properties, and consequently the building was sold at auction by the church society in 1881. This society is one of the oldest in the city, dating back to 1699, at which time their first meeting-house was erected in old Brattle Square. This edifice was replaced by a larger and less primitive one in 1778, which was called the "Manifesto Church." This church was used as barracks by the British soldiers during their Revolutionary occupancy of the city, and their treatment of it illustrated well the Christian spirit shown by the old country in her attempt to bring to submission her rebellious child. In the wall of the old building a cannon ball sent by the Continental battery in Cambridge was long imbedded. Among other noted pastors of the old Brattle Square church was Edward Everett.

The fine statue of Lief Ericsson is one of the latest additions to Commonwealth Ave., and constitutes a worthy testimonial to the character and services of the famous discoverer, as well as to the discriminating appreciation of the "Hub," and its cosmopolitan spirit.

HOTEL BRUNSWICK.

Boylston street is considerably older than Commonwealth Ave., and by reason of the many famous buildings situated on it, not less widely known. The Hotel Brunswick, on the corner of Boylston and Clarendon sts., ranks among the first in this country, and is one of the most magnificent buildings in the city. It was built in 1874, at a cost of nearly a million dollars, and was still further enlarged in 1876. It is 224 by 125 feet in dimensions, covering more than half an acre of ground; is six stories high, and contains 350 rooms. The frame is of brick, with dark sandstone trimmings, and the front with its variegated and artistic abutments, presents a stately and beautiful aspect. Its internal arrangements are fully on a par with the exterior, the parlors and dining rooms being especially celebrated for their magnificence. Here are often held college-class and alumni dinners, and it is also a favorite resort of the noted literary and other societies of this society-given city. The attractiveness of the Brunswick as of the Vendome, consists not a little in its situation, not only because it is at once in close proximity to the railroads, and also the loveliest part of Boston, but the great number of large, majestic buildings surrounding it give a rich setting that is rarely obtained by hotels in this country. It is also one of the obvious advantages of the Back-Bay, that it contains many justly world-famous hotels, which add to its fame and help to make known its beauties. Among other well-known hotels in the Back-Bay are the Berkeley, Victoria, Huntingdon, and Oxford.

The Boston Society of Natural History, on the corner of Berkeley and Boylston streets, adjoining the Institute of Technology, is also one of the intellectual landmarks of the city. It is constructed of brick and freestone, and with its great Corinthian pillars and Parthenian roof, partakes of that mingled charm of stateliness and substantiability that distinguishes so many of the buildings of this section of the city. It is 80 feet in length, and its front on Berkeley street measures 105 feet. The seal of the society, bearing the head of the great French naturalist Cuvier is sculptured over the entrance. The first floor is divided into a lecture room, library, offices, and rooms containing geological and mineralogical collections. There is a grand hall on the second floor sixty feet high, with balconies, and here in profusion are natural objects and specimens of great interest. The collections of birds, insects, plants and skeletons, contain many most remarkable curiosities and beauties of nature. The museum is free to the public on Wednesdays and Saturdays, on other days a slight fee is charged for admittance. The Society was incorporated in 1831, and has counted among its members and benefactors many of the most distinguished Bostonians. The late Dr. W. J. Walker, whose benefactions aggregated about $200,000, was its chief benefactor. The building now occupied was erected in 1864, at a cost of $100,000. It is one of the marks of the true Bostonian spirit, that an institution of this character should be so successfully developed almost entirely by private means, the State only giving the land on which it is now situated, and the work of the Society having been always self-supporting.

The Massachusetts Institute of Technology, about opposite the Brunswick, ranks among the first educational institutions in the land, and its fame for bestowing a thorough and practical scientific training is international. It was first incorporated in 1861, for three distinct purposes: to institute and maintain a Society of Arts, a Museum of Arts, and a School of Industrial Science. The Society has at present a membership in the neighborhood of three hundred. The Museum contains an extensive and valuable collection of machinery, models and drawings, casts, prints, architectural plans, etc. The School of Science has upward of five hundred pupils, and is constantly extending its range of influence and resources. It receives aid from the National Government by virtue of the Act of Congress to promote instruction in Agriculture, Mechanical Arts and Sciences, and Military Science and Practice, all of which are liberally provided for in its curriculum. Its President is Gen. Francis A. Walker, the chief of the Census Commission of 1880, and a distinguished political economist and statistician. Under his guidance the school has made great advances in recent years. The main building is a large classic structure of brick with freestone trimmings, and presents an impressive appearance with its immense steps and high Corinthian pillars. A new building alongside of the first has been erected within a few years, and both are admirably adapted to the practical experimentation and practice which necessarily constitute the greater part of the instruction. The large number of machines, models and apparatus, are all of the best type, and the opportunities offered for work and study are of the highest in the country. There are ten courses, each of four years, civil and topographical engineering, mechanical engineering, geology and mining engineering, building and architecture, chemistry, metallurgy, natural history science and literature, physics and an elective. The department of mechanic arts is especially famous for the scope and value of its manual instruction. The School of Industrial Design, maintained by the Lowell Institute Fund, is another highly advanced and well known part of the Institute. Visitors are always welcomed and will find much of great interest in these buildings, representative of the spirit and progress of the age.

Among the numerous buildings of great beauty in this immediate vicinity, the Boston Young Men's Christian Association Hall, erected within a few years, takes a prominent place. The great beauty of its exterior is more than surpassed by the elegance and convenience of its interior arrangements. The reception room and parlors are fitted up in the highest style of refinement and artistic comfort, and the young men of Boston are certainly exceptionally blessed in the advantages offered by this institution. The gymnasium, though not among the largest, is one of the most thoroughly equipped and complete in the country. Every possible form of gymnastic exercise is here offered and indulged in. The large lecture hall of the Association is generally regarded as the best owned by any Y. M. C. A. in this country, and ranks among the best lecture halls of Boston. Several valuable courses of lectures are given here every season by the Association, and every department of this vast and influential work is maintained with great enthusiasm and vigor.

BOSTON YOUNG MEN'S CHRISTIAN ASSOCIATION, BOYLSTON AND BERKELEY STS.

The present attractive building of the Association was dedicated nearly two years ago. With the exception of the Brooklyn Association building which has just been dedicated, it is the largest building of the kind which has been erected for many years, and in this sense may be called new.

The Association building is 105 feet front, 100 feet deep, 105 feet high at the highest point. The land cost $97,000; the building and furniture, $208,000; the largest donations were one each of $25,000 and $10,000; twelve of $5,000; one of $3,000 and $2,500, (two in number); $1,000, forty in number. Alexander Cochrane was chairman of the Finance Committee; Charles H. Freeland was chairman of the Building Committee; the architects were Messrs. Sturgis & Bridgham.

The building contains the following rooms: Association Hall, seating 900; Choral Hall, seating 350; Lyceum, seating 200; Lecture Room, 250; Parlors, Library, Reading Room, Recreation Room; Class Rooms, fourteen in number; Lavatory; Coat Room; Gymnasium, 40x95, with dressing roooms for 942.

The exterior is deceptive in regard to size. It was intended by the architects to look like a great mansion. One does not realize the amount of space inside until he passes through the building.

The illustrations of the building give us as fair a representation of its appearance as may be expected from pen and ink sketches. The general plan of the interior is controlled by two ideas: first to place the rooms in daily use on the first and second floors, those used twice or three times a week on the third floor; those used once a

On the Staircase.

week or once a month on the fourth and fifth floors. Second, to separate the departments of work so as to prevent them from disturbing each other. The Choral Hall for music classes is on the fifth floor. The floors between the Association Hall and Reading room, Library, and Reception and Recreation rooms are thoroughly deadened. The noise from the Gymnasium is scarcely ever heard in the building. The second floor on which are the working rooms of the Association, viz:— parlor, secretary's office business office, library, reading room, recreation room, chess and checker room, lavatory, chapel and coat room is so arranged that it can all be thrown together, making a splendid series of reception

Y. M. C. A. GYMNASIUM.

In the Recreation Room

BOSTON Y. M. C. A. INTERIOR VIEWS.

rooms for special occasions. Fully five thousand people can move around in the building. The library has 4500 volumes, with frequent additions of new books. The reading room has twenty-nine dailies, seventy-five weeklies, three semi-monthlies, and forty-two monthlies. The gymnasium is one of the best equipped and best managed in the country. Its bathing facilities are the very best; its systems of exercise are the result of long years of study on the part of its superintendents. There are two paid instructors, and a staff of experienced volunteer teachers. Eight young men have been graduated as superintendents for other gymnasiums and more are studying for similar positions. About 1470 different young men belonged to the gymnasium last year.

The Boston Young Men's Christian Association was first organized Dec. 22, 1851, and is the oldest Y. M. C. A. in this country, being preceded by only one other on the North American continent, that of Montreal, which was organized a week earlier. The first president of the Boston Y. M. C. A., was Francis O. Watts. When first organized it occupied rooms on the corner of Washington and Summer streets, afterward from 1853 to 1872 in Tremont Temple, and from 1872, until it moved into its present building, a large structure on the corner of Tremont and Elliot streets. Five hundred of its members enlisted in the defence of the Union during the civil war, and its Army Relief Committee raised $333,237.49, which was devoted to the work of the Christian Commission, in alleviating the condition of the soldiery. After the Chicago fire, also, over $34,000 was collected and sent to the sufferers, in addition to goods valued at $210,000. The present membership is between three and four thousand, and the influences for good it has inaugurated among the young men of Boston are incalculable.

Back-Bay is further distinguished by the possession of two of the most beautiful church edifices in the new world, namely the New Trinity, and the new Old South. The former is, taking all things into account, the "finest church edifice" in New England, and in many respects in the United States. This great edifice was completed in 1877, at a total cost of $750,000, and the society being very wealthy, without any incumbrance or debt. It is in the shape of a Latin cross of the French-Romanesque type, and a semi-circular apse is added to the eastern arm. The great central tower rises to the height of 211 feet, and the beauty of its architecture passes all description. The width of the church is 121 feet and the length 160 feet; the tower is 46 feet square on the inside; the chancel is 57 feet deep by 52 wide. The stone employed in the body of the Church is Dedham granite, with brown free stone trimmings, and the mosaic work of polished granite is especially beautiful. The interior is finished throughout the body of the church in black walnut, the vestibules with ash and oak, and the decorations are known among the most beautiful work of the celebrated New York artist LaFarge. The architects were Gambrill & Richardson, also of New York. The magnificent stained-glass windows were imported direct from Europe. The Trinity Society is one of the oldest in the city, and of the Episcopal Church, in the country, dating back to 1728. Many of the most famous preachers and bishops of America have been among its rectors, and the present rector is Dr. Phillips Brooks, known throughout the country for his great eloquence, and as a leader of Christian thought. He is intimately connected with Harvard University, and with the highest interests and noblest movements of Boston.

The New Old South was erected in 1872 by the society formerly occupying the famous "Old South," about which cluster so many inspiring memories. Erected in 1729, the scene of so many celebrated events, escaping narrowly from destruction in the fire of 1872, and already being encroached upon and threatened by its surroundings, a most determined effort is being made by all who love the noble history of old Boston to perpetuate it for future generations. The new building on the corner of Dartmouth and Boylston streets, is, with the exception of Trinity Church, the finest church structure in New England. It was completed at a cost of $500,000, the exterior material being Roxbury stone and freestone, and the interior finished in cherry. The area covered by the church is 200 by 90 feet, and the great tower rising at the southwest corner is 235 feet high. This magnificent triumph of architecture is one of the landmarks of the Back-Bay, and immediately impresses one with its stately yet delicate beauty. The whole exterior is most artistically built, and the interior is famous for its rich and elaborate coloring. The arched screen of Caen stone with pillars of Lisbon marble, which separates the church from the vestibules, is one of the handsomest pieces of architecture in the city.

The Back-Bay numbers many church edifices, all of which are attractive and substantial, many besides those we have mentioned, of great beauty. Among the best known of these are The First Church, Unitarian, Dr. Rufus Ellis, pastor, on Berkeley street; the Arlington Street Church, Dr. Channing's old church, on the corner of Arlington and Boylston streets; the Central Church, Congregational, corner of Berkeley and Newbury streets, Dr. Joseph T. Duryea being its pastor, and which cost over $325,000, also possessing the highest steeple in the city, 236 feet; the Church of the Disciples, of which the learned and esteemed late Dr. James Freeman Clarke was pastor; the Berkeley Street Church, Congregational, under the pastorate of Dr. Wm. Burnet Wright; and the Memorial Church to Theodore Parker, of the Twenty-eighth Congregational Society, of which that gifted man was once pastor. The religious spirit to which Boston has been devoted since the earliest days, is still maintained and cultivated earnestly.

The Boston Museum of Fine Arts, corner of Dartmouth street and St. James avenue, may well engage the most careful attention of all visitors and admirers of Boston. Already its fame as a center of the most beautiful and inspiring art of the continent is becoming transatlantic, and all lovers of the æsthetic and artistic can here find almost unending enjoyment. In its exterior appearance it is one of the most beautiful buildings in this garden of beauty, where it is situated. It is not yet entirely completed, but rapidly assuming harmonious proportions. The chief building material is red brick, the friezes, mouldings, copings, and all the decorative work being of red and buff imported terra cotta, which is for the first time here used on a large scale in this country and presents a most pleasing effect. There are two large and magnificent facades upon the front of the building, one representing the "Genius of Art," by illustrations and types from remote antiquity until the present day, the other representing the union of "Art and Industry." Along the front are heads of distinguished artists, among whom are Copley, Crawford and Allston. The main entrance is one of the most beautiful sights in the city, with its wide marble steps, its tall columns of polished granite, and terra cotta decorations. The first floor is devoted to antiquities and statuary, the second floor to paintings, engravings and bric-a-brac. The Egyptian and Greek Rooms contain antiquarian collections of exceptional value and interest, a goodly supply of mummies and hieroglyphics, the Greek vases, the Cyprian discoveries of Gen. di Cesnola, and the celebrated Olympian casts being the most generally admired. The works of Michael Angelo in the Roman and Renaissance rooms, constitute one of the most valuable features of the whole collection. The Ariadne of the Vatican is a most striking and beautiful figure, which meets one on the stairway. Among innumerable other attractions, we might mention as especially worthy of study, the masterpieces of Stuart, Copley, Allston, Reynolds, Rubens, Courbet, Fromentine, LeBrun, Guido, Correggio and Velasquez. The "Belshazzar's Feast," of Allston, and "King Lear," by Benjamin West, and a number of pieces by the modern French School, are of commanding interest. The Royal French Tapestries, the Persian fabrics, the Chinese, Japanese, Dresden, Sèvres, Delft, and Wedgewood wares, the Venetian glasses, and the Lawrence Room, also possess a high flavor for the initiated into the rare beauties of art. The Gray collection of Engravings, and the cartoon by Delaroche, "Christ the Hope and Support of the Afflicted," should also be seen by those unwilling to miss some of the greatest attractions of this grand collection. The Boston Water Power Company, which was largely interested and influential in the creation of the Back-Bay, presented the land on which the Art Museum now stands, to the city, with the condition that it should be used for a public square, or for the site of a museum of the fine arts. In 1870, this lot, containing 91,000 square feet and enclosed by streets on all sides, was entrusted by the city to the corporation which had been recently formed. By the subscriptions of the public nearly $250,000 was raised, and the building was commenced in 1871, the architects being Sturgis & Brigham of this city. The part now completed was opened in 1876, and since that time has been one of the most popular resorts in the city, next perhaps to the Public Library. When entirely finished the building will constitute a vast quadrangle enveloping two great courts, after the style of the European palaces. During the first three-fourths of 1878, the visitors to the Museum were about 100,000, and this number has since been steadily increasing. In response to an appeal made to the public by the institution, in 1878, while only $100,000 was asked for, $125,000 was subscribed, and a large addition made on the St. James avenue side to the original section. Harvard University, the Institute of Technology, the Lowell Institute, the Athenæum and the Public Library, are all represented in the Board of Trustees, as is also the City and State and City Boards of Education. The Museum is open daily on week days from 9 A.M. to 5 P.M.; on Sunday from 1 to 5 P.M.; on Saturday and Sunday admittance is free, at other times the fee is twenty-five cents. One has hardly seen Boston without a considerable acquaintance with its highly developed artistic side as represented in this superb institution.

The Boston Art Club, though somewhat overshadowed by the fame of its younger contemporary, is widely known for the rare beauty and value of its collections. It was organized by the artists of Boston in 1855, and has exerted a strong and beneficent influence in the evolution of art in Boston. At its club rooms on the corner of Newbury and Dartmouth streets, fine exhibitions of paintings, etchings, etc., are given in the winter and spring of every year, and these events are of great importance in the art season. Many of the most cultured people of Boston are members of this society.

Already this section of the Back-Bay is witnessing the erection of a new building which, for many reasons, will be one of the most celebrated in the city and the country; we refer to the New Public Library. This institution, which since its inception in 1848, has held so influential a position in the life of the city, has been rapidly out-growing its present quarters on Boylston street, and will soon occupy the most magnificent public library building in the world. The architects, Messrs. McKim, Mead & White, of New York and Boston, have been working upon the design of this immense and costly building for a year, and now that work has begun, a description of how the new library will appear among the other great art works of the Back-Bay, when it is completed, which is expected to take about three years, cannot fail to be of great interest to all lovers of Boston. The estimate of the building places the cost at $1,175,000, and it is the determination of all interested, that money shall not be spared in creating a structure worthy of the city's fame. The lot which the building is to occupy is situated on Copley Square, and is 254 by 264 feet in dimensions. The old Roman style has been chosen as most in keeping with the stateliness and simple grandeur of the institution, and the mingled richness and charming naturalness of its exterior, must prove of striking beauty, situated as it is among so many other buildings of a more complex and elaborate style of art. The building will be constructed of Milford granite, whose rich warm color and extreme durability are well known. It will be very nearly 218 feet square, and along the upper half of all four sides will run a beautiful arcade with its strong restful lines, in perfect harmony with the rest of the structure. The great windows of stained glass in this arcade will furnish an abundant supply of light, which will be increased by windows opening into an inner court 100x135 feet, the plan being to make a quadrangular building on a similar principle as the Art Museum and English-High and Latin School is constructed. This inner court will form a most delightful retreat, having in its center a large fountain, and seats for readers during the warm summer days. The doorway in the center of the front will be triple arched, and of the same stern and noble style as the rest. On each side will be groups of statuary representing the Arts and Sciences, and in the center solitary figures of Philosophy and History. Semi-circular granite seats add to the attractiveness. Within the door one will find himself in a great vestibule 55x16 feet, through which he passes into the grand marble entrance hall, 87x44 feet. Then comes the grand staircase, leading from the first floor, which will be devoted to the working departments of the library, up to the reading room. This staircase will be of the finest Sicilian marble, each step being twenty feet long, and will be resplendent in its whiteness and purity. The reading room, to be known by the familiar name of "Bates Hall," on the second floor, will be the most magnificent room in the building It will extend along the whole two hundred and eighteen feet, and be forty-two feet wide and fifty high, with a grand vaulted roof. The woodwork will be of polished oak, and the effect of its brilliantly decorated and gracefully arched ceiling, and the tessellated pillars on its sides with the art windows intervening, will be unparalleled by anything at present on this side the water. At the two ends of this immense hall will be small semi-domed spaces, separated from the rest of the hall by carved oaken screens. The rest of the lower and upper floors, with the exception of those parts of the two sides opening into Bates Hall, immediately contiguous to it, will be devoted entirely to the storing of its immense collection of books, and before the century closes it is probable that this building will contain one of the largest libraries the world has ever known. The shelves on which the books will rest will be arranged in six stories, each seven and a half feet in height. The well-grounded pride which Bostonians have always taken in their inimitable public library will not unnaturally or unreasonably be steadily increased, as during the next three years this grand structure develops into harmonious proportions; and when it stands forth in its perfected beauty it will mark, not without deep significance, the presence of a new era in the education of the people, when what Carlyle calls the "true university," a great library, will have reached a position unrivalled in history.

Hitherto our study of the Back-Bay has been chiefly confined to Commonwealth Avenue and Boylston Street. With all their beauty, however, these do not contain the only or the greater part of its beautiful attractions. In former days, old Beacon street was the street of Boston, but since the genesis of the Back-Bay, its sometime glories have slowly paled before the more modern spirit and enterprise of the avenues in this section. The prolongation of old Beacon street into the Back-Bay, commonly known as the Mill-Dam, was the favorite racing and pacing thoroughfare of the city. But its honors have also paled before that of a younger rival — namely, the famous Brighton Road. When the Mill Dam was first completed in 1821, it was generally considered a gigantic achievement, but more recent workings in the Back-Bay district have overshadowed it considerably. The six hundred or more acres of flats, which it originally enclosed, have all been rescued from the tide, and the Dam itself is now no longer a dam but a well-regulated, high-toned avenue with many beautiful and famed private residences upon it. During the height of its glory, that is to say up to within a few years, a most lively scene could be witnessed here daily, as the proud owners of the fastest horses in the city drove dashingly along to the tune of 2.80 or lower. In the winter, when the jingling sleighbells, and laughing maiden voices touched with silver the frosty air, the scene was one of continual beauty and fascination. But its glory has departed, and quieter days come upon it, so that it now threatens to become as staid and slow-going as its ancient namesake, with its hoary traditions looking loftily down upon the Common it has known for some two hundred and fifty years. Perhaps the change is for the better, and it certainly is more in accord with the elegance and style which have made the residences immediately facing upon the water among the handsomest of this whole select region. One has not to go far, however, to see the repetition of these old Mill-Dam days, for new Beacon street runs into the "Brighton Road," where the racing is even faster, and the sleighing more exuberant than of old. This famous course, like the Boulevard of New York, is well known throughout the land to all the modern "equites." West Chester Park, though not a park at all, is one of the best known and most beautiful of the Back-Bay avenues. It crosses Commonwealth avenue five blocks above the Vendome

Hotel, and runs from the Charles river, turning at Falmouth street, completely across the city, developing into an actual park toward its latter end. Being 90 foot wide and most carefully and pleasantly laid out through the Back-Bay district, it is destined to be one of the most beautiful avenues in the vicinity, or the country, and already some of the handsomest and costliest residences of the Back-Bay have been erected upon it. A bridge is to be built, running across the Charles River from the end of West Chester Park into Cambridge, which will be the shortest and pleasantest route from Harvard University into Boston. Its completion will be a valued public work.

THE VICTORIA HOTEL.

Among the other fine avenues of the Back-Bay, Huntington, Columbus, at its upper end, and St. James avenues, Newbury and Marlborough streets, are perhaps most worthy of mention. Each is distinguished by many beautiful buildings, and the carefulness and superior beauty with which it is laid out. Huntington especially, is sure to become one of the most famous in the city. Many handsome residences have been laid out upon it, and, in 1881, a most noteworthy building, the permanent exhibition halls of the Massachusetts Charitable Mechanic Association. This building cost $400,000, and is one of the largest ever erected in the country. Its front on Huntington avenue is 600 feet, and on West Newton street 300 feet, being 345 feet wide in its widest part. The space covered amounts to 90,000 square feet. The style of architecture is after the Renaissance, with considerable freedom in the treatment, and the material used was red brick with free-stone trimmings and terra-cotta ornaments. Graceful arches rise one above another almost to the roof, and many symbolical art representations are portrayed on the outer walls. Among these are the heads of Franklin, representing electricity, and Oakes Ames, representing railroads. The eastern end of the vast structure consists of an octagonal tower, forty feet in diameter and ninety feet high. The immense entrance on Huntington avenue is a massive and imposing piece of work, constructed of stone and brick intermingled, and with a fine tiled roof. The interior arrangements are as tasteful and convenient as extensive. Offices, administration rooms, a great exhibition hall, the main hall at the west end, art exhibition rooms with balconies, studios, and a large music hall, answer admirably and exhaustively every purpose which could be asked for in the immense exhibitions given by this association every few years, known throughout New England and the Atlantic States as the "Mechanics Fair." The value and necessity of the building is demonstrated by the enormous crowds which fill it to overflowing week after week. This association is one of the oldest of its kind in the country, and has exercised a great influence in the industrial progress of the Bay State. It was founded in 1795, and incorporated in 1806. It formerly occupied a handsome building in Chauncy street, which cost $325,000 and is a very wealthy association.

Among many other notable and handsome buildings within the range of the Back-Bay, may be mentioned the Odd Fellows Hall, on the corner of Berkeley and Tremont streets, a five story building, covering 12,000 square feet of ground, and of imposing appearance; Notre Dame Academy and Convent, on Berkeley street, near Boylston, not unworthy in its appearance of its surroundings; and the great depot of the Providence Railroad, which is within a minute's walk of Boylston street, and ranks among the most beautiful railroad depots in the world, being too well known to need detailed description here.

Back-Bay Park from its character and that of such streets as Commonwealth Av., Boylston and West Chester, is in reality one of the most beautiful of parks. There are, however, several smaller parks here, both in existence now and to be in the future, not unworthy of mention. The great park of the Back-Bay will not be completed for three or four years, although much has been already expended upon it. With two such parks as the Common and the Public Garden, most large cities would have rested content, but the "Hub" has displayed its usual spirit in planning a series of great parks, the first of which is to be situated on the water side of the Back-Bay district. The first step in this movement was taken in 1874, when a commission, consisting of the Mayor, two aldermen and three citizens at large, was appointed to study and devise concerning the matter of new parks. This Park Commission was authorized by the City Council, in 1877, to purchase not less than one hundred acres of land on the flats of the Back-Bay, to be converted into a magnificent water-side park, the land not to cost over ten cents a foot. In this way, three great ends were achieved: the work of redeeming the land in this section was forwarded, and a great step was taken in beautifying this lovely section, and an admirable basis was obtained by its relation to Commonwealth avenue and the Public Garden for the proposed series of parks, which is to include all parts of the growing city, all being connected by park-roads on the plan of Commonwealth avenue, thus making this city even more worthy of the preëminence already achieved among the most beautiful cities of America. In 1877, a loan of $450,000 was authorized by the city government to forward this movement, and in February, 1878, yet more land was purchased, so that this park when completed will have but few equals in size in this country. In addition, $16,000 more

THE PUBLIC GARDEN.

was appropriated for the purchase of land, and $25,000 for filling, grading, surveying and laying out the park. The sides of the park will rest partially in Beacon street, Brookline avenue, Longwood avenue, and Parker street, having an entrance from each. This magnificent park, which will be nearly three times as large as the Common, and five times as large as the Public Garden, though it will lack the historic traditions of the two latter, will yet in time have a glory all its own not unworthy of comparison, and can but add in an almost unimaginable measure to the continually increasing beauty of the Back-Bay.

Our sketches hitherto have been chiefly of the external appearance of the Back-Bay, as represented by many of its greatest features. Into its inner life it is not given to those outside, nor for that matter to many of those within it, to penetrate very far, yet a few references can help, perhaps, to picture the life that animates this center of the social sphere of the Hub. Most of the light on this side of Boston, the Back-Bay, will be found in the numerous novels that have been written about the city and its inhabitants, such as James' "Bostonians," Howell's "Silas Lapham" and "The Minister's Charge." The social exodus into the Back-Bay and its revolutionary effects, to a great extent are fresh in the memories of all. It is not merely a matter of the "*Nouveau riches*," but many of the old families have left their ancestral halls, until the greater part of the *bon-ton* have become residents of the old time flats, but now beautiful "*new land*"; and so a manner of life has been developed far different from any that the old Puritan fathers and founders of the city could have imagined. Indeed, it is not likely that it has ever had an exact parallel in the world's history. Luxury there is in abundance, yet tempered by an intellectual tone which makes it, on the whole, of a higher, more cultivated sort than any other form of luxury known to this country, at least, and which removes the glare and false show entirely, which so often attends wealth of less than a half-dozen generations' growth. Exclusiveness, too, is not without a place in the social economy of the Back-Bay, and yet it is so affected and permeated by the old "Yankee" quality of sturdy independence of thought, that it seems more of an intellectual cast than of the purely gilded or old-family type. Perhaps there is no large city in the world, where intellectual and artistic power are more readily or widely appreciated and honored, apart from all other considerations, than in this center of American thought, and even in the exclusive Back-Bay. One cannot study what extra Bostonians of this and other countries attribute to it as faults for any length of time without finding them linked very closely with some very appreciable virtues. The old New England flavor of character and life yet lingers and touches with its strong colors the life of the Back-Bay and its inhabitants, and though Bostonians themselves are not blind to faults within their own borders, yet the merits of all its various sections are not rated much too high. The kindly spirit of the Back-Bay folk is thoroughly evidenced in every good work, with which no spot on earth, in all probability, is more blessed than Boston. The innumerable efforts for the nurture of unfortunate children, the help and advancement of the poor, the especial care which is given to the education of the young people, the large avenues through which the church work penetrates all parts of the city, all meet with cordial sympathy, and most earnest forwarding in this region. Many societies such as those of which the "Society to Encourage Studies at Home," under the management of Miss Anna E. Ticknor, and other Boston ladies, is a marked example illustrating the spirit which yet prompts and dictates the duty-loving activities of Boston's rich society. On the more social side, the brilliance yet quiet refinement of the society life in the Back-Bay is the characteristic which is perhaps most striking. A feeling of rivalry is sometimes declared in other great cities of the continent, but it finds little echo here. If there is one thing above another for which all Bostonians are remarkable, it is their supreme *self-containedness*, if we may coin the word. They do not feel the need, as a general rule, (though perhaps it would be too much to say that there are not exceptions,) of looking to any other center, be it American, or English, or French, for the main principles and customs of their social life. In this it would seem that the influence of the life which centers about the Back-Bay, cannot but be of great good at this period of our country's history. The influence of the great leaders in literature, art and science, who have for generations been nurtured in Boston, and who today form so large a number of the leading men and women in the social life of the Back-Bay, is felt throughout it all. As we said before, however, it is but glimpses, scattered here and there, that can be obtained by temporary acquaintance with this part of the Hub, and this applies even more forcibly to the social life than to its outward form and artistic expression, in the representative local sketches of places, institutions and buildings which we have given. The commercial life of the Back-Bay is necessarily and chiefly of a retail and miscellaneous character. Within the borders of the Back-Bay are situated some of the highest and most reliable retail firms in the city, and almost every branch of commerce has representatives, although from its nature there is little or no manufacturing of great extent. All these industries are fittingly represented in the immense displays which are given by the M. C. M. A. at their fairs. The fact should not be forgotten that this district is the home of the largest number of most successful business men of the city, and it is of course evident that nowhere else will be found such magnificent results of the old New England thrift, industry and genius for commercial enterprise, which other people, in vain emulation, have been wont to dub as the "Yankee spirit." This region is its paradise on its material side, and the old fact though new doctrine of the "survival of the fittest," finds a brilliant exemplification here in the financial prosperity of the descendants of these stern-hearted people, whose integrity was as unflinching as their faith. From whatever side we approach it, the Back-Bay, its appearance, its inhabitants, and its life, form a most interesting study, worthy of a modern epic, which perhaps will yet be written by some of its literary sons. The side glances which we have given here show but a very small part of its beauty and power, for a complete picture of which volumes would need be compiled; but if we shall have succeeded in portraying points of interest to those who have never seen them, and given familiar touches to things recognizable by those who have long loved what appertains to Boston, as only Bostonians can, we shall not have traversed this lovely region in vain. Nor can we refrain from the hope that those to whom all these things we have mentioned are yet pictures of the mind, may have been excited to a livelier appreciation of them, and to an effective resolution to see and judge of for themselves, what has never yet been, and, not unlikely, never will be adequately described by the pen, the superb and delightful Back-Bay of Boston.

LEADING BUSINESS MEN

OF THE

BACK-BAY.

"The Belmont" Natural Spring Water, George H. Cotton, Prop., Office and Depot 71 Chestnut Street. Pure water is at least as essential to health as pure air or pure food, and the more sedentary the occupation of a person is the more careful should he be to use *Pure Water*, as where there is not a great deal of outdoor exercise taken, the use of impure water is especially harmful. The general prevalence of Kidney disease, Constipation, Dyspepsia, etc., is largely due to the harmful effects of the impure water drank, and it is now conceded by the most advanced physicians that the cure or alleviation of any of these dangerous disorders is best effected by dieting and exercise rather than by the medicines, and that a really pure water is a powerful and well nigh indispensable aid to recovery. Pure water is unfortunately not so common an article as many people believe it to be, but still it may be had if sought for in the right place, and no better place can be found than the headquarters of "The Belmont Spring Water," at No. 71 Chestnut St., Boston. "The Belmont" Spring is located on high land in the town of Belmont, Mass., and being isolated and elevated above all sources of contamination, supplies a *drinking water* that is cordially endorsed by physicians, and is highly recommended for people troubled with the diseases before mentioned, as well as for everybody that believes "an ounce of prevention is worth a pound of cure" and wants to be secure against all such disorders. This water has been supplied to the public since 1876, and is firmly established in popular favor. The proprietor of the spring, Mr. George H. Cotton, has, in response to the solicitation of many customers, made arrangements for aerating the water, and as these arrangements have proved most efficient and satisfactory, he now places on the market not only "The Belmont" Natural Spring Water but also the same water aerated, together with "The Belmont Spring Standard Soda Water. These carbonated waters are conceded by good judges to be superior to any others, either Foreign or Domestic, and have met with a very large sale. "The Belmont" Natural Spring Water is brought fresh daily in glass vessels from the spring to the Boston Depot, 71 Chestnut Street, and is delivered in quantities to suit the purchaser at moderate rates. Every provision is made for the accommodation of patrons and a trial order is sure to be followed by others.

J. G. Godding & Co., Apothecaries Dartmouth Street, cor. Newbury. There are certain peculiarities about the business of the apothecary which give it a unique position among other trade-enterprises, for it is indisputable that an educated and competent apothecary is at least as much of a professional man as he is a merchant, and in fact the ordinary outcome of the hazy views held by the general public on the matter, is that he is judged by the standards applicable to both pursuits, and condemned if he be found wanting in either of them. To successfully conduct a first-class city pharmacy is therefore, as will readily be seen, no light task and on this account all the more credit is due to those who have solved the problems involved in so doing and gained an extended reputation for reliability and strict integrity. Such a record has been made by the concern known as J. G. Godding & Co., located at the corner of Dartmouth and Newbury Streets and there are few if any similar establishments which have won so high and assured a position during the comparatively few years which have elapsed since operations were begun. Messrs. J. G. Godding & Co., opened their present store in 1884 and now do a business as remarkable for its character as for its magnitude, as a specialty is made of prescription trade and a large proportion of the many orders received are included within this department. One floor and a basement, are occupied and it is one of the most elegantly appointed pharmacies in Boston and enjoys a large patronage among the leading families in the Back Bay, and a fine and complete assortment of Drugs and Medicines is carried. Five assistants are employed and orders filled at all hours without delay and at reasonable rates.

E. J. H. Trask, Upholstery and Draperies, Window Shades and Wire Screens a Specialty. Venetian Blinds, Brass and Nickel Rods. 174 Columbus Avenue. It is in the furnishing and draping of a house, in the tasteful selection and arrangement of the many articles going to fill out the bare shell of the building, that a pleasing and home-like effect is obtainable and it is just here that many people make a mistake in relying on their individual judgment when they might be materially aided and the result of their labors greatly improved, by the counsel and direction of some one who has made a special study of house decoration. Such a one is Mr. E. J. H. Trask, doing business at No. 174 Columbus Avenue, and no one can converse with this gentleman on the subject mentioned without being impressed by his thorough knowledge of it and his evident desire to assist his customers to the extent of his ability in cases where his guidance is requested. Mr. Trask was born in Boston and is a member of the Free Masons. He opened his present store in 1887 and has already been favored with many orders, his business showing a marked and steady increase week by week. One floor and a basement are occupied of the dimensions of 25x55 feet and employment is afforded to five efficient assistants. Upholstering of every description will be done at short notice and in a thoroughly satisfactory and durable manner, for every facility is at hand for the filling of such orders and repairing is given particular attention. Window-Shades and Wire-Screens are also made a specialty and Venetian Blinds, Brass and Nickel Rods are largely handled. Mr. Trask's prices are very low and all articles leaving his establishment are warranted to prove as represented. Mr. Trask's customers are among the leading families of the Back Bay and also in the suburban districts. Among the elegant residences decorated by him we take pleasure in referring to the following: Mr. Oakes Ames of Newbury Street, Mr. J. B. Kendall of Commonwealth Avenue, Mr. C. H. Andrews of the Boston Herald Men. Wentworth of Commonwealth Avenue. "The Abbotsford" at 300 Walnut Avenue, Highlands, owned by J. N. Smith. The Gen'l Burnside estate of Providence R. L., Walter Potter of Nantasket, C. H. Crump and Major Shreve of Shreve, Crump and Low.

Office of Brewster, Cobb & Estabrooke, 35 Congress Street, Boston.

Mr. E. J. H. Trask—Dear Sir:

It gives me pleasure to say that all the work you have done for me is very satisfactory, and has been done promptly and in a first-class manner. Yours truly. C. H. Watson.

———

T. H. Duggan & Co., No. 141 Dartmouth Street, Plumber and Sanitary Engineer, Dealer in Fine Plumbing Materials and the latest Sanitary Specialties. First-class work only. Reasonable Rates. Orders from All Parts and Jobbing promptly attended to. Telephone No. 4165. Everybody is familiar with one type of Plumber—the man who knows it all and who refuses to be taught anything new. It makes no difference how valuable an improvement may be submitted to him—he don't want anything to do with it. Show him a patent trap which avoids much of the danger from Sewer Gas, and he will smile contemptuously and say that "they didn't use such things when he learned his trade and he guesses he can get along without them now." Now this picture is not overdrawn. There are plenty of such fossils right here in Boston, and as we all want to have our Plumbing and Repairing done by a man who is alive to the needs of the hour and who is fully up with the latest scientific progress in his business, we should use some care in the placing of our orders. No mistake will be made if Mr. T. H. Duggan, of No. 141 Dartmouth Street, be patronized for this gentleman has not only had long experience in Sanitary Plumbing but is known to do first-class work only. His trade is very largely in the Back Bay section, and specimens of his work will be found in many of the finest residences. He makes a specialty of the use and sale of fine plumbing materials and the latest and most approved sanitary specialties. He was in business on Tremont Street, some ten years but removed to his present quarters in 1885. This store is a spacious one being 20x60 feet in dimensions and contains a very large and varied stock, employment being given to from 12 to 20 competent assistants. Mr. Duggan's rates are very reasonable and orders and jobbing work of every description will be promptly and thoroughly attended to. Telephone 4165. Mr. Duggan's residence is at 130 Camden St., where in cases of emergency he can be found after working hours.

———

P. Edwards & Son, Fine Groceries, Under Hotel Berkeley. It would probably be difficult to find another establishment in the city enjoying precisely the same class of trade as that carried on by Messrs. Edwards & Son, under Hotel Berkeley, for this house have, from the inception of their business in 1832, made it an invariable rule to handle only such supplies as they could conscientiously recommend, and, as a consequence, have secured the patronage of the most exclusive class of trade. There is one floor occupied, of the dimensions of 60 x 70 feet, and the premises contain as fine an assortment of the very choicest family stores as is to be found in New England. It has been carefully and personally selected, for the most part, by either the senior or junior member of the firm, and is offered at the very lowest rates at which it can be handled at retail. The productions of some of the most famous manufacturers in the world are included within it, and in the line of Canned Goods alone, inducements are offered which are well worthy of careful attention. The Table Condiments, Sauces, Relishes, etc., in stock are such as have received the repeated and enthusiastic endorsement of the most noted bon vivants and epicures, and nothing is sold that cannot be fully and unreservedly warranted. Under these circumstances it is not surprising that the utmost confidence has been established between this concern and its patrons, and that the sales show a marked annual increase. Ten competent assistants are employed and the most prompt and courteous attention shown to all callers.

O'Brien Brothers, Fish and Oysters, Park Square and 63 Charles Street, also Beverly Farms and Manchester by the Sea. The man who said that "he preferred beef to any kind of food except when he was eating fish" is not the only one who holds similar opinions, for that fish is one of the most popular foods the world over, is known and appreciated by everybody. Well, there is certainly no reason why it should not be, for it is not only healthful, finely flavored and easy to cook, but is one of the cheapest food products in the market. Of course its goodness depends in a great measure upon its freshness and cleanliness, and the only practical way for the consumer to satisfy himself that he is supplied with fish that is all that could be desired in these respects is to purchase it of a concern both reputable and enterprising. Such a firm is that of O'Brien Bros., doing business in Park Square, and everything coming from their store may be unquestionably accepted in the perfect confidence that it will prove just as represented in every respect. No doubt it is to the early public appreciation of this fact that the house alluded to owes much of its rapid and exceptional success, for operations were only begun in 1877 at Charles Street, and the Park Square store opened September 1887, and a fine and growing trade has already been established. The members of the firm are Bostonians by birth and give close personal attention to their business. The stores occupied measure 30 x 50 feet, eight assistants are employed, and a very large and desirable assortment of Fresh and Salted Fish, Oysters, Clams, Lobsters, etc., offered at prices as low as the goods are superior.

George S. Mansfield, Upholsterer and Cabinet Maker, 26 Charles Street. There are few if any housekeepers that would not be glad to learn of an upholstery establishment where the very best of work is done, and this information would be all the more acceptable were it accompanied by the statement that the prices charged were as low as the work done was first-class. Therefore we are sure that many of our readers will thank us for calling their attention to the enterprise carried on by Mr. George S. Mansfield at No. 26 Charles Street, for both the good points we have alluded to are secured by placing orders here. Mr. Mansfield began operations in 1880 and has since executed many especially difficult commissions. He has every convenience at hand for the accomplishment of satisfactory results and employs three assistants who are capable of doing first-class work. The premises occupied, measure 22x40 feet and are centrally located and very easy of access. A postal card dropped to Mr. Mansfield, will result in work being called for and the same will be returned promptly when completed without extra charge. Parlor, Dining Room and Library Furniture stuffed to order. Old furniture restuffed and repaired. Drapery made to order. Old ones changed to modern styles. Mattresses and Spring Beds made to order or repaired. French Mattresses a specialty. Shades furnished to order. Particular attention given to cushions for Yachts, Window Seats or Furniture and warranted to fit. Curtains taken down and carefully packed away. Laces and Shades washed. Carpets taken up, beaten, refitted and laid in the best manner at reasonable prices. General repairing of furniture, etc., and jobbing work of all descriptions.

Kenny & Clark, Established 1829., 22 Charles Street, Chas. Kenny, E. L. Clark. Everybody recognizes that sometimes money is "spent" and sometimes it is "invested." If a man buys Real Estate at a fair price, he does not "spend" his money—he "invests" it—or in other words—he places it where he expects a return from it, and cannot be called extravagant, even if he makes use of all his available funds. Now many people never think of putting out money for horse-hire; "extravagant," "can't afford it" they say. Is that money really spent? Suppose an overworked business man, clerk, book-keeper—anything you please—is the money, he puts out for the hire of a horse that will take him into the open air, wake him up, straighten him out, put his heart to beating with some vim and energy, and in short "make a new man of him"—is such money "spent" or "invested?" Answer that question in the only way it can be answered and then go around to Messrs. Kenny & Clark's Stable on Charles Street, No. 22 and put a few dollars where they will do the most good. These gentlemen have the ability and the desire to give their customers a full return for every cent they may leave with them, as they furnish the most stylish, speedy and reliable turnouts in the city. It is the largest of its kind in this country. Two more stables, conducted by these gentlemen are to be found in this city, one at No. 4 Byron Street, and another at 104 Mt. Vernon Street. Over one hundred men are employed, and at least two hundred horses are at these airy and well-ventilated Stables, Vehicles of all kinds to the number of about one hundred and fifty are constantly on hand, not including the large assortment of sleighs, which this enterprising firm furnishes during the winter months. Carriages are always to be found at the "Brunswick" "Vendome" "Victoria" and Young's Hotels, as offices for this special purpose are kept at each of those hotels, with clerks attached to them furnished from the head office at 22 Charles Street. During the summer months stables are also to be found at "Nahant." The premises on Charles Street are 125x 100 feet in dimensions, and comprise three floors. This establishment has been in existence since 1829, and Messrs. Kenny & Clark, the present well known and genial proprietors, understand their business thoroughly in every detail, and being liberal, courteous and well known in society they control the best trade.

The Allen Gymnasium for women and children. Bowling Alley and Tennis Court, corner Botolph and Garrison Streets. The day when physical debility was accepted as an almost inevitable accompaniment of mental strength, and vigorous health was deemed an essentially masculine attribute wholly incompatible with the ideal of delicate womanhood, has passed by, never to return let us hope, for a more mischievous doctrine it is almost impossible to imagine, and the numerous evils it carries in its train are now too widely appreciated to require mention here. Strong oaks do not spring from seeds nor stalwart men from puny, undeveloped women, and for the future of the race if for no other reason, let us hope the now familiar maxim—"A sound mind in a sound body," shall be observed in the case of one sex equally with that of the other. Physical exercise is now doing for the American people what all the drugs known to science could never accomplish, and should its influence continue to spread, the day will soon dawn when the significant title "A Nation of Dyspeptics" can no longer in justice be applied to us. To Miss M. E. Allen, more than to any other one person, should credit be given for the present facilities available in this city for the physical culture of women and children, for since she first became identified with this movement, ten years ago, at No. 503 Washington Street, she has worked with an enthusiasm and single-mindedness that were bound to carry everything before them. The ninth year of the enterprise under her charge opened in the new building specially erected for it, corner of St. Botolph and Garrison Streets, November, 1886. This structure is, in one sense, a substantial token of the appreciation felt for the practical value of Miss Allen's labor, and by its erection Boston is given the finest gymnasium for women and children in the country. Space does not permit a description of it in detail, but we may say it contains a hall 34 feet in height and 96 x 63 feet in dimensions otherwise and also 66 dressing rooms, bath rooms, costume closets, etc. The most approved apparatus is in use and the heating and ventilation may be said to be as nearly perfect as the present condition of sanitary engineering will permit. The work is graduated to the strength of the weakest pupil and is under the personal direction of Miss Allen or her assistants, and is conducted slowly, carefully, progressively. As for the character and aim of the work—these are best presented in the words of Miss Allen herself, as follows: The aim of the work is to promote symmetrical bodily development; to straighten curved spines; to correct uneven hips and shoulders; to draw down projecting shoulder blades; to deepen and broaden the chest, and give vigor to the system by judicious deep breathing; to develop ease of step and grace of movement in walking and running; to round and make supple the whole figure, not to accomplish marvelous feats and dangerous tricks; to force every muscle to perform its legitimate function, with the least possible expenditure of nerve force, thus producing free and unimpeded circulation of the blood throughout the system, —which means *Health*. Now no one will deny that a course of treatment that will bring about such results cannot be too highly praised, and such is evidently the opinion of many of our leading physicians for they cordially testify to the admirable work which the Allen Gymnasium is doing and bespeak for it the continued hearty patronage of the public. Miss Allen may be consulted every day except Saturday, between the hours of 2 and 3 P.M. and will be happy to send explanatory circulars to such as feel interested. She is prepared to give private instruction when desired and her class rates are equitable and moderate. Patients sent by physicians will receive special care, and all using the apparatus will do so under the direction of Miss Allen or her assistants, all injurious exercises being thus avoided. In the Allen Gymnasium Building, are for rent six finely equipped Bowling Alleys, each 72 feet in length, and unsurpassed in the city. The rooms at the head of the alleys are so arranged that they can be used separately, one for each two alleys, or they can all be thrown into one. The entrance is from Garrison Street, and everything connected with the alleys is pleasant and inviting. There is also to let, evenings and Saturday afternoons, a Double Tennis Court, 96 x 52 feet, finely lighted, with a height of 30 feet. Miss Allen also conducts a Normal Class. A broad field having been opened for teachers of gymnastics, for women and children, within the last few years unusual interest has been aroused in physical training and the demand for teachers who understand bodybuilding is growing each year. The requirements for culture and refinement are as great in this department of the education of the future as in any other, and the supply runs far below the demand. Positions are waiting for educated and accomplished gymnasts, but they are not to be found.

Tighe & Burke, Grocers, No. 3 Charles Street. Charles Street is remarkable in more respects than one among our Boston thoroughfares, but it is especially so from the large proportion of old established business enterprises to be found in it. A canvass of the more prominent establishments from one end of the street to the other, brings out the interesting and significant fact that a score of years does not more than cover the average term which the several premises have been occupied in the carrying on of a special line of business, and in some instances it is found that forty years and more have passed since the inception of operations. Take the establishment conducted under the firm name of Tighe & Burke, at No. 3 Charles Street, and we find that a grocery store has been located here for just about forty years, and that the present firm began operations in 1869. One floor and a basement are occupied of the dimensions of 20 x 90 feet, and an immense trade is carried on, employment being afforded to ten efficient assistants. A large and extremely varied stock of Groceries and Family Stores is carried, and the quality of the goods offered is equal to any in the market. Indeed there are few groceries where such choice grades of Tea and Coffee are obtainable, and we question if so desirable an assortment of Table Condiments and fine Canned Goods could easily be found elsewhere. All the standard and popular brands of Flour are also sold at low prices, and customers are guaranteed not only reliable goods but also prompt, courteous and willing attention.

P. H. Murphy & Co., Plumbers and Gas Fitters, Hotel Glendon, cor. Columbus Ave. & Cazenove Street, Boston. "An ounce of prevention is worth a pound of cure," so runs the old saying and its wisdom is to be seen every day in affairs of all kinds. But in nothing is it more worthy of being heeded than in the care of the complicated system of piping to be found in our modern houses and on which we depend for our supply of water, our supply of gas and the expeditious carrying away of the waste products from our sinks, etc. The damages that may be caused by the bursting of a water-pipe by reason of frost or over-pressure, are of course in many cases unavoidable as there is no previous warning given that such an accident is likely to happen, but in the case of a defect in the drainage or a leak in the gas-pipe, it is easy to see that something is wrong and measures should be taken at once to remedy the trouble. The best way to do is to notify a Plumber or Gas Fitter who is known to be skilful and thorough in his work, and a house that combines both these branches of industry and has won a high reputation for attaining the best results is that carried on by Messrs. P. H. Murphy & Co., at Hotel Glendon, corner of Columbus Avenue and Cazenove Street. Business was begun in 1880 and many commissions have since been executed throughout the Back Bay and vicinity in a thoroughly first-class and satisfactory manner. Mr. Murphy was born in New York and is known as one of the ablest Plumbers in this city. He takes pride in doing only the best of work and those favoring him with their patronage may feel assured that there will be no occasion to regret it. Jobbing orders are given particular and prompt attention, and a sufficient force of skilled assistants and every facility, are at hand to undertake the doing of anything in this line with the certainty of success.

J. M. Newell, Fancy and Small Wares, 173 Columbus Avenue. It is a great convenience to the public to have a number of Fancy Goods stores scattered about throughout the city, as it permits purchases being made without being obliged to go "in town" for every trifling article and, aside from the saving in time thus made, when such establishments are conducted in the manner noticeable in that carried on by J. M. Newell at No. 173 Columbus Avenue, there are many other advantages to be gained by patronizing them. The enterprise alluded to was started in 1835 and has already built up a most desirable trade. The premises in use comprise one floor and a basement, measuring 20x45 feet and the stock on hand is varied and complete, being displayed to most excellent advantage. The proprietor is a native of this city and has a large circle of friends in the community. Close personal attention is given to the business and the interests of customers is considered in every respect, knowing that such a course cannot fail to be the most successful in the long run. Fancy and Small wares, Toys etc. of every desciption are handled extensively, prices being quoted at the lowest market rates, pains being taken to assure that every article sold shall prove just as represented. Agency for the Boston Hotel and Steamboat Laundry and Dye House. Special attention is given to Dress and Cloak Making, also stamping. Employment is afforded to two well-informed and polite assistants and customers are invariably accorded prompt service and courteous treatment. Painting and needlework, Lessons given in Oils, Water-Colors, China and Lustre Painting. Punto Tirato and Art Needlework are taught by Miss Amy Dawes.

J. KEEFE,
Express, Furniture and Piano Moving.
Stand at cor. Columbus Avenue and Clarendon Street.

Miss H. F. Parker, Troy Laundry, Small Wares, Fancy Goods and Stationery, 143 Dartmouth St., near the Bridge. But little inquiry is necessary to establish the fact of the popularity of certain enterprises even in a great city like Boston, where it would seem that individuality would be surely lost in the vast number of interests to be considered, but the store carried on by Miss H. F. Parker at No. 143 Dartmouth Street, near the bridge, is well known and highly regarded in the vicinity, and the popularity it enjoys shows that true enterprise and an honest desire to serve the public in the best possible manner are sure to meet with due appreciation. Miss Parker is a native of Maine, and began operations in her present line of business in 1885. She carries an assortment of Small Wares, Fancy Goods and Stationery in stock that is at once varied and complete and is prepared to furnish anything in this class of goods at the lowest market rates. Perfect dependence may be placed on the articles obtained at this establishment as Miss Parker strives to handle only reliable goods of standard quality, and her ability and experience enable her to intelligently discriminate in the selection of her stock. We must not omit mention of the fact that a Troy Laundry Agency is here conducted, for a large business is done in this line and laundry work done that is as good as the best while the methods employed are entirely non-injurious.

Haines & Murphy, Grocers, 61 Charles, cor. Mt. Vernon Sts. These gentlemen are in a position to extend the best possible service to the public. They recently succeeded to the business established by B. F. Shattuck, who conducted a first-class Family Grocery store at No. 61 Charles Street, corner of Mt. Vernon, and that their efforts are appreciated is shown by the general satisfaction that is expressed at their business methods. They have already built up a most promising business that is already sufficiently extensive to require the employment of three experienced and efficient assistants. The premises utilized, measure 20 x 50 feet, and include one floor and a basement. There are few retail grocers in the city that can show so extensive and skillfully selected a stock as is carried by Messrs. Haines & Murphy, and the prices they quote on the same are remarkably low for goods of standard quality and of perfect freshness. We have not the space to particularize, but may simply state that both as regards Fancy and Staple articles, the assortment is exceptionally full and desirable, and the prompt response given to orders is also worthy of especial mention.

Newcomb & Frost, Grocers and Tea Dealers, and Importers of Foreign Wines, Cigars and Condiments, No. 297 Boylston Street, also 307 Columbus Avenue, Telephone 4020. Careful, intelligent and continuous efforts toward the achievement of any given object, is pretty sure to win success finally, provided the goal striven for is not absolutely inaccessible, and therefore it is but natural, and no more than was to be expected, that Messrs. Newcomb & Frost have attained the purpose they have had in view since inaugurating their present enterprise, and established an undisputed reputation for handling a uniformly high and satisfactory grade of goods. Operations were begun by them at 307 Columbus Avenue in 1878, and at Boylston Street in 1885, and the large patronage they now enjoy has been honestly won by strict attention to the wants of the special class of trade to which they cater, and by furnishing the best of materials at the lowest attainable rates. This concern are Grocers and Tea Dealers and Importers of Wine, Cigars and Condiments, and the gentlemen constituting it are Messrs. C. H. Newcomb and W. E. Frost, both of whom are natives of this State. One floor and a basement are occupied at each store measuring about 90 x 30 feet each, and there is employment afforded to eight efficient assistants at each place. The Groceries handled by this house will be found uniform and reliable in character, while the Teas sold are absolutely the finest flavored in the city. No expense is spared either in their purchase or in the measures taken for their preservation to secure and retain the full virtue of the natural leaf, and in this way not only the palatableness but the healthfulness of the product are assured. The Wines, Cigars, etc., in stock are also carefully selected and are well worthy of the trial and appreciation of connoisseurs. Boylston Street store is connected by telephone 4020.

F. P. Snyder, Upholsterer and Cabinetmaker, 21 Charles Street, over the Arlington Market. Ingenuity and good taste are certainly of prime importance in the carrying on of the Upholsterer's business, and it is chiefly owing to the lack of one or both of these that so many fail to achieve success in this line of industry.

But there is some compensation, for when the attributes are present the appreciation of the public is generally prompt and decided. Such has been the case with the enterprise carried on by Mr. F. P. Snyder, at No. 21 Charles Street, over the Arlington Market, for although this gentleman did not begin operations until 1879, he has already received a liberal share of patronage, and his business is now steadily and rapidly growing. Upholstering and Cabinet making are carried on in the most skillful and satisfactory manner. A large and complete line of all grades of furniture are constantly kept on hand or furnished direct from the manufacturer; Cabinet work of all kinds finely executed, and "fancy chairs" in great variety as well as odd ones are always on hand or furnished to order. To give a complete list of every article to be had here would almost fill a whole volume, but it is absolutely necessary to mention the well stocked department of Shades, Screens Drapery Work, Awning and Carpet Work, which comprise a large portion of this complete assortment of all articles coming under the heading Upholsterer's Department. All kinds of work pertaining to the outfitting of Yachts, is paid special attention to, as Mr. Snyder has had many years of practical experience in that line, having fitted up the yachts Mayflower, Volunteer, Sachem, Marguerite, etc. Employment is given to from ten to twenty-six assistants, all of whom are among the most reliable and the most competent in their line of business. New work will be made to order if desired, but great attention is also paid to restoring and repairing, and in this line as well as in all of those belonging to his business, he has made a record that is equalled by that of no other upholsterer, either as regards the quality of the work done, or the satisfactory character of the price on the same. Only strictly first-class material is used, and Mr. Snyder never sacrifices strength to beauty when the one can be attained without injury to the other, so that durability is one of the most distinguishing features of his work.

William Trainer & Co., Plumbers, and Dealers in Plumbing Materials, No. 8 Park Square. Very few men would think of employing an inferior physician because he charged fifty cents less a visit than a man of good repute and accomplished skill, for they would justly argue that health is beyond price, and consequently that no reasonable expenditure to retain or recover it could be called extravagant. Yet many people will fit their houses up with cheap and ineffective plumbing appliances, when it must be known to everybody who can read, or even hear, that there is no more constant and deadly menace to health than that afforded by defective methods of Plumbing and Drainage. The most improved appliances do not cost much more to begin with than those which experience has condemned, and when the question of repairs and comparative durability is considered, we doubt if any pecuniary saving is made by the use of the latter. Doctor's bills count up rapidly, and the loss of even a week's time by reason of sickness, may occasion more of a deficiency than would be made up by the entire cost of the most improved system. "Get the best" is a good motto, and the way to carry it into practical effect is to place your orders with Messrs. William Trainer & Co., at No. 3 Park Square. This concern is one of the best known in the city in the contracting and jobbing line, and is prepared to supply Plumbing Materials of the most approved description at bottom prices and short notice. The firm is made up of Messrs. William Trainer and John C. McCoole, both of whom are active and energetic business men, the former being a member of the Odd Fellows. Employment is given to sixteen competent assistants, and any one wanting a job of plumbing done with the maximum of neatness and despatch, has only to place his order with this highly popular house. Their rates are very low for first-class work, and the use of the best material assures the permanency of the operations conducted.

C. B. Worster & Co., Dealers in Foreign and Domestic Groceries, Teas, Wines, Preserves, Fruits, Etc., 216 Clarendon, cor. Boylston Street. The carrying on of such an establishment as that conducted by Messrs. C. B. Worster & Co., at No. 216 Clarendon Street, corner of Boylston, must be a work of no small magnitude for it is but rarely a store is found in which such elaborate provision has been made for the accommodation of the one thousand and one articles handled in a first-class modern grocery or in which so carefully selected and varied a stock is carried. This enterprise had its inception in 1887, and perhaps the best commentary that could be made on the character of the management it has received is that afforded by the patronage already bestowed upon it, which is not only very large but as yet shows no signs of diminution in its rate of increase. Both members of this firm were born in this city, and recognize the fact that their success thus far has been largely due to the uniformly high grade nature of the commodities they handle, and therefore may be depended on to fully maintain the high standard they have established for this firm in this respect. One floor and a basement of the dimensions of 40x80 feet are occupied, and the stock of Foreign and Domestic Groceries carried, shows careful and intelligent selection and a determination to cater to the most fastidious class of trade. Teas and Coffees of full strength and delicious flavor, Wines of the choicest vintage, preserves put up by the most reputable houses, all these articles are supplied at the lowest market rates and the employment of five efficient assistants allows prompt service to be guaranteed.

C. M. & J. W. Cox, No. 214 Clarendon Street, corner Boylston. Artists' Materials, Fine Stationery, Students' Supplies. Among the numerous minor but significant indications of a person's culture and breeding, that afforded by the stationery used is one of the most important and conclusive. We have reference of course to the stationery employed in social correspondence, for that devoted to business purposes is entirely out of the question. The difference between the cost of fashionable, appropriate and desirable stationery and that of which the opposite may be said, is not sufficiently great to warrant any educated person in using the latter from motives of economy, and indeed in the majority of cases where such is used, we believe it is owing more to carelessness than any other one thing. A call at the establishment of Messrs. C. M. & J. W. Cox, No. 214 Clarendon Street, will disclose the fact that the latest novelties in fashionable stationery are obtainable at very low prices, and this house always has a complete stock on hand to choose from; also, Artists' Materials, Students' Supplies, etc. This firm makes a specialty also of Artistic Picture Framing and Society Engraving and have also a full line of Choice Confectionery. This enterprise was inaugurated in 1885 and greatly increased in patronage and appreciation as the liberal methods of its originators became more generally understood. The store is 20 x 65 feet in size and every effort is made to keep the stock on hand so well supplied in every department that all delay will be avoided.

Charles Pierce, Dealer in Gas Fixtures and Fittings, Locksmithing and Bell Hanging, Electric Bells, General Jobbing; also in store an assortment of Kitchen Furnishing Goods and Hardware, 52 Charles Street. The discussions and the arguments which have occupied the newspapers of late years regarding the comparative dangers and advantages of "Water Gas," have doubtless been of no small use in educating the public as to the character and general nature of illuminating gas, and have accomplished much good, even if they have done nothing but to bring home to everybody the importance of keeping the gas service of our houses in first-class condition. Like many other things that are used in every-day life, gas makes a good servant but a bad master, and it is much easier, and inexpensive to keep this agent under control than to repair the damage done when this control is temporarily shaken off. It is therefore not only the part of wisdom but also of economy to give prompt attention to any trouble in the gas fixtures or supply pipes, and the importance of employing a competent and reliable gas-fitter can hardly be overestimated. Mr. Charles Pierce, of No. 52 Charles Street, has carried on his present enterprise since 1862, and makes gas-fitting a specialty. He is thoroughly competent in every department of the trade, and as he employs only skilled and careful assistants, orders entrusted to him are ensured proper carrying out. The premises occupied measure 18 x 80 feet. Mr. Pierce also does considerable in the line of locksmithing and fits keys and does general repairing at short notice and low rates. He has built up a large business during the past twenty-six years, and his reputation for turning out desirable and durable work is unsurpassed.

James Delay, Florist, 81 Boylston Street, next to L. P. Hollander & Co. Choice Roses. Funeral Designs, and Wedding Decorations. Although philosophers tell us that natural laws are unchangeable by man and that the operation of these laws is never interrupted but goes on by day and by night, in frost or in heat, still it almost seems as if in some fields of effort the ingenuity of man had actually brought about at least a suspension of some of these, for how also could we have delicate flowers in the utmost profusion during the bleak month of January, or wear roses while ice and snow still covered the ground? Of course this has been brought about, not by defying nature's mandates but by carefully studying them and turning them to individual account; but for all that the results attained are none the less wonderful, and the progress made in floriculture of late years shows the eminent ability of the men engaged in that pursuit. Among our Boston florists none bear a more deservedly high reputation than Mr. James Delay, doing business at No. 81 Boylston Street, next to L. P. Hollander & Co., and this reputation has been won, not alone by the furnishing of uniformly reliable flowers, etc., but also by the maintenance of a scale of prices as low as the lowest. Mr. Delay is a native of this State, and inaugurated his present enterprise in 1879. His salesrooms occupy one floor of the dimensions of 20 x 70 feet, and four greenhouses are utilized, measuring from 20x100 to 20x50 feet respectively.

C. E. Ridler, Stationery and Students' Supplies, Fancy Articles, Drawing Materials, etc., Circulating Library, corner Berkeley and Boylston Streets, under Hotel Berkeley. One of the most completely stocked stores of the kind in the section of the city wherein it is located is that conducted by Mr. C. E. Ridler, at the corner of Berkeley and Boylston Streets, under Hotel Berkeley, and this holds especially good as regards the department devoted to the sale of Students' Supplies, as Mr. Ridler pays particular attention to this important branch of his business, and strives to fully meet the demands of his customers both as regards the quality and the variety of the goods he offers them. He is a native of this city and began operations here in 1885, having already built up a large and rapidly growing trade. The premises in use measure 40 x 50 feet, and the goods in stock are as varied as they are numerous, comprising, besides the Student's Supplies previously alluded to, Fashionable and Commercial Stationery, Fancy Articles, Drawing Materials, etc. A well selected and quite extensive Circulating Library is also at hand for the accommodation of patrons, and is constantly receiving new accessions in the shape of the latest and most popular novels and sketches of travel or biography, while books are issued without any of that "red tape" and exasperating delay so common in the larger public libraries. Sufficient assistance is at hand to allow all customers to be assured prompt and courteous attention, and Mr. Ridler's prices will be found as low as his goods are attractive.

Norton Brothers, Florists, Hotel Berkeley, Berkeley and Boylston Streets, Greenhouses at Dorchester. It may be safely accepted as a practically invariable rule that the greater the culture of a community, the more demand there will be for the products of the florists, and hence it is not surprising that Boston offers a grand field for the practice of this profession. Residents of this city have the reputation of being critical but appreciative, and this characterization holds good in business as well as in social relations, so that our most successful retailers have been those who have recognized this fact and have endeavored to supply uniformly superior articles. A prominent case in point is that afforded by the well-known house of Norton Brothers, whose business was established over a quarter of a century ago, and whose products have long ranked with the very best attainable. This firm have an office and salesroom in Hotel Berkeley, and maintain extensive greenhouses at Dorchester, equipped with every modern facility, and capable of supplying the choicest flowers in any desired quantity. Owing to the long and varied experience Messrs. Norton Brothers have had in their chosen business, they are thoroughly conversant with the nicest points pertaining to it, and their taste as shown in the design and execution of the many emblems offered to choose from is correct and pleasing. Roses and cut flowers of every description are supplied at short notice in quantities to suit, and all promises made regarding the goods, etc., will be strictly adhered to, as this firm make it a rule never to disappoint their customers.

Samuel Appleton, Manufacturer of Fine Shoes, on Artistic & Anatomical Principles, Y. M. C. A. Building, 176 Boylston Street, Chiropodist and Manicure Department. Skillful Lady Operators. Agency for Dr. J. Parker Pray, of New York. His Preparations and Instruments Wholesale and Retail. The time when it was thought that man could improve upon his Maker as regards the shaping of the whole or portions of "the human form divine" has happily passed by with all people of culture at least and as a consequence there is now a chance that future generations' feet should be preserved as nature intended them to be, and not warped out of shape, by deformity. That a decided gain is attained in the general health as well as in beauty and symmetry by the wearing of properly shaped foot-coverings is a fact too evident to call for proof and no one who has not had personal experience in the matter, can even imagine the added capacity for long-continued exertion on the feet that the wearing of truly "perfect fitting" shoes ensures. Mr. Samuel Appleton, whose place of business is at No. 176 Boylston Street, Y. M. C. A. Building, and who became identified with his present enterprise in 1878 is probably as well known as any man in New England in the manufacture of Fine Shoes on Artistic and Anatomical principles and his productions are generally conceded by physicians and others qualified to judge, to be excelled by none in the market, Mr. Appleton is a native of this city and gives the most careful personal attention to his business. By the use of the best material obtainable and the employment of the most highly-skilled assistants, he seeks to fully maintain the enviable reputation his goods have won and strives to fill all orders without delay in a uniformly satisfactory manner. A Chiropodist and Manicure department is in operation, skilful lady operators being at hand and an agency is conducted for the sale at wholesale and retail of the celebrated preparations of Dr. J. Parker Pray of New York, a full assortment being constantly carried.

William H. Agry, Dealer in Choice Groceries and Provisions, 58 Clarendon Street, corner Chandler, Boston. It would be remarkable if, during the twenty-three years which he has been engaged in his present business, Mr. Wm. H. Agry had not gained an accurate and comprehensive idea of the wants of the public so far as his branch of trade was concerned, and that he has in fact done so, needs no further proof, than that afforded by the very extensive and select patronage with which his establishment is favored. Mr. Agry was born in Bath, Me., and is a member of the Odd Fellows. To say that he is one of the leading retail Grocers and Provision dealers in the city, is but to express a fact known to all who are familiar with the comparative standing of Boston's business houses, and it is equally well known that Mr. Agry has won his way to his present position by sheer force of energy and perseverance, and that although his ability is unquestioned still his prominence has been largely brought about by the "genius of hard work," for he has ever given strict attention to the details of his undertaking and has not hesitated to labor early and late to secure the interests of his customers. One floor and a basement are utilized of the dimensions of 25 x 60 feet, and employment is afforded to seven experienced and entirely competent assistants. The uniform excellence of the commodities supplied by Mr. Agry is too generally appreciated to call for detailed mention here, but we may say that no city house bears a more enviable reputation in this respect. Choice Groceries of every description and a complete assortment of Meats, Poultry, Game, Country Produce etc. are always to be found here; a specialty being made of choice creamery butter, and fresh laid eggs, and orders are filled without delay at the lowest rates consistent with the quality of the goods.

H. Summers & Co., 38 Charles Street Boston. Repairer of Silver Ware, etc. Cutlery Ground. Restorer of every description of China, Costly Fans, Parians, Glass, Rich Vases, Marbles, Dishes, Statuettes, Plaques, Turcons, Art Metal, Bronzes, Terra-Cotta Groups, etc., etc., Missing Parts made up to avoid detection. Umbrellas and Parasols Repaired and Re-covered, Lock-Smithing, Speaking Tubes, and Electrical Bell-Hanging are Specialties. The philosopher who declared that it is not what is used but what is wasted that makes men poor," was undoubtedly pretty nearly correct, for no observing person can fail to notice decided examples of waste every day. A piece is chipped off a costly china dish, an article of ornamental glass ware is broken, a delicately wrought fan is injured—any one or all of these accidents are constantly occurring, and the usual result is that the damaged article is either put aside in some closet where it is of no use to anybody, or else is thrown into the ash-heap to be carried off. Now this is simply wanton waste, for there is an establishment in this city where all such injuries as we have mentioned, as well as countless others are repaired promptly, and so skillfully that in most cases the article treated is actually "as good as new." Even missing parts will be made up in so perfect a manner as to defy detection and the prices charged are very reasonable considering the difficulties of the work done. Mr. H. Summers, the proprietor of this enterprise, does business at No. 38 Charles Street, and has been identified with the industry to which we have reference for the past ten years. He thus combines skill with experience and it must be a pretty badly demoralized article that cannot be restored to its original beauty under his magic touch. Mr. Summers repairs Statuettes, Art metal, Bronzes, Plaques, Parians, the most costly Fans in existence, Rich Vases, China of all kinds, and Terra Cotta Groups, the latter of which are very hard to mend; also Silverware; Cutlery ground, and any kind of Trunks, as well as Speaking Tubes, in fact anything however delicate will be accepted by him, for he has the facilities and the knowledge to repair all articles in this line. Umbrellas and Parasols are also repaired and re-covered and Lock-smithing and Electrical Bell-hanging are given special attention and all orders filled without delay at moderate rates.

P. Kelley, Confectionery and Dining Room, 41 Charles Street. Judging from the number of Confectionery stores in this city, there must be a large proportion of the population that is fond of sweets, and indeed this is not to be wondered at for there are really but few things more agreeable to the taste than a fresh and well-made piece of Confectionery. Unfortunately it is not every dealer in candy that supplies his patrons with goods that can be described as "fresh and well-made," but there are a good many reliable establishments and one of the most popular of them is that conducted by Mr. P. Kelley, at No. 41 Charles Street. Mr. Kelley occupies a store of the dimensions of 20x50 feet and carries on a dining-room in connection with his enterprise at which appetizing food may be had at reasonable prices, the service being prompt and polite and the cooking first-class in every particular. Employment is given to four efficient assistants and the prices charged are sure to be satisfactory to all reasonable persons. Mr. Kelley began operations in 1870 and has reason to congratulate himself on the present condition of his business. Not only is a large patronage enjoyed, but the trade shows a rapid and constant increase that promises the most brilliant results in the future.

F. C. Lord & Co., Fancy and Family Groceries, 85 Boylston St., and Park Sq., opp. Prov. Depot. It is but rarely that we come across an establishment which impresses us so favorably as that conducted by Messrs F. C. Lord & Co. in Park Square, and indeed there are few stores of the kind, wherein the stock is of so uniformly a high character or is displayed to better advantage. That we are not alone in this estimate of the attractiveness of the enterprise in question, may be seen by the large and constantly growing patronage bestowed upon it and those who have made the most exhaustive trial of the resources of the establishment are loudest in their encomiums on its management and capabilities. The inception of this undertaking was in 1869 and the firm has long been considered as one of the leaders in the city, in its special branch of trade. Family and Fancy Groceries of every description are carried in stock at all times and the assortment is so large and complete that all orders are assured prompt and accurate filling. The premises utilized are 25x136 feet in size and employment is afforded to six efficient and courteous assistants who are at all times ready to extend instant and polite attention to callers. Every effort is made to avoid mistakes, either in the representation or delivery of goods, but as "accidents will happen" we can assure our readers that in case anything ordered from this house should prove deficient in any respect, it may be returned, and that, in any event, the policy of the firm to extend fair dealing to all will be rigidly adhered to. F. C. Lord & Co., also manufacture the celebrated Castilian Cream (awarded a Diploma—First Prize—at 16th Exhibition, Massachusetts Charitable Mechanic Association, December, 1887) removes Grease and Paint from Clothing, will also remove gloss from Woolen Cloth and Black Silk. An excellent preparation for Cleansing Black Crêpe. For sale by Weeks & Potter, Doolittle & Smith, Carter, Carter & Killam, Geo. C. Goodwin, C. F. Hovey & Co., R. H. Stearns & Co., R. H. White & Co., D. R. Emerson, N. D. Whitney & Co., Theo. Metcalf & Co., Jos. T. Brown & Co., Melvin & Badger, and others. Used by the following houses: L. P. Hollander & Co., Macullar, Parker & Co., Messenger Bros. & Jones, Miner, Beal & Co., Continental Clothing House, Robt. H. Vivian, Boston Cab Co. F. C. Lord & Co., Props., 85 Boylston St., Boston.

D. J. Keefe & Co., Sanitary Plumbers, 186 Charles Street. It is an invariable rule that with increased comforts come increased responsibilities, and we need not look far to see examples of this truth on every side. Our houses are so arranged as to furnish light, heat, water and drainage in the most convenient fashion, but the more complicated the system the more keen should be its inspection, and such inspection can only properly be done by one who is an expert in that particular line. The first requisite of a healthful house is good drainage, and the first duty of the inmates should be to see that the drain pipes, etc., are not allowed to remain out of repair. When repairing is necessary, be sure and place your order in competent hands, and in this connection we may say that no better course can be followed than to patronize Messrs. D. J. Keefe & Co., who do business at No. 186 Charles Street. These gentlemen have been known as first-class Sanitary Plumbers for the past ten years, and their reputation for reliability is unsurpassed in this city. They employ a force of sixteen competent assistants, and although the very best of work is done they put their prices at very low figures. Orders are carried out promptly and thoroughly, and every precaution is taken to avoid errors of any description.

M. C. Curry & CO., Harness and Saddle Makers, Charles Street. Driving, and more especially horseback riding, are beginning to be more fully appreciated as regards their health-giving qualities, and the result is to be seen in the increased demand for harness and saddlery goods. The importance of having a well-proportioned and well made saddle, is known to every experienced rider, and in fact only such people can really appreciate the difference noticeable between a good and a poor article of this kind. There is one house in this city that makes a specialty of the manufacture and sale of fine saddles and harness, and so superior is the quality of the article turned out, that we take pleasure in calling the attention of our readers to them, as we know that the result is sure to be satisfactory. The concern referred to is that of M. C. Curry & Co., doing business on Charles Street, and although the premises occupied have been utilized as a harness manufactory, since 1863, they have never produced a higher grade of work than since the present occupants took possession. Mr. Curry became interested in the business in 1872, and became sole proprietor in 1881. The store is 20 x 60 feet in dimensions, and employment is given to ten competent and careful assistants. Both a wholesale and retail business are done, and order work is also given prompt and painstaking attention. The harness on sale here will be found to be of late and fashionable design, and that intended for carriage use is of especially light and elegant appearance. But strength is also provided for and the goods are certain to prove durable as well as ornamental.

BOSTON HIGHLANDS.

That delightful suburban district of Boston, familiarly known as the "Highlands," (née Roxbury) is one of the brilliant examples in this region, of the principle of "natural selection." The old town of Roxbury has a history vying in age and interest with that of the most famous cities and towns in the State, to which history we shall have frequent occasion to refer. Incorporated as a town but a few days after the same sponsorial act had been performed in Boston herself, the two towns grew up alongside each other for many years like twin sisters, until the overwhelming fame of the only "Hub" hid its more retiring companion from view and finally threw the veil of her name over the other's distinct personality. In those days, hardly to be imagined now, when the old Puritan settlers were first laying out their stakes along the shore of the "Bay," nothing, probably, seemed more remote or impossible to them than that "Trimountain," the little village down there on the point, should throw out her all-embracing arms and unite in indissoluble wedlock with the similar little villages scattered around within some half dozen miles. They burned and trimmed their clearings, with more difficulty than we now erect immense buildings, constructed those primitive cradles of liberty, the log-cabins, went on and raised their log meeting house, met and counseled in most solemn seriousness, until that unique and admirable institution—New England town government, was evolved, without a thought that they were building for others, perhaps, better than they knew, and that other men should reap a harvest unexpected. But it was not long after the first quarter of the present century before the "growing pains" of Boston began to cry out for more room, and though they created vast tracts of land where before the sea and mud had had their own sweet way, it did not take many more decades for thoughtful observers to see that the extinction of the individual existence of the town of Roxbury was only a question of time, that it was destined inevitably to succumb to the insatiable appetite of the expanding young giant of a city. And so, foreshadowed by many long and not untroubled years in advance, its appointed destiny came to pass in 1868, January 6th, when it was incorporated with Boston. Not easily, however, do long cherished names and traditions yield up the ghost.

The old name of Roxbury, which old acquaintance and usage had long made so dear, still lingers lovingly about its ancient haunts, and to the stranger in Boston this conflict of names has sometimes caused more or less confusion. The two cities had so long crowded into one another, that sentiment could never have kept asunder what everything else in the universe had joined. Complications innumerable, amusing and distressing, were removed by the union. Houses, part in Roxbury and the rest in Boston, had led the boundary line an extremely tiresome hunt to find itself throughout its whole course, and it had about given the chase up, when the change put an end to it forever. The separation of families that had ensued when many a husband sat down to dinner in Boston, while his wife, on the other side of the table, was in Roxbury, was happily alleviated and became merely an amusing tradition of the neighborhood. The large valuation of the city of Roxbury at the time of union, $26,551,700, went, in truth, to swell the "general coffers" of the Hub's resources; but, on the other hand, Boston assumed the debt of Roxbury, which was, however, very light, about $180,000. The two decades that have passed since the union, have welded the two cities so closely, and every sign of division has been so thoroughly obliterated, that the "Highlands" now seem to have always been an integral part of Boston. Thus London and Paris have rolled their vast waves of population in ever widening circles, until it is often impossible to tell where the engulfing process, which has been so frequent, took place, and the various towns have merged their individuality in the great whole. These last twenty years have been by far the most progressive in the history of the "Highlands." An immense amount of building has been going steadily on, and a large part of it has now come to assume the compact arrangement of a large city. Some old landmarks have had to go, but the old Roxburians have been most tenacious in defending these, to their honor be it said. They have, in fact, throughout their whole history, shown a marked trait of hero worship, as many streets and monuments in honor of distinguished citizens can abundantly testify. If the advancing growth of Boston goes on proportionally for another century, the Highlands will long ere that have become the very heart of the city, and those relics of the past will have to endure the same unwearied assaults which the "old South" and other memorable landmarks are now undergoing. The intellectual cast, however, which has ever distinguished the Bostonian mind, offers far more hopes of immortality to these memorials of a noble history, than most communities would afford. May their idealism never wax old or cold.

The name of Warren is one of the most honored in all Roxbury's history, and on the house now standing where his residence formerly stood, is a tablet to his honored memory. When he left Roxbury, on that fatal morning, June 17, 1775, many patriotic citizens of Roxbury followed and supported him in the great struggle, and his glorious fall on the field of Bunker Hill will ever hallow and ennoble the scenes of his life and work in the "Highlands." Beside the commemorating tablet on the "Warren House," one of the largest and most beautiful avenues is named in his honor. Many other of the honored sons of the town are commemorated in a similar way, as Dudley, Eustis and other streets show. In this connection it is but just to say that the avenues in the Highland district constitute one of the most beautiful and attract-

ive features of Boston. For great and uniform breadth, for picturesqueness of scenery
noble shade trees and handsome residences with generous and entrancing environment
of lawn and flowers, for all the qualities which go to make a quiet drive or stroll delightful, these avenues are not excelled by any in the vicinity of Boston, or what is
about the same thing, in a general character, anywhere in the country.

Warren street, referred to above, and Walnut
avenue are generally regarded as the most beautiful, and correspondingly popular, while there are

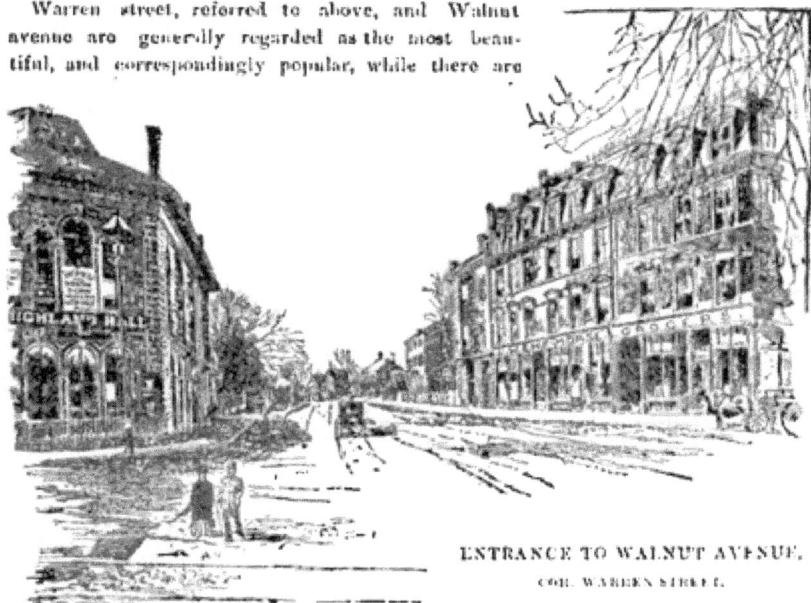

ENTRANCE TO WALNUT AVENUE,
COR. WARREN STREET.

others possessing their own peculiar charms. The residences on Elm hill are especially famed for their elaborate and distinguished adornments in the way of floriculture and architecture, in which fame other parts of the Highlands deservedly share.

The parks in the Highlands also claim attention. Washington park, on Dale and
Bainbridge streets, is the largest and best known of these. Its nine acres of cultivated
grounds are replete with shrubbery and all natural beauties, and it is very popular in
this section. Other parks, also noted for their general beauty and attractiveness are :
Madison Square, between Marble, Warwick, Westminster and Sterling streets, covering three fine acres ; Fountain square, corner of Walnut avenue and Munroe street,
with a recreation square of two and a half acres ; Walnut park, the favored resort of
residents between Walnut avenue and Washington street ; Linwood park, corner of
Center and Linwood streets, a charming bit of green ; Lewis park, corner Highland
and New streets ; Longwood park, corner Park and Austin streets, a beautiful half
acre plot of breathing space for many frequenters ; and Orchard park, between Chadwick and Yeomans streets, two acres in extent, and most carefully cultivated and preserved. The æsthetic common sense of Boston is most undeniably exemplified in her
numerous and delightful parks.

One of the most celebrated and valued relics of old Roxbury is the ancient burying ground on the corner of Eustis and Washington streets, where lie interred the bones of the good John Eliot, the first missionary to the Indians, translator of the Bible into the Indian language, and one of the great religious leaders of New England, besides those of many other great and noble sons of the old town of Roxbury. Forest Hills cemetery, though not included in the present limits of the Highlands, is yet peculiarly connected with this region, and with the local history of Roxbury, of which it was a part when it was originally established by that town before the middle of the present century, being consecrated in 1848. It is now one of the most beautiful cemeteries in the country, being adorned and preserved with remarkable care. The gateway at the entrance is an elaborate and costly piece of work, constructed of Roxbury stone and Caledonian freestone, with the following inscription beautifully inscribed on the outer side:

"I AM THE RESURRECTION AND THE LIFE."

On the inner side, inscribed in golden letters, are these words:

"HE THAT KEEPETH THEE WILL NOT SLUMBER."

The grounds are highly renowned for their exquisite and immense display of floral decoration, in extent and beauty vieing even with "Greenwood" in Brooklyn, and is one of the most entrancingly delicate and grand sights in the way of horticultural triumphs, in the world. Yet, even more highly valued than the outward beauty of the place are the noble memories and traditions of the past which cluster about it. Sons of the greatest and noblest men of the state and nation here lie at rest, "after life's fitful fever." Hither were removed and placed in the Warren family lot on the summit of Mount Warren, the treasured remains of Roxbury's greatest son, General Joseph Warren, whose early death at Bunker Hill, after strenuous efforts in behalf of liberty, has enrolled him among the immortal heroes of America. A handsome monument on Dearborn hill commemorates Gen. H. A. S. Dearborn, the original projector of the cemetery. Admiral Winslow, who maintained the honor of the town-on-the-sea, is commemorated by a huge block of rough granite, reminding one of Emerson's noble tombstone in its simplicity and strength. Also worthy of highest regard, is the beautiful soldier's monument, affectionately erected here by the citizens of Roxbury, in memory of her martyr sons. It was designed by Martin Milmore, and was erected in 1867. The statue is of bronze, representing a soldier of heroic size, and rests upon a granite pedestal six feet in height. About the monument and within the granite railing surrounding the lot, rest the bones of a score of Roxbury's soldier sons, many of whom fell at Antietam, within two months after they left the state, being members of the gallant thirty-fifth Massachusetts, which bore such terrible losses on that day. The monument is under the watchful care of Thomas G. Stevenson Post 26, G. A. R., of the Highlands. The following inscriptions are engraved upon the pedestal of the monument:

4

ERECTED
BY
THE CITY OF ROXBURY
IN HONOR OF
HER SOLDIERS,
WHO DIED FOR THEIR COUNTRY
IN THE REBELLION OF
1861 — 1865

1867

"FROM THE HONORED DEAD
WE TAKE INCREASED DEVOTION
TO THAT CAUSE FOR WHICH
THEY GAVE THE LAST FULL
MEASURE OF DEVOTION."
President Abraham Lincoln,
at Gettysburg.

The innumerable objects of beauty and interest to be seen within the two hundred and twenty-five acres of Forest Hills cemetery, can be but very partially described here. Situated only five miles from the center of the city, it is easily accessible and affords one of the most beautiful trips in the vicinity. To have passed through its floral avenues, over the picturesque hills, and by the little lakes nestling in the valleys all adorned in the height of their summer glory, is a life long memory, but not to be experienced in any measure, save by personal visiting and enjoyment. The main entrance to Forest Hills is situated on Scarborough street, and there are side entrances on Canterbury and Walk-Hill streets. The carriage drives are exceedingly delightful and very much frequented. The rustic observatory on Consecration hill, a unique and attractive structure about twenty-five feet in height, is well worthy of a visit and inspection. The four Eliot hills, named after Roxbury's ancient missionary, and Chapel hill, also possess many beautiful features. It is said that the finest receiving tomb in the country is situated here. Its portico is a magnificent piece of architecture in Concord granite, and is thirty feet square. Within are contained two hundred and eighty-six catacombs, each having space for a single coffin, and all being most carefully arranged. Forest Hills is not so old as Mount Auburn, which has peculiar beauties of its own, but it is larger, and it can safely be said that a visitor has not seen one of the most important sights in Boston, and certainly not in the Highlands district, without having seen Forest Hills.

Among the other notable and prominent features of the Highlands is the great stand-pipe of the Cochituate water-works, erected here in 1869. It is situated on the "Old Fort" lot, between Beach street, Glen and Fort avenues, being raised one hundred and fifty-eight feet above tide level. The pipe itself is of large cylindrical shape, eighty feet long, and is surrounded by a thick wall of brick, between which and the pipe itself, and winding around the latter, is a staircase which leads to the lookout tower on the top. The exterior is artistically conceived and produces a striking and pleasant effect. The value of this pipe to the water service and the city has been tested by many years of successful operating, and is admired no less for its simplicity than its perfection. The entire cost of the structure and the attendant pumping works was not more than $100,000, and its successful results obviated the former necessity of maintaining the reservoir on Beacon Hill. The grounds around the stand-pipe are tastefully laid out, and form another small park in this much and pleasantly be-parked city.

The center of the old town is Eliot square, and here are several points of interest. The old First Unitarian church is the oldest in the Highlands, and in all Boston, excepting the First church of old Boston town. It was settled soon after the latter, in the early history of Massachusetts Bay colony, and has for centuries exercised an important part in the religious thought and life of New England. Among the many well known clergymen who have presided over its interests, the Rev. Dr. Geo. Putnam, for half a century was a prominent leader in all the highest interests of this community. The church edifice is of the substantial and quiet type of architecture which marked the churches built in the first half of the present century, and about

ELIOT SQUARE.

it are gathered many of old Roxbury's dearest traditions. The whole square has the refined and retired aspect which are associated with honored longevity, and is one of the strongholds in this section of the old New England aristocracy, which Dr. Holmes has called the "Brahmin" race, tracing their ancestry back to the Puritan fathers. The residences have spacious and beautiful grounds, and these less pretentious structures of an earlier time, form a quiet and pleasing contrast with the more stylish modern villas which are scattered all around on the heights of the Highlands. The square has retained its earlier aspect, though city influences have been folding in about it more and more, and will probably do so for many generations to come. The Norfolk House adds a touch of brightness and stately elegance, by its fine building, to the square, which is one of the most attractive in the vicinity.

The Roxbury Charitable Society is one of the oldest and most efficient benevolent associations in New England. It was founded nearly a century ago, in 1794, and ever since has earnestly and thoroughly carried out its purpose then stated, "the relief of the poor and the prevention of pauperism." It is noteworthy as being among the earliest societies in this country or the world, which in addition to donating and aiding, give to charitable benevolence a systematic and scientific character. Among other useful articles distributed through a skilled and trained agent, are clothing, food, fuel and also carefully regulated supplies of money, the aim being to encourage and foster self-help, rather than support idleness. The work is exclusively in the Highlands district, and is one of the best applied charities in the country, the society having a large income from legacies and subscriptions. Under the care of this society, the Roxbury Dispensary, which was founded in 1841, is conducted and maintained. The office of the agent is at 118 Roxbury street.

Another well known charity in the Highlands is the Home for the Aged Poor, which was founded in 1870 and incorporated in 1872, by a Catholic associated sisterhood, the "Little Sisters of the Poor," and has since been doing a most estimable work. This sisterhood was instituted in St. Servan, France, by a poor priest and two working girls. It now has a membership of two thousand sisters, and has twenty thousand old people under its support. So long as the applicants are sixty years old or over, of good character and destitute, they are received here and tenderly cared for, irrespective of religious belief or nationality. It is maintained by the collections of the sisters and the gifts of generous friends, among the most helpful of whom has been Mrs. Andrew Carney, whose husband established Carney Hospital, beside being well known for many other charitable deeds. The new building of the society, which was completed in 1880, has accommodations for two hundred persons, and eligibly situated on the corner of Woodward avenue and Dudley street. The management and work of the institution are all carried on by the voluntary efforts of the sisters, and many an aged person has had good reason to bless their thoughtful minds and kindly hearts.

Yet another widely famed and important charitable institution in the Highlands, is the "House of the Angel Guardian," at 85 Vernon street. It was planned and founded by the Rev. George F. Haskins, who graduated at Harvard University, and from its establishment in 1851 until his death in 1872, he served it with greatest fidelity and exertion, as rector and treasurer, devoting from his own property $20,000 to its founding and maintenance. It is now under the charge of a Catholic order, the Brothers of Charity, whose supervisor is W. J. Becker. It occupies a large and handsome building on commodious grounds, and is both richly endowed and possesses property of more than $87,000 in value. Its main object is to rescue and educate orphan and destitute children, of whom there are about two hundred here annually. A carefully graded educational system is maintained, there being many scholars from outside the regular inmates, and thorough instruction is given in English branches, mathematics and commercial studies. The institution is among the most famous in the state for its efficient management and system, and its widely beneficent results. These representative institutions can convey the just impression that the people of the Highlands are not behind the well known character for generosity and kindliness for all, especially the unfortunate, for which Boston is so widely famed throughout the United States.

The Roxbury Latin School is one of the oldest and most famous in the country. It was established in 1645, only nine years after Harvard College, and has proved a powerful force in the intellectual development of this region. John Eliot and Governor Thomas Dudley were among its founders, and among its early teachers are the honored names of Judge William Cushing, Gen. Joseph Warren, Gov. Increase Sumner, and the Rev. Bishop Samuel Parker. Under the direction of such men, it has steadily risen to a commanding position of influence and character. It was incorporated in 1789, and throughout its history has been marked by liberality and thorough scholarship. The only school of its class older than it is the Boston Latin School, founded in 1635, and the two schools have grown up together like honored cotemporaries, each forming an important preparatory school to Harvard University. It is managed by a board of trustees, incorporated as a close corporation, but the school is free to residents of Boston. The support is partly obtained from the voluntary subscription of some leading citizens of Roxbury, partly from the income of past bequests, and partly from the support of the city of Roxbury itself. In the present century it has numbered among its teachers and pupils some of the most honored literary and scholarly men of New England. There are two distinct courses, the English, including all common and higher school studies, and the college preparatory, fitting for any, but especially for the comprehensive and thorough entrance examinations of Harvard. Each course is six years in length. The original name of the school was "The Grammar School in the easterly part of the town of Roxbury." The present school building, situated on Kearsarge avenue, is of large dimensions, plain and substantial in appearance. The Roxbury Latin School, though free to the public, is not under the government of the city, and is in reality a private institution. The public schools of the Highlands are maintained at the highest standard known in this educational center at Boston, and every department of this most important work is cared for most thoroughly and scientifically. The private schools in the Highlands are also famed for their high character and efficiency. Among the best known of these is the boarding and day school conducted by the Sisters of Notre Dame, a Catholic institution. It is a large four story brick structure with fine granite trimmings, situated on Washington street, in one of the most beautiful parts of the Highlands, and in large and delightful grounds of six acres in extent, with many adornments and fine facilities for exercise. The school was founded in 1854, and has been conducted on a self-supporting basis ever since. The Instruction and discipline is of a very high character, and the number of pupils is limited to one hundred. Part of the building is devoted to the training of novitiates in the Sisterhood. The whole annual charge is $200, including both board and tuition.

Among other educational and charitable institutions which are doing a grand work for good in this part of Boston, the Marcella Street Home for Neglected and Pauper Boys, should not pass unnoticed or without high praise.

The branch of the Boston Public Library in the Highlands is one of the largest of the eight, and since its union with the Fellowes Athenæum, has been especially powerful and widely utilized by the reading public of this region.

The New England hospital for women and children is an unique and well known institution, situated in the Highlands, on Codman avenue. It was established in 1863 with a three-fold purpose: "To provide for women medical aid of competent physicians of their own sex; to assist educated women in the practice and study of medicine, and to train nurses for the care of the sick." In all of these lines and in others it has accomplished a wide and beneficient work. It grew out of a movement instituted by Dr. Marie E. Takrzewska for the establishment of a clinical department of the Female Medical College of Boston. Its building and real estate cost $100,000, and is admirably adapted for its work. The annual number of patients treated in its hospital wards exceeds 200, and in the dispensary from 8000 to 4000 receive advice, medicine and surgical treatment. There are a number of free beds in the hospital, but most of the patients are received at light charges, requisite to cover expenses. The medical, surgical and maternity wards are all conducted with the thorough care and good results, which, despite the predictions of the old school, have attended the entrance of women into the realm of practical medicine. Yet another example of the generosity and kindly sentiment manifested in the Highlands is St. Luke's Home, which is situated on Roxbury street, and furnishes gratuitously to all women convalescing from sickness the best of medical treatment. It has accommodations for forty patients, and in connection with it there has been established in the town of Falmouth, a country sanitarium, where thirty-five patients can enjoy all of nature's invigorating resources at first hand. The Home was founded in 1870, and incorporated two years later.

To turn from these kindly yet sad themes to those of a lighter character, we find that the Highlands are not without many popular forms of amusement. There are several large halls, where first class entertainments are given. Highland hall, Bacon's hall, Orienta, Palladio hall, and Dudley Street Opera House, are well known places of high class entertainment.

Washington market is situated near the indefinite, almost imaginary, boundary line between the South End and the Highlands, and is patronized largely by citizens of the latter place, being the only large market so far up town. It is at 1833 Washington street, and was erected in 1870. It is a large handsome building, two hundred and fifty feet long and one hundred and twenty feet wide, and is a model in every respect.

Perhaps there is no city in New England which received a more appropriate name than the old town of Roxbury, which is said to have been so called on account of its large rock quarries. These have been largely developed since the settlement of the town until now the "Roxbury" stone ranks among the most popular in the state, and thus through the durable monument of granite fame, the name of the old town will be preserved for many generations after it has long vanished as a living fact. A few reminiscences of the old town can hardly fail to be of interest to those who have loved it in the past, and to whom, probably, it will always seem like a separate town. Roxbury was settled among the earliest towns in America, and in the same year with Boston proper, 1630, which seems to have been a year of marked prominence in the emigration of the Puritans to this country. The first settlers were mostly from London, and all of the respectable, middle class which formed, and forms to-day, the backbone of old England as well as of New. Consequently the settlement was begun under the most favorable moral influences and so continued for many years. According to the report of a visitor in its early history: "One might dwell there from year to year, and not see a drunkard, hear an oath or meet a beggar." Like many another New England settlement, the first few years were spent in mingled and bitter privation and fear. The year 1633 marked a great accession to their numbers, and after that time growth was steady and increasing.

The first church of Roxbury, which we have already mentioned, was founded in 1632, having but few converts in the state. In this we see the independence and energy of the inhabitants in their earliest history. Thomas Welde was the first pastor of the church, and in November, 1632, the honored apostle to the Indians, John Eliot, who had already come to the front as a man of great intellect and deep sympathies, was appointed teacher in the church. The first building had no shingles to adorn its exterior, or pews to render it comfortable within, being a plain log building. The people of the town were distinguished from the beginning by the deep interest which they took in the subject of education, of which the "Roxbury Latin School" is now one of the shining examples. In fact owing to their universal intelligence and the leading of Eliot, Stone and others they early took a leading part in the development of these interests, among others the establishment of Harvard University. For the "Free School in Roxbury," the far-seeing colonists spent large amounts, as those times went, and sacrificed many things. Mr. Samuel Hayburne led in the good work, and sixty of the people promised to give certain sums for the school every year, pledging even their barns, houses, orchards and stock. The influence of these measures was felt powerfully both without and within the town itself. After long and steady development, the town in 1790, possessed five schools, with an aggregate of 225 pupils, and throughout the history of this region the progress in this department has been great and beneficent.

The Second Parish Church which was built in 1773 is famous for having been the first settlement of the great preacher Theodore Parker. The earliest interment in the old burying ground of Roxbury was in 1633. It is an interesting comparison, and shows the growth of the Highlands, in that instead of the two churches, which for many generations were sufficient for its religious work, now there are over forty churches here, making the region one of the most favored with churches in proportion to its population in the world.

The history of the Highlands during the Revolution vies in interest and glory with the other famous sections of this historic region. In all these exciting incidents, the rejection of the stamp-act, the destruction of the tea in Boston harbor, the skirmishes in Boston with the first British troops and the gallant resistance which the detachment sent to Lexington and Concord met, the citizens of Roxbury were actively and earnestly engaged. After the disdainful redcoats had been driven back into Boston like whipped curs by the enraged farmers, all the heights about Boston, except Dorchester were immediately seized by the rebels and Roxbury became one of the most important centers and rallying points of all the whole series of fortifications which now penned the British up in the town of Boston, as if in a rat-trap. The Americans did not know where the impatient and hitherto invincible soldiery of old England would attempt to break through, so they had to keep watch all around the line. Gage, Howe and Clinton, the British generals, at first planned to seize Dorchester, but the Americans hearing of the attempt, poured large reinforcements into the camp at Roxbury, and the plan was likewise counter-checked by the fortifications thrown up by the alert and intrepid freemen on Bunker and Breed hills. During this memorable conflict, which in all future time will rank among the great and decisive battles of the world, both from the spirit shown by the defenders of liberty, and great issues which turned upon it, the men of Roxbury fought with distinguished gallantry. And here General Joseph Warren, fighting in the ranks, though he might have commanded the whole force, and nobly seeking the most dangerous position, reveals to the world what heroic men the old Puritan blood and discipline have produced in the new land, and how much a single hero can accomplish among his fellows. Throughout this short but sanguinary conflict, the British artillery in the South End had been shelling the Americans entrenched in the Highlands at Roxbury. At this time the Roxbury heights were occupied by Rhode Island troops, under the command of Gen. Nathaniel Green, and so thoroughly did they fortify their position, that Gen. Washington on his arrival praised the works as the best on the line. After the division of the army by Washington, General Artemas Ward was commander of the right wing, and occupied a palatial residence known as the Brierly mansion on Parker hill. On this hill the immense and precipitous rocks formed a great natural fortification behind which the American line ran, and the region roundabout was covered with tents. The works which flanked these rocks were known as High Fort from their commanding situation, and most telling use was made of the position in cannonading and harassing the usurping inhabitants of Boston. The main encampment in Roxbury was on Meeting-House hill, and was noted as being the cleanest and most orderly in the Continental army.

An amusing anecdote is related of this corps and its commander, Brig. Gen. John Thomas, who was expecting an attack from the British, and by marching his seven hundred men round and round Meeting-House hill, whose front was in plain sight of the British camp in Boston, for several hours, until he had made them think there were several thousand of the fiery rebels. Thus the war scenes of the time were not unrelieved by lighter touches of grim humor.

Behind Meeting-House hill was the highest fortification known as the "Upper Fort," or "Roxbury High Fort," and this was the spot which received the brunt of the cannonading, both during the battle of Bunker Hill on the 17th of June, 1775, and at other times. The night after the battle, the newly arrived troops lay awake under arms all night during a tremendous artillery engagement, hourly expecting an attack. Both the upper and lower forts were strongly and carefully constructed, despite the fact that the British cannonaded the soldiers here a large part of the time they were building them. A reward was offered for those who should bring in a cannon ball to headquarters, and the soldiers would chase them after they had fallen and pluck out the fuse, though several made unfortunate mistakes in trying to stop them too soon, and losing a foot or a hand.

Among other buildings which were torn down to build into the two forts, was the old dwelling house of the Dudley family, whose founder was so prominent in early Bostonian history, and which stood where now the Universalist church is. The old Warren homestead, since torn down and replaced by a more modern structure, was

WARREN ST., COR. DUDLEY ST.

then used as a barracks by the troops. The line of circumvallation is carried completely across the Highlands, not even the old burying grounds being spared, but suffering all the indignities which follow in war's train. The roads are all obstructed by this blockade of trees, etc., and all outlying houses are used for skirmishing. On the stage of the Highlands, thus arranged for the bloody play, many exciting scenes of strategy and danger take place between June, 1775, and March, 1776. A large part of the Highlands during this time was debatable ground, given over to skirmishes and parties of ravaging soldiers. The outpost of the American forces was at George's tavern, and the British picket came up to what was known as Brown's chimneys about a mile away. The British seized on Enoch Brown's house at this point near the rock early in the seige, but did not hold it long, as the American cannon soon battered it nearly out of shape. Several volunteers attempted to burn down the remains, but all were slain, until on the 9th of July, 1775, a detachment of two hundred men under Captains Tupper and Crane, surrounded the mass, drove out the garrison, and burned it to the ground. The British, however, succeeded in keeping their picket post at the chimneys that were left for several months longer, and moreover by a counter-rally soon after burned down the George's tavern, and scattered its gallant defenders. Thus for some nine months the Highlands were one constant scene of rallying and counter-rallying. The skirmishers of each army picked off each others' sentinels, and occasionally an encounter of some magnitude would end in a great deal of spilt blood. The whole region was devastated and burnt, neither public nor private property, buildings, trees or crops were spared, and when the storm of war had passed, the place looked like a desert. There is no country so unhappy and desolate as that lying between two hostile armies and fought for by each. Many an unburied victim in scarlet coat or homespun lay uncared for in this sad sepulchre, whose modern beauty and shining front hides many an unwritten tragedy. In this desultory warfare neither side gained permanent advantage, though the Americans were practically victorious so long as the British could not drive them away. The final move in this game of war had the Highlands as its basis. During the 2d, 3d and 4th of March, 1776, the flower of the army, amounting to some five thousand men were massed here, unknown to the enemy. Washington was planning his masterly seizure and fortifying of Dorchester heights.

The night of the 4th of March, 1776, was probably the most exciting and critical the Highlands had or have ever seen. The battalions were forming for a dangerous march across the neck to the heights of Dorchester, two thousand four hundred men being in line. Great trains of wagons carrying tools, fascines, hay and other material for a hasty fortification were drawn up in waiting. As soon as darkness had settled, the word was given and the long line of march started through the streets of Roxbury, down to the Neck. Here a halt was made as the Neck was swept by the enemy's cannon, and discovery meant defeat and destruction by an enfilading cannonading. The side of the road toward Boston is protected by a bulwark of hay, and under a protecting artillery fire from Roxbury, Cambridge and Charlestown Neck the long column passes over without detection, and mounts the heights in safety. All night they work with unceasing vigor, and just before morning, having thrown up a strong fort, they are relieved by three thousand fresh troops from Roxbury. This move was the checkmate of the baffled Britons. Gen. Howe at first planned a similar attack to that at Bunker Hill, but was unable to carry it through, and thoroughly beaten set sail on the 17th of March, '76, leaving Boston and the Highlands to a well-earned peace, since undisturbed. The ravages which it had suffered did not disappear from the Highlands for many years, however, and today in some parts can be found traces fast disappearing of this sanguinary and troubled time.

After the Revolution the town progressed steadily, depending chiefly upon manufacturing, and so escaping many of the fluctuations and panics which beset the sea-going towns of the state in the early part of the century. If the statement of a visitor named Wood, in 1634, "it is a fair and handsome country town, the inhabitants of it being all very rich," did not continue to be exactly true, it is still certain that its growth has been one of the most healthy, evenly prosperous of any town in the state, and that it has had a very small share of earth's poverty and misery. By the time it received the city charter in 1846, a very extensive and valuable manufacturing interest, including foundries, tanneries, machines, soap, watches, breweries, candles, phosphate, etc., had been built up, which has since largely increased. The Highlands is also the place where one of the most famous picture and lithographic establishments in the world is situated, the beauty and purity of whose work is international, and whose buildings are among the most interesting to visit in the neighborhood of Boston.

The population of Roxbury at various periods has been as follows:

1790,	2,226	1850,	18,373
1810,	3,669	1860,	25,137
1830,	5,247	1870.	34,772
1840,	9,089		

At the time of the civil war the city had taken a prominent place in the Commonwealth, and throughout that struggle exerted the most strenuous and honorable efforts. A large and full quota of men were sent to the field, and many of her noblest sons offered up their lives in behalf of liberty and justice. Gen. T. J. C. Amory, and Col. Lucius M. Sargent, were among the number of distinguished patriot martyrs.

A few biographical references to prominent citizens of Roxbury from its foundation until the present, seems pertinent. The most influential man in the settlement of the place was William Pynchon, from Chelmsford, Essex, England. He came to America as a companion of John Winthrop of Boston fame, and was esteemed "a gentleman of learning and religion." According to the early chronicler, he was "the principal founder of the town of Rooksbury, and the first member who joined in forming the Congregational church there." Up to 1636 he was the leading man of the new town, but in that year he led to Connecticut a company of colonists, and founded the town of Springfield in that state. His mind seems to have been of a broader, more liberal cast than his fellow Puritans, for he published a book opposing the cold Calvinism of the age, which was deemed heretical at the time, but has been accepted and surpassed by the orthodoxy of today. The book was burned, and its author suffered much persecution for his honesty and faith, until, wearied of the narrowness of the religious spirit, he returned to England, where he died in 1661. A street in the Highlands is named in his honor, and he was certainly one of the most remarkable and worthy men of his generation in New England, although the early records say of his book, that it was "full of errors and weakness and some heresies," which from the standpoint of the present seem its highest characteristics.

John Eliot's history is so interwoven with that of Roxbury, and in fact with all early colonial history, that references to him have already been necessitated. A few further facts are valuable in connection with this eminent and kind-hearted man. He was born in Nazing, Essex, England, and was a graduate of Jesus college, Cambridge. He arrived in Boston, Nov. 2, 1631, and though the people of that town wanted him

to stay with them he decided to accept the call given to him by the people of Roxbury. Here he labored as teacher and pastor for fifty-eight years, from 1631 to 1688,
and exerted an incalculable influence for good in all departments of the town's growth
The title by which he is known in history, "the Apostle to the Indians," was attained
by his efforts as the first and most laborious of all the American colonists to convert
the Indians to christianity. His great task, the translation of the Bible into the Indian tongue, required a vast outlay of time and labor, forming a colossal monument
to Eliot's untiring devotion, and one of the most interesting memorials of early American literature. In the matter of literature, Roxbury was an early and influential
leader, no less than three of her sons, Pynchon, Calef and Eliot writing works so
abounding in truth and liberality, in other words, heresy, that the ecclesiastical council thought they must be burned to prevent them from exerting a great influence.
Eliot, in his loving zeal for the Indians, used to undertake long missionary tours into
the interior, and gained a great influence over the savage, though his efforts were
neutralized by the cruel treatment of some of the English. Eliot's translation of the
Bible consumed twelve years of hard, steady working, the language having no alphabet when he began, so that this had also to be created. The New Testament was
published at Cambridge in 1661, and the whole Bible two years later. Two editions
were published, the last of two thousand copies in 1686, and copies are so highly valued now that a thousand dollars have been given for one. Eliot was the founder of
the Roxbury Latin School, and his influence in educational matters was felt throughout New England. He was the author of several notable books, beside the translation
of the Bible, and his great intellectual powers were attended by a disposition of self-
sacrifice and charity, which made him universally beloved. Many anecdotes are related of his unfailing and wide benevolence. Unceasing in his toil for others, his own
habits of life were always temperate and frugal. His saying about wine has become
famous: "It is a noble, generous liquor, and we should be humbly thankful for it, but,
as I remember, water was made before it." Both as a man, and as an intellectual and
spiritual leader, the memory of John Eliot will be cherished among the most revered
of this country's early patriots. His death which occurred May 20, 1690, was universally and deeply mourned.

The Warren family was one of the oldest and most honored in Roxbury. The
Warren estate was bought in 1687 by the grandfather of the great general, and it remained in the family for many generations. Here Joseph Warren was born, June 11,
1741. He graduated at Harvard college, practiced as a successful physician, and was
an influential teacher of the Roxbury Latin School. His parents had been among the
leading people of the town, and he admirably maintained the prestige of the family
His brilliant genius as an orator and writer in the struggle for liberty, was matched by
a noble, generous disposition which endeared him to all who knew him. He was a
hero in private as well as public life. His character and powers placed him naturally
in the van of the great movement preceding the Revolution. His great oration on
the "Boston Massacre," March 5, 1775, was a performance of great danger, as well as
genius, and his eloquence awoke and inspired the people as if by fire. He seemed to

be omnipresent during the early days of the Revolution, being the leading spirit in
the battle of Lexington, and the beginning of the seige up to the battle of Bunker
Hill. At this time he was president of the Congress of Massachusetts, and chairman
of the Committee of Safety, practically occupying the chief position in the new commonwealth. Three days before the battle of Bunker Hill, he was appointed a major
general. Although he thought the Charlestown movement unwise on account of scar-

DUDLEY ST., OPP. BAPTIST CHURCH.

city of ammunition, his clearer judgment being afterward manifest, he joined in the
movement with a devotion which cost him and the country an invaluable life. His
heroism on that occasion is too well known to be recounted. A monument to his
honor stands on Bunker Hill, but it is one of the strange things about Roxbury, that
she has never erected a monument to Warren, whom the whole country has and will
delight to honor as her greatest son. His fame will be tenderly kept as long as the
sentiment of veneration remains in the human heart. The "Joseph Warren Association," organized in 1860, has long been endeavoring to obtain a fitting statue for commemorating Warren. The stone cottage upon the Warren estate today was erected
by Dr. John C. Warren in 1846, superseding the original homestead erected in 1720.
Several brothers of General Warren were prominent in the Revolution and in the affairs of Massachusetts since that time.

The Dudley family, also of Roxbury, has been among the most famous of Massachusetts. The founder was Thomas Dudley, who achieved fame in England before coming to America in 1630. His father, of cavalier blood, was slain in the civil war of England, 1642–8, and he received his education in the family of the Earl of Northampton. He received a full legal education, and served with distinction in the French wars of the 17th century, under Henry of Navarre, where he won a captaincy. He was one of the four most prominent men in the settlement of the Massachusetts Bay colony in 1630, locating first at Newton and afterward at Roxbury, to be near John Eliot, whom he much admired. He was appointed Sergeant Major, the highest military office in the colony in 1644. In 1634, 1640, 1645, and 1650, he was elected governor, and served as deputy-governor in the intermediate years, up to the time of his death, July 31, 1653. He was widely honored for his remarkable power of judgment, his untouched honor and fidelity, and his devotion to the upbuilding of the colony. His strong convictions placed him among the most intolerant of the persecutors of Quakers, Anabaptists, and other so-called heretics. Some harshness characterized his treatment of his opponents, and his quarrel with Gov. Winthrop is one of the great topics of early history. Arising from a hot dispute on some purchases of Dudley's, not without some blame on both sides, it continued several years and was finally ended in 1638, when these two most prominent men in the colony were reconciled in the new settlement fittingly called Concord. The family of Dudley has been one of the most celebrated in the literary annals of New England. Among other descendants, have been Oliver Wendell Holmes and Richard H. Dana. His daughter, Annie, afterward married to Gov. Bradstreet, produced the first volume of poems (1642) in America, and though not of the highest value, they are still important as the first fruits of the New England mind. Thomas Dudley contributed to a degree hardly equaled by few others, to the foundation and upbuilding of New England, and through his descendants he strongly affected the growth of the state. His son Joseph was born July 23, 1643, in the town of Roxbury, when his aged father was already seventy years old. Though educated for the ministry, Joseph turned early and naturally to public life and served as a member of the general court from 1673 to 1675. He was a commissioner to the Narragansett Indians in 1775, being present at the last desperate battle fought by King Philip, and arranging the terms of the treaty. He was a commissioner of the United Colonies from 1677 to 1681; deputy governor from 1676 to 1685; and president of New England from 1685 to 1686, receiving his commission from James the Second. He made a voyage to England in 1682, being one of the commissioners appointed to endeavor to save the old charter of Massachusetts, but not being successful, and being considered as wanting in firmness and patriotism at that time, he gained a bad reputation among his fellow citizens in Massachusetts, which was not changed for many years. He made many friends in England, among others the celebrated essayist of the Spectator, Sir Richard Steele, who said that "he owed an abundance of those fine thoughts and the manner of expressing them, which he since presented to the world (Spectator and Tattler), to his happy acquaintance with Colonel Dudley." He returned to New England as a member of Governor Andros' government council, of which he served as president, and chief justice of the supreme court from 1687 to 1689, which added to his unpopularity, and when the Andros government was overthrown in 1689 by the liberty-loving spirit of the people, he suffered with it, being arrested at Providence, R. I., and thrown into prison along with the governor at Boston. After nine months of distressing imprisonment he was released, and appointed by the English government as chief justice of New York, where he served 1690–1692. He returned to England in 1693, where he remained until 1701, when he received the appointment of governor of Massachusetts, and came back with honors to his native colony, which shortly before had thrust him out. He was unpopular yet for six or seven years even in his native Roxbury, but finally by judicious administration and high character, he conquered their prejudices and was honored thereafter to the end of his life in 1720. His term of governorship ended in 1715, on the accession of a new sovereign, George I, to the throne, the chief feature of his term being the able manner in which he conducted the French and Indian wars ending in 1713 with the treaty of Utrecht. He lived a retired life on his farm at Roxbury from 1715 to 1720, and his funeral was celebrated with great honors. So completely had the people changed their minds that the chief paper, the Boston News Letter, speaks of him as "a singular honor to his country, early its darling, always its ornament, and in age its crown." He was a man of distinguished abilities as a statesman and lawyer, but of rather unsteady will, and none too scrupulous in his choice of methods in obtaining the ambition of his life. He was the first American who sat in the English parliament, representing Newton, England, in 1701, and was very much esteemed at the English court, which was not a high recommendation at home. He was one of the most influential in advancing the interests of Harvard College, helping to give its charter a permanent character. He left £50 in his will to the Roxbury Latin School, and contributed much to the upbuilding of educational interests in this region. He was one of the most gifted sons that Roxbury ever produced, and equaled by but few.

Paul Dudley, son of the preceding, was born at Roxbury in 1675, graduated at Harvard in 1690, and afterward at the law school in the Temple, London. He returned to New England with his father in 1702, and was appointed in that year attorney general of the colony. He was elected a member of the legislature, of the executive council, and speaker of the house; a justice of the supreme court in 1718, and from 1745 until his death in 1751, was chief justice of Massachusetts. The great work of his life was in the legal profession and he was a born leader. As a lawyer and a judge he was among the most talented and preëminent that the state has had, and left a fame which has not yet died away. Many of the great reforms and improvements in the state courts of law were due to his efforts. He was deeply interested, like his father, in the educational affairs of the colony, founding a lectureship, among other things, at Harvard. He was elected a member of the Royal Society of London, a rare distinction for an American. He did much for his native town of Roxbury, where he was always highly honored. He was also, together with his brother, chief-original proprietor of the town of Dudley, Mass.

Among other honored members of the family were Colonels William and Joseph Dudley. The former was the youngest son of Gen. Joseph Dudley, born in 1686, graduated at Harvard in 1704, and occupied a commanding position in the civil and military affairs of the state. He served with honor as a colonel in the expedition against Port Royal in 1710, as a member and speaker of the house of representatives, and as a member of the governor's council. He was one of the greatest orators of his time, and a man of great powers and noble character. His son, Col. Joseph Dudley, served with honor during the Revolutionary war, and afterward in civil life. He was the last great man of this distinguished family, who, taken as a whole, have produced more men of genius and power than any other of Roxbury's great families, though their glory has now passed away. The Universalist church in the Highlands is now situated on the site of Governor Dudley's old mansion, which in its time was one of the most elaborate and beautiful in the colony. It was razed to the ground soon after the battle of Bunker Hill, and its brick foundation walls formed the corner of the fort already mentioned as having been erected on Meeting-House hill. It was occupied at the time by a tory, named Isaac Winslow.

Among other great governors which Roxbury has given the state, the name of Increase Sumner deserves an honored place. He was born Nov. 9, 1746, in an old-fashioned house, back of where Hall's block on Roxbury street now stands. He attended the Roxbury Latin School, of which he was later a master, after his graduation from Harvard in 1767. He was a prominent lawyer of the town during the Revolutionary period, and was elected a member of the state convention to ratify the Federal Constitution in 1789. Here he took a leading part and gained a great reputation for ability and judgment. He was elected governor in 1797, and was the first governor to occupy the new state-house which was opened in the following year with appropriate ceremonies. He was re-elected in 1798 and 1799, but did not live to administer the duties of the office a third time. The oath was administered to him on his death bed, and his funeral was said to have been the most solemn and grand the state had ever seen up to that time. Business all through the state was suspended and signs of mourning were universally displayed for one of Massachusetts' greatest and most beloved sons. In personal character and powers of mind, and in every grace of social intercourse with men he was one of those rare men who seem born to be admired and followed by their fellows. He came of an old and honored family, active in the affairs of the eighteenth century, and the revolutionary war, and his son, Gen. Wm. H. Sumner, was a prominent leader in the military affairs of the state. The Sumner house is yet in existence, having been moved back from the street early in the century and is one of the antiquities of the town.

Gen. William Heath was another military hero from Roxbury. He was descended from one of the oldest families in the town, which was founded by William Heath of Nazing, England, who settled here in 1632. He was early enamoured of military life, and was appointed captain of the Ancient and Honorable Artillery Company of Boston, in 1770. One of the moving spirits in the agitation and movements leading up to the Revolution, it was chiefly due to his efforts that the minute men service which proved so important at the outbreak of war, was put upon a good working basis. He was unanimously chosen captain of the first company of Roxbury, in 1774, and in the same year made a colonel of a Suffolk county regiment. He served as a leading member in the provincial Congress of 1774 and 1775, and on the committees of correspondence and safety. One of his most important services was rendered at Lexington and Concord on the famous 19th of April, 1775, where he was the only general officer, and contributed a large share toward the final repulsion of the British soldiers. He led the pursuit of the baffled brigands, and began the seige of Boston by posting guards at Charlestown neck that same night. For these and other notable services he received the commission of major-general in June, 1775, which was confirmed by Con-

WASHINGTON PARK, DALE, COR. BAINBRIDGE STREET.

gress in the following August. During the war he rendered Washington constant and valuable aid, and was appointed by him to command West Point, after the treason of Benedict Arnold. After the war he served the state as member of the convention to ratify the constitution in 1789; as state senator from 1791 to 1792; as judge of probate in Norfolk county from 1793 until his death in 1814. He refused the office of lieutenant-general of the state to which he was elected in 1806. He was one of Washington's most trusted generals, and held as his highest honor a letter of high praise given him by the commander-in-chief, at West Point, when he was the last general in the army to disband his troops. The ashes of this staunch patriot and noble man now rest in Forest Hills cemetery; though no memorial has ever been raised to his memory, he will ever remain among the most honored sons of Roxbury.

Gen. John Greaton was another prominent Roxburian in the revolution. He was a companion and adviser of Warren and Heath through the preliminary struggle of the war, and performed very valuable services at Lexington. Rising rapidly through

10

the grades of major, lieutenant-colonel, and colonel of Gen. Heath's regiment, his gallant services during the seige of Boston attracted wide attention. He engaged in the fateful expedition to Canada in 1776 where he barely escaped death. He performed important services in the Jersey campaigns, at Princeton and Trenton in 1777, and the campaign against Burgoyne in 1779. Though his gallantry and great services were equalled by few other officers, Congress was ungratefully slow in recognizing them, and did not bestow the honor of brigadier-general upon him until the close of the war in 1783. He spared himself in no way throughout the war, and came home at its close so utterly exhausted that he died soon after, Dec. 16, 1788. He sleeps the last, long sleep from which no reveille awakes him, in the old burying-grounds of Roxbury, his grave unmarked by any stone. Roxbury would seem ungrateful in the matter of honoring her gallant sons, but it is not perhaps so much that, as that she honors them more in a quiet way, and has so many of high rank and fame there is no special endeavor to honor the memory of one, but they all rest untouched by the lapse of time, forever safe in the loving regard of her citizens.

Prominent among the names of the families that have exercised a great influence in various periods of the town's history, are those of Alcock, Allen, Amory, Auchmuty, Baker, Bartlett, Bowen, Brewer, Bowman, Crafts, Curtis, Davis, Dearborn, Denison, Daggett, Dorr, Draper, Eustis, Felton, Gardiner, Gore, Griggs, Hatch, Hawes, Howe, Johnson, Lamb, Lewis, Lyne, May, Mayo, Mears, Munroe, Newell, Parker, Payson, Perrin, Pierpont, Porter, Reed, Richardson, Ruggles, Seaver, Smith, Stevens, Thompson, Walter, Weld, Whiting, Whitney, White, Willard, Williams and Young. By comparing these names with the map one can see how Roxbury streets were named after her best people, and had in their time some living significance.

The Williams family was noted for its military character, having for four officers in it Captains Nathaniel, John, Eleazar, and Col. Joseph, the chiefest of whom was Joseph, as usual, for who dare say there is nothing in a name. Col. Joseph Williams was one of the old standbys of the town. He was born here in 1708, and died in 1798 at the age of ninety. He cared not much for public office or he could have had more, indeed all he wanted of it. As it is, his name appears in the town records more often than any other. For a great many years successively he was a leading selectman and moderator of town meetings; also a member of the general court. He gained his colonelcy in the French wars, winning bright laurels at Fort George on the Mohawk river. His influence told greatly in the preparatory struggles of the Revolution, as he was a staunch and most out spoken patriot. He was very remarkable for his physical strength, as well as his intellectual powers, both of which he transmitted to his fifteen children in an extraordinary degree.

Gen. Joseph Palmer was another military man, to which class, indeed, Roxbury seemed to offer special attractions, who came there during the eighteenth century. He was a native of England and arrived in the town in 1746. His first work was to establish extensive salt works on Boston neck, where he was the constructor of a great dam, long known by his name. He was very prominent as a patriot, statesman and general during the revolutionary war. His chief services were rendered in the provincial congress, of which he was a member in 1774 and 1775, and as a brigadier-general of the state militia in the campaign in Rhode Island, 1778. He died by a sudden stroke of palsy, contracted through his exertions in completing his dam for the salt-works, December 25, 1788. It is perhaps worthy of note, that if they had celebrated Christmas day in his time, old Gen. Palmer might have lived many another long year in peace and happiness. "Thus even the whirligig of time bring in its revenges."

Governor William Eustis of Roxbury, was one of the most powerful public men the state has had since its beginning. He was born here and graduated at Harvard College, being a favorite pupil in the Latin School of Gen. Warren. He was present as surgeon at the battle of Lexington, and at many other important battles during the war. After it was over he practiced his profession with great success for a time, but was soon drawn irresistibly into public life. He was elected a member of the legisla-ture in 1788, and passed soon, his abilities being immediately recognized, into the national congress. He served as secretary of war in President Madison's cabinet up to 1812, when not agreeing with the war policy, he received a transfer to the place of minister to Holland, which he occupied from 1815 to 1818. In 1823, 1824 and 1825, he was elected to the gubernatorial chair of the state, giving very popular ad-ministrations, and dying in office during his third term, exactly like Governor Sumner before him. This is one of the remarkable instances of history's repeating itself. His death occurred February 6, 1825, and was universally mourned. During Lafayette's visit to New England and Boston in 1824, he was the especial guest of Gov. Eustis at Roxbury, who exerted himself strenuously to provide the most elaborate entertain-ments, and in them he was heartily and actively supported by the people of Roxbury. An amusing anecdote is related of the French general's tour through the country: Having occasion at one time to ask a social acquaintance the question, "Are you mar-ried?" he replied to an affirmative answer with an emphatic "Happy man!" At anoth-er time when the same question elicited a self-congratulatory "No," he whispered in his friend's ear, "You're a lucky dog." Who but a brilliant Frenchman could have differentiated the two conditions with more witty epigrams and salient truth.

Governor William Shirley was another leader who hailed from Roxbury. He was born in London, England, and educated there at Cambridge University. His success-ful law practice in England made him the confidant and friend of Sir Robert Walpole and the Duke of Newcastle. After coming to Boston in 1731, he practised here with much honor and renown, and ten years later, in 1741, he was raised to the governor-ship by the hearty and combined efforts of his powerful friends at home and the peo-ple here. He was the organizer and chief director of the great military movement in Canada, in 1745, which ended in the capture of Louisburg, and a vital wound being inflicted on the French power in America. Other strong and popular measures marked his administration which ended in 1749. He then went to England, and was appoint-ed one of the commissioners to arrange the American boundary line. Gov. Shirley was appointed a major-general in 1755, and governor of the Bahamas in 1756. He returned to his great Roxbury mansion in 1769, where he died two years later, widely mourned in this country and England. His mansion, one of the most elegant in the American colonies, did not descend to his posterity, but was afterward occupied by Gov. Eustis, and is now one of the most stately of the old New England mansions.

A reference to Caleb Fellowes, who founded the Fellowes Athenæum, is necessary in any account of the honored men of Roxbury. He was a native of Gloucester, Mass, but settled in Roxbury in 1810, where he made a large fortune, most of which he left to found the library which bears his name, and will ever render it honored in the Highlands.

This account of the honored men of the Highlands is necessarily incomplete from the very large number of great men which this region has produced; indeed, in examining the records, we are convinced that no other place in the state, outside of Boston, can show a longer list of more eminent names, and the memory of their services are recorded for all time in the progress and glory of the old Bay State, both in military, civil and literary domains. A list of the mayors of Roxbury from the time of incorporation in 1846, until united with Boston in 1867, is as follows:

John James Clarke,	1846–47.
H. A. S. Dearborn,	1847–51.
Samuel Walker,	1851–53.
Louis Bacon Comins,	1854–55.
James Ritchie,	1855–56.
John Sherburne Sleeper,	1856–58.
Theodore Otis,	1859–60.
William Gaston,	1861–62.
George Lewis,	1863–67.

As we remarked at the beginning of our sketch, there can be no doubt that, materially speaking, Roxbury has made vast and unprecedented progress since she was married to Boston and christened the Highlands. There seems to be no use whatever in lamenting this union as it was plainly in the inevitable tendency of things and the survival of the fittest is the law of civilization. That she will continue to advance, and in time in all lines, under her new name and auspices is not only the deep desire, but the not unreasonable assurance of her friends.

LEADING BUSINESS MEN

OF

BOSTON HIGHLANDS.

Griffith's Steam Laundry, W. B. Merrill, Proprietor, No. 173, 175 and 177 Dudley Street, Corner Harrison Avenue, Highlands. If public laundries continue to increase in numbers and in patronage as rapidly as they have of late years, the familiar horrors of a domestic "wash day" will soon become a mere tradition, and one fruitful source of discomfort and strife will be banished from our households. As in the case of all improvements, they had to encounter strong prejudices and oppositions at first, but the superiority of the work they turned out was so plainly manifest and the prices charged were so low that they soon overcame all objections, and secured a firm and lasting hold on popular favor. Steam has worked wondrous changes in about every industry to which it has been applied, but it is a question if in any of them the changes have been more radical, the standard of improvement higher, and the benefits to the public more pronounced, than in the Laundry business. Once it could be said that everybody's clothes were washed at home, but now with equal truth it might be asserted that they were brought to the Laundry. This is due to a variety of causes, of course, as is any other great popular change, but chief among them are the facts that the work could be done easier, cheaper and better in this way, and that the system of receiving and distributing the goods soon became so perfect as to almost ensure against loss or even serious delay. The best-appointed and most largely-patronized Laundry in New England is that carried on by Mr. W. B. Merrill, at No. 173, 175 and 177 Dudley street, under the name of the Griffith's Steam Laundry. This establishment was founded about ten years ago and was soon taken into popular favor, its business having been a steadily-growing one from its inception. This great success was largely due to the enterprise and ability of Mr. Merrill, who has been indefatigable in his efforts to improve the reliability and efficiency of the laundry, and has thus gained the confidence of the public in a marked and unusual degree. The business was formerly conducted at the corner of Warren and Dudley streets, (under Palladio Hall) but owing to the rapid increase of the business Mr. Merrill erected the present building No. 173, 175 and 177 Dudley street, and in the spring of 1883 moved his extensive machinery, etc., to this building. Here every convenience is at hand for turning out the immense amount of work done at short notice. The machinery which is of the most expensive and improved description is run by a large steam engine located in the basement, where are also located the immense boilers for boiling the clothes. From 90 to 100 hands are employed and as every department of the business is under Mr. Merrill's close personal supervision, the quality of the work done is first-class in every respect. The very finest goods can be sent here without damage either to fabric or color as no injurious chemicals are employed in the cleansing process. In addition to the principal office on Dudley street, Mr. Merrill has almost a hundred agencies in different sections of the city and suburbs. In spite of the immense business transacted the same careful attention is given to each order however small intrusted to the laundry, and if the trade continues to increase the next ten years as rapidly as it has the last, the present building, large as it is will have to be enlarged. Orders may be sent by postal card or telephone and goods will be called for and delivered, four teams being employed for this purpose.

Frank Ferdinand, "Blue Store," Furniture, Carpets, Stoves, Bedding and House Furnishing Goods, No. 2360 Washington Street. The "Blue Store" was established in 1867, just twenty-one years ago. It was at first rather a small affair, but it was a very healthy infant and was cared for with skill and liberality. Of late years its proportions have become immense, but unlike some other enterprises that could be mentioned, this increase has not brought about the use of "red-tape" to such a degree that a man must expend five dollars' worth of time in buying a one-dollar article; and the smallest as well as the largest buyer will find that his or her interests are guarded, and that any misunderstandings that may occur where thousands of dollars' worth of goods are sold weekly will be promptly and cheerfully corrected without the least compulsion or ill-feeling. How do we know this? Well, we have "been there" ourselves, and speak from personal experience. Then, again, think for a moment. Mr. Ferdinand has carried on business here for over twenty years. He is located near no depots, has never appealed to out-of-town buyers for the bulk of his custom, but has sold at least seven-eighths of his goods right here in the Highlands within a radius of two miles. Everybody knows the kind of people who make up the majority of the population of the Highlands, and therefore everybody knows that they will submit to neither imposition nor extortion. What, then, is to be concluded when we see the marvelous development of the "Blue Store's" trade? Has it a monopoly? The idea is absurd on its face. Numerous other dealers handle House Furnishing Goods, selling the same for cash or installments, numerous other dealers employ competent and polite salesmen; but where can another "Blue Store" be found? The only "monopoly" Mr. Ferdinand enjoys is that given him by his ability to supply reliable goods at prices below those of his would-be competitors, and there you have the whole story. His establishment is a credit to the city. It is the most extensive of the kind in New England, and every inch of space has a legitimate use. Visit it; it will cost you nothing. On the contrary, if you have furniture to buy, you can save a liberal percentage and can be sure you are getting just what you think you are, for one of Mr. Ferdinand's "cast-iron" rules is, "No misrepresentation." Every article necessary to furnish a house from garret to cellar is sold by him, and he guarantees both his goods and his prices to be satisfactory in every respect.

Norfolk Billiard Hall, E. B. Wood, Proprietor, corner of Washington and Vernon Sts., Boston, Mass. It may at last be said that Roxbury has a Billiard Hall worthy of the section in which it is located, for there can be no dispute that the establishment now carried on by Mr. E. B. Wood at the corner of Washington and Vernon Streets, is the largest and finest appointed in the city. The Norfolk Billiard Hall was formerly located a few doors from its present situation, but its quarters proved too small to accommodate the rapidly increasing business and on the completion of the magnificent building it now occupies, the enterprise was transferred to the spacious room utilized. The Hall is conducted on a *strictly temperance basis* and no liquors are tolerated on the premises at present. It is 70x100 ft. In dimensions and is without doubt the best lighted in the city, as it has windows on three sides and four gas burners to every table. The draperies and furniture are elegant and even luxurious, and the twelve billiard and three pool tables with which the place is equipped are of the most approved manufacture, being made by A. W. Bailey, and are maintained in first-class condition. Balls, cues and every article used in the establishment are subjected to a careful and rigid inspection daily, and patrons are spared the annoyance of having to search for properly tipped cues or asking for chalk, as such wants are anticipated and fully provided for. A rifle range of 75 feet is at hand for the convenience of those interested in marksmanship, and the rifles furnished being of the Ballard and the Winchester manufacture, are not the toy weapons usually found in shooting galleries, but costly, serviceable guns of standard weight and strength, capable of throwing a ball half a mile with accuracy, so that a man who shoots well in this hall can shoot equally well in the field or woods. Two handsome Hallet & Davis upright pianos are also at the disposal of patrons. This is an attraction seldom found in a billiard room and will be appreciated by all gentlemen fond of music. The proprietor of this popular enterprise is Mr. E. B. Wood, who is a native of Boston, and is to be congratulated on having solved the oft-repeated problem: Who is to furnish the Highlands with a first-class billiard hall?

Wm. W. Bartlet, ph.g., Pharmaceutical Chemist, 675 Shawmut Avenue. The professional Pharmacist is one who operates effectively in times of need in arresting and alleviating the ailments and ills of the human body, and therefore deserves the most thankful and appreciative consideration on the part of the public. Mr. Wm. W. Bartlet has since 1873 been actively engaged in the pharmaceutical profession. He graduated in that year with honor at the Massachusetts College of Pharmacy, and for several years was a member of its board of trustees. He is also a member of the the Mass. State Phar. Association, of the Boston Druggists' Association, of the American Phar. Association of which he is committee on prize essays, and of the Mass. Druggists' Alliance, and now occupies and controls a fine and well appointed Drug Store at No. 675 Shawmut Avenue, where is conducted a large business in this line. The premises utilized by Mr. Bartlet cover an area of 20 by 40 feet, and are fitted up with every possibility requisite for the prosecution of the extensive retail trade and manufacture of the following well-known preparations: Peptocarb (or Pepsinated Charcoal); Peptocarb Tablets, small; Aromatic Elixir, Pepsin Compound; Aromatic Saccharated Pancreatin; Bartlet's Concentrated Meat Juice; Pancreat Emulsion Cod Liver Oil; Saccharated Pepsin; Pepsin Porci; Essence of Jamaica Ginger; Sarsaparilla and Iodide of Potassium; Bartlet's Camphor Ice and Glycerine; Beef, Iron and Wine; Anodyne Corn Remover; Orange Cream. Mr. Bartlet keeps a full line of Pure Drugs, Proprietary Medicines, Chemicals and Toilet Articles, and has a well developed prescription trade, and in this department of the business the house takes rank with the first in the city for purity of drugs, and the accuracy and care with which medicines are compounded. Mr. Bartlet is a native of Newburyport and a highly respected citizen of the community. He is a member of the Royal Arcanum. The success of this house is as well merited as it is prominent.

G. R. Soderbery, Carpenter and Builder, 24 Warren Street, Boston. Jobbing promptly attended to. We feel sure that all those familiar with the business methods of Mr. G. R. Soderbery, who is located at 24 Warren street, will bear us out in selecting him for special mention in this book. He is very widely known. The premises occupied are of the dimensions of 25 x 50 feet, and employment is afforded to about ten men on the average. Mr. Soderbery is well prepared to undertake any job in the line of carpentering on the shortest notice, and his facilities are such that he is able to do the best of work at the lowest prices. All orders are given the personal attention of Mr. Soderbery, and satisfaction is guaranteed in every respect.

Highland Creamery, W. E. Davis, Proprietor; Wholesale and Retail Dealer in Choice Butter, Cheese, Eggs, Lard and Beans, No. 1901 Washington Street. In the division of retail trade up into specialties, which has been steadily going on for some years, one of the most noticeable points is the prominence that has been accorded to the handling of butter, cheese, eggs and other country produce, and it has been learned that when a concern confines its business to the sale of these indispensable commodities it is generally able to quote lower prices on them, as well as furnish them in better condition, than those houses that deal in many other products, and only make the supplying of dairy goods, etc., a subordinate feature of their business. Mr. W. E. Davis, of No. 1901 Washington street, has achieved the name of carrying as finely flavored and in every way desirable a stock of butter and cheese as there is to be found in this city, and it is also conceded that his prices are as low as the lowest, when the quality of the goods is considered. He only began operations in 1887, succeeding Mr. J. C. Atkinson, who founded the undertaking in 1881, but he has already built up a large and growing patronage, and neglects no means to ensure a continuance of his present success. The store is a spacious and attractive one, and being fitted up especially for this line of business contains every facility for properly storing and caring for the goods dealt in. Both a wholesale and retail

trade is carried on, and goods are sold on commission, prompt returns being made and satisfaction guaranteed. Butter, cheese, eggs, lard, beans, etc., are furnished in quantities to suit, at positively the lowest market rates, and the employment of two efficient assistants allows of prompt and courteous attention being assured to every customer.

R. S. Margeson, Dealer in House Furnishing Goods, 2329, 2331, 2333, 2335, 2337, Washington Street. "Nothing succeeds like success," says the proverb, and what more striking commentary on the methods employed and inducements offered by Mr. R. S. Margeson in the line of House Furnishings, etc., can be given than that afforded by the patronage given the enterprise under that gentleman's control since it was inaugurated in 1883. Those familiar with the premises first occupied know that they contained the right goods at the right prices, and hence a thriving trade was soon established that grew and grew until finally the present beautiful, spacious and convenient edifice was built, and the establishment transferred to its new quarters. Here four floors are occupied, each measuring 60 x 90 feet, and the magnificent show-windows give tempting glimpses of and hints at what is within. The same methods that built up the enterprise, are depended upon to still further increase its magnitude, and the constantly lengthening list of patrons shows that this dependence is fully justified by the results attained. Mr. Margeson is not a man to be content with any but a leading position in the line of business which he carries on, and he makes it a rule to allow no concern to undersell him or to offer more liberal inducements to purchasers. To those who have never visited his establishment we would say, "Do so by all means." There may be found as fine and complete a selection of House Furnishing Goods as New England can show, and every article in the immense stock is fully warranted to prove as represented in every respect. Whether you occupy a three room "flat" or a thirty room mansion Mr. Margeson can furnish it for you, complete in every detail—kitchen, dining-room, parlors, chambers, halls, and all, can cover the floors with any material desired, from a Velvet Wilton to a Straw Matting, hang the walls with Pictures, furnish Decorations in any quantity desired, and do it all at as low a figure as can be named by any one on similar goods. He employs ten energetic and polite assistants.

D. H. Everett, provisions, 1935 Washington Street. Notwithstanding there are many provision stores to be found throughout the city, there is always a demand for information regarding a thoroughly reliable establishment of this kind, and therefore no excuse need be made for asking our readers to give their attention a moment to these few words regarding the enterprise carried on by Mr. D. H. Everett, at No. 1935 Washington street. We said information relating to *reliable* establishments, and really know of none that could be more truthfully described in those words than that alluded to, for Mr. Everett makes it a point to offer only such goods as he believes to be satisfactory and will at all times be found ready and willing to repair and make due amends for any mistake that may occur. He is a native of New York, and founded his present undertaking in 1883, meeting with instant and pronounced success, as the public was quick to see the genuine merits of his goods and his prices spoke for themselves, as indeed they do now more strongly than ever. The premises occupied comprise one floor and a basement of the dimensions of 25 x 40 feet, and very completely fitted up. There are four efficient and polite assistants employed, and hence very little delay is met with at any time in being waited upon, a fact which has done much to give this store the popularity it now enjoys. Meats of all kinds are always in stock, and from the choicest and costliest cuts down to neck and soup pieces, are sold at bottom rates. The trade is rapidly increasing and the percentage of "regular" customers is very large.

Fred Hoeffner, Upholsterer, 40 Warren Street, Opposite Post-office. It requires no argument to prove that Upholstering is either good or bad, for to eyes experienced in such work an imperfect job of Upholstering is wholly bad and should not be tolerated by anybody. But our readers may inquire how they are to know the good from the bad; and as the easier way to answer this question we would refer them to the establishment conducted by Mr. Fred Hoeffner at No. 40 Warren Street, opposite the post-office. Here they will find some of the finest specimens of Upholstery Work to be seen in the city, and we have but little fear that they will be imposed upon by incompetent upholsterers after they have seen what can be done in that line. Mr. Hoeffner has no desire and no intention of thriving at the expense of other people, but his work speaks for itself and we need say no more concerning it. He is a native of Roxbury and inaugurated his present enterprise in 1832, since which time a large business has been built up. Two floors and a basement are occupied, measuring 20 x 70 feet, and four experienced and careful assistants employed. Upholstered Furniture is largely dealt in, and a specialty is made of individual and uncommon designs. Window Shade and Carpet Work is given prompt, careful and thorough attention, and satisfaction is warranted to customers. Mattresses are made to order, or old ones will be renovated so as to be as good as new, while Shades and Lace Curtains will be thoroughly and permanently cleansed without injury and at low rates. Mr. Hoeffner is a member of the Ancient Order of United Workmen, and has many friends throughout this portion of the city.

M & H. H. Collins, Practical Plumbers, No. 121 Dudley Street. Modern plumbing is becoming more and more of a science every day and the march toward perfection in this line, is a steady and constant one. The methods of ten or even five years ago, have already been almost entirely superseded, and caution should be used in the placing of orders for plumbing work, to see that they are intrusted to men who are progressive as well as practical. No firm holds a higher reputation for good work, moderate charges and enterprising methods, than does that of Messrs. M. & H. H. Collins, doing business at No. 121 Dudley street, and as this house has been before the public since 1876, there has certainly been abundant chance to observe what its merits are. Both partners are well known here, both in and out of the trade, and the steady increase in the business of the firm from year to year, is the best possible proof that it satisfies its customers and is worthy of the liberal patronage received. Practical plumbing of every description is done at the shortest possible notice, and as employment is given to ten competent and experienced assistants a large amount of work can be very quickly disposed of. Contracting is an important branch of the business, and the complete piping and general fitting up of new houses are given special attention, estimates and specifications being furnished when desired and strictly adhered to in the practical carrying out of the work. Jobbing of all kinds is also largely carried on, and prompt, faithful service assured to every customer. The most difficult jobs will be undertaken, and reasonable prices and durable work guaranteed in every instance.

F. J. Williams, Dealer in Provisions, Fruits and Vegetables, No. 127 Dudley Street, Revere Market. The "Revere Market" 127 Dudley Street, known to all residents of Roxbury and vicinity, was established over thirty years ago; the business has been conducted by a number of able gentlemen, but has never been more successfully carried on than at present, by Mr. F. J. Williams, who has built up a large and appreciative trade. He first became connected with the enterprise in 1885, his methods of business are strictly honorable, his efforts to cater satisfactorily to cultivated tastes have been amply rewarded by the just appreciation of the public. Mr. Williams is a native of Boston, extremely well known to many in and around Boston. The premises occupied in carrying on his business consist of one floor and a basement 20 x 50 feet. Two capable assistants are always at hand, and Mr. Williams gives his personal supervision to the strict and prompt filling and delivering of orders. Beef, Mutton, Lamb, Pork, Poultry, fresh Vegetables and Fruits in their seasons are dealt in to a large degree; canned fruits and vegetables, and all kinds of pickles, etc., are in stock, in fact everything to be found in a first class provision store, is to be had here.

Richard G. Jacobs, Martin L. Catc, Walter B. Phipps, Boston Office, 50 Kilby Street, and Roxbury Office, 2380 Washington Street, Room 8. Insurance in all its branches on Mercantile and Manufacturing Buildings and Blocks, Hotels, Apartment Houses and Dwellings, Stables and Contents, Household-furniture, Store and Office Fixtures, Rents, Leases and Profits of Business for long or short terms. Agents for Ætna Insurance Company of Hartford, Conn., capital $4,000,000; net surplus $3,345,038.04; surplus for policy holders $1,345,-058.04; losses paid in sixty-nine years $61,830,000. Scottish Union and National Insurance Co. of Edinburgh, Scotland. Statement United States Branch, January 1, 1888: assets $1,421,748.74; liabilities $748,497.08; surplus to policy holders $1,073,251.66. Fireman's Fund Insurance Co. of San Francisco, Cal., capital 1,000,000; net surplus $130,948.92; surplus for policy holders $1,380,948.92; losses paid in Boston's great fire $180,903.89. National Fire Insurance Co. of Hartford, Conn., capital $1,000,000; net surplus 651,712.18; surplus for policy holders $1,651,-712.18. Franklin Fire Insurance Co. of Philadelphia, Pa., capital $400,000; net surplus $963,-386.23; total assets $3,181,248.55. Holyoke Mutual Fire Insurance Co. Salem, Mass., guarantee capital $100,000; net surplus $546,763; losses in Boston's great fire over $225,000 without any assessment on its members. German Fire Insurance Co. of Pittsburgh, Pa., capital $200,000; net surplus 932,166.37; total assets $471,547.39 Abington Mutual Fire Insurance Co. of Abington, Mass., total assets $71,119.03; net surplus $33,073.79; contingent assets $180,780. Has never made an assessment, and its dividends have steadily increased.

J. M. Sheehan, Practical Plumber, 47 Warren St., next door to the Post Office, Boston Highlands. Personal supervision given to all orders. Ventilation of soil and waste pipes a specialty. Jobbing and Contracting promptly attended to. Prices reasonable and all work warranted. Particular pains should be taken in the placing of orders for plumbing work to see that they are intrusted to a respectable and reliable house, for unless this precaution be taken not only waste of money but loss of health may ensue, as on the perfect plumbing and drainage of our houses does our health largely depend. One of the best concerns known to us is that of Mr. J. M. Sheehan, of 47 Warren Street, next door to the post office. He has labored as apprentice, journeyman and employer on Warren St., for the past twenty-three years, doing business for himself the past eleven years, during which time he has contracted for and carried out to the entire satisfaction of the owners, the plumbing of many of the best buildings and residences in the Highlands, including the Dudley opera house, Armory Hall Warren Street, Parochial School, Forest Street, Merrill's new laundry, Dudley Street, Isaac Fenno's block, Warren Street, and many others, to the owners of which he would be pleased to refer. He employs seven skilled workmen and fills all orders promptly. Mr. Sheehan gives his orders his own personal supervision, and all his work is guaranteed to be the best and prices reasonable and compatible with such work.

O. G. Moonr, Dealer in Boots, Shoes and Rubbers; Repairing done; No. 1999 Washington Street, between Ball and Arnold Streets, Boston Highlands. The gentleman whose card we present above, is conceded to be one of the leading shoe-dealers in the Highlands and the South End, and those who are aware of the vigor and ability with which that line of business is prosecuted in those portions of the city, will require no further evidence of his capacity as a business man. Mr. Moonr is a native of Boston, and inaugurated the enterprise with which he is connected in 1870. He occupies one floor and a basement, measuring 20 x 90 feet, and enjoys a very large patronage, for his establishment has for years been recognized as one of the most absolutely reliable in the city, and his prices are as low as his goods are trustworthy. Some of our readers may consider low prices and reliable goods a somewhat strange and very rare combination, and so perhaps they are, but nevertheless such a combination is surely to be found at Mr. Moonr's, and if any one doubts this assertion, let them prove its truth or falsity by the easiest and most natural means imaginable—calling at that gentleman's store themselves, and examining his goods and prices. This is not hard to do, as his establishment is conveniently located at No. 1999 Washington Street, between Ball and Arnold Streets, and even should no purchases be made, Mr. Moonr will be found willing to show goods cheerfully and without delay. He employs two efficient and polite assistants, and carries a stock so complete that it must be seen to be appreciated. Repairing is neatly done, and satisfaction is confidently guaranteed.

J. E. Ryan, Upholsterer and Cabinet Maker, 61 Warren Street, (up stairs). Furniture Repaired, Upholstered and Polished; Carpets Made and Laid; Window Shades and Screens of all kinds made to order; Window Shades and Lace Curtains laundried in first-class style; Mattresses made to order and made over. Although the work of the old-time cabinet maker has, to a great extent, been superseded by that of machinery, still enough people remain who prefer the individual production of an artist, in his line of trade, to any stereotyped pattern however elaborate and showy. Prominent among well known cabinet makers and upholsterers in the Highlands is Mr. J. E. Ryan, doing business at 61 Warren street. He began operations in 1880, and has established a considerable trade by the high grade of the work he turned out and his reasonable prices. Furniture manufactured to order and repaired, upholstered and polished; window screens and shades made to order—also mattresses made over and altered; window shades and lace curtains laundried in the best manner. Mr. Ryan is a native of Boston, where he has many friends. One floor 20 x 45 feet in dimensions is occupied, and a competent assistant is employed to give every attention to orders, which are executed with promptness.

S. H. L'Heureux, Watchmaker and Jeweller, 2400 Washington Street. The "big clock" over the door of the store occupied by Messrs. Currier & L'Heureux, at No. 2400 Washington street, corner of Dudley, has stared people in the face for a number of years, and it stares now as hard as ever, although Mr. L'Heureux is now the sole proprietor of the establishment in question. Passers-by glance at the thermometer in the doorway, up at the clock and into the show-window, and then if they admire tastefully displayed jewelry, etc., they are very apt to linger a while, as the window mentioned is always attractive and has contained some of the most beautiful jewelry ever shown in the Highlands. At all events, whoever looks in is pretty sure to see watch repairing going on, for this industry is given particular attention by Mr. L'Heureux, and he is prepared to undertake the most difficult and delicate jobs in this line and guarantee satisfaction to his patrons. One floor and a basement, of the dimensions of 25 by 60 feet, are occupied, and a beautiful and varied stock is carried, comprising the latest novelties in jewelry, wedding and engagement rings, optical goods of various descriptions, watches of standard make and warranted accuracy and durability, and all the many articles generally found in a first-class store of this kind. The prices quoted on these goods are moderate and equitable, and everything bought here is sure to prove just as represented, and if it should not the purchase money will be refunded if desired or the goods exchanged. The enterprise was inaugurated nearly forty years ago, and it has long been one of the representative undertakings of the Highlands.

Dr. F. J. Macfarlane, Surgeon Dentist, 67 Warren Street, corner Dudley. One of the incidental drawbacks to the highly civilized state in which a larger portion of mankind has lived during the present century, is the grave injury which the habits and the food indulged in under such circumstances has worked on the teeth. It is a fact, too obvious to all to require illustration, that as a general thing the ruder and more primitive the habits of a race of men are, the better are their teeth, and this despite the fact that such a people take no care of their teeth whatever, but allow them to remain continually unbrushed and uncleansed. Now not only should a person in civilized life take excellent care of the teeth, but not allow them to go a great while without examination by a skillful dentist who could be depended upon. An expert can be found in this city in the person of Dr. F. J. Macfarlane, whose office and operating rooms are at No. 67 Warren street (Armory building). The doctor has been established since 1883, and graduated that year from Boston Dental College, where he has gained and held the office of Demonstrator, a well deserved reputation for thoroughness and skill in dental operations. Two large rooms are occupied and every comfort is at hand for the convenience of patients. Dr. Macfarlane, since he opened his office here has gained a large circle of friends and patients. The illustration of Armory building, corner Warren and Dudley streets, gives a view of the exterior of his office.

B. W. Felton, Manufacturer of Felton's Patent Furnaces and Ventilators, Stoves, Ranges, Furnaces and Kitchen Furnishing. A full assortment of Registers and Refrigerators, Laundry Stoves, Oil Stoves, Parlor Stoves, Tin, Sheet-Iron, Zinc and Copper work done at short notice. Nos. 2 and 4, Warren St, Roxbury, Mass.

Heating and ventilating go hand in hand, and no house or no apartment can be economically and properly heated unless ventilation be also taken into account and scientifically provided for. This fact being granted, the importance of intrusting the work of providing heating facilities for a building to one who is also competent to undertake its ventilation, becomes at once apparent, and in this connection we would invite the attention of our readers to the furnaces and ventilators patented and manufactured by Mr. B. W. Felton, for these are designed and constructed on correct scientific principles, as has been proved not only by theory but by years of practical use. Even did the purpose of this work permit, we could not spare enough space to make the arrangement of these heaters and ventilators clear to our readers, but if those interested will call on Mr. Felton at Nos. 2 and 4 Warren street, they will be received with courtesy and given every opportunity to familiarize themselves with the practical details of the appliances in question. Mr. Felton began operations in 1872, and his business has grown steadily and rapidly, his present quarters occupying five stores of the dimensions of 40 x 125 feet, and has the largest store of the kind in the state. He is a native of Vermont, and gives employment to fifteen experienced assistants. A very large stock is carried, comprising, in addition to furnaces and ventilators, a full selection of stoves, ranges and kitchen furnishing goods in general, registers, laundry stoves, oil stoves, parlor stoves, etc. Refrigerators are also extensively dealt in, and those supplied by Mr. Felton will be found economical of ice and very effective in operation if properly cared for. Tin, sheet iron, zinc and copper work will be done at short notice, and especial attention is given to furnace and range setting up and repairs in general. Smokey chimneys, or any unsatisfactory working of furnaces, ranges and stoves, or their connections, will be remedied and all charges will be found moderate and just. Mr. Felton is the manufacturer of the celebrated Felton Low Furnace, which is the lowest furnace made, only fifty inches in height, good pitch to hot air pipe and requires no digging pits in low cellars.

Artist and Photographer, 2332 Washington Street, Boston Highlands. Egleston Square or Forest Hills Horse Cars pass the door every seven minutes; no stairs to climb. Of the many Photographic establishments in this city, none have gained a higher reputation for more uniformly artistic and reliable work than that conducted by Mr. W. H. Partridge at No. 2332 Washington Street. Founded over ten years ago, it early established a high record for its productions. The premises occupied are of the dimensions of 25 x 50 feet, and are on the first floor, thus avoiding stairs to climb. As several courteous and capable assistants are employed, all orders are assured prompt and satisfactory attention. The various instruments and appliances in use are all of the latest and most improved design and construction, and together with the skill and experience possessed by the proprietor and his assistants sufficiently explain the large patronage enjoyed, and the high artistic merit of the portraits made. All styles of pictures are made, and while a good likeness is guaranteed, the re-touching, or finishing as it may be called, of the portrait is so skillfully done that the best points of the features are brought out and an artistic picture, and not a mere photo., is the result. The prices will be found very reasonable and delivery prompt. A specialty is made of Crayon, Ink, and Portraits at residences. Owing to the superior character of the work done by Mr. Partridge, his custom is not confined to the neighborhood, but he has patrons from all sections of the city, Dorchester, Jamaica Plain, Brookline, etc. There is every accommodation offered for those coming in carriages, and the Forest Hill and Egleston Square cars pass the Studio every seven minutes.

Centennial American Tea Co., 2187 Washington Street, Bacon's Building, Boston. That there is often a great difference between theory and practice all of us are aware, but it is seldom this truth receives a more complete demonstration than that afforded in the case of the Centennial American Tea Company, which has a Branch Store in charge of Mr. W. J. Mills, at No. 2187 Washington Street, Bacon's Building. For instance, the theory of many people is that no company or no man can sell choice Teas and Coffees at the lowest market rates and also give rich and useful presents to customers. This theory is supported by numerous arguments that are convincing in the extreme, and that would doubtless have converted everybody in the Highlands to the same way of thinking, were it not for the fact that hundreds of people have visited the store in question, have purchased Teas and Coffees, have found them to be of uniformly superior quality, have discovered that they are supplied at literally bottom prices, have been presented with really valuable gifts which in some cases would bring nearly as much at retail as the tea or coffee with which they were given, and so have been forced to believe in spite of all statements to the contrary, that the Centennial American Tea Company can and will do all, and even more than it promises. The store under notice was opened in 1877, and a very large patronage has long since been established. One floor and a basement are occupied, 20 x 70 feet in size, and three competent assistants employed. A very large and choice assortment of Teas, Coffees, etc., is always carried, and the most fastidious buyer can find brands here perfectly suited to his or her taste. The lowest market rates are quoted at all times, and even were no presents given, the customer would get full value for his money under all circumstances. The manager, Mr. Mills, has shown himself to be the right man in the right place, and may always be depended upon to use every means in his power to ensure satisfaction to all patrons.

Bouve, Crawford & Co., Manufacturers. Our shoes can only be obtained at our own Retail Stores. The "Crawford" shoe has only been on the market a short time, but during that time it has attained such great and even phenomenal popularity that it is already one of the best-known articles of the kind before the public. This popularity has been gained solely by legitimate methods, for no effort has been made to decry the productions of other manufactures, no abuse has been lavished upon competitors, but every energy devoted to making so perfect and desirable an article of foot-wear, that its merits would be discernible at once, and the most powerful arguments for its purchase furnished by the experience of its wearers. The "Crawford" shoe is elegant in design, strong and durable in construction, the easiest and most comfortable to be found anywhere and it is sold at $3.00 and $4.00, the latter price being put on a hand-sewed shoe that is seemingly incapable of further improvement. There is no use in denying these facts for they are self-evident, and that they have been accepted as such by the general public is shown by the truly remarkable way in which the business of the manufacturers of the "Crawford" shoe has developed, at the present writing, there are sixteen stores devoted entirely to the sale of these goods, eventually there can be no doubt (judging from past experience) but that this number will be increased to twenty or more. This gives an idea of the increasing demand for the "Crawford" shoe, which is not to be had excepting at the retail stores of Messrs. Bouve, Crawford & Co. Its sole manufacturers. Those who have hitherto considered it necessary to purchase a large and ungainly shoe to ensure comfort, should give this shoe a trial, and we venture to predict that the result will be more business for its manufacturers and better satisfaction for consumers, as each branch store carries a full assortment of sizes, the most difficult feet can be fitted and it should be remembered that every shoe is fully guaranteed to prove as represented. The model factory at Brockton, which is run at its full capacity for the exclusive make of the "Crawford" shoe, and the extensive supply store No. 611 Washington street, should be visited by all who are interested in new ways of doing business. All will say this firm deserves success.

George A. Bolster, Apothecary, corner of Warren and Dudley Streets. The corner of Warren and Dudley streets is a very conspicuous and convenient location for a drug store, and it is not surprising that its advantages were soon recognized and that it has been utilized for this purpose for the past thirteen years. The store is a very handsome and convenient one, and has been under the control of its present proprietor, Mr. Geo. A. Bolster, since 1880, during which time the patronage has materially increased. This growth has been aided very perceptibly by the liberal policy of the proprietor, for Mr. Bolster seeks to serve the public to the best of his ability, and begrudges neither time nor labor in accommodating his patrons. He carries a very complete assortment of the articles usually found in a first-class drug store and quotes very moderate prices in every department of his business. One floor and a basement, 25 x 60 feet in size, are occupied, and there is employment given to two competent and polite assistants. The compounding of physicians' prescriptions is given special and careful attention, and although there is no other branch of the pharmacist' business in which so long a time is required to establish a reputation as in this, Mr. Bolster has no reason to complain of the manner in which his prescription department is referred to, for it is clearly evident that the care and skill manifested therein have been noticed and appreciated by the public, and no stronger proof of this can be asked than the steady increase of orders of this kind. The drugs and medicines handled are selected with great care, and no pains are spared to ensure accuracy in their compounding, while the scale of prices is a very moderate one.

George H. Ash & Co., Manufacturers of fine grade Upright and Pedal Pianos; pedals applied to Piano-Fortes of any style; also repairing of every description of Pianos and Organs. Orders for tuning and regulating will receive prompt and careful attention. No. 42 Warren Street. The house of Messrs. Geo. H. Ash & Co., of 42 Warren street, carry on a business so successful that concerns of greater size might well envy them. They began operations at their present place about 1885, and have already built up an enormous trade, for the work

executed at the above-named place is done in such a perfect manner as to have gained the firm a high reputation. One floor 40 x 60 feet in dimensions is occupied, and competent workmen are employed. Upright and pedal pianos of the finest grade are manufactured here and repaired, every description of piano and organ pedal are applied to piano-fortes of any style. Orders for tuning will receive prompt attention, as Mr. Ash gives his business, in all branches, his personal supervision. Both a wholesale and retail business is carried on, and terms will be found to be very reasonable.

J. J. May, Provisions, Fruits and Vegetables, Butter, Eggs, etc., No. 30 Warren Street. In analyzing the popularity that the enterprise carried on by Mr. J. J. May, at No. 80 Warren street, unquestionably enjoys, we find that it does not seem to be due to any one thing, but rather to the impression made by the method of doing business when considered altogether. Mr. May does not claim to sell cheaper than every body else, although he does offer his goods at the lowest market rates. The variety of stock always on hand is such that all tastes can be suited. He strives to fully satisfy every customer, and gives a dollar's worth of value for every dollar received. Mr. May is a native of Boston and has carried on the undertaking with which he is now identified since 1887, and has many regular customers, as well as a large "transient trade," as it may be called. One floor and basement, 20 x 50 feet in dimensions, are occupied, and three assistants are employed. Meats and provisions, fruits and vegetables in their season, and butter, eggs, etc., are dealt in extensively. Orders are called for and goods delivered free of charge in any part of the city, while his prices are such that parties in buying goods at this place may be sure of getting as good a return for their money as may be had at any other like establishment in the city, with everything as pure and fresh as the market affords. Mr. May has built up a good trade by furnishing first-class goods at low prices, and when once a customer trades here a change is seldom desired.

C. R. Hatch, No. 465 Dudley Street, Boston Highlands, Dealer in American and Foreign Dry and Fancy goods. A business very prominent and successful, but of quite recent establishment, is that conducted by Mr. C. R. Hatch located at No. 465 Dudley Street, who carries a good and varied stock of Foreign and American Dry and Fancy goods, small wares, etc. As agent for the Universal Patterns he is well known, as the patterns have gained a reputation since their introduction into Boston some years ago. Being a native of Boston, Mr. Hatch is well informed as to the demands of the public, his experience in the business he carries on, has been large and varied, he endeavors to please his patrons' tastes, and is even willing to procure goods to order that he does not carry in stock. Low as are his prices his goods are of the best. The premises occupied are of the dimensions of 20 x 60 feet, two assistants are in attendance and courteous and prompt attention is guaranteed to all.

James P. Fallon, Furnishing Undertaker, Warerooms No. 145 Dudley Street, corner Warren, Boston Highlands. Hacks to let and Wreaths furnished, Plates Engrossed, etc.; night orders promptly attended to. Although good sense forbids there being too much stress put on the thought of death under ordinary circumstance still it is but the part of common prudence to be prepared to act with promptness and decision in any emergency and therefore we feel that the information we propose to supply regarding the establishment conducted by Mr. J. P. Fallon, corner of Dudley and Warren Sts., will be neither out of place nor neglected. Mr. Fallon is fully prepared to assume entire control of funerals and to supply everything required at equitable rates. All branches of the undertaking profession are carried on in a strictly first-class manner. The premises occupied are 18x25 feet in size and are appropriately fitted up for the purposes for which they are used, and every facility is at hand that is necessary to the undertaking. (See Illustration of building corner Dudley and Warren Sts.)

R. E. Boyd, Plumber and Gasfitter; Jobbing promptly attended to. Estimates cheerfully furnished; 10 Dudley Street, Boston Highlands. The dispute between the advocates of book learning as applied to plumbing and those of practical experience will probably never be satisfactorily settled, for of course there is a great deal to be said on either side, although a judicious mixture of both study and experience is undoubtedly the more desirable and sure way to master a trade, but if only one can be had, of course the practical experience is to be preferred, for as books are but the outcome of experience they can much better be dispensed with. A plumber who combines experience with careful study of the subject is Mr. R. E. Boyd, who has been engaged in the business since 1883, at 10 Dudley Street. He occupies premises 18x50 feet in dimensions and employs six skillful workmen. He is prepared to fill all orders for plumbing and repairing, and owing to his familiarity with both the old and new systems of plumbing, is especially well equipped to do all kinds of repairing. His prices will be found to be very reasonable and all work entrusted to him is assured only faithful performance.

A. D. Mowry & Co., Druggists, 329 and 365 Warren Street, Highlands, also at Grove Hall and 90 Blird St., Dorchester. We have rarely, if ever, witnessed so rapid a growth as the business now carried on by the present firm, has assumed since its establishment about ten years ago. Starting with but one store, the extensive trade now requires the occupancy of four separate establishments, each carrying a full and complete stock, and doing the leading drug business in the section in which each is located. This business has attained its present high standing in the mercantile community solely by dint of hard and persistent work, honorable business methods, and particularly by handling only strictly reliable articles. At 365 Warren Street is carried a full line of Mixed Paints, Oils, Varnishes, etc. The new store at 329 Warren St., which was finished in the spring of the present year, is, without exception, the handsomest and most complete one of its kind we have ever seen. The store is large and commodious, and is finished in cherry, the ceilings are elegantly frescoed, and the interior of the store presents a most attractive appearance. Large plate-glass windows afford ample day light, and at night, when illuminated, the brilliant effect is heightened. Near the prescription counter, and for the convenience of lady patrons there is an elegant reception room handsomely carpeted and furnished. This innovation is appreciated by the many ladies who visit the store. Messrs. A. D. Mowry & Co. make a specialty of physicians' prescriptions, which are carefully compounded, and orders are answered with care and dispatch. The stock of medicines are complete and warranted of the best quality. The extensive retail trade of this house requires the assistance of several competent clerks, and the utmost care and precaution is used to guard against mistakes. In conclusion, we would say that in dealing with this house, every advantage is offered, both as regards the quality of the goods and the prices, and the cause of their exceptional success is thus explained.

Francis Vallee, Carpenter and Builder, No. 1100 Harrison Avenue, corner of Dudley Street, Boston Highlands. Residence, 81 Dudley Street. Jobbing attended to. A concern which deserves special mention in any history of the industrial development of the Highlands, is that conducted by Mr. Francis Vallee at No. 1100 Harrison Avenue. This gentleman began operations at his present place in 1882, and soon gained a reputation for the excellence of his work, and the high standard of business honor which has ever been lived up to. Mr. Vallee is prepared to enter into contracts for building of any kind, carpentering work, and jobbing is given special attention. One floor 20 x 50 feet in dimensions is occupied, and employment is afforded to a number of skilled workmen. The terms will be found as reasonable as those charged by any other builder of first-class reputation. Orders can be left at 81 Dudley Street, if Mr. Vallee is not at his place of business, where it is almost impossible to be at all times, as his business is very extensive and calls him to all parts of the city.

A. A. Burnham, Jr., Druggist, 450 Dudley Street, Boston. A favorite and largely patronized drug store is that conducted by Mr. A. A. Burnham, jr., at 450 Dudley St. This establishment was opened in 1885. the present proprietor assuming control in 1887. He occupies one floor and basement 20x50 feet in dimensions. Mr. Burnham was born in Gloucester and has had practical experience in the compounding and dispensing of drugs and medicines, and as he constantly carries a full and fresh stock of all descriptions, he is especially well prepared to fill prescriptions promptly with most scrupulous care and the highest skill. An elegant stock of fancy goods and toilet requisites is also on hand, offered at prices which will prove satisfactory to all. A full assortment of all the popular and standard patent medicines is kept. All customers are assured of prompt service and honorable treatment. Also proprietor of Burnham's Spanish Lung Balsam, for the cure of Coughs, Colds, Hoarseness, Bronchitis and other troubles of the throat and lungs. Burnham's Cream Lotion, a most effectual remedy for Chapped Hands or Face, and Eruptions or Irritation of the Skin. For chapped hands it is unrivalled.

G. H. Pearson, Fine Groceries, Teas, Coffees and Flour, a specialty. No. 531 Dudley St. The extensive grocery establishment of Mr. G. H. Pearson located at No. 531 Dudley Street, was opened in 1883. The business has grown rapidly since it was opened in this section, Mr. Pearson having been located for the previous sixteen years at the South End, and the transactions of the house are indicative of a remarkable healthy growth. The space occupied is 25x80 feet in dimensions, and is fully equipped with all kinds of choice teas, coffees, sugar, butter, and canned goods of the best quality. Mr. Pearson is a native of Maine, but has resided for the past twenty-five years in Boston, and having carried on the same business at the South End for sixteen years, his experience in this particular line must necessarily be large. He has many friends, both in business and social circles. He is noted for being a careful buyer; all his stock being selected from the best in the market. Four competent assistants are employed. Orders are promptly filled and delivered, and courteous attention given to customers.

Mrs. W. Gaul, dealer in Fancy Dry Goods and Underwear and also Dressmaking to order, 37 Warren Street. There is perhaps no class of business which must depend more in the long run on the intrinsic excellence of the goods handled than that pertaining to the dry and fancy goods business. A concern in the Highlands which, although of recent establishment, has gained a high reputation, is that conducted by Mrs. Gaul at No. 37 Warren Street. All kinds of dry and fancy goods are dealt in, in great variety. Laces and ready-made children's dresses are constantly on hand and everything to be found in any similar establishment in Boston is to be had here. Mrs. Gaul also does a large dressmaking trade—all kinds of ladies' garments made to order at the shortest possible notice and at rates as low as are to be found elsewhere. One floor 20x50 feet in dimensions is occupied and two assistants are employed. Mrs. Gaul is a native of Boston and is well known and highly esteemed.

Wm. Bramhall, Plumber and Gas Fitter, Dealer in Stoves, Furnaces and Ranges, 10 and 12 Blue Hill Avenue, Near Dudley Street, Boston Highlands; Sole Agents for Richardson & Boynton Co.'s Celebrated Furnaces, a full and complete stock of repairs for the above Furnaces.

As improving the sanitary condition of the people, the occupation of the plumber, apart from the general usefulness of his work, becomes one of the most important industries of all cities and towns. Among those in Boston Highlands who are recognized as masters of their art is Mr. Wm. Bramhall, who holds a prominent place, and whose services are called into constant requisition on work of the most important character. This business was inaugurated by Mr. Bramhall in 1880. The proprietor of this establishment is a practical plumber and gas fitter, and his house is supplied with every facility for executing all work in his line in the most scientific and satisfactory manner. Mr. Bramhall occupies two floors of the building located at Nos. 10 and 12 Blue Hill avenue near Dudley Street, each 30 x 45 feet in size, where in connection with the Plumbing and Gas Fitting business he carries a very extensive assortment of Stoves, Ranges, Furnaces, etc. He is sole agent for Richardson and Boynton Furnaces, and carries a full and complete stock for repairs of the above furnaces. Ten competent workmen are employed, and satisfaction is guaranteed as to prices and quality of merchandise and workmanship. Mr. Bramhall is widely known, and his house is daily growing in favor and its patronage is steadily increasing.

E. Robinson & Co., Warren Market, 63 Warren street, also Oak Grove Farm Milk and Cream. No one at all experienced in housekeeping, needs to be told the advantages of doing business with a house that may be depended upon to furnish first-class supplies at all times, but to those who have not as yet had an extended experience in the housekeeping line, we would say, "be sure that those with whom you deal will furnish you with as reliable goods when you send for them as they do when you call and select them in person." It is owing in no small degree to the invariable policy pursued in this respect that the establishment conducted by E. Robinson & Co., successors to Geo. Witherell at No. 63 Warren street is so popular and its trade so extensive and increasing, for since operations were begun in 1870, no pains have been spared to convince the public that the interests of customers are carefully regarded at all times. Those who have had dealings with this firm have learned that they strive to satisfy every patron and that their stock is always sufficiently extensive to permit of all tastes being suited. One floor and a basement are occupied, of the dimensions of 30 x 60 feet, and choice meats, vegetables and fruits are always to be had here, while fish and oysters are also handled very extensively. Employment is afforded to five competent and courteous assistants, and one of the most popular features of the business is the promptitude with which customers are attended to and orders delivered.

William Barton, Watchmaker and Jeweler, No. 2182 Washington St., Boston Highlands. This gentleman carries on an establishment for the manufacture and sale of fine watches, repairing of the same is also given special attention. All styles of jewelry and optical goods are offered to the public at prices equal to those to be had at larger and more pretentious houses down town. One floor is devoted to the business, which is carried on in a strictly honorable manner. Mr. Barton is a native of Boston and has been in his present business since 1887, but had a previous experience of several years, consequently he has had ample opportunity for extensive experience, his terms are so reasonable for the work executed that he has gained a large patronage. Everything will be found as represented in this establishment.

E. E. Richards, Real Estate, Insurance and Paper Hangings, 75 Warren Street, corner Glenwood, Roxbury, down town office 266 Washington, corner Water Street. The Highlands have long been a favorite place of residence, but of late years they have come into more prominence than ever and the demand for houses, tenements, etc., has been more brisk than even the most sanguine property-holder could have believed possible a dozen years ago. People who desire first-class accommodations in a good neighborhood, but who do not wish an entire house to themselves, are especially pleased with the provision made for their welfare in this section of the city for in no other portion of it can such desirable tenements be obtained at such reasonable rates. Mr. E. E. Richards, of No. 75 Warren Street, corner of Glenwood, is particularly well able to offer exceptional advantages in this line, for he has given special attention to the needs of small families, having 700 tenants, and as about 10 per cent are changing, has at his disposal from 50 to 100 vacancies and the finest and largest list of apartments designed expressly for such uses, to be found in the city. Having tenants also in West Roxbury, Dorchester, Brookline, Cambridge, Somerville, Charlestown, Chelsea, East Boston, South Boston, and Winthrop. No one wishing handsomely and conveniently fitted rooms in a quiet and healthful location, should on any account miss seeing what he has to offer, for if they do the result is very apt to be disappointment. Mr. Richards controls other property of course but his specialty is as we have stated, apartment houses. He is also interested in the insurance business and can place insurance, in standard companies, being agent for the Imperial of London, United Firemen and the Reliance of Philadelphia, on the most favorable terms. A down-town office is maintained under the name of E. E. & H. N. Richards, at No. 266 Washington Street, corner of Water, and employment is given to five assistants. At his Warren Street store Mr. Richards displays a very tastefully selected stock of over 5,000 rolls of choice paper hangings, and callers will find all the most popular and late patterns represented. He is in a position to offer exceptional bargains in this line, and the magnitude of the business done shows that these inducements are taken full advantage of.

MORSE BROS.' NEW STORE,

Recently Erected at Grove Hall.

L. W. & H. F. Morse, Grocers, and dealers in kitchen furnishings, Nos. 1, 5 and 9 Walnut Avenue, Boston Highlands; also Morse Brothers, 479 Blue Hill Avenue. There is no section of this city that contains more first-class and enterprising grocery houses than that known as the "Highland District," and to say that a certain concern is a leader in this branch of trade in the section alluded to, is to give it very high praise indeed. Yet such can honestly be said of the firm of L. W. and H. F. Morse, doing business at Nos. 1, 5 and 9 Walnut Avenue, and we feel no doubt whatever but that all who have had dealings with this highly popular concern, will agree with us in the estimate we have expressed. This firm was formed in 1870 and its trade has steadily increased in magnitude, until now three connecting stores each supplied with a basement and each 22x60 feet in dimensions, are required to accommodate the heavy stock carried at 1, 5 and 9 Walnut Avenue, and meet the demands of patrons in that locality. Fine family and fancy groceries are very extensively handled, and kitchen furnishing goods are also given special attention and offered in great variety at bottom prices. There being employment given at this store to 5 assistants, customers can receive prompt attention and orders are delivered at short notice

A full line of all the goods which are usually found in a first-class grocery store are to be had here, and the assortment of table condiments, sauces, relishes, canned goods, etc., is especially full and complete and contains goods that cannot fail to suit the most fastidious. Many useful novelties in kitchen furnishings are shown, together with all the staple articles in this line and any housekeeper will find himself well repaid for a visit to this establishment. The proprietors constitute the firm of Morse Brothers, doing business at No. 479 Blue Hill Avenue, and are among our most enterprising and successful business men. Owing to their rapidly extending trade at Grove Hall and other sections of Dorchester, the old store at 470 Blue Hill Avenue was too small for their large business transacted. They therefore erected on the opposite side of the street 479 Blue Hill Avenue, the elegant brick building now occupied by them. This structure is 42x73 feet in size and is four stories above basement. The building is not only an ornament to the neighborhood but is one of the most completely stocked and finest arranged stores in the city devoted to the sale of choice groceries, kitchen furnishings, etc., and the select patronage they enjoy among the leading families in the neighborhood is extending from year to year.

S. W. Keene & Son, Real Estate and Fire Insurance, 800 Warren Street. Estates managed and rents collected at reasonable rates. Boston is sometimes called "slow" and "conservative" by many of her sister cities, and unfavorable comparisons are made of her growth as contrasted with that of certain other communities. It is true that many western cities have gained in population by leaps and bounds and attained a position in a few decades that it has taken Boston almost an equal number of centuries to reach, but it is questionable after all if such phenomenal progress is to be desired, for indications have not been wanting of late years that "slow but sure" is perhaps the most satisfactory and truly healthy mode of growth when everything is considered. Boston is growing steadily and at no mean rate of increase, and the continually improving demand for real estate in the Highlands, Dorchester, etc., is one of the surest signs that could be afforded of such a state of affairs. The question of rapid transit is receiving universal attention and is apparently nearing a practical solution. The air is filled with rumors of "cable" roads, "elevated" roads, etc., and it is certain that there is no time like the present for those who contemplate an investment in Highland real estate. A call at the office of Messrs. S. W. Keene & Son, doing business at No. 800 Warren Street, will demonstrate the fact that these gentlemen are well prepared to assist in the selection of desirable property for investment purposes and not only that, but also to render efficient aid in the choosing of dwelling houses and flats. The firm in question control some very desirable real estate, and the premises of which they have the disposal, are varied enough in location and in price to enable all tastes and purses to be suited. Messrs. S. W. Keene & Son make a specialty of the managing of estates and the collection of rents, and non-resident owners may safely put every confidence in their fidelity and discretion. Their rates are reasonable and their standing is unimpeachable. Fire insurance is placed in the most reliable companies by this firm, and they are in a position to offer inducements to customers equal to those attainable anywhere.

J. P. Lang, Bakery, 1950 Washington St. It is true that some people have a prejudice against public bakeries, but if all of these establishments are run on the same principles that have characterized the management of that carried on by Mr. J. P. Lang, of 1950 Washington Street, these prejudices could not possibly long continue, as they would not have the slightest foundation in fact. Mr. Lang began business at the above-named place in 1878 and has built up a trade that shows that honest, intelligent efforts to please, are sure to be appreciated. The success gained is by no means the result of luck or chance, but is the legitimate outcome of hard work, large experience and good management. The materials employed in the making of the bread, cakes, pastry, etc., that are offered to the public are not selected solely with an eye to their cheapness, but on the contrary are chosen with the purpose of producing a superior article that cannot fail to please. The result is that many who would otherwise depend upon home-made productions find it not only easier but also more agreeable to patronize this popular store. One floor 20x60 and basement are utilized and employment is afforded to three skilled and efficient assistants. Low prices prevail and all goods guaranteed satisfactory.

Mrs. E. S. Aiken, 171 Hampden Street Dry Goods and Small Wares. An enterprise that is conducted on strictly honorable and upright principles is that of which Mrs. E. S. Aiken is the proprietress. The premises occupied by this lady are located at No. 171 Hampden Street, and are of the dimensions of 20x50 feet, a full line of every mentionable article in the fancy goods line is kept, as is also a well selected variety of Dry Goods. Mrs. Aiken who was born in New York, became identified with her present enterprise in 1880, and her style of doing business was so well appreciated by the patrons who were attracted to her tasteful little establishment, that she soon built up an extensive and lasting trade. Three courteous and polite assistants are given employment and all callers may be assured good service, and everything will be found to be exactly as represented. Mrs. Aiken is also agent for the well known Troy Laundry. A very fine assortment of Gent's furnishings may be obtained here too at prices as reasonable as can be found in town.

N. O. Whitcomb & Co., Merchant Tailors, No. 2182 Washington Street. Those who prefer custom-made garments (and the proportion of such people is rapidly increasing) should bear in mind that perfection of style and fit is quite unattainable at the so-called "cheap" tailors for the simple reason that first-class cutters and skilful journeyman tailors are not so common as to be at the command of everybody, and that the best of work brings a premium in the tailoring business the same as in any other. On the other hand, there is no necessity for paying the exorbitant prices demanded at certain fashionable establishments for, as a call on Messrs. N. O. Whitcomb & Co. at No. 2182 Washington Street will demonstrate, the very highest grade of tailoring is to be had, while their very moderate business expenses enable them to quote prices much less than the more costly down town locations. The enterprise carried on by the firm mentioned, was started in 1848 by Mr. R. W. Molineux who in 1883 associated with him Mr. N. O. Whitcomb forming the firm of Molineux & Whitcomb, Mr. Molineux retiring in 1879. The present partnership being recently formed by the admission of Mr. J. P. Kees, late with L. P. Hollander & Co. Both partners are practical men and the establishment under their control has long been known as one of the few in the Highlands where strictly first-class garments were produced at all times and in every case. A fine stock of Imported and Domestic Woolens etc. is at hand to select from and a perfect fit and the most thorough making are positively guaranteed. The rates charged are very low for such clothing as is here produced, and when everything is taken into consideration, will bear comparison with those of any other establishment in the city.

11

Geo. R. Bakeman & Co., dealers in Furniture, Carpets and Ranges. Misfit Carpets and Remnants on hand, No. 2132 and 2136 Washington Street. The house-furnishing goods business has assumed great prominence in Boston of late years and anyone thinking of furnishing a house is much more apt to be puzzled by the number of firms that stand ready to supply him than he is by any other one thing. It is not our place of course to draw comparisons between rival firms in the same line of business and we have no intention of doing so, but yet there can be no objection to making mention of those popular favorites in the community and prominent among such is unquestionably that conducted by Geo. R. Bakeman & Co., at No. 2132 and 2136 Washington Street. Mr. Bakeman began operations in 1870 and has proceeded from the first to give full value for money expended in every case, being confident that such a course would be appreciated and duly rewarded as a consequence. His patronage is large and constantly increasing. Two stores in which are six floors 30x125 feet each are utilized, and furniture, ranges, bedding, oil cloth, carpets and all house-furnishing goods are carried in great variety. Mr. Bakeman is a native of this city, is a Free Mason and a well-informed man in his line of business. He realizes that in order to sell low he must buy low and give close personal attention to his business in every department.

Charles H. Sefton, House, Sign and Fresco Painter, Graining, Glazing and Gilding Hardwood Doors a Specialty, No. 2070 Washington Street, Boston. Orders by mail promptly attended to. A house that is prominent among those of similar description, is that carried on by Charles H. Sefton at No. 2070 Washington St. Mr. Sefton began business in 1881, and has an extensive and growing trade; he is well known; is a member of the Royal Arcanum, of the order of Redmen and order of Haptosaphs. The premises occupied by him are of the dimensions of 25x60 feet, and a force of seven men is employed, who are very skillful in their trade. House, sign and fresco painting is done, and he also makes a specialty of graining, glazing and gilding; all orders are given prompt attention and executed at the shortest notice. Mr. Sefton may be said to be an artist in his business, so beautifully is his work done, and at prices too that are very low.

Henry L. Hadcock, Apothecary, No. 2700 Washington Street, Corner of Dale, Boston Highlands. It is impossible to find a more truly popular apothecary store in the Highlands than that conducted by Mr. Henry L. Hadcock, at 2700 Washington, corner of Dale Street. This store was established upward of 30 years ago, and the present proprietor assumed control about 15 years ago. An extremely large and varied stock is carried and whether drugs, medicines, chemicals, toilet or fancy articles be wanted, Mr. Hadcock can supply the same to the satisfaction of all concerned. Physician's prescriptions are filled with the utmost care and as only fresh and unadulterated ingredients are employed, the full efficacy of the compound is preserved. Customers will be served with promptness and courtesy, and the lowest prices consistant with the nature of the commodities handled are always maintained. Mr. Hadcock employs an experienced assistant.

G. W. Chesley & Co., Dealers in Hay, Straw, Flour and Grain, 2078 Washington Street, Boston. Few people have any conception of the immense trade carried on in Hay, Straw Flour, Grain, etc., in this city, any more than they had of the important work done by horses in Boston, until the famous "epizootic" of 1872 came along, and by depriving us of the services of many of these useful animals showed us how indispensable they were to the proper transaction of business under existing circumstances. Messrs. G. W. Chesley & Co. of 2078 Washington Street, carry on an establishment which is very advantageously located, to be sure, but that is not the only reason of their doing a large business, for although location is doubtless of importance, still there are other things to be considered if great success is to be won in this line of trade. A large stock must be carried, and this stock must be sufficiently varied to meet all demands; and not only this, but the goods themselves must be uniform in quality and low in price. We believe that all of these conditions are fulfilled at the establishment to which we have reference, and indeed it is obvious that many inducements must be there obtainable, for although operations were not begun until 1881, an immense trade is now carried on, both at wholesale and retail, and this trade is constantly increasing. Mr. Chesley is a native of New Hampshire, and gives strict personal attention to the many details of the numerous orders received. They are General Agents for the Boston Prepared Food Co. A spiced food specially prepared for horses and cattle, of which it has no superior for all diseases of these animals. It not only is one of the greatest invigorators for the blood, but it is a sure preventive of Colds and Colic, and is on° of the best things to clear an animal of worms, which many horses' are subject to. Where the animal is off its feed, a small bag of the food fed three times a day with his ordinary feed will at once produce an appetite. Prices: 12½ lbs. bag, $1.00; 25 do., $1.90; 50 do., $3.50; 100 do., $6.50; in bbls, 200 lbs., $12.00. G. W. Chesley & Co General Agents.

William W. Morse, No. 3077 Washington Street, Choice Family Groceries, Fine Teas and Pure Coffees, Provisions, Fruits and Vegetables, Fresh Eggs a Specialty, also Coal and Wood, (Egleston Square). A gentleman who has had a large experience in the retail grocery and provision business and who commands trade, is Mr. Wm. W. Morse of No. 3077 Washington St., who opened his present establishment some time in 1876. One floor and a basement 20x80 feet in dimensions are occupied, and completely stocked with a varied assortment of the finest groceries, teas, coffees, etc. Fruits and vegetables are handled to a great extent in their seasons and are always to be found fresh and of the best quality. Meats of every description are largely dealt in and a specialty is made of fresh butter and eggs. Mr. Morse is a native of Roxbury, and a member of the Royal Arcanum and also the Legion of Honor. He gives employment to three competent assistants who are always on hand to afford attention to customers, everything will be found as represented and prices below comparison.

N. S. Cate, dealer in Stoves, Ranges, Crockery Ware, and a complete line of House Furnishing Goods, Stove and Range Linings and Grates a Specialty. Storage for Furniture. 1895 Washington St., Washington Market Building. The bewildering variety of goods in common use in a modern house is not appreciated except by the initiated, and when the average young man of small means but large ambition decides to "set up housekeeping" and starts out accompanied by his bride he is very apt to sigh for a return of primitive savagery when a haunch of venison and a good appetite were considered the chief indispensables in household economy, but for all that if one but knows where to go to purchase house-furnishing goods a supply may be easily obtained at a moderate outlay, and no better establishment in many respects can be visited than that of Mr. N. S. Cate, located at 1895 Washington Street. Here two floors of the dimensions of 40x60 feet and a good-sized basement is occupied, containing a vast and varied amount of crockery, woodenware and house-furnishing goods in general, stoves, ranges, and linings for the same are made a specialty of. During the 30 years that this enterprise has been established, an enormous trade has been built up. Mr. Cate is a native of this city and is universally known and highly respected. He keeps constantly employed two or more men who thoroughly understand the business, and orders for repairs may be left with the full assurance that they will be executed with alacrity. Furniture stored with safety. Everything is as represented and prices will be found reasonable.

Miss A. M. Kerr, Dry and Fancy Goods and Millinery, 3105 Washington Street. A business that has been carried on for more than twelve years successfully is certainly worthy of mention in a work of this kind. Miss A. M. Kerr of No. 3105 Washington Street, began her present enterprise in 1876 and has established an extensive trade in dry and fancy goods, and also millinery. Bonnets and hats made and trimmed to order at reasonable prices. One floor and a basement 25x55 feet in dimensions are occupied, which is well supplied with fancy goods of all descriptions—hosiery, laces, ribbons and small wares. Employment is given to two competent assistants, and the proprietress is always at hand to superintend the business. Orders are taken for Griffith's Steam Laundry and Barrett's Dye House which are given careful attention. A visit to this store will amply repay the time devoted to it.

McCabe & Strange, (Successors to Wm. F. Farrington), Plain and Decorative Painters, 1196 Harrison Avenue. The firm of McCabe & Strange, House and Sign Painters, is certainly very deserving of mention in our book, for they have gained a very high reputation for excellent work in the comparatively short time they have been established. They began business in 1886, at No. 1196 Harrison Avenue. They occupy premises there measuring 15x25 feet and give employment to four competent and reliable assistants. Contracts are made and work is executed in as short a time as by any other concern of a similar nature and in a great many cases much less time, as the firm can command a much larger force of workmen when necessary. Both members of the firm are well-known citizens, having a large circle of friends in Roxbury and vicinity. House painting, graining, tinting and wood-work finishing in all its branches is done, and also screen doors and window screens varnished and painted to appear like new. Sign painting and lettering are made a specialty. Prices will be found extremely reasonable.

S. S. Strout, Dealer in Choice Groceries, No. 3112 Washington Street, Egleston Square. The establishment carried on by Mr. S. S. Strout, at No. 3112 Washington Street, is first-class in every respect. The gentleman began operations in 1847, and his business has grown to such an extent since then, that no other evidence of his good business methods is necessary. Mr. Strout is a member of the Free Masons and belongs to the G. A. R. He was a member of the 30th Maine Co. E. and was wounded in the battle at Pleasant Hill, on the 9th of April 1864. He is very highly respected by all who know him. The premises occupied by this gentleman are 30 x 50 feet in dimensions, and are completely stocked with a choice line of groceries, tea, coffee, sugar and finest of flour largely dealt in, a large assortment of canned goods are carried, fancy groceries are also kept. A capable assistant is employed, who affords polite attention to all. Orders called for, filled and delivered promptly.

Mt. Pleasant Ice Cream and Confectionery Parlor, 484 Dudley Street. About as useful a bit of information as can be given a person is any relating to the whereabouts of an Ice Cream Parlor, for everybody is interested in learning where to obtain an appetizing dish of ice cream at a reasonable price, and therefore we are assured that this article will receive a careful reading. Since Messrs. Keith & Hastings opened their establishment in 1887 located at 484 Dudley St.—they have built-up a large and deserving trade—they have never given their patrons cause for the slightest complaint of the creams supplied, either as regards quantity or quality. The premises occupied comprise one floor and basement 20 x 45 feet in dimensions and are conveniently fitted up for the accommodation of customers. Confectionery of all kinds, Cigars and Tobacco of the finest grades are kept constantly in stock, also stationery and fancy goods. Orders for ice cream are filled at the shortest possible notice for entertainments or private use. Three attendants are always on hand and good service is guaranteed.

J. F. McDonald, Merchant Tailor, 18 Blue Hill Avenue, Boston Highlands. In spite of all the many wonderful inventions and discoveries of the age, no substitute has been found as yet for experience, and if one wants a thing done well he must entrust it to somebody who has had long practice in that particular kind of work. When a man has worked in a certain business for twelve years, he cannot have failed to gain a practical mastery of it during that time, and so may be depended upon to conduct it in the very best manner. Such an experience has been enjoyed by Mr. J. F. McDonald, merchant tailor, whose place of business is now located at No. 18 Blue Hill Avenue. He possesses a most thorough knowledge of the tailoring business in all its branches. He occupies one floor of the dimensions of 20 x 40 feet, and employes five assistants specially selected for their skill and experience. Those wishing anything in the tailoring line should not fail to give him a call, as his work is of the best quality and done at very reasonable rates. Fitting is an art that is acquired only by study and practice, and as Mr. McDonald has had exceptional opportunities for both, he is in a position to give perfect satisfaction. A fine line of the latest novelties in suitings is constantly carried, and all work is done at short notice and in the best manner, as an examination of any of his finished garments will show.

Cephas Drew, dealer in Fine Groceries, Teas, Coffees, Sugars, Flour, Butter, Cheese, etc., No. 43 Dearborn Street, Boston, Mass. A retail grocery establishment which is extremely well known and regarded with great favor by the citizens of this section of Boston is that carried on at No. 43 Dearborn Street by Mr. Cephas Drew, successor to G. F. James. The inauguration of this grocery establishment took place many years ago and has been under the enterprising management of Mr. Drew since March 1888. Mr. Drew is a native of Quincy and as might be expected from one of his ability and experience, "has the grocery trade at his fingers' ends" as one might say, for he understands it perfectly in all its branches. His store covers an area of 20x40 feet, and the trade is not only large but select, and an examination of the heavy stock he carries will show that it is made up largely of the finer grades of goods, although all classes are represented, and any demand in the grocery line can be supplied. Two assistants are in attendance and the most prompt and polite service is accorded to customers. Those wishing and appreciating a fine article in this line should certainly give Mr. Drew an early call.

Goff & Randall, dealers in Provisions, Fruits, Vegetables, Poultry, Etc., No. 47 Dearborn Street. One of the popular and largely patronized provision stores in this section of Boston, where so many excellent establishments of this kind exist, is that carried on at No 47 Dearborn Street, by Messrs Goff & Randall. These gentlemen began business here in 1886, and have so successfully managed it that today they are the proprietors of the above-named and well-known provision establishment. Their store is of the dimensions of 20x55 feet and is well supplied with facilities for carrying on a first-class business, ample assistance being at hand to assure customers prompt and courteous attention. A very fine stock of provisions of all kinds is carried; also fruit, vegetables, poultry, etc., and pains is taken to provide for all tastes and purses by furnishing goods of sufficient variety to satisfy every want. Orders will be promptly and accurately delivered, and are filled at the lowest market rates. Messrs. Goff & Randall are both members of the Odd Fellows and Grand Army, Mr. Goff having enlisted in the 12th Maine Regiment and Mr. Randall in the 10th Maine Regiment.

James Tizley, Practical Watchmaker, No. 9 Blue Hill Avenue; Watches, Jewelry and Optical Goods. Probably not a few of our readers are aware that it is one thing to buy a watch and another to keep it in running order, even the best-made watches cannot stand everything, and some of the shocks received in the course of business, or by some unavoidable accident, are enough to stop a thrashing machine almost, to say nothing about a watch. But if a good watch be bought originally, it can generally be repaired at a comparatively small expense if it be brought to the right place, and in this connection we would call attention to the establishment conducted by Mr. James Tizley located at No 9 Blue Hill Avenue. This gentleman is most admirably fitted both by ability and experience to undertake the watch-making and jewelry business in all its branches with a guarantee of satisfaction. The store utilized by Mr. Tizley covers an area of 18x20 feet and is stocked with a fine assortment of Watches, Jewelry and Optical goods and some very pronounced bargains are offered in these goods, which are worthy of examination. All orders are promptly attended to in a careful manner. Mr. Tizley established himself in business in 1880 and is altogether too well known and highly esteemed in this locality to render further personal mention necessary.

William F. Eells, Manufacturer and Dealer in Stoves, Ranges and Furnaces, Fine Hand-Made Tin, Copper and Sheet Iron Ware, 486 Dudley Street, Corner of Shirley Street, Mt. Pleasant. Tin Roofing, Furnace Repairing and Jobbing of all kinds promptly attended to. One of the business houses well known in Roxbury

is that of Mr. William F. Eells, manufacturer and dealer in stoves, ranges and furnaces, at 486 Dudley St., and although of recent establishment this house has built for itself a name that might be envied by older houses. Zinc, and home made copper and sheet iron ware, are dealt in to a great extent, while stoves, ranges and furnaces of the most improved and latest designs are handled, among which are the well known Winthrop Ranges and Fuller, Warren & Co.'s Top Return Fine Furnaces, the best made and most powerful heaters in the market. Repairing of these articles is also done, and roofing and jobbing are done at the shortest possible notice. The quality of all work executed guaranteed to be the best found. One floor 20 x 40 feet in dimensions is occupied and an assistant is always at hand, and all orders are assured prompt attention.

H. G. McGlauflin, Dealer in Meats and Provisions, Butter, Cheese, Eggs, Beans and Canned Goods. 923 Albany Street, Boston Highlands. Boston, like every other large city of this country, is constantly growing, both in importance and population, and one of the many effects of this growth is to be seen in the steadily increasing number of provision stores, to be found on our streets. People must eat, and the more people, the more stores, this is one of the prime rules of trade and it is one that is sure to go with and foster healthy competition. The establishment of which Mr. H. G. McGlauflin is the proprietor was only founded in 1887, but it has "come to stay" without a doubt, for the business done by him is already large and is rapidly growing. This gentleman is a native of Maine and carries on operations at No. 923 Albany Street. The premises in use are some 20 feet square and are pretty thoroughly occupied by a large and varied assortment of Meats and Provisions, comprising Butter, Cheese, Eggs, Beans and Canned Goods in great variety. Polite assistants employed, and the present policy of standard goods at bottom prices, gives them all the work they can easily handle.

A. W. Barton, Stationery, Cigars, Tobacco and Periodicals, 481 Dudley Street. The store occupied by Mr. A. W. Barton at No. 481 Dudley street, is tastefully and neatly arranged and devoted to the sale of stationery of the latest design, weekly, daily and monthly newspapers and periodicals, and a large stock of the choicest brands of cigars, both foreign and domestic is carried. Tobacco of all kinds and smokers' goods in general are to be had in great quantities. Goods are purchased direct of manufacturers and importers, and are therefore offered to the trade and the public on favorable terms. All goods sold here are marked at the very lowest rates that such goods can be retailed for. Mr. Barton is a native of this city and the business he has built up since he began operations, shows how his methods are appreciated.

John Oliver, Carpenter and Builder, Jobbing Promptly attended to, 1206 Harrison Avenue, near Warren Street. Prominent among the many others in business, stands Mr. John Oliver, of No. 1206 Harrison Avenue. This gentleman is a native of Boston and began business at 816 Shawmut Avenue in 1876, removing to his present quarters in 1887. He soon became known to those who were in search of one to perform work in his line, for the excellent manner in which everything that was undertaken was executed, and as a result he rapidly built up a very extensive trade. He now employs five skilled assistants and is prepared to undertake carpentry work of any kind. All those leaving orders at his office may feel assured that their work will be done in a first class manner. One floor is utilized, 20x40 feet in size. Mr. Oliver will be found to be as reasonable in his terms as is consistent with good work.

J. H. Aldrich, Boarding Stable, 24 Blue Hill Avenue, near Dudley Street. "A merciful man is merciful to his beast" says the proverb, and in no way can mercy be more plainly shown than by taking pains to see that the "beast" is properly fed and kindly treated. Horse owners cannot be too careful of the animals in their possession, for a horse that is properly fed and housed, will do more and better work than one that is not, to say nothing of the treatment that an intelligent and faithful an animal deserves at the hands of its master. Among the many boarding stables located in this portion of the city, we know not one that we can more heartily and unreservedly recommend than that conducted by Mr. J. H. Aldrich at No. 24 Blue Hill Avenue. These premises have been utilized for stable purposes since 1878, and have been under the present management since 1883. That he is thoroughly acquainted with the business, and is determined to run an establishment second to none, his record so far abundantly proves, and his promise that "the best of care and personal attention will be paid to boarders" and to all orders connected with the business has been faithfully lived up to. Mr. Aldrich is a native of Boston and is connected with the Odd Fellows and Knights of Pythias. The premises occupied comprise two floors, of the dimensions of 40 x 60 feet and employment is given to five assistants. A coupé is kept for Theatres, Calling, Shopping, etc.

F. B. Woodbury, No. 189 Centre Street, corner Old Heath St., Roxbury. This establishment was opened in 1872 by Frank Duard and on the death of that gentleman in February the present proprietor assumed control. The store has undergone a thorough renovation and everything is now arranged in the most attractive style, and the stock carried comprises a complete line of pure drugs and medicines, fancy and toilet articles, stationery, periodicals, cigars and confectionery. The best soda with pure syrup is sold at five cents per glass. Prescriptions are compounded with the greatest care and only the purest drugs and medicines are carried. Mr. Woodbury has enjoyed a long experience in prominent drug stores, and brings to the business a thorough knowledge of every department. The store is 20 x 30 feet in size and being at the junction of Pynchon, Old Heath and Centre Streets, is very conveniently located.

Ferguson & Co., dealers in Foreign and Domestic Dry Goods, Gent's Furnishing Goods a specialty, 1110 to 1114 Tremont St. One of the deservedly popular and representative establishments in this section of Boston is the well-known dry goods house conducted by Ferguson & Co., and located at Nos. 1110 to 1114 Tremont Street. This establishment was founded in 1874 by its present management, and during the fourteen years since elapsed, has been conducted with distinguished honor and success. A commodious and attractive store is utilized, consisting of two floors and basement each covering an area of 60x40 feet which is well stocked with a choice assortment of foreign and domestic dry goods, also a full and desirable line of gent's furnishing goods. These goods are in every respect equal to all they are claimed and guaranteed to be, and can be confidently depended upon. The prices are most reasonable and many fine bargains are kept constantly in stock. Ten competent and courteous clerks are employed in the various departments, and show every attention to those inspecting the fine and varied stock of the house. Mr. Ferguson is a native of St. John and merits the position he has so honorably won among the dry goods merchants in this section of Boston.

J. Pennie, Baker, No. 1007 Tremont Street. One of the best-known business enterprises in this section of the city is that conducted by Mr. J. Pennie. This time-honored establishment was founded twenty-five years ago, and has been under the control of its present proprietor since 1884. One floor and basement, each 20 x 50 feet in dimensions, are occupied, and an extensive retail trade is done, four assistants being required to handle the many orders received. The establishment, which is located at No. 1007 Tremont street, is completely stocked with a fine variety of fresh daily-made bread, cake and pastry of all kinds. Mr. Pennie is a native of Scotland, and an enterprising and progressive business man. The residents of this section will find this establishment a most satisfactory place at which to trade, for while the daily product is fresh and first-class, customers receive the most courteous attention, both from the proprietor and his efficient assistants.

Arthur F. Pepper, Photographer, work finished in Crayon, Ink and Water Colors, No. 1051 Tremont Street. Among the many complete and reliable photograph galleries in this part of Boston, is that conducted by Mr. Arthur F. Pepper, located at No. 1051 Tremont street. There he occupies a suit of three rooms, covering an area of 20 by 60 feet, and admirably fitted up and arranged for his business. Mr. Pepper established his business here in 1880, and has had a prosperous career. Photographic work of every description is executed by him, a specialty being made in crayon, ink and water colors. Mr. Pepper employs able and experienced assistants and does a very extensive photographic business in this section. His work will always be found of excellent character, for which most reasonable prices prevail. Being very anxious to please all patrons, none ever leave his studio without a feeling of satisfaction. Mr. Pepper, owing to his long experience, can guarantee a first-class likeness. He is highly esteemed by all who know him, and his list of business and social friends is very large. We commend his establishment to all wishing any work in his artistic line.

F. J. Herthel, Jr., Real Estate, 212 Ruggles Street. From the inception of the above house, it has been recognized as among the principal realty concerns in this section of the city, where could be found an extensive list of the most desirable city and suburban property, farms and land. Since January 1888, the proprietor of this enterprise Mr. F. J. Herthel, Jr., has been intimately connected with the business interests of this section of Boston, and he has in consequence made the venture a great success. His office is prominently located at No. 212 Ruggles Street, where he is pleased to meet and accommodate in any way those interested in the purchase, sale, or renting of property. In addition to his real estate business, he is prepared to loan money at lowest rates on approved securities in any amount, and he will be found a safe medium for transacting business of this nature. Mr. Herthel is a native of Roxbury, and a member of the Pilgrim Fathers association. He is well and favorably known throughout this section.

J. C. Lafreniere, dealer in Ranges, Stoves and Furnaces, 1362 Tremont Street. No better illustration of the perfection which has been attained in the manufacture of stoves and ranges can be found than by an inspection of the stock of Mr. J. C. Lafreniere whose establishment was founded in 1878, and which has ever since its inception been recognized as among the leading ones in the stove trade of this section of Boston. At his store which is located at No. 1362 Tremont St. may be found everything needed in the line of stoves, ranges and furnaces, together with a large and select stock of custom-made tinware, kitchen goods, etc., also oil stoves of all kinds. The premises utilized for this extensive retail trade comprise a store 20x60 feet in dimensions. Four assistants are required in the various departments of the business, and special attention is given to all kinds of job work and a large variety of stove linings and grates are always on hand. Mr. Lafreniere is closely identified with the material advancements of his line of business, devoting his entire time and attention to the furtherance of the interests of his customers. Prompt and reliable in all his dealings, the extensive business he has established has followed as a natural result. He will be found worthy of the extensive patronage he enjoys and therefore we commend his house to this community.

HEALTH AND COMFORT

CAN BE HAD BY USING

LAFRENIERE'S

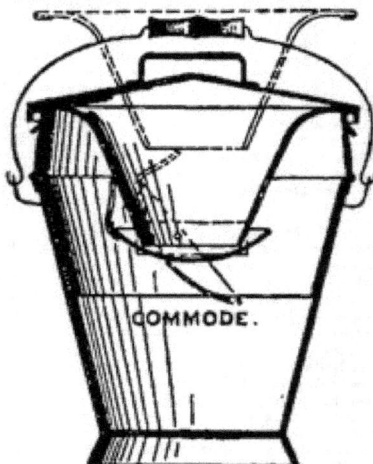

COMMODE.

Commode is perfectly odorless and indispensable to sick room, for it is a comfort to the sick and a help to the nurse, and by its use a great amount of labor is avoided in the sick room or where there are no sanitary improvements in the house. For sale only by J. C. Lafreniere, 1362 Tremont Street, Boston.

C. B. Faunce, Grocer, No. 204 Pynchon Street. Standing among the first-class houses in this line of trade, in this section of Boston, is the well-known store conducted by Mr. C. B. Faunce, situated at No. 204 Pynchon street, cor. New Heath. The premises occupied by him consist of a store and basement, each 25 x 60 feet in dimensions, with store house, stable and yard adjoining, and are entirely filled with a complete stock of goods in his line of trade, embracing everything in the grocery line, including the finest grades of Teas, Coffees, etc., also Flour, Grain, Hay and Feed. His prices are the very lowest to be obtained for first-class goods. Two assistants are employed, and the details of the business are ably managed. This well-known house was established by Mr. Faunce on Tremont street in 1804, removing here in 1883, and the store is among the most reliable in the Highland District. The business is conducted in a prompt and systematic style, and merits that liberal patronage which gives to it a commanding influence. Mr. Faunce is a native of Boston and a member of the Royal Arcanum, Knights of Honor and Good Fellows. He has made his house a favorite one for those who appreciate the advantages he offers in quality, quantity and prices, and we bespeak for him a continuance of the patronage he so well deserves.

Eugene Babo, Pharmacist, 1277 Tremont Street. The gentleman whose card we print above has not carried on his present establishment for a very long period of time, but he has has already succeeded in building up a promising business, although as our readers know there are many similar enterprises seeking the patronage of the public. Mr. Babo owes what success he has won, first, to his intimate knowledge of pharmacy, and second, to his evident devotion to the interests of his customers. The former gives him the ability to serve the public to the best advantage, and the latter shows that he is determined to do so. The stock on hand is a large and carefully selected one, and comprises drugs, medicines and chemicals of standard purity, together with full lines of fancy goods, toilet articles, etc. Those who are accustomed to think of "drug-store prices" as necessarily high, should call at this store and learn their mistake with their own eyes. Mr. Babo is a careful and discriminating buyer, and he gives his customers the benefit of whatever bargains he may make. An important and rapidly growing branch of his trade is the sale of various preparations bearing his name and designed expressly for the relief and cure of some of the more common physical indispositions. These preparations are compounded of carefully chosen ingredients, and will be found as efficient as they are cheap, harmless and agreeable. Physicians' prescriptions are prepared at short notice, and it should be stated that Mr. Babo gives careful personal attention to the filling of all such orders. He has every facility at hand that tends to lessen the possibility of mistake, and as he is fully aware of the responsibility devolving upon him, may be entirely depended upon to avoid the slightest error. Low prices rule and satisfaction is guaranteed.

J. B. Cassidy & Bro., Hack, Livery and Boarding Stable, No. 7 Station Street. Night calls promptly attended to. Picnic and Sleighing Parties accommodated. J. J. Franey, proprietor. Although the day of stages has passed away the demand for the livery business has only increased with advancing wealth and refinement, and the first-class livery stable is now as much as ever, and as it will continue to be, a practical necessity in every cultivated community. The livery business now conducted by Mr. John J. Franey was established by J. B. Cassidy & Brother (which firm name he still retains) in 1836, and has been under the sole management of Mr. Franey since 1878, and has continued uninterruptedly since then to meet all demands upon its service in the most prompt, courteous and satisfactory manner. The fine stable now occupied is a four-story structure, and is fitted up and stocked in the most modern and approved style. It contains thirty-five stalls and has ample accommodations for sixty carriages. Horses and carriages are constantly kept in readiness for driving, funerals, weddings, etc., and the most satisfactory and agreeable terms can be made at any time for any of the requirements of a first-class livery and boarding-stable. Our readers will also find the best opportunities here for the boarding and baiting of their horses. Six capable and experienced assistants are employed, and the advantages of this stable and the liberal and reliable methods of its able proprietor are too well known to the residents of this community to need any commendation. Mr. Franey is a member of the Foresters.

C. E. Chamberlain, dealer in Carpenters' Tools, Builders' Hardware, Paper Hangings, Paints, Oils, Varnishes, Window Glass, etc. etc., No. 1380 Tremont Street, (Roxbury Crossing). The well-known establishment of C. E. Chamberlain, located at No. 1380 Tremont street, which was founded twenty-four years ago, has attained to a position of prominence among the leading retail houses of Boston. The premises occupied for business purposes consist of a store 20 by 30 feet in dimensions, with a three-story building in the rear used as a store-house in which an immense stock is carried. The store is fitted up in a convenient manner, a new front having been recently built, and no facility is wanting for extending his trade. The magnitude and variety of the stock carried is at all times prepared for the demand upon it, and embraces a large assortment and variety of carpenters' tools, builders' hardware, paper hangings, of which he carries a very full line, paints, oils, varnishes of every description, window glass, etc. etc. Mr. Chamberlain makes it a point to carry only the most reliable goods, and such as he can confidently recommend to his customers. The assortments are full and choice, and very low prices are quoted. It is, without doubt, one of the leading hardware stores in this part of the city, and is conducted by Mr. Chamberlain on strict business principles. He established his business here in 1864. He is energetic and progressive, a gentleman of integrity and personal worth, and enjoys a large patronage throughout this community.

E. W. Wright, dealer in Boots and Shoes, 1386 Tremont Street, Railroad Crossing. There is nothing which contributes more directly to the metropolitan character of a city than the establishment of enterprising and reliable houses, thereby augmenting the facilities of supply and inducing trade to the given centre. Among the important accessions to this branch of trade (namely, boots, shoes and rubbers), is the house of E. W. Wright, which was established in 1875, and since his death has been conducted under its original name by Mrs. Wright. The premises occupied are located at No. 1386 Tremont street, and cover an area of 20 by 80 feet, and are stocked with every variety of the most desirable boots and shoes for men, women, boys, youths, misses and children, of all the various grades suited to the market. The facilities enjoyed by the house embrace the most desirable relations with manufacturers for supplying that class of goods they can with confidence commend to the trade. In conclusion, we would say that with experience in the business and possessing those essential qualities of progression which keep pace with the spirit of the times, the management presents to the public unsurpassed advantages.

James F. Curley, Fish and Oysters, 1211 Tremont Street. The Retail Fish and Oyster establishment of Mr. James F. Curley, is one of the popular sources of sea food supply in this section of Boston, and since the business was established eight years ago, it has been a most popular market for the retail trade in this section. This fish market was established in 1880 by the present proprietor, Mr. James F. Curley, at No. 1211 Tremont street. Mr. Curley occupies a store covering an area of 20x40 feet, and his facilities for supplying fish, oysters, clams, lobsters and sea food generally, of standard excellence at fair prices, are unsurpassed by any competitor in this section of the city. Orders delivered personally, by customers, or otherwise have prompt attention, and merchandise is delivered to all parts of the city. The most delicious goods are always obtainable here in season, warranted fresh. Mr. Curley is held in highest esteem for his probity and worth, and his success in catering to the people of the Highlands District is the logical sequence of his business ability and energy.

Kenneth Mackay, manufacturer of Fine Harness, 1394 Tremont Street (Crossing). In writing a commercial history of Boston and her present enterprises, we find some firms who have, by superior workmanship, steadily gained a

patronage and rank among the solid and well-tried houses of this city. One of these is the harness manufacturing establishment of Mr. Kenneth Mackay, located at 1394 Tremont st., and we are glad to call the attention of our readers to this honorable and reliable house. Mr. Mackay has in stock all kinds of the very best of fine harness. He employs only skilled workmen, and occupies premises covering an area of 20 x 45 feet. Mr. Mackay is a practical harness maker, and has been established at his present location since 1878, having enjoyed a previous experience of twenty-nine years. Being a manufacturer of his harness it enables him to place his goods upon the market at such wonderfully low prices that they cannot be easily duplicated. He has a large custom and retail trade among the citizens of this vicinity, which is yearly increasing, and a specialty is made in manufacturing gentlemen's driving harness, having made harness for several well-known horse owners. He is prompt in executing all orders, whether for repairing or manufacture, and we may say has established an enviable reputation.

Thomas J. Mitchell, Dealer in Groceries and Provisions, choice brands of Wines, Liquors and Cigars, 146 and 148 Ruggles, and 160 Cabot Street, Boston Highlands. Largely engaged in this line of trade, we would mention Mr. Thos. J. Mitchell, who for the past sixteen years has been recognized as a prominent and successful dealer in groceries and provisions in this section of the city. This business was established in 1872 by Mr. Mitchell, and from its inception gave promise of vitality which the succeeding years have only rendered more apparent, and at the present time is classed among the first-class retail houses in this line of trade in this locality. The premises occupied by him for trade purposes are located at Nos. 146 and 148 Ruggles and 160 Cabot streets. The stock carried is very complete and embraces a full line of choice family and fancy groceries; also a desirable assortment of provisions, which enables the proprietor to suit the large variety of tastes catered to. Aside from the above-mentioned lines of merchandise the stock embraces choice liquors. All these are offered to consumers at guaranteed lowest prices, and are warranted to be genuine and of the best quality. Four assistants are required in the orderly management of the business, which is exclusively retail in character. Mr. Mitchell is a native of Boston, and is widely known and esteemed throughout the community.

E. D. Conklin, Boarding and Livery Stable, Hacks, Barges and Boat-Sleighs to let, 50 Lynchon Street, Boston Highlands, (telephone connection). One of the important livery establishments of this part of Boston is that conducted by Mr. E. D. Conklin, and located at No. 50 Lynchon street. The business established by this enterprising gentleman in 1882, has rapidly grown in public favor. The needs of the business demand the services of eleven experienced employees. The stable comprises a three-story structure, covering an area of 40 by 60 feet, with ample accommodation for the care of eighty horses and seventy carriages, and an air of neatness pervades the entire establishment. Mr. Conklin has on hand, at all times, a large variety of teams for livery purposes, including single and double teams, hacks, barges and boat-sleighs. These will be furnished for all occasions on short notice and at most reasonable terms. Mr. Conklin spares no pains in his efforts to please the public. The stables have a good location and the genial and obliging proprietor deserves the continued success which is assured to him. Mr. Conklin is a native of Boston, and a member of the Grand Army, having enlisted in the 45th Massachusetts Regiment, Co. B., and was in the engagements at Kingston Bridge and Newbern, and many others during our late rebellion.

M. Kerr, Dealer in Dry and Fancy Goods, Cloaks, etc.; Agent for Household Sewing Machines; Machine Supplies on hand; also Agent for the Original Barrett's Dye House and Domestic Patterns; Millinery in all its branches; No. 1247 Tremont Street, Boston, Mass. One of the most enterprising business houses in this part of the city, and one in whose history and business methods are brilliantly set forth the sure results of energetic, honorable and persevering work, is the well-known business represented and conducted by Mr. M. Kerr of this city. This house was established over fifteen years ago, and has been under the sole control of Mr. Kerr since 1886, who has since carried it forward with great ability and merited success. The store occupied is 20 x 60 feet in dimensions, with a basement of the same size, located at No. 1247 Tremont Street. The trade of this house has assumed large proportions, being undoubtedly one of the largest in its line in this vicinity. The stock of the house includes Fine Dry and Fancy Goods, Cloaks, Sacks and Jerseys of the most reliable quality, also a large line of Furs; and in addition to the above-mentioned goods, Mr. Kerr is agent for the Domestic Pattern Co.; and the original Barrett's Dye House. Mr. Kerr also deals in the Household Sewing Machines. Needles, Belts, Oils and Machine Supplies are constantly on hand. Machines are bought, sold and rented by the month. Machines are cleaned and repaired at short notice. One department of this house is devoted to the Millinery line of trade in all its branches, a specialty being made of Mourning orders at short notice. Eight competent assistants are constantly employed to meet the growing demand of the retail trade. Mr. Kerr ranks among our energetic and enterprising business men.

Walter Mott, M.D., Free Dispensary, No. 1250 Tremont Street, hours: 9 to 12 a.m.; 7 to 9 p.m.; and 75 Chester Square, hours: 1 to 3 p.m. A great convenience to the residents of upper Tremont Street, is the Free Dispensary of Dr. Mott. This gentleman graduated in 1870 at Long Island College Hospital at Brooklyn. Removing to Boston in 1878, he opened his present office in June 1887. The idea of the present enterprise is to furnish free advice to all classes, particularly those who are unable to pay for such, and charge only the regular prices for the medicines furnished to patients. The advantage of this plan will be readily seen as they obtain equal service as at the hospitals, and patients find this a much more convenient place. The doctor is at his office at 1250 Tremont St., from 9 to 12 and 4 to 6 and 7 to 9 daily, and no charge whatever is made for advice, unless he is called upon to visit a patient at his residence. In addition to his large practice at his dispensary, he has another office at 75 Chester Square, where he makes a specialty of Diseases of the Rectum, and his patients visit him from distant portions of the United States as well as a large city practice.

Essex Market, E. R. Lowe, dealer in all kinds of Beef, Pork, Lamb, Mutton, Veal, Poultry, Fruit and Vegetables, No. 1337 Tremont St., cor. Station. Among the prosperous retail houses of Boston Highlands, whose extensive operations entitle them to our consideration, we note with pleasure the one above named, the character and extent of whose business furnishes a fitting example of that class of houses whose success is the best evidence we can offer for the consideration of the purchasing public. This enterprise which is among the most complete meat markets in this part of Boston, was founded in 1835 by Mr. C. R. Lowe, its present proprietor. This establishment is popularly known as the Essex Market, and located at No. 1337 Tremont street, corner of Station, and comprises one floor and basement, each 20 by 45 feet in dimensions, which are well stocked with a choice variety of beef, pork, lamb, mutton; veal, poultry, fruit and vegetables. The extensive retail trade requires the services of three capable assistants, and all orders received are promptly filled and delivered. Mr. Lowe is well known in social as well as business circles of the community, and is a member of the Odd Fellows.

H. Bradford, Grocer, 1191 Tremont Street. The age and importance of the grocery trade entitles it to a leading position among the most influential industries of the world, and its representatives in this city and vicinity are not surpassed for reliable dealings or business enterprise by any of their *confreres.* Prominent among the grocers of this section of Boston, Mr. H. Bradford is recognized as an honorable and progressive merchant. The establishment now conducted by him was founded thirteen years ago, and has been under the sole management and control of Mr. Bradford since 1887, and he has met with continuous and deserved success. The premises utilized for this grocery business are located at No. 1191 Tremont street,

and consist of one floor and basement, each covering an area of 20 by 50 feet. The stock of choice staple and fancy family groceries carried is first-class and reliable in every respect, and rated at prices considerably below the average. Mr. Bradford employs only courteous and competent assistants, and commands a fine retail trade in this part of Boston. He has won the respect and regard of his fellow-citizens for the striking and honorable qualities of mind and character, which, in his case, have been the fitting fore-runners of success.

J. B. Walker, Stationery, Fancy Goods, Valentines, Birthday Cards, Toys and Periodicals, 1302 Tremont Street, (crossing of Providence Railroad). This establishment, which ranks among the leading business houses in this part of the city, is one of the most popular dealing in stationery, fancy goods and books. Mr. J. B. Walker, the present proprietor, established the business in 1873, and to his superior skill and able management and untiring industry, is due, in a great measure, the progress and success which has been attained during its career. A large and varied stock is carried, including stationery, books and periodicals of all kinds, fancy goods, valentines and birthday cards of every description; also a large variety of toys. Mr. Walker possesses every facility known to the trade for giving his patrons and friends extra inducements, both in low prices and excellent quality of goods sold. The store occupied covers an area of 20 by 50 feet. It is eligibly located at No. 1302 Tremont street, and is filled with as large and reliable a stock as can be found in any similar establishment. Mr. Walker is a native of Boston, enterprising and energetic, and his business standing and general reputation, as well as the liberal manner in which the business is conducted, is a subject of the most favorable comment,

---

J. A. Anderson, Dry and Fancy Goods, 1305 Tremont Street. Among the many well-known Dry and Fancy Goods houses in the section of Boston known as the Highland District, is the one conducted by J. A. Anderson who is located at No. 1305 Tremont Street. From its foundation in 1865, it took a leading position among similar establishments. The premises utilized by Mr. Anderson comprise one floor and a basement each covering an area of 29 x 55 feet, which are conveniently fitted up for the tasteful display of the large stock handled, which embraces a fine line of Dry and Fancy Goods. A number of experienced assistants are constantly employed, and in addition to the line of goods already mentioned Mr. Anderson carries a fine assortment of Berlin Knitting Yarn, for which he is the General Agent. He is also agent for the Universal Fashion Patterns, and it is with pleasure we commend his goods and establishment to the favorable attention of all our readers who have not patronized him. Here they can obtain fresh goods, and patterns of the latest designs and newest fashions at fair and reasonable prices. Mr. Anderson is thoroughly experienced in all the details of his business and well deserving of the success he has achieved.

Hannon Bros., Dealers in Groceries and Provisions, 24, 26 & 28 Heath Street. If there was anybody that mistrusted the ability of Hannon Brothers to make a success of the enterprise they established at Nos. 24, 26 and 28 Heath street in 1885, they must have long since changed their opinion, for, as a matter of fact, these gentlemen have scored a genuine "hit" and do a business that is large now and is growing larger every month. Two stores are occupied, and groceries and provisions of all kinds are dealt in very extensively. The firm is made up of Messrs. M. A. and D. P. Hannon, both of whom are energetic business men and thoroughly acquainted with the many details of the business they conduct. From the very beginning of operations but one course has been followed—furnishing the best possible goods at the lowest possible prices, and the result of this method of management is to be seen in the preference which those who have done business here show for dealing with this firm. Orders are filled without delay, and a sufficient number of assistants are employed to make it possible to serve customers with politeness and dispatch. The stock carried is a very heavy and varied one, and comprises about everything that is usually sold at a first-class grocery and provision store. Teas, coffees and flour are offered at bottom rates, and meats of all kinds are also handled very largely and supplied in quantities to suit, at prices within the reach of all.

Frank Schwartz, Upholsterer and Furniture Repairer, 17 Blue Hill Avenue, Roxbury, and 406 Washington Street, Dorchester. The demand for the requisites for making our homes attractive, has of late years steadily increased, and the skill and taste of manufacturers of articles entering into the adornment of dwellings has been taxed to supply the essentials called for by the cultivated tastes and refinement of to-day. In no particular of house decoration, has such marked improvement been manifest as in that relating to upholstery, and the artistic styles evolved by those who cater to the people in this regard, have added manifold attractions to "the palaces of the rich and the cottages of the poor." Prominent among the establishments devoted to this line of trade is that conducted by Mr. Frank Schwartz, upholsterer, located at No. 17 Blue Hill Avenue, Roxbury, and 406 Washington St., Dorchester. Mr. Schwartz began business here in 1884, and during the four years since elapsed, has conducted it with such energy and tact as to develop the extensive trade now enjoyed in this locality. Mr. Schwartz's facilities for supplying the latest and best goods, and executing all orders in the most satisfactory manner are all that could be desired. Hair Mattresses made over and to order; carpets taken up, beating, cleaning, sewing, fitting, planning and put down; all kinds of furniture repaired and made to order; window shades, curtains and draperies cleansed, fixed and made to order; work done at residence if desired, at reasonable prices; good work guaranteed; a postal card will receive prompt attention. Mr. Schwartz is a native of Germany, and enjoys the esteem and confidence of the residents of this community to a marked degree.

F. L. Hazelton & Co., 57 Chadwick Street, and 20 Yeoman Street. It is agreed by physicians, and also by others who have made the matter a study, that the moderate use of cooling beverages is one of the best aids towards retaining perfect health during Summer's heats, and the first point to be observed is, that these drinks are light in quality and pure in composition. Without the least desire to disparage the productions of other makers, it must be acknowledged that those bottled by Messrs. F. L. Hazelton & Co., are very hard to equal, either as regards the purity of the materials entering into them or the delicacy and desirability of the flavoring, and that the public in general sustains us in this opinion is shown by the large and steadily growing demand for the goods bearing the name of the firm mentioned. Business was begun in 1876 and has now reached such proportions that thirty men are required to supply its demands. The premises utilized are located at Nos. 57 Chadwick Street, and 20 Yeoman Streets, and comprise three floors of the dimensions of 50x100 feet together with a storehouse of considerable capacity. Messrs. F. L. Hazelton & Co., bottle Summer Drinks of every description including Tonic beer, Mineral Waters, Lager beer, Porter, Ale, Cider, etc., and have reason to be proud of the reputation their productions have in the market for uniform superiority of excellence. They do an exclusively wholesale business, which is by no means confined to this city but extends for some miles around it, and despite the fact that unusual pains are taken in the manufacture of their goods, their prices will bear comparison with those of any firm engaged in a similar line of business. Dealers should place their orders with this house as they will supply a product that will sell.

Krug & Beck, Manufacturers of Bologna Sausages, &c.; also Dealers in Beef, Pork, Lard, Hams, Vegetables, &c., 23 Station, cor. Mendora Street. There are few articles of food that are more universal favorites than sausages, and, indeed, it would be hard to find anything in the eating line that contains more nutriment in the same space, is easier to prepare for the table, or is more truly economical to use. It is to our German fellow citizens that we owe the general introduction of sausages, and the manufacture of them is almost entirely in the hands of men of this nationality. Among the most successful sausage manufacturers in Roxbury are Krug & Beck, doing business on Station street, and the way in which these gentlemen's trade has grown since it was started in 1885 is as unusual as it is marked. Both partners were born in Germany, and make a specialty of the manufacture of Bologna and Frankfort sausages, doing both a wholesale and a retail business, and occupying one floor and a basement of the dimensions of 22 x 50 feet. They are both men of skill and experience in their line of trade, and produce articles that are equal to the best and are made of selected material carefully seasoned and warranted all right in every respect. They employ three competent assistants, and their prices are as low as can be quoted on really first-class articles.

Day & Gould, Boots and Shoes, 1303 Tremont Street. Among the best-known houses engaged in the sale of boots, shoes and rubbers in this section of the city, is that of Day & Gould, located at No. 1303 Tremont street. This business was established in 1872, succeeded by the present firm in 1883, and during the sixteen years which have elapsed since starting the store has been carried on in a highly satisfactory manner, to both Mr. Day and his numerous customers. The store is 25 by 70 feet in dimensions, and is finely stocked with a full assortment of ladies' and gentlemen's boots, shoes and rubbers, and the prices will be found as reasonable as any in the city. The extensive retail trade of this house requires the employment of four salesmen, who will be found attentive and polite, and everything possible will be done to give entire satisfaction to all their patrons. Mr. Day has had thirty years' experience in this business, and they both deserve great credit for the manner in which the business is conducted, and we would earnestly recommend this as an enterprise worthy of patronage. The trade is large and rapidly extending.

Fallon Bros., Plumbers, and dealers in plumbing Materials; Jobbing promptly and personally attended to; No. 1246 Tremont Street. Among the many successful houses engaged in the above-named trade in this section of Boston, is that of Fallon Bros. which was established in 1882, and has been conducted by them in a most commendable manner. This establishment is located at No. 1246 Tremont St, and covers an area of 20x50 feet, and is fitted up with every facility for the systematic prosecution of the work engaged in, which embraces everything in the plumbing business. In every branch of the business Messrs. Fallon Bros. are prepared to compete with any of their contemporaries, and they may be implicitly depended upon to perform all contracts with promptness and satisfaction. The general stock is complete, extensive and valuable, and embraces all materials requisite for the plumbing business. The extensive jobbing and contract work transacted by this firm, requires the services of six thoroughly capable and skilled assistants. Jobbing promptly and personally attended to, and all orders by mail executed promptly and satisfactorily. Messrs. Fallon Bros. are life-long residents of Boston and have established a reputation, which admits of no cavil, while the interest they take in all matters tending to the advancement and material prosperity of their trade, entitles them to the wide-spread esteem they enjoy in this community.

Newell Paine, Apothecary, 1181 Tremont Street. The profession of the apothecary is one which demands a wide knowledge of medical and Pharmaceutical science, which only comes as the result of long years of study and practice, and also a rare executive ability in the administration of the delicate and highly important duties which are intrusted to him. In our day and city there are few who adorn this position and fulfil its duties with the highest ability and success, and none have proved themselves more worthy of this distinction than Mr. Newell Paine, one of our first-class druggists. He has been settled in business here since 1872, with a previous experience of fourteen years, and has won extended recognition among our citizens of the Highland district, as being eminently fitted to fulfil all duties devolving on him. The premises occupied by him are located at No. 1181 Tremont Street, and comprise one floor and a basement each 20 x 40 feet in dimensions, where is carried a large and complete stock of pure drugs and medicines of every description, and his counters are also adorned with many beautiful and tasty fancy articles. Every department is managed on the strictest principles of honor and fidelity, and great care is taken in the putting up of prescriptions for the thoroughness and absence from all mistakes, in which department the house bears an honorable reputation. Mr. Paine is one of our most respected and reliable citizens.

E. D. Woods, Grocer, 1265 Tremont Street. The special attention of our many readers is directed to the well-known house of E. D. Woods, located at 1265 Tremont street, retail dealer in choice staple and fancy family groceries. There are probably few articles so hard to obtain unadulterated as groceries, and only by the greatest care in purchasing, either by the consumer or retailer, can the quality be assured. This enterprising house was established in 1877 by its present proprietor. In consequence of the unrivaled superiority of his goods his trade has rapidly increased, necessitating the employment of two capable and reliable assistants. The premises utilized comprise a store and basement, each 20 by 60 feet in dimensions, and a large retail trade is done. The stock embraces a fine selection of staple and fancy groceries, a specialty being made of flour. Mr. Woods is a member of the Odd Fellows, Knights of Honor, Legion of Honor and Pilgrim Fathers. The equitable manner in which his business is conducted, as well as the excellent quality of goods handled, are guarantees sufficiently obvious why consumers would do well to place their orders with this progressive and representative house.

J. Woodward, Locksmith and Dealer in Hardware and Wall Paper, No. 1278 Tremont Street. The business of the locksmith and hardware dealer, above almost all others, increases in importance as the country grows older and more thickly settled, but the degree of perfection which is attained, is due to the energy of individuals, who have been for many years connected with the business. Such a one is that conducted by Mr. J. Woodward, which was established in 1867, and during the twenty-one years since elapsed, he has succeeded by his ability and practical knowledge of the business, in building up a large retail trade, as locksmith and dealer in hardware and paper hangings. This establishment is located at No. 1278 Tremont street, and comprises one floor and a basement each 20 x 40 feet in dimensions. The fine stock comprises everything under the head of hardware, also glass and a large assortment of paper hangings. Mr. Woodward makes a specialty of the locksmith business in all its

branches, and keys are made and fitted for all
kinds of locks; saws filed, etc. Two thoroughly
competent assistants are employed, who understand the business in all its details. Mr. Woodward is a native of Boston, an enterprising business man, studying the wants of his trade, and
by handling a reliable quality of goods at fair
prices, has built up his present prosperous business.

Taylor & Carey, Dealers in Stoves, Furnaces, Furniture, Tinware and Kitchen Goods,
Crockery and Glass, No. 1267 Tremont Street.
To obtain as much heat as possible from the
fuel consumed, has long been the aim of those
scientists and inventors, who have turned their
attention to the designing of stoves, furnaces,
etc., and the progress made in this direction
during the last score of years is simply wonderful. So pronounced is it that in more than one
instance with coal at present prices, a man
would save money by throwing away the old-
fashioned stove, or furnace he now has, and procuring one fitted with the latest fuel-saving devices, and not only has great progress been made
from an economical stand-point, but also from
an artistic one, as the stove of the present day
has been changed from an ugly black cylinder,
to what may justly be entitled, "a thing of
beauty." To inspect and secure the latest improvements in these goods visit an establishment which makes a point of handling the
latest novelties as well as dealing in articles of
standard celebrity, and as good an example of
this kind of a house as can be found is that
lately established and conducted by Messrs.
Taylor & Carey, whose finely arranged and attractive store is located at No. 1267 Tremont
street. These gentlemen are thoroughly conversant with all the details of the business, both
having been engaged in this line of trade
for many years. Mr. Taylor was formerly of
the firm of Taylor Brothers of Charlestown,
and Mr. Carey has been for several years connected with the Magee Furnace Co. The stock
carried embraces all the latest and most improved styles and inventions in stoves, furnaces, etc.; also a complete and fine assortment
of furniture, tinware and kitchen goods, glass-
ware and crockery. Their present patronage

shows that the public appreciate liberal and
enterprising business methods, and an examination of their stock and prices will give sufficient explanation as to the reason of their exceptional success, already attained. All callers
will be courteously served and given all desired
information in regard to anything in their line.
Everything handled by this firm is fresh and
first-class in every respect, and all articles are
warranted to prove as represented.

A. Nicholson, Meat Market, 1189 Tremont
Street. The provision trade of Boston is yearly
assuming greater proportions, and she can
boast of many large and enterprising firms in
this line as any city in the state. Among them
and one which has exhibited marked ability in
this direction is that of Mr. A. Nicholson. This
market was established by Mr. Nicholson in
1888, and although of such very recent inception has succeeded in gaining an extensive retail trade, and the services of two capable assistants are required. The market is eligibly
located at No. 1189 Tremont street. It is 20 by
40 feet in size, and is well stocked with a choice
assortment of meats of all kinds. This market
is very neat and attractive, and goods are arranged in the most inviting manner. Mr. Nicholson enjoys a fine retail trade among the best
citizens in this part of the city. This is due, in
part, to the superiority of the goods carried and
in part to the prompt filling and delivery of all
orders, as well as the courteous treatment given
to patrons. Mr. Nicholson is a native of Prince
Edwards Island, an honorable and enterprising
business manager, and it is with pleasure that
we commend this establishment to all who read
this notice.

John J. Curley, Florist, dealer in Plants,
Bouquets, Cut-Flowers and Floral Designs, No.
1336 Tremont Street, opposite Station Street.
Nearly every locality of any magnitude affords
some enterprising concern prepared to conduct
the florist's business on a large scale, and in a
manner that will insure customers fresh flowers
and first-class plants, in large variety, and at
reasonable prices, and when we consider the
large number of these used for decorations,
weddings, funerals, etc., we can form some idea
of the vast quantities that must be cultivated to
supply the great demand for them. The florist
business was established in this section of the
city by Messrs. Butler & Curley in 1887, and
after a career of a few months Mr. Curley, the
present proprietor, assumed full control, and
since then has built a reputation for dealing in
a fine variety of flowers. His retail store is located at No. 1336 Tremont street, where an elegant and varied assortment of cut-flowers and
plants may be obtained. All orders are promptly filled in a reliable manner. Mr. Curley's energy and tact have met with a well-merited
success, and we bot reflect the public sentiment
when we testify to the high esteem in which he
is held for honorable character and fair and
liberal dealings.

C. T. Mooar, Retail Dealer in Boots, Shoes and Rubbers, No. 1307 Tremont Street. As the boot and shoe trade of Boston forms a significant element in the make-up of the city's enterprises, in referring to the above house it may be stated that the special line to which its best energies are confined, is the handling of medium and first-class lines of boots, shoes and rubbers. This house was originally established under the firm name of Mooar Brothers and continued until 1834, when Mr. C. T. Mooar the present proprietor assumed full control of the business, since which date this gentleman has so successfully managed his retail trade that today his house ranks among the best in this section of the city engaged in the shoe trade. Premises located at No. 1307 Tremont Street, and covering an area of 25 x 60 feet are utilized, and the assistance of four experienced clerks is required in addition to the close personal supervision of the proprietor. Mr. Mooar is a native of Massachusetts, and conducts a similar store in Worcester, Mass., and in conclusion we will remark that while we do not wish to indulge in laudation of any house in particular, it shall be within our province to state that if one would have his interests highly advanced, the acquaintance of this house should be made.

B. F. Ansart, dealer in Choice Family Groceries, Fine Teas, Coffees and Spices, Wines, Spirits and Bottled Ales, etc., 6 Pynchon St., opposite Railroad Crossing. The importance of an enterprise of this character in a large city like Boston Highlands, is too apparent to need comment. We have here a business devoted to the family grocery trade an industry of great importance to the thrift of the city, and serving an important purpose in the community. The house of Mr. B. F. Ansart, grocer, was established by its present proprietors in 1876. Since his decease in 1885, the house has been conducted by Mrs. Ansart. She occupies a neatly arranged and well-stocked store located at No. 6 Pynchon Street, covering an area of 20x55 feet, where she is prepared to offer to the citizens of the Highland District, on advantageous terms, a superior quality of staple and fancy family groceries, including the best brands of flour, teas, coffees and spices, and in connection with the above-mentioned goods, Mrs. Ansart deals largely in wines, spirits, bottled ales, etc. The trade of this house is steadily increasing requiring the services of three very capable assistants, and its resources are ample to meet all demands made upon it, while its policy entitles it to the consideration of the purchasing public, who will find assured advantages in dealing here.

John C. Kelly, Plumber, Plumbing and Sanitary Work, No. 1376 Tremont Street. No account of Boston's industries would be complete without containing at least some mention of the enterprise conducted by Mr. John C. Kelly at No. 1376 Tremont street, which must rank with any of its contemporaries in this section of the city. This house was founded about fifteen years ago by Mr. Kelly, whose business has been successfully managed during the years since its inception, and whose reputation has been so well established as to place it among the representative houses in that line of business. Mr. Kelly is an experienced and practical Plumber, all work being neatly and promptly executed by the skilled workmen of whom fourteen are employed. He does an extensive business in all branches of Plumbing and Sanitary Work, and his prices will be found as reasonable as any in the city. It requires premises 18x45 feet in dimensions to handle the varied stock carried. A large local retail trade is done, which is annually increasing. Mr. Kelly is a native of Roxbury and resides at No. 6 Haud square. He is a practical man, capable of pleasing the public in this line of business, and the success which has been attained by him is as well earned as it is richly merited.

F. O. Lowe, Dealer in Chicago Dressed Beef, Fowl and Game at all seasons. No. 1365 Tremont Street. The public has been for some time familiar with Chicago Dressed Beef, and that its verdict has been distinctly favorable is proved by the many houses established for the sale of it throughout the country, and one of the popular agencies located in this city, is that conducted by Mr. F. O. Lowe, and located at No. 1365 Tremont Street. These premises have been utilized as a market for the past twenty years, and have been conducted by Mr. Lowe since 1870. They cover an area of 35 x 70 feet, and are stocked with a choice assortment of Chicago dressed beef, and meats of all kinds, also fowl and game at all seasons. Seven thoroughly capable and experienced assistants are constantly employed and orders are taken and delivered free of charge. Mr. Lowe is a native of Boston and a prominent member of the Free Masons. So high a reputation does this house bear, that a guarantee from it is universally considered as final and conclusive, and this trust has not been established in a day, but is the legitimate result of long years of business integrity.

A. W. Bradford, Dealer in Groceries and Provisions, Flour, Teas, Coffees, Butter, Cheese, Lard, Eggs, etc., Choice Meats, Fruits and Vegetables, 2672 Washington Street, Boston Highlands. A concern that has for its proprietor a gentleman who has enjoyed an active business experience of many years duration may reasonably be expected to offer goods at as low rates, and be able to extend as satisfactory services to the public as any similar firm in the city, and indeed in the case of Mr. Bradford, the gentleman to whom we have reference, we are sure that such expectations will be realized. This concern carries on business at No. 2672 Washington street, the store occupies a space of 20 x 40 feet. Mr. Bradford began operations in 1878, and has built up a large and successful trade, his store is well stocked with flour, teas, coffees, butter, cheese, lard, eggs, etc.; a fine line of choice fruit and vegetables is to be found here in their seasons; beef, mutton, veal and pork, both fresh and salted, are carried and sold at prices that will bear comparison. Four assistants are employed, who will be found competent and attentive, goods delivered promptly and free of expense.

F. L. Whitcomb, Registered Pharmacist, No. 117 Hampden Street, Boston Highlands. The drug trade of this country can surely invite comparison, both as regards the character and ability of those engaged in it, and its importance to the community at large, with any other branch of commerce. Whatever its nature may be, there are many reliable and successful houses engaged in it in this city, but none are more highly regarded than is that of Mr. F. L. Whitcomb, doing business at 117 Hampden St., though of comparatively recent establishment. Mr. Whitcomb has gained for himself an enviable reputation for perseverance and honorable business methods. The perfect familiarity of this gentleman with both the theory and practice of his chosen business, has had much to do with the great confidence placed in this house by the general public. One floor 20 x 40 feet in size is occupied, and employment is afforded to experienced assistants. The variety, freshness and purity of the stock carried, enables Mr. Whitcomb to fill all orders with precision and at the lowest rates, as a dispenser of standard pharmaceutical preparations, a business is done that is second to few and is constantly and rapidly increasing.

W. H. Waitt & Co., Plumbers, No. 18 Zeigler Street, between Washington and Warren Streets. Jobbing promptly attended to. W. H. Waitt, Residence 20 Bartlett Street, Boston Highlands. We doubt if there is any firm better known in the vicinity in which it is located than is the house of W. H. Waitt & Co., who have carried on their business at No. 18 Zeigler Street, since 1833, they gained at the outset a very extensive reputation for doing good work at reasonable prices, and have as a consequence built up a large and growing trade. Mr. Waitt is a native of Boston, and has had a large experience in his particular line of business, he is capable of doing all kinds of plumbing work in a very superior manner. Contracts for plumbing houses and buildings of all kinds are entered into, and as good if not better terms can be made with this house as with any other in the Highlands. Jobbing and repairing are made a specialty, and all orders for the same will receive prompt attention, a force of eight men are constantly on hand, so no delay is necessary. One floor 20 x 55 feet in size is occupied, where orders are received for all kinds of work in their line, within business hours.

Thomas F. Dolan, Manufacturer of Fine Coach, Chaise, Express, Buggy and Double Harness. Repairing neatly and promptly done. Harness Oiled and Blacked; 83 Hampden St., Boston Highlands. No man who really appreciates a horse can bear to see one trying to work with improper harness on, and no person who is not familiar with horses has the least idea of what a difference it makes, whether their harness are well designed and well made or not. Mr. W. F. Dolan, of 83 Hampton Street, is a harness manufacturer of wide experience and has given the business very careful study. When making a harness to order, he strives to make it suit the peculiarities of the animal for which it is intended and hence that horse is often able to do better than ever before after being supplied with a harness of Mr. Dolan's manufacture. It was in 1882 this gentleman opened his present store, and has already attained a high degree of success. Two floors 20x25 feet in size are occupied, and harness, whips, horse blankets, combs and horse clothing of all descriptions are very extensively handled. Experienced men are employed and the lowest market rates are quoted.

Chase Refrigerating Co., Manufacturers of Cold-Blast Refrigerators. In the general advance made in scientific knowledge during the past score of years, there has been a much clearer understanding gained of the true principles of heating and of refrigerating artificially; for strange as it may seem at first, it is nevertheless a fact that the same general laws govern both operations. We have not space for a detailed explanation of the difference between the old and the new systems of supplying artificial heat or cold, but briefly stated, it may be said that while the old idea was to apply heat or ice to a confined apartment in which there was little if any circulation of air, the improved method is to provide a constant current or "blast" of hot or cold air which finds an outlet after doing its work, and thus makes room for a fresh supply — furnishing ventilation as well as heat or cold. The celebrated "cold-blast" refrigerators made under the Chase patents supply the most perfect application of this principal with which we are acquainted, and as a consequence they are truly unrivaled for efficiency and economy of operation. Mr. Chase's inventions were formerly manufactured and put upon the market by the Cold-Blast Refrigerator Company of this city, but in 1885 this Company was succeeded by the present firm, Childs, Chase & Co. The factory is located in the Highlands, on Washington Street, and is well adapted to the uses to which it is put, being of brick, substantially fitted up. The Chase Refrigerators are built in all sizes, and are therefore suitable for the use of Private Families, Markets, Hotels, Dining Saloons, Dairies, Steamboats, Cold-storage Warehouses, Railroad Cars, etc. Over three thousand railroad cars are now equipped with these refrigerators, and utilized for the transportation of meats from the West to the East, and many trans-Atlantic steamers are also supplied with facilities for preserving fresh meat and vegetables for an indefinite period. The firm makes a specialty of the manufacture and sale of the Chase Drying Process Apparatus, and also manufacture the Chase system of Tramways, which in connection with the Cole Patent Switch affords the most economical and labor-saving method of handling dressed meats, no floor space being taken up and the mechanism being simple and positive in its action. Mr. Chase is a native of Augusta, Me., and is probably one of the best known business men in the city. A large and increasing demand exists for his productions, and they are supplied at very reasonable rates.

H. J. Seiler, Caterer and Confectioner, No. 140 Dudley and No. 2150 Washington Streets. The success of an occasion in which a collation bears a prominent part, is so dependent upon the quality of the refreshments furnished and the character of the service provided, that too much care cannot be exercised in the selection of the caterer who is to supply these things. There are many excellent caterers in this city and it is far from being our purpose to exalt one at the expense of all the rest, but it is the general opinion among those best qualified to judge, that Mr. H. J. Seiler is the leader in this line of business in the Highlands, and certainly the years of experience he has had, should give him an intimate knowledge of what the public wants and how to supply those wants in the most satisfactory manner. His store is located at No. 140 Dudley street, and orders by mail or by telephone will receive equally prompt attention to those given in person. The establishment is very thoroughly equipped, and the most elaborate banquets can be supplied at short notice, trained waiters and in fact everything required on such occasions being provided at reasonable rates. Mr. Seiler makes a specialty of out of town catering, and in no department of his business have his efforts been more successful. The ice cream, sherbets, etc., manufactured by him, have an unsurpassed reputation for uniformity and delicacy of flavor, and are delivered at the residences of customers in quantities to suit. Confectionery of all kinds is also largely handled, and those wishing a pure article in this line, will find that sold at this store is all that could be desired. A year or more ago Mr. Seiler opened a branch establishment at No. 2150 Washington street, where a specialty is made of bread, cake, pastry and confectionery. This venture has proved a decided success, and the liberal patronage accorded it, shows conclusively that the public appreciate the efforts made to furnish articles of superior quality at popular prices.

W. Ballantyne, Carpenter and Builder, No. 108 Dudley Street. The business of the wood-worker or carpenter is divided and subdivided into many departments, and the trade is one calling for special aptitude and experience with tools. Mr. W. Ballantyne, of No. 108 Dudley street, is one who has a high reputation for prompt and thorough work in this line, and the size of his trade shows that faithful effort is by no means unappreciated. Although Mr. Ballantyne only opened at his present place in 1884, his success has been of steady growth. Mr. Ballantyne is a native of Scotland and is prepared to give estimates on all kinds of buildings to be erected in this or any other vicinity. His experience is very extensive and varied, so he will be found equal to the task he has undertaken. Employment is given to upward of fifty men, who are all first-class workmen, and one floor, 20 x 50 feet, and a large yard are used in carrying on the business. The very best of work is done, and the prices are made as reasonable as possible.

James N. W. Emmons, Boots, Shoes and Rubbers, No. 2212 Washington Street, Opposite Ruggles Street. The oldest shoe store in the Highlands if not in Boston, is that now conducted by Mr. James N. W. Emmons at No. 2212 Washington Street. It was first opened as a shoe store by a Mr. Childs about seventy-five years ago. Mr. Emmons succeeded John B. Currier in 1878 and has since built up a large and rapidly increasing trade. In addition to a full line of boots, shoes and rubbers, Mr. Emmons makes a specialty of calf button, congress or lace to order for $4.00, also a workingmen's shoe at $2.50; the latter are made of kip and are intended for laboring work. When shoes are made to order at such prices as those quoted by Mr. James N. W. Emmons, it is a question if they are not really more economical to buy than nine-tenths of the ready-made goods in the market. They are certainly surprising bargains, and those who have taken advantage of the opportunity to secure a perfect-fitting boot or shoe at a nominal price, are loud in their expressions of satisfaction at the treatment received and the high character of the work done. Mr. Emmons started his present enterprise in 1878, two stores being occupied at Nos. 2212 and 2214 Washington street, of the dimensions of 22 x 60 feet each. Employment is given to competent assistants and no pains is spared to fill orders without delay and in a perfectly satisfactory manner. A fine and varied stock of boots, shoes and rubbers is constantly carried, and low prices are the rule in every department, a fine retail business being done and mail orders given prompt and careful attention.

J. H. Riley, Rugby Clothier, 2168 Washington Street, Roxbury. Few if any of the business enterprises now carried on in this section, were watched with more interest and attention during their inception than that conducted by Mr. J. H. Riley, at No. 2168 Washington Street, for Mr. Riley, who is a native of Boston, is one of the best known of our Highland business men, and previously occupied a position in which he added largely to his list of friends and well-wishers by the uniformly courteous and obliging manner in which he discharged his duties. "Riley's Rugby" was regarded as a bold experiment by many people who, while they recognized the ability of the proprietor, still considered that the clothing trade of the vicinity was sufficiently provided for. Mr. Riley thought differently. He fitted up his establishment, which is 25 x 60 feet in dimensions, without regard to expense, illuminated it by both gas and electricity, stocked it with one of the most varied and desirable assortments of Men's, Youth's and Boys' Clothing and Furnishing Goods ever got together in the city, put his prices down to the lowest possible figure and awaited results. He had not long to wait. Customers came. Some were attracted by friendship, some by curiosity, some by seeing the goods displayed in the magnificent and tastefully arranged show windows; but at all events the store was crowded. People saw that no goods were misrepresented in the slightest degree; they saw that courteous attention was given to all, and that genuine bargains were to be found on every side. There could be but one result. A large trade was at once established and this trade has since steadily and rapidly increased, and cannot help continuing to do so as long as the present methods are adhered to. Mr. Riley is a careful and expert buyer and the articles he offers are always fashionable and desirable, to say nothing of the low prices he places on them. This is a representative establishment and fully deserves the liberal support accorded it.

A. W. Newman, Carriage Maker, Eustis Street, Boston Highlands. The enterprise conducted by Mr. A. W. Newman on Eustis Street is of exceptional interest in more respects than one, and not the least remarkable thing concerning it, is the fact that it was inaugurated as far back as the year 1824, the present proprietors having been here for almost 61 years. Since the gentleman who now carries it on assumed control the old reputation of the establishment has been fully maintained and in fact no similar shop in this city has more reason to be proud of its record as regards faithfulness and diligence in filling of orders. The premises occupied measure 40x60 feet and carriage and wagon manufacturing and repairing is extensively carried on, employment being given to three assistants. Notwithstanding the fact that this is one of the most unpretentious establishments of the kind in Roxbury, and that Mr. Newman is not given to calling attention to the superiority of his work, it still remains true that many people have all their carriage and wagon work done here and consider that no other shop offers such solid advantages. One thing is sure at least, and that is that when repairing or anything of the kind is done here, it is done to stay and in fact one of the main reasons of the popu-

larity enjoyed by this house, is the durability of the work it turns out. Mr. Newman is a native of Roxbury and is extremely well-known in the vicinity. His charges are always moderate and orders are attended to at short notice.

Martin's Improved, Double Flanged, Gas Tight Furnace, four sizes, Manufactured and For Sale by J. M. Martin, 2225 Washington St., Boston Highlands. One of the most economical and efficient heating appliances that has ever

been put on the market, is that manufactured and sold by Mr. J. M. Martin, known as the "Martin Improved, Double-flanged, Gas-tight Furnace. This is a very powerful heater, is constructed in the most durable and skillful manner, is extremely economical of fuel, and being made in four sizes can be furnished in just the right capacity for the work required of it. Our space forbids a detailed description, but Mr. Martin will be happy to give any additional information that may be desired, and will put the furnace in under a guarantee that it will do what it is promised to. The gentleman alluded to is a native of New Hampshire, and a member of the Free Masons. His place of business is at No. 2225 Washington Street, and he is an extensive dealer in Stoves, Ranges, etc., occupying one floor of the dimensions of 25 x 60 feet, and affording employment to three assistants. Tinsmithing and Plumbing are carried on to a considerable degree, and all kinds of sheet iron work will be made to order at short notice. Especial attention is given to the repairing of stoves and furnaces, and no one should allow an article of this kind to remain out of order, as aside from the danger of such a course the saving of fuel will generally soon make up for any expense that may be incurred. Mr. Martin has been engaged in the carrying on of his present enterprise since 1882, and has gained a reputation for fair dealing and moderate prices of which he may well be proud.

Eliot Square Hack, Boarding and Livery Stable, opp. Norfolk House, J. Austin Rogers, Proprietor. One of the most hopeful signs of the future that can be seen at the present day, is that afforded by the increased attention given to recreation by those who need it the most—business men and their wives. The American people are just about discovering that "all work and no joy makes Jack a dull boy" both mentally and physically, and that no real gain is made by devoting every available moment to "business" and none whatever to recreation. Among recreations most truly worthy of the name, that of driving must ever hold a foremost position, for even a tired man can enjoy a ride behind a good horse, and find relief from pressing anxiety in the swift motion and constant changes of scene. But very few of those living or doing business in the city, find it convenient to keep a horse of their own, but that need not deter anybody from enjoying the benefits of driving, at least not so long as such an establishment as that conducted by Mr. J. Austin Rogers in Eliot Square is in operation. This enterprise was begun about a quarter of a century ago and is one of the best known as it one of the most meritorious in the city. The stable contains about sixty stalls and is fitted up in a manner that ensures the health and comfort of the horses kept within its walls. Employment is given to 11 competent assistants, and a large Livery, Boarding and Hacking business is done. Mr. Rogers is moderate in his prices although first-class in his accommodations, and is prepared to furnish carriages for Weddings, Funerals, Parties, the Theatre, etc., at short notice and in any quantity.

Dudley Market, James F. Wise, Beef, Mutton, Poultry, Game, and Dairy Products, 7 Dudley Street, Boston Highlands. Americans consume immense quantities of meat as compared with those of other nationalities, but probably the reason for this is found in the fact that although we may not be fonder of flesh food than other people we certainly are better able, generally speaking, to buy it. The advocates of a vegetable diet may say what they please regarding the alleged advantage of that kind of food, but as long as our country maintains its present leading position among nations, we may be well content to rely on that which has served us so well in the past, not only to live on, but also to work on, and even to fight on, and no better place can be found to replenish our exhausted forces than that of Mr. James F. Wise, located at 7 Dudley Street. His stock consists of the choicest of Beef, Mutton, Lamb, Game, in its season, and all the products of the dairy, particular attention being given to choice Butter. A full line is carried of Foreign and Domestic Preserves and Condiments, etc. The premises occupied by Mr. Wise are one floor and basement, 30 x 60 feet in dimensions. He affords employment to three assistants. "Dudley Market," which is the first market in Norfolk County, was established in 1826, and continued by Mr. Wise since 1884, when he assumed control. He is a native of Boston and has hosts of friends and patrons. Orders have his personal supervision, and every article is guaranteed as represented.

W. A. Bonney, Grocer, Eliot Square. Ten years is not considered a very long time in which to build up a business, under ordinary circumstances, and indeed it is by no means always that so large a trade can be obtained during that period as has been accorded to the establishment conducted by Mr. W. A. Bonney, in Eliot Square. This gentleman began operations in 1878, and his store soon became popular with the general public, for it was at once evident that the goods furnished were of the best, and all could see that the prices were as low as the lowest. The premises occupied are 25 x 60 feet in size, and comprise one floor and a basement. The stock on hand is not only extensive but also choice in quality, for Mr. Bonney puts his prices at such figures as to ensure early sales, and consequently is in a position to constantly renew his assortment and to avoid having to carry a "dead" supply of unsalable goods. When every department is so well supplied as is the case with the establishment under mention, it is difficult to call attention to any special feature, but we think that unusual efforts are made by Mr. Bonney in the handling of Tea, etc., and at all events this portion of his stock is worthy of careful inspection. Flour, Sugar, and other staples are of course given due attention, and pure Creamery Butter is also to be had here at all seasons, at the lowest market rates. Callers are shown prompt and polite attention, and orders are delivered without delay.

Tower's Pharmacy, Eliot Square, Boston Highlands. To say that the pharmacy conducted by Mr. Walter S. Tower in Eliot Square is worthy of the utmost confidence, may seem a superfluous statement to those who are already conversant with that gentleman's methods, but as not a few of our readers, even among those residing in the Highlands, have not had an opportunity to learn the relative merits of our more prominent druggists, we feel that such information as we can give will prove acceptable, especially as we propose to confine our statements within such bounds that their truth can be easily demonstrated. The establishment alluded to was opened in 1817 by Henry White and has been under Mr. Tower's control since 1873. The dimensions of the premises occupied are 20x35 feet, and the stock carried is of itself such as to give Mr. Tower the ability to fill all orders without delay, for it is very complete in every department and is made up of Pure Drugs, Chemicals and Medicines, carefully selected and obtained from the most reputable manufacturers and wholesalers. Fancy and Toilet articles are dealt in to some extent, but not enough to cause the more important branches of the business to be neglected, for the proprietor recognizes the fact that the true province of a dispensing chemist is to render the best possible service in the filling of physicians' prescriptions, etc., and indeed we know of no other pharmacy where such orders are given more conscientious and painstaking attention. No means are neglected to ensure both absolute accuracy and reasonable speed in the compounding of prescriptions, and as the best materials are used and no exorbitant rates charged, it is but natural that a large business should be done.

Highland Drug Store, 2224 and 2226 Washington Street, Boston Highlands. This portion of the city is particularly favored in the matter of Drug Stores, and it is probable that so large a number of generally excellent establishments of this kind, cannot be found in any other section of no greater extent or population. This being the case, of course it is evident that a very high degree of merit is essential to the gaining of especial distinction in this line of business hereabouts, and it is just because the "Highland Drug Store" possesses this merit that its popularity is so great and its patronage so extensive. It is located at Nos. 2224 and 2226 Washington Street, and is one of the oldest established business enterprises in town, having been inaugurated in 1834. The present proprietor, Mr. N. Adams, who has been here for ten years, and succeeded Geo. B. Codwell who had been here fifty years, is a native of Massachusetts, and has done much to build up the reputation and the trade of the undertaking to which we have reference. This has been accomplished by carrying a full stock of every thing usually found in a first-class Drug Store, by giving prompt, careful, and polite attention to all, by trying to accommodate the public as completely as possible, and finally by selling goods at reasonable prices at all times and under all circumstances. One floor and a basement, of the dimensions of 35 x 55 feet, are occupied and employment is given to three competent and affable assistants. No pains has been spared to provide everything essential to the quick, accurate and satisfactory filling of physicians' prescriptions, and the assortment of Drugs, Chemicals, etc., is so complete that every necessary ingredient is sure to be at hand. Very low prices are quoted in this department and it is but natural that a very large business should be done.

Thomas Wild, House Painter, Grainer, Glazier, Whitener and Colorer, 28 Eustis Street. Next in importance to keeping a house well-painted, comes the question of who shall be employed to do the work, and on the answer given, depends in a great measure the frequency with which the problem must be solved. Of course the weather and a number of other things have a more or less important influence on the durability of a painted surface, but for all that much depends upon the stock used and the men who use it, and it is without doubt the truest economy to place such orders with houses that may be trusted to execute them thoroughly as well as promptly. Such a record is held by Mr. Thomas Wild who does business at No. 28 Eustis Street, and as he began operations in 1876, his record may be deemed firmly and correctly established. One floor is occupied, of the dimensions of 20 x 50 feet, and employment is given to eight efficient assistants. House Painting, Graining and Glazing are some of the branches of industry carried on, and Whitening and Coloring are also done in first-class style and without injury to furniture or carpets. Mr. Wild uses reliable stock and employs careful help, and as he puts his prices as low as is consistent with satisfactory results, it is by no means to be wondered at that his business is a large one and is steadily growing.

Joseph S. Waterman & Sons, Funeral Undertakers and Embalmers, 2302 Washington Street. By general consent, the undertaking establishment conducted by Messrs. Joseph S. Waterman & Sons, is given the leading position among similar enterprises carried on in this section of the city, and this concession is only what is rightfully due to an establishment of such long standing and unblemished reputation. Operations were begun in 1859, and the present co-partnership was formed a few years ago, the existing firm being made up of Messrs. Joseph S., George H., and Frank S. Waterman, all of whom are natives of this city. The premises occupied at No. 2302 Washington Street, are conveniently and appropriately fitted up, and there is always carried therein a full supply of Caskets, Coffins and everything needed at Funerals, this house being one of the very few in the city, that manufacture the Caskets supplied by them. Embalming, and every necessary operation connected with the burial of the dead is given prompt and skilful attention, and in cases where the entire direction of funerals is entrusted to this firm, they may be depended upon to see that everything is attended to, as their experience has been both extensive and varied and they are equally well prepared to assume charge of the largest public or the quietest private ceremony of this kind. The office is open day and night, and telephone connection enables orders to be quickly transmitted from any part of the city.

Frederick Slader, Gas Fixtures. Gas Fitting and Repairing, 45 Warren Street, Boston Highlands. It is easy to get used to about anything, and for this reason we accept things as a matter of course that would otherwise be a constant source of trouble and alarm. All of us know that illuminating gas, although perfectly harmless when properly used, is still a very dangerous thing when out of place and under certain circumstances, yet too many of us will permit men to repair or adjust our gas fixtures, who are entirely incompetent to undertake such work. But it may be asked. "How are we to know who is competent and who is not?" Very easily. Place your orders only with men of good repute, and whenever possible, patronize those who give their attention exclusively to Gas Fitting and Repairing. Such a man is Mr. Frederick Slader of No. 45 Warren Street, and his experience is as great as his reputation is high, for he has been engaged in this line of business since 1861. The store he occupies, comprises one floor and a basement, measuring 25x60 feet, and Gas Fixtures and Fittings of all descriptions are furnished at reasonable prices. Any grade of gas fixture, from the plainest and cheapest, to the most elegant and costly, can be furnished by Mr. Slader and his prices will be found to compare favorably with those of other dealers. Buildings will be fitted up in the most approved manner and in a thoroughly workmanlike style, and orders will be filled without delay, satisfaction being guaranteed. Repairing of all descriptions is given special attention, and as employment is given to four skilled assistants, the most extensive jobs can be quickly completed.

John Thomas, Practical Horse-Shoer, No. 50 Eustis Street, Boston Highlands. The subject of "scientific horse-shoeing" has secured a great deal of attention of late years and some very remarkable theories have been advanced concerning it. Some gentlemen (who claim to have given the matter great study) solve the problem of how to shoe a horse, by declaring that he should not be shod at all, basing their arguments on the statement that if horses had needed shoes, they would have been created with them on. On the same principle, they should have been born with harness on, if a harness were necessary, but as it is rather difficult to make practical use of a horse without a harness, so it is to utilize one without shoes. That many a hoof and many a horse has been spoiled by bad shoeing is undeniable, but this simply proves, not that the principle is wrong, but that the *application* of it should be entrusted to proper hands. No man can learn horse-shoeing from a book, any more than he can learn yacht-sailing in the same way, and if he tries to do it, the result is apt to be like that reached by the individual who thought he had mastered the latter art after reading a number of works on the subject. He tried to sail a boat across the harbor and might perhaps have succeeded, had he not been so sea-sick that he couldn't stand up. It is easy to shoe a horse—on paper, but when it comes down to practical work, it is an excellent idea to have a practical workman. Mr. John Thomas of No. 50 Eustis Street, is well known as a practical horse-shoer, and well he may be, for he has carried on his present enterprise over forty-four years, and does a very extensive business in that line. The establishment of which he is proprietor has been a blacksmith shop since 1812 and is the largest in New England. It contains every facility for the doing of blacksmithing in all its branches. The premises are 40x60 feet in size and employment is given to twenty skilled assistants. Mr. Thomas is prepared to fill orders with neatness and dispatch, and the uniformly high and durable character of the work done at his shop, is too well known to require further mention. All shoes are hand made. His charges are moderate and satisfaction is guaranteed.

Alex. Blackwood, Bell Hanger and Locksmith, Speaking Tubes put up, Keys Fitted, 2080 Washington Street, Boston Highlands. House-work is hard enough under the most favorable circumstances and when the expense of fitting up a residence with the necessary bells, etc., is so small as is now the case, and the saving in steps and worry is so decided, there should be no hesitation felt about taking advantage of this labor-saving device to lighten the cares of housekeeping as much as possible. One of the most skillful Electric and Mechanical Bell Hangers in this city, is Mr. Alexander Blackwood of No. 2080 Washington Street, and those who want anything in this line given prompt and careful attention may rely upon his ability to give perfect satisfaction. Mr. Blackwood occupies one floor of the dimensions of 30 x 25 feet and employs three competent assistants. Locksmithing in all its branches, including Electric Locks for apartment hotels is carried on, and keys will be fitted at short notice and at moderate rates. Orders by mail will receive as prompt attention as those given in person, and an important branch of the business is the putting up of Speaking Tubes, such work being done without unnecessary expense, and satisfactory results guaranteed. Trunk-locks will be repaired or replaced at low prices, and secure locks of all kinds are extensively dealt in. Mr. Blackwood warrants all goods sold to prove as represented and his business is steadily increasing.

Miss K. E. Riley, Fashionable Millinery, 2087 Washington Street, Boston Highlands. Notwithstanding that there is an immense demand for Millinery Goods in a great city like Boston, it is quite difficult to build up a successful trade in these articles, for the reason that the field is already well occupied and but very few openings present themselves. But still, exceptional merit will be recognized, if backed by the requisite business enterprise and ability, and hence the large patronage that has been attained by Miss K. E. Riley, since she opened her present establishment in 1883, is only what might legitimately have been expected by those previously familiar with the lady's pronounced taste and business ability. Miss Riley is a native of this city, and has made Fashionable Millinery a special study. As a result, she is well equipped to assure satisfaction to the most fastidious of her patrons, and her success in arranging the leading styles to suit the varying requirements of her customers has been the subject of much favorable and even admiring comment. The premises utilized measure 28 x 30 feet and contain a very complete assortment of hats, bonnets and trimmings of various kinds, both trimmed and untrimmed head coverings being offered for sale, and the very latest Parisian styles on exhibition. Employment is given to four skilled assistants, and order work is done with a celerity and thoroughness that, combined with the low prices quoted, have done much to give this establishment the great popularity that it enjoys.

Roxbury Clothing Co., Northerly Cor. Washington & Vernon Sts., S. O. Hadley Uniforms a Specialty. Much of the prejudice that formerly existed regarding the wearing of ready-made clothing has now passed away, and indeed there is no longer reason for its continuance, as ready-made garments are now produced that are practically equal to the best custom clothing, and that are far superior to the "thrown-together" productions of cheap tailors with which the market is flooded. Of course Ready-made Clothing is sold to-day, that deserves all the ridicule that used to be cast at "slop-shop" garments in general, but there is no necessity for anyone being imposed upon through ignorance, for everybody has had an opportunity to inspect high-grade ready-made garments and hence should know what can be done in this line. The "Roxbury Clothing Company," doing business at the northerly or "down-town" corner of Washington and Vernon Streets, has done good work in the past in educating the public up to a point where only the best of garments will prove acceptable, for it has never been satisfied to accept a second position but has endeavored to maintain its position as a leader in the production of well-fitting, well-made and fashionably out clothing. Such has been its policy during a career of nearly thirty years, and the result is to be seen to-day, not only in the magnitude of its trade, but also in the high standing the concern has for probity, fair-dealing and enterprise, in the best and truest sense of that much-abused term. The enterprise of this company does not consist of sharp dealing, and is not exemplified by its success in palming off damaged or superannuated goods on its customers by one pretence or the other, but is shown in the low prices quoted on standard and fashionable clothing and in the liberal provision made for the comfort and convenience of patrons. The manager, Mr. S. O. Hadley, is a well-known business man of established reputation. Every article sold is guaranteed to prove as represented, and Uniforms are made a specialty.

H. B. Smith, Harness Maker, No. 33 Roxbury Street, Boston Highlands. That the harness a horse is furnished with has much to do with his effectiveness as well as his appearance, no one at all acquainted with the subject will dispute, and it still remains as true as it ever was, that to get a good harness you must patronize a good and reliable maker. Mr. H. B. Smith of No. 33 Roxbury Street (2nd door from Mr. Wm. Sullivan, Horse shoer) has carried on business in his present quarters since 1885, and has made and sold a great number of harnesses of all kinds during that time. There has not been, so far as we have learned, the least complaint from any of his customers, up to date, while on the contrary the expressions of satisfaction have been many and pronounced. This fact, taken in connection with the evident superiority of the goods produced as seen by inspection of those on hand, warrants us in declaring that those who may favor Mr. Smith with their patronage may be assured of receiving complete satisfaction, while the prices at which the various articles are sold, are so low as to commend themselves to all. Both a wholesale and retail business is done and Whips, Oils, Soaps, and Horse-furnishings and Sundries in general are extensively dealt in. Second-hand Harnesses are bought and sold and particular attention is given to repairing, which is done at short notice and in a uniformly durable, neat and thorough manner. Mr. Smith employs two competent assistants and produces the best work by using the finest stock and giving it careful and skillful handling.

B. E. Howard, Cor. Dudley Street, and Albany Ave., Boston Highlands, Dealer in Dry & Fancy Goods, Stationery. Agency for Mme. Demorest's Reliable Patterns. In no line of trade is experience of more practical value than in that devoted to the handling of Dry and Fancy Goods, etc., and as Mr. B. E. Howard (who does business at the corner of Dudley Street, and Albany Avenue) has carried on his present enterprise for nearly fifteen years, it is but natural that he should be able to offer his patrons such frequent and decided inducements as to gain for his establishment great popularity and a steadily increasing trade. The premises utilized, measure 20x55 feet and comprise one floor and a basement, being well-filled by an assortment of Dry and Fancy Goods, Stationery, etc., that is both large and varied, and contains articles suited to everybody's needs and quoted at prices adapted to everybody's means. Mr. Howard acts as agent for Mme. Demorest's celebrated patterns and can supply anything in this line at the lowest attainable rates. These patterns are too well known to require description, suffice it to say that they well deserve the name "Reliable" and will be found equal to any in the world. Employment is afforded to two efficient and obliging assistants and not the least popular feature of the establishment is the prompt and painstaking attention extended to every caller.

G. W. Andrews & Co., Dealers in Choice Family Groceries, Tea, Coffee, Butter and Flour, 91 Warren Street. That the business of the grocer has been extended and widened in scope of late years, must be apparent to all who have given the matter their attention, and indeed even a casual observer can hardly have failed to notice that with the more general introduction of canned goods and the raising of the standard of popular taste, the demands made upon the resources of a first-class grocery become more varied than ever. The enterprise conducted by Messrs. G. W. Andrews & Co., at No. 91 Warren Street, was inaugurated in 1881, and has, from its inception, been characterized by liberal management and corresponding success. The firm is made up of Mr. G. W. Andrews and Mr. W. S. Melcher, both of whom are natives of Boston. The premises utilized comprise one floor and a basement, measuring 22 x 60 feet, and containing a very large and desirable assortment of Choice Family Groceries, Tea, Coffee, Butter and Flour. Employment is afforded to three courteous and efficient assistants, and all callers may depend on prompt and willing service and fair and equitable treatment. The line of Groceries handled is one that has been selected expressly for the trade to which this house caters, and will be found exceptionally complete in every department and containing nothing that cannot be unreservedly recommended. The Teas and Coffees offered are fine-flavored, full strength and low in price, and it only needs a trial of these goods to demonstrate their superiority over those sold in the average grocery store. Fresh Creamery Butter is always obtainable here at the lowest market rates, as are also fresh country eggs, while Family Flour is handled very extensively, and is supplied by the bag or barrel at bottom prices.

John H. Rowe, Upholsterer, 1 Roxbury St. Furniture repaired and polished, Window Shades made. The cares of a household are onerous enough at the best, without adding to them any more than is possible, and the assistance that can be rendered by an experienced and careful Upholsterer should by all means be taken advantage of and utilized to its full extent when "house cleaning" is in progress. There are many Upholsterers in this city, and not a few in the Highlands, but Mr. John H. Rowe bears a reputation as high as any of them, and during the twenty years that he has carried on his present business, he has certainly had ample opportunity to become thoroughly acquainted with it in every branch and detail. Mr. Rowe may be found at No. 1 Roxbury Street, where he utilizes one floor and a basement, measuring 20x100 feet and gives employment to six experienced and efficient assistants. He makes a specialty of the repairing and general renovation of Furniture, Repolishing and Reupholstering it at short notice and doing the work in so thorough and effective a manner as to make the articles look like new in every respect. Window Shades will be made to order and put up, so as to ensure their smooth working, etc., carpets will be made and laid to order as well as taken up and cleaned. All of Mr. Rowe's work is done in accordance with the high standard that the public have become accustomed to use in judging of his efforts and his prices are as moderate as can be quoted on thorough and careful work. Orders are promptly acted upon, and finished work immediately delivered.

H. A. Davenport, Dealer in Teas, Coffees, Spices, Fruits, Nuts, etc. 123 Warren Street. Among those establishments that seem to us to be exceptionally worthy of honorable mention in these pages, that of Mr. H. A. Davenport, located at No. 123 Warren Street deserves a prominent position, for this enterprise was inaugurated in 1873 by Mr. G. O. Alden and has been under the control of its present owner for about ten years. Mr. Davenport is a native of Boston and is engaged in handling Fine Groceries, Teas, Coffees, Spices, Fruits, Nuts, etc. The store utilized by him is of the dimensions of 30x55 feet and is well worthy of a visit, for it contains as skilfully selected a stock of the articles we have mentioned, as can be found in the whole city. These goods have been chosen with an eye to the requirement of the most fastidious trade, and they are offered at such prices that no one can fail to find something therein suited to his purse as well as his palate. There are, after all, but comparatively few establishments where really high-grade teas and coffees are obtainable at fair prices, and hence it is only natural that this department of Mr. Davenport's business should be of the utmost importance, and that a very large and constantly growing trade should have resulted from the inducements he has to offer. His spices are also pure and finely-flavored, and the assortment of Foreign and Domestic Fruits shown, is one that pleases the eye as much as it stimulates the appetite, for the articles comprising it are ripe, tempting and neatly arranged.

W. B. Cutter, Doors, Windows and Blinds, Paints, Oils and Glass, Nos. 17 and 19 Warren Street, Boston Highlands. That the establishment conducted by W. B. Cutter, at Nos. 17 and 19 Warren Street, is one of the most prominent of the kind in this section, is a fact that admits of no dispute, for long before Mr. Cutter moved into his present quarters, his business was so large that more room became an imperative necessity. The premises now occupied are very spacious, comprising three floors and a basement, and measuring 40 x 60 feet, and the stock carried is very heavy and varied and complete in every department. Doors, Windows and Blinds are very extensively handled, and the assortment of Paints and Oils is large enough to contain goods suitable for all kinds of work, while window-glass is also dealt in largely and all the standard sizes kept in stock. Mr Cutter is a native of Boston, and has been engaged in his present business for twenty-seven years, having occupied the premises now utilized since 1885. The goods handled by him bear a high reputation among those best qualified to judge of their merits, and there are few buildings put up in Roxbury or vicinity without Mr. Cutter's being called upon to furnish a greater or less proportion of the material necessary to their completion. He has always made it a point to be reasonable in his charges and is in a position to quote bottom prices, as the magnitude of the business done enables him to buy to the best advantage. There is employment given to two competent assistants, and prompt attention is promised all customers.

I. Rosenkranz, Clothier, Hatter and Gent's Furnisher; Trunks, Bags, Umbrellas, etc.; Watches and Jewelry bought and sold, 2201 Washington Street. Mr. I. Rosenkranz of No. 2201 Washington Street, (Dean's Block) has carried on his present enterprise since 1862 and has built up a large trade by selling reliable goods at prices much lower than the same class of articles can generally be bought for. He is a native of Germany and occupies a store 20x70 feet in dimensions, which is filled with a splendid assortment of Ready-made Clothing, Hats, Caps, and Gent's Furnishings in general, together with Trunks, Bags and Umbrellas of all kinds. The Overalls, Jumpers and Shirts sold here, are manufactured by Mr. Rosenkranz for his own trade and he can consequently warrant them to be as represented. Watches and Jewelry, Musical Instruments and Fire Arms, both new and second-hand, are dealt in very extensively and some decided bargains are offered to cash buyers by Mr. Rosenkranz who carries on the Highland Loan Office in the same store and loans money on Diamonds, Watches, Jewelry, Musical Instruments, clothing and Personal Property of every description. This is a very popular department of the business, as the highest cash prices are paid and every transaction is considered as strictly confidential. Those temporarily embarrassed, should make this establishment a call as they are assured fair and liberal dealing, and whatever is done will not be known outside unless they themselves tell it. Mr. Rosenkranz does a large and growing business, and fully deserves the high degree of popularity his establishment enjoys.

Greene & Stevens, Grocers, Tea, Coffee, Butter and Flour Specialties, 304 Warren Street, Corner Clifford Street. In these days, business is almost entirely divided up into specialties, and in order to purchase to the best advantage one must be acquainted with the houses giving particular attention to the handling of certain products. Take for instance the enterprise conducted by Messrs. Greene & Stevens at No. 304 Warren Street. These gentlemen do a general grocery business and carry a large and well-selected stock of Staple and Fancy Groceries in great variety. The firm only began operations here in 1888, and consequently have a new and fresh assortment that contains no unsalable goods of any kind. The firm is made up of C. C. Greene, formerly with F. O. White, and T. N. Stevens, formerly with L. W. & H. F. Morse; both partners have a long experience in the business. Despite the fact of their not being established a great while, they do a very large business, and why? Simply because people have discovered that family supplies can be purchased of them to most excellent advantage, and that prompt and careful attention is given to every order. The store is 22 x 50 feet, with a basement, and is one of the handsomest and best arranged in the Highlands. A speciality is made of Tea, Coffee, Butter and Flour and some really surprising inducements are offered in these lines. Lovers of a good cup of Tea or Coffee should most certainly place an order with this firm, for they handle goods of the choicest flavor and are very reasonable in their prices. Pure and Fresh Creamery Butter is also supplied at bottom rates, and the Flour in stock includes the most approved brands for family use, being furnished by the bag or barrel at very low figures.

S. Isaacs, Dealer in all Kinds of Fresh and Salt Fish, also Smoked and Pickled Fish, Fancy Fish of all kinds. All orders promptly attended to, 353 and 647 Warren Street, Boston Highlands.

Fish is a very popular article of food among all classes of people, but in spite of the active demand that exists for it, those who handle it at retail must be both experienced and able if they wish to attain the highest success. In order to build up a desirable class of trade, it is necessary to carry a large and varied stock, and to keep the same in a neat and attractive condition, and it is largely owing to his observance of these points that Mr. S. Isaacs has won such success since he began operations at 353 Warren Street in 1884. This gentleman is a native of Boston, and has had about twenty years' experience in the fish business, catering to the best kind of trade, and becoming thoroughly conversant with the wants of the public. He carries on two stores on Warren Street, one at No. 353 and the other at No. 647, and employs six competent and polite assistants. The latter store was opened in February, 1888, and has already received the liberal patronage of those residing in its vicinity, for Mr. Isaacs has won an enviable reputation for dealing in reliable goods, and his prices speak for themselves. An assortment of Fresh, Salt, Smoked and Pickled Fish is carried at all times and especial attention is given to the handling of Fancy or Game Fish. Prompt and careful attention is given to all orders, and callers are treated with uniform courtesy and consideration.

D. B. Macdonald, Successor to Geo. W. Reynolds, Winthrop Market, 121 Warren Street. Americans are said to be the most fastidious eaters in the world, and it is charged that an average American family throws away enough in a week to live upon another week, but however this may be, it is a fact that about everyone wants to know where the best of meats, the best of vegetables, the best of fruits and the best of butter, etc., are to be had, and therefore all will be interested when we answer "At Macdonald's, Winthrop Market, No. 121 Warren Street, Warren Block." This business was started in 1871 by Mr. Geo. W. Reynolds, who was succeeded in 1886 by the present proprietor. One floor and a basement are occupied, measuring 20 x 55 feet, and as employment is afforded to five efficient assistants, customers are assured prompt and polite attention. Mr. D. B. Macdonald is a native of Nova Scotia, and is thoroughly acquainted with every detail of his present business. The finest cuts of Meats, the tenderest and finest flavored Steaks, Chops, Cutlets, etc., are to be had here at all times and at prices as low as the market will permit. Fruits and Vegetables in their seasons are given particular attention, and those wanting fresh and full-flavored articles of this kind, may always find them here if anywhere. Butter and Cheese are received direct from the dairies, and purchasers are fully guaranteed that every article in this line will prove as represented in every respect. Mr. Macdonald believes in "quick sales and small profits" and hence his stock is constantly fresh and desirable.

George W. Downs, House and Sign Painter, 165 Warren Street. Any man who owns a handsome residence, may be pardoned for exercising considerable care in the selection of a painter to work upon it, as painting when unskilfully or carelessly done is neither useful nor ornamental. Hence we take pleasure in mentioning the facilities enjoyed by Mr. George W. Downs, of No. 165 Warren St., in the filling of orders of this kind, for we know that he will give satisfaction to such as may employ his services, and we also know that his terms are very reasonable for first-class work. He has carried on business for twenty-five years, and has been in business for himself since 1880, and has executed many important commissions in a style that has done much to build up the extensive patronage now enjoyed. The premises utilized measure 20 x 40 feet in size, and employment is afforded to four skilled and experienced assistants. The shop is supplied with every appliance, etc., that is required to carry on the business economically and successfully, and an important part of the industry is here conducted, that of Plain and Ornamental Sign Painting. Some beautiful work is done in this line, and not only beauty but durability is regarded.

D. Danahy & Son, Manufacturers of Tin and Sheet Iron Ware, Proprietors of Danahy & Son's Plate Iron Furnace, all sizes. Furnaces, Ranges and Stoves Repaired; Tin Roofing Warranted, 2044 Washington Street. No experienced

householder needs to be told that the selection of the stoves to be used for heating or cooking purposes in a house is a matter of the first importance, for it only requires a small amount of familiarity with domestic life to impress this fact very forcibly upon the mind. The choosing of a furnace is still more difficult for there are any number of such heaters in the market, and although many of them are constructed on correct principles, still there are not a few of which this cannot be said, and which are both high in first cost and wasteful of fuel. Danahy & Son's Plate Iron Furnace is not the invention of men who have had no practical experience in the heating of houses, but is the result of years of observation of the defects found in the great majority of furnaces designed for domestic use. It is simple in plan, strong and durable in construction, easy to manage, economical of fuel, capable of supplying an enormous amount of heat or of being so controlled as to avoid overheating a house during a "warm spell." It is in fact as perfect a furnace as we have ever seen, and we would advise all of our readers who are dissatisfied with their present heating facilities, to call at No. 2044 Washington Street, and consult the firm on the subject, for it is well to prepare for next winter before the "rush" comes in the fall. Messrs. D. Danahy & Son began operations in 1872, and occupy one floor and a basement at the address given. They can supply the furnace mentioned in all sizes, and fully guarantee it to do all that is promised for it. Ranges and Stoves are also extensively dealt in, and will be repaired at short notice and in a thoroughly workmanlike manner at low prices.

Tin Roofing and Plumbing are also given special attention and parties wishing a durable roof which will be positively warranted, would do well to place their orders with this popular firm. Both partners are natives of Boston, and there are employed two efficient and careful assistants.

H. R. Hunting, Dealer in Choice Family Groceries, Flour, Teas, Coffees, etc., Cigars and Tobacco, 126 Dudley Street, Boston Highlands. Groceries are so universally used, that it is hardly possible to devote too large a share of this work to a consideration of the more important houses engaged in handling the same in this vicinity, and we are sure that those familiar with the establishment and business of Mr. H. R. Hunting will agree with us concerning the propriety of giving him honorable and prominent mention within these pages. He occupies one floor, measuring 20 x 40 feet at 126 Dudley Street, and carries a finely selected stock, among which may be found Flour, Teas, Coffees, and a fine line of Fancy Groceries, Foreign and Domestic Cigars, Tobacco, etc. Mr. Hunting is a native of Boston and a member of the Odd Fellows and Good Fellows. He began operations about 1881 and has given unmistakable and repeated signs since then that he understood what was wanted by the public. Owing to the large increase in his business Mr. Hunting contemplates enlarging and improving his store shortly. He has established a reputation for selling honest goods in an honest fashion, of which he may well be proud.

James O'Brien, Florist, 63 Union Avenue, and 3171 Washington Street, Jamaica Plain, and 2301 Washington Street, Boston Highlands. It is generally desirable to purchase directly from the producer whenever possible and this is particularly the case when buying such perishable articles as cut-flowers, bouquets, etc., as in no other way can they be obtained in so fresh and hardy a condition, to say nothing of the gain made in economy by so doing. Mr. James O'Brien, although he only opened his retail establishment at No. 2301 Washington Street, last year, is a Florist of long experience, and that this experience has brought skill, is proved by the many prizes awarded to him by the Massachusetts Horticultural Society for the artistic arrangement of flowers, etc. His prices are moderate in the extreme as he grows his own flowers (utilizing six large green-houses, covering a space of nine thousand square feet with glass) and owing to the large scale on which he conducts operations, the cost of producing a given number of flowers or plants is reduced to a minimum. Mr. O'Brien has carried on business at Jamaica Plain for a score of years and occupies premises at No. 63 Union Avenue and No. 3171 Washington Street in that section. Choice Cut Fowers, Artistic Floral Designs, Plants, etc., fresh every day are supplied by him at bottom prices, and all who have given him orders for Wedding or Funeral Emblems, speak in the very highest terms of the taste displayed in filling the same and the spirit of accommodation manifested by Mr. O'Brien and those in his employ. He already does a large business at his Roxbury store, and it is rapidly increasing, by reason of the liberal and enterprising methods followed

Potter's Hotel and Restaurant, 2143 & 2145 Washington Street, George M. Potter. Proprietor. Potter's Hotel and Restaurant are known to every resident of the Highlands, and occupy a position such as is held by no other similar enterprise in that section. The undertaking was founded in 1846 and for nearly half a century has afforded an example of what an institution of the kind should be. Potter's Hotel has a reputation for hospitality and freedom from exasperating "style" and for liberty without license, that is richly deserved, and those who wish to stop at a house where any part of the city can be quickly reached, and which is at once prominent and retired in situation, might go a great deal further and fair a great deal worse. Three floors and a basement are occupied of the dimensions of 40x60 feet and there are forty rooms available which are let by the day or week at very reasonable rates. Ten employees are in attendance and perfect neatness and prompt and willing service are among the advantages observed by those staying at this popular house. The Restaurant is the most celebrated in Roxbury and enjoys a reputation for the choicest food cooked in the best manner, such as any similar establishment in the city might well be proud of. Game, Chicken and Oyster Suppers are given special attention and will be furnished at short notice to parties of any number. The seating capacity of the dining rooms is sufficient to accommodate sixty guests and the arrangements are such that that number can be promptly and satisfactorily served. The finest Wines, Brandies, Cordials and liquors of all kinds are supplied at low prices as are also imported and domestic ales, etc., while choice cigars are made a specialty.

Ames Bros., Grocers, 125 Roxbury Street. That there are many grocery stores to be found in the Highland District, our readers need not be told, for the fact is plainly evident to any one who has even a slight acquaintance with that section, but it requires something more than a slight acquaintance to become posted as to the relative merits of these establishments and therefore whatever information we can give in that line is quite sure to be acceptable. In this connection we should like to call attention to the enterprise of which Ames Brothers are the proprietors, located at No. 125 Roxbury Street, for we believe that no better goods are to be found in the market than are obtainable here and we are sure that no more honorable business methods can be practiced anywhere. One floor and a basement are utilized, of the dimensions of 20x45 feet, and employment is afforded to two obliging and well-informed assistants. An extremely large and varied stock of Fine Groceries is carried, comprising choice Teas and Coffees, Pure Spices, all the favorite brands of Flour, etc., and the prices quoted are very reasonable, especially when the superior quality of the goods is remembered. Messrs. Ames Brothers have not conducted this establishment for a very long period of time, but they have carried it on long enough to make it evident that success is assured. Under a continuance of the present liberal and enterprising management.

Geo. W. Stacey, 2196 Washington Street, Roxbury, Mass. Stationer and dealer in the "Domestic" Paper Patterns adjustable Dress and Skirt Forms, also Laundry agency. The gentleman whose card we print above, has carried on his present business for very nearly a score of years and his establishment at No. 2196 Washington Street has long been one of the most popular in the Highlands. It is but natural that it should be so, for Mr. Stacey spares no pains to afford his customers complete satisfaction and carries a fine assortment of fashionable stationery etc., and a full line of Lovell's Library together with Fancy articles of various descriptions, which he offers at the lowest market rates. One floor is occupied, of the dimensions of 30x25 feet and the stock on hand is tastefully arranged and displayed to excellent advantage. A popular article handled by Mr. Stacey is the "Domestic" adjustable Dress form, which is indispensable to every lady making or altering her own dresses and which will more than save its cost ($6.50) in a single season. The Domestic Skirt form at $4.00 and the Folding Skirt form (recently improved) at $3.00 are also of great value to ladies and it is not surprising that Mr. Stacey should sell many of them as they are superior to any others in the market and are offered by him at manufacturer's prices. He is a native of York, Maine and is connected with both the Odd Fellows and the Grand Army. He was a member of Co. F 3d Massachusetts during the Rebellion and served under Gen. Banks in La., and with Gen. Sheridan in Shenandoah Valley. Everything coming from his establishment may be strictly depended on, as he chooses his goods with the utmost care and never misrepresents an article.

Samuel C. Nason, Dealer in Fish, Oysters, etc., 2107 Washington Street. There are very few people who don't like fish, and it is well that this is so, for no more healthful and generally desirable article of food exists, and it is in most cases as cheap as it is good. We need not say that much of the palatableness and nutritive qualities of fish depend on the treatment they receive after being caught, and it is largely owing to the precautions observed to avoid all injury and to preserve perfect freshness, that the members of the finny tribe furnished by Mr. Samuel C. Nason of No. 2107 Washington Street, opposite Eustis, enjoy so high a reputation for fineness of flavor and uniformity of excellence. Mr. Nason has been concerned in this line of business since 1866 and is thoroughly conversant with every detail of the trade. He is a native of Roxbury and a member of the Good Fellows and it would be hard to find a man more generally known or a more universal favorite. "Nason's Orchestra" is one of the most popular organizations of the kind in town and is in great request during the dancing season for parties, balls and such occasions. To those who have never favored Mr. Nason with their patronage, we would say that his stock is always as complete as the market will permit. His prices are invariably reasonable and fair, every representation made may be strictly depended on. One floor and a basement, measuring 20 x 60 feet are occupied and employment is given to two polite and competent assistants.

T. D. Mulrey, Marble and Granite Works, Nos. 2355 and 2357 Washington Street, Boston Highlands. The Marble and Granite Works carried on by Mr. T. D. Mulrey at Nos. 2355 and 2357 Washington Street, were established in 1849 and are undoubtedly the best known in this section of the city. It is not, however, entirely on account of their old standing by any means, that these works are so popular, for much of the celebrity they enjoy is due to the high character of the work turned out, and it may be truthfully said that no similar enterprise in the state is capable of filling orders in a more thoroughly artistic and satisfactory manner. The premises occupied comprise three buildings of the dimensions of 70 x 100 feet, and employment is afforded to twenty skilled hands. Although order work is executed at short notice, there is carried in stock a magnificent assortment of Marble and Granite Monumental Tablets, Foreign and American Marble Chimney Pieces of the most approved and fashionable designs. This assortment comprises goods suited to all tastes, to all circumstances and to all purses, and is well worthy of a careful examination by those interested. Mr. Mulrey will be happy to permit an inspection of his finished work at any time during business hours, and even if he does not happen to have in stock just what is wanted by the customer, such an inspection will generally result in finding out precisely what the patron desires. The facilities for filling of orders without delay and at the least possible expense, are of the best, and Marble and Stone Work of every description will be supplied on the most reasonable terms, and satisfaction guaranteed.

John C. Martin, Merchant, Tailor 2363 Washington Street. The genial gentleman whose card we print above, is one of the best-known and most highly esteemed of our Highland business men and fully deserves the success he has won in the carrying on of his present enterprise. Mr. Martin is a native of Boston and is connected with the Free Masons, the Ancient Order of Workmen and the Foresters. He assumed control of his present undertaking in 1883 and has built up a large trade during the comparatively short time that he has conducted the industry in question. This is not surprising when his methods are taken into consideration, for everybody likes fair dealing, everybody likes courteous treatment, everybody likes fashionable and thoroughly made garments, and everybody likes to secure a first-class article at a moderate price. All of these likings can be and are satisfied by Mr. Martin, and his popularity follows as a matter of course. At No. 2363 Washington Street, his establishment is located, and there is always carried in stock a fine assortment of Foreign and Domestic cloths embracing goods suited to all conditions of wear, particular attention being paid to suitings especially adapted to young men's requirements. One floor and a basement are occupied, of the dimensions of 20x60 feet and employment is given to five skilled assistants. Mr. Martin guarantees satisfaction as regards style and fit and his experience thus far has been that those who patronize him once almost invariably come again. He has just received his fall importations of Fine Woolens, etc. which he is making up at very reasonable prices. His prices are extremely low for the fine quality of work done, and we can commend his garments to the most fastidious dressers.

H. J. & W. J. Shine, Dealers in Fresh Fish, Lobsters, Smoked Fish, Oysters, Clams etc. 2328 Washington Street, Boston Highlands. Without a doubt the handsomest fish-store in the Highlands is that occupied by Messrs. H. J. & W. J. Shine at No. 2328 Washington Street and those who associate the handling and sale of fish with a dingy, dirty store and poor accommodations, should pay this establishment a visit and see that such association is by no means always justified. Both members of the firm are natives of Boston and thoroughly acquainted with the requirements of the best city trade, as may be seen by their successful efforts to fully satisfy their patrons. The premises occupied are of the dimensions of 30x50 feet and comprise one floor and a basement, a splendid show-window affording excellent opportunity for the display of goods. Fresh fish of all kinds is carried in stock, including such game fish as pickerel, black bass, etc., and a full assortment of Smoked and Pickled Fish is also on hand as are Lobsters, Oysters, Clams, etc. These are offered at moderate prices and customers are always given prompt attention and treated with courtesy and consideration. One of the most popular customs pursued by this firm is the calling at the houses of patrons for orders, and this service is strictly reliable and may be entirely depended upon. Orders are also delivered with promptness and accuracy, and will be sent at the time they are promised.

J. P. Kelley, Practical Plumber and Engineer, Dealer in Water Closets, Boilers, Baths, Sinks, etc., No. 10 Roxbury Street, Boston Highlands. Mr. J. P. Kelley began operations just about ten years ago, and has consequently been long enough before the public for some definite conclusion to be arrived at concerning his skill and reliability. That the verdict has been a distinctly favorable one need hardly be said, for were it otherwise, the large business he now carries on would be quite out of the question. One floor and a basement of the dimensions of 25 x 60 feet are utilized, the premises being located at No. 10 Roxbury Street. Mr. Kelley is an extensive dealer in Water Closets, Boilers, Baths, Sinks, etc., and offers the latest and most approved models of these goods at bottom rates. He will furnish estimates on any contemplated line of work, and can give the very best of references as to character and responsibility. Employment is given to sixteen efficient assistants, and jobbing orders are attended to without delay and given careful and painstaking attention. Mr. Kelley is a Practical Plumber and Sanitary Engineer, in fact as well as in name, and will undertake the laying of drains, the placing of soil-pipes, etc., in accordance with the latest scientific methods. The dangers that lurk in every house are too well understood nowadays to require detailed mention here, but they are many and deadly, and can only be put at defiance by the adoption of every sanitary precaution. Mr. Kelley is perfectly competent to assume the direction of such work and will do so at very moderate rates.

Norfolk Clothing Store, F. B. Snow and F. E. Merrick, 2321 Washington Street, Boston Highlands. Those people that think all ready-made clothing to be practically alike as regards fit, cut, durability, etc., make a very great mistake, for there is as much difference in ready-made garments as there is in those made to order; and if any one doubts it, let him examine the stock exhibited by those carrying on the "Norfolk Clothing Store," and compare it with the assortment shown by certain other dealers not a thousand miles away. The "Norfolk" was established in 1885, and has already gained an amount of patronage that has fairly astonished those who are not personally familiar with the advantages extended to customers. Its proprietors are Messrs. F. B. Snow and F. E. Merrick: the former is a member of the Odd Fellows, while the latter is connected with the Free Masons. These gentlemen are thoroughly acquainted with the Clothing and Gents' Furnishing business, and have so successfully catered to the wants of the public that their trade is as varied as it is extensive. Whether you have five dollars or five times that sum to invest in clothing, you will have an opportunity to expend it to the best advantage at the "Norfolk," and you run absolutely no risk of imposition, as every article is fully warranted to prove as represented, and is sold at the lowest market rates. The store is located at No. 2321 Washington Street, and measures 25 x 100 feet, a large stock being carried that is complete in every department. Style and fit are guaranteed, and the garments sold here are better finished than many of the so-called "custom-made goods" with which the market is flooded. Gents' Furnishings are offered at bottom prices, and all customers are assured prompt and polite attention.

J. B. Howard, Dealer in Boots and Shoes, 2189 Washington Street. As a result of the constant changes incident to city life, it is very rarely that an establishment can be found that has been occupied for the carrying on of one line of business for a third of a century, but such is the record of the store of which Mr. J. B. Howard is the proprietor, located at No. 2189 Washington Street, for business was begun here in 1855, and it has been confined to the sale of Boots and Shoes ever since. Despite the many years this establishment has been known to the public, it was never before more popular than it now is, for since Mr. Howard assumed control in 1853, he has proved to the satisfaction of all, that he knows a thing or two about shoes himself and proposes to give his patrons the benefit of his knowledge. In what way do you ask? Well, by dealing in goods that are what they appear to be, by endeavoring to sell nothing that will not give perfect satisfaction, by ascertaining by personal inspection if the representations made by the manufacturers of goods handled by him are justified by the facts, and by making it an invariable rule to avoid all over statements in the sale of commodities dealt in. These are Mr. Howard's business methods, and that they are well advised, his heavy patronage proves. He is a native of this state and very well known in the community. One floor and a basement, measuring 25 x 70 feet are occupied, and the stock carried is as varied as it is carefully selected.

Parker Bryant, Hack, Boarding and Livery Stable, 46 and 861 Warren Street, Boston Highlands. Telephone 47-79-2. Carriages and Coupes furnished, with careful Drivers, for Parties, Funerals, and other occasions. It is

only necessary to call at the establishments conducted by Mr. Parker Bryant at No. 46 and 861 Warren Street to gain an idea of the first-class character of the accommodations furnished, for the stables carried on by that gentleman at the address given, are undeniably among the very first in the city. Particular attention is given to the boarding of horses, and the facilities at hand for the proper care of a large number of animals, are as complete as the latest improvements and an unstinted expenditure of money can make them. These stables have been erected but a few years and they are models of convenience and cleanliness in every respect. Some fifty-five stalls are to be found on the premises and employment is afforded to eight careful and experienced assistants. The rates of board are very reasonable, and the very best of care and the most healthful surroundings are guaranteed. Mr. Bryant is a native of this city, and carries on another and similar enterprise at No. 361 Warren Street. Carriages and Coupes will be furnished for Parties, Funerals, Weddings, the Theatre, etc., and careful drivers are supplied, who will be found very civil and well acquainted with the city and suburbs. A very extensive Livery business is done and no wonder, for the teams coming from both of Mr. Bryant's establishments, form a refreshing contrast to those generally supplied the public and will be found entirely acceptable by the most fastidious. Gentle and fearless horses especially fitted for ladies' driving may be obtained here at reasonable rates, together with vehicles that are both easy riding and easy to get in and out of, and for those who desire a speedy and spirited animal, there is every provision made. Orders by Telephone No. 45 77-3 will receive prompt attention and Mr. Bryant's charges for all services will be found reasonable and just.

Emond & Quinsler, Manufacturers of Fine Carriages, 2113 and 2115 Washington Street. There is no question that American Manufacturers produce the finest light carriages in the world and indeed the same may be said of all our productions in the line of vehicles where lightness and strength must be combined. Those who have become familiar with the carriages manufactured by Messrs. Emond & Quinsler, of Nos. 2113 and 2115 Washington Street, opposite Eustis, speak in the highest terms of the design and workmanship of these vehicles, and the firm were awarded a medal at the 14th Exhibition of the Charitable Mechanics Association held in 1881, for a Goddard Pattern Buggy of their manufacture. Messrs. Emond & Quinsler began operations in 1873, and the growth of their business during the past fifteen years shows that their efforts to supply a superior article at a fair price are appreciated by those interested. The premises occupied are of the dimensions of 60 x 70 feet and comprise a five story building, the shop being well supplied with improved machinery which is run by steam, some twelve horse power being required. There are twenty assistants employed and all the many operations from the time the "raw material" is taken in hand, to when the finished carriage resplendent in paint and varnish comes forth, are conducted with a care and skill that go far to explain why the productions of this house are durable as well as handsome. A fine assortment of vehicles is open for inspection in the spacious warerooms, and no one wanting a stylish, strong, light, and thoroughly made carriage can afford to omit an examination of what this firm have to offer.

C. W. Richardson, Carriage and Sign-Painting, 50 Eustis Street, Boston Highlands. That carriage-painting calls for special skill and special training, is too obvious to admit of question, for it is easy to see that carriages and such vehicles are so exposed to the weather and so subject to excessive wear in a number of other ways, that their painted surfaces need very careful treatment as well as the use of the best of stock. Mr. B. Richardson of No. 50 Eustis Street, was for many years one of the best-known carriage painters in the city, for he began operations in 1853 and continued until 1880, when he was succeeded by his son Mr. C. W. Richardson who has proved himself entirely competent to maintain the ancient reputation of the house. The shop measures 40x60 feet in size and employment is given to a sufficient force to allow all orders to be filled without undue delay, and at the same time without such haste as is inconsistent with the attainment of the best results. Not only carriage but also sign-painting is done in a thoroughly first-class manner, and those who want an attractive and durable sign should favor Mr. Richardson with their order, for his work is equal to the best and his prices are always moderate. He has produced some unique and beautiful designs in this line and will cheerfully give such information or advice as may be desired.

E. W. King, Upholsterer, Warren Street, near Walnut Avenue. We are sure that our readers (especially those of the gentler sex) will be interested in learning of an establishment where first-class upholstery work is done at moderate rates, for there is not a household but what affords opportunity for some works of this description, and it is often possible to make a set of furniture look as good as new at a comparatively trifling expenditure, if the task is entrusted to the right party. Mr. E. W. King is located on Warren Street, near Walnut Avenue, and has been identified with his present enterprise since 1882. He has attained an enviable reputation for the thoroughness of his work and the reasonableness of his prices, and is prepared to guarantee satisfaction to all customers. One floor is utilized, and all the necessary appliances are at hand to carry on the business in the most economical and thorough manner. Mr. King is a native of this city, and has had a great deal of experience in the Upholstery trade. He supplies at low prices an assortment of goods such as are used in this industry, and gives every order prompt and careful attention.

W. S. Knowles, Dealer in Provisions and Fruits, No. 99 Eustis Street. The importance of the provision business is not generally understood, except by those who have given the matter some study, for although everybody knows of course that we must "eat to live" and that provisions form an important portion of our food, still few realize the magnitude of the provision trade of this city taken as a whole. It seems smaller, being carried on by so large a number of comparatively unpretentious establishments, but these stores, as a general thing, are in the hands of enterprising business men and the trade is never allowed to stagnate but is kept lively by the energy and "go" that are put into it. Not the least energetic of our provisions dealers, by any means is Mr. W. S. Knowles of No. 99 Eustis Street., and the best possible proof of this statement may be found in the manner in which his business has increased since it was founded in 1893. One floor is occupied, measuring 20x50 feet, and employment is given to three wide-awake and courteous assistants. The assortment of Provisions shown is complete in every detail and comprises Meats of the finest quality as well as Vegetables and Foreign and Domestic Fruits in their seasons. The prices quoted, are as low as can easily be named on first-class goods, and orders are promptly delivered.

Alvin F. Bradley, Photographer, 18 Blue Hill Avenue, Boston Highlands. The elements which enter into a complete and artistic photographic portrait are so many and various, that it is little wonder that photographers capable of turning out work of this description are literally "few and far between." Hence we find that among those sitting for their portraits, perfect satisfaction is the distinguished exception, and considering the immense number of photographers doing business, it is but rarely that we find one who as a rule and in the regular course of affairs produces what may truthfully be called a "Speaking Likeness." When we do, we may be assured that this artist leaves nothing to chance but exercises the most intelligent care in every detail of his work from the time the plate is exposed to when the finished portrait is produced. It is by the pursuance of just such methods that Mr. Alvin F. Bradley of No. 18 Blue Hill Avenue, has built up the high reputation he now enjoys for the furnishing of photographs of the very highest order of excellence, and under these circumstances it is not to be wondered at that this gentleman's Studio is becoming one of the most popular in the city among those who appreciate really artistic work. The enterprise he conducts was inaugurated in 1883, by Mr. Laming, who was succeeded by Mr. Bradley in October, 1856. A beautiful collection of finished work is on hand and Mr. Bradley invites all interested to give him an early call, when he will be happy to show samples from Miniature to Life Size direct, or finished in Crayon, Pastel or Water Color. Any desired information will be cheerfully and courteously given, and appointments can be made in advance, thus serving the interests of all parties concerned.

F. S. Eldredge, Dealer in Choice Family Groceries, also Fine Teas, Spices, Cigars and Tobacco, 191 Hampden Street, Boston Highlands. A great deal of the annoyance to which householders are subjected, might be obviated if more care were used in the selection of the firms which are depended upon to furnish the housekeeping supplies and if we may be allowed to offer a word of advice in this connection, we would say. "Choose your grocer carefully, and then having chosen him and found him reliable, do not transfer your custom to some other and unknown dealer, because he offers sugar a half cent cheaper or announces that he is prepared to 'defy competition.' Let him defy it as much as he chooses, but place your orders where they are sure to be satisfactorily filled." Mr. F. S. Eldredge of No. 191 Hampden Street, began operations in 1894. He occupies one floor and a basement, measuring 20 x 60 feet, and carries a well-selected stock of Choice Family Groceries, comprising all the commodities usually found in a first-class store of this description. The best Family Flour is given special attention, and Mr. Eldredge's prices on it by the bag or barrel will be found as low as the lowest, for goods of equal merit. The assortment of fine Teas, Coffees and Spices, is likewise one worthy of careful inspection, and smokers will find the Choicest Cigars and all the favorite brands of Tobacco for sale here on the most favorable terms. Customers are assured cheerful and prompt service.

John H. Ryder, Dealer in Groceries, Flour and Produce, Coal and Wood, 2938 Washington Street. It would hardly seem to be necessary to call the attention of the public to the advantage gained by purchasing certain commodities at establishments where they are sure

to be found first-class, but there are so many inferior places that we take great pleasure in bringing to notice the establishment conducted by Mr. John H. Ryder, located at No. 2938 Washington Street. One floor and basement are occupied measuring 20 x 60 feet, which are well supplied with a fine assortment of all kinds of Groceries, Flour of the finest grades, and first-class Produce. Coal and Wood are sold in large or small quantities. A large retail trade is carried on in all the above-mentioned articles. Two assistants are given employment and customers are always assured of the best attention. Prices will be found to be as low as the lowest. Mr. Ryder is also one of the proprietors of the PIONEER CARD Co., and all orders for job printing receive prompt attention and low prices.

People's Market, John F. Newton, Dealer in First-Class Provisions, Fruit and Vegetables, Fresh Fish and Oysters, No. 2234 Washington Street, Corner of Warren and Palmer, Boston Highlands. The "People's Market" is a very attractive name to give a business enterprise, but the name itself would amount to but little unless the establishment to which it was given was managed in a style in harmony with the title. Well, the enterprise to which this article has reference, that conducted by Mr. John F. Newton at No. 2234 Washington Street, Corner of Warren and Palmer Streets, was inaugurated in 1845, so that abundant chance has been given the public to determine whether it is worthy of its name or not. The answer is to be found in its continued existence and prosperity. There is not a similar establishment in this vicinity, enjoying a more liberal share of patronage, and new customers are constantly being added to those already on the list. Mr. Newton is a native of Roxbury and a member of the Free Masons. Of course a man of his experience is prominent in the community, and none of our Roxbury Merchants have shown greater public spirit than Mr. Newton in numerous instances that might be mentioned. The premises utilized by him comprise one floor and a basement, of the dimensions of 50 x 80 feet and there is employment given to six efficient and polite assistants. A very heavy stock of first-class Provisions of every description is constantly carried, and Fruit and Vegetables are also largely dealt in. The assortment of the most popular brands of Canned Goods is a most complete one, and Fresh Fish and Oysters are extensively handled, and offered at the lowest market rates for strictly first-class goods. Orders are promptly delivered and will be called for if desired.

Nelson S. Putnam, Grocer, Eliot Square, Opposite Norfolk House, Boston Highlands. The establishment carried on by Mr. Nelson S. Putnam in Eliot Square, opposite the Norfolk House, is one of the best-known in Roxbury, for it was conducted under the firm name of Faunce & Putnam for many years, and has in fact been in operation for over half a century. The premises occupied are very spacious, comprising three floors and a basement of the dimensions of 35 x 50 feet, and the stock carried is in harmony with the accommodations provided for it, for it is very varied, and is exceptionally complete in each of its many departments. Fine Family Groceries of every description are included within it and it is not to be wondered at that this establishment is a favorite with the public, for the same latitude of choice is afforded as can be obtained at any down-town store and the prices are as low as can be named on standard goods. To attempt to catalogue even, all the articles dealt in, would more than exhaust our available space, but we may at least call attention to the fine line of Canned Goods shown, and also to the superior quality of the Teas and Coffees offered, for special pains is taken in these departments, and the result is worthy of appreciation and encouragement. Orders are promptly delivered and all articles fully guaranteed to prove as represented.

Edward Beard, 2033 Washington Street and 1 Hunneman Street, Boston Highlands, Dealer in New and Second Hand Furniture, Chamber Sets, Bedding, Oil Cloths, Ranges, Stoves, etc. Furniture Repaired and Upholstered at moderate prices. "A word to the

wise is sufficient" says the proverb, and if this is the case, we feel that even though our limited space does not permit of our treating of all the advantages to be gained by patronizing the establishment of which Mr. Edward Beard is the proprietor, located at Nos. 2033 Washington and 1 Hunneman Streets, with workshops in the rear, still we can say enough to induce such of our readers as may want anything in his line, to give that gentleman a call. He is a native of England and has conducted the enterprise in question since 1880. One large floor and a basement are utilized with a workshop in the rear and you may be sure that none of this space is wasted, for Mr. Beard carries one of the largest and most complete stocks of New and Second Hand Furniture to be found in the Highlands. But Furniture is by no means all he sells. House Furnishing Goods of every description are also very extensively handled and such indispensable articles as Bedding, Oil Cloths, Ranges, Stoves, Refrigerators, etc., are to be purchased of him at bottom prices. Especial attention is paid to the Repairing and Upholstering of Furniture in a neat and workmanlike manner at short notice, and every facility is at hand to do such work at the least possible expense. No one who wants to furnish a house or a single room, can afford to let the advantages offered by Mr. Beard go unimproved, and at all events it will cost nothing to visit his establishment and see what he has to offer.

Mrs. M. M. Davis, Home Cooking, 95 Warren Street. All of our readers know that "Bakers' Bread" however excellent (and some of our city bakers can make as good bread as can be had anywhere) is still not "home made" bread by any means, and there are very few people but in the long run, prefer the latter to the former. The difficulty has been, that in many households circumstances rendered it inexpedient to bake bread, and therefore recourse of necessity was had to that obtainable at some of the many bakeries in the vicinity. Mrs. M. M. Davis, being a practical housekeeper herself, observed this fact and likewise observed, as have doubtless most of our readers, that even that which was called "home made" bread at some establishments, was actually so in name only. As an experiment therefore, she secured the use of the premises now occupied by her at No. 95 Warren Street, and proceeded to furnish bread that was "home-made" in fact as well as in name. Her success was great and almost immediate. Operations were not begun until 1887, but already a thriving trade has been built up, and this is by no means entirely confined to those who are unable to bake at home, for it has been discovered that as Mrs. Davis bread is equal to any that can be produced, and as it is fresh daily it is hardly worth while to eat stale home made bread when she can furnish that which is satisfactory in every respect at a moderate price. Cake and Pastry are also supplied cooked in home fashion, and hot biscuits are on hand twice a day. Lunches will be served at all hours and callers will always receive prompt attention and satisfactory service. Mrs. Davis is to be congratulated on the success of her venture, and the public also have reason to appreciate her enterprise and skill.

Edward F. Otis, Successor to E. A. Alden, Apothecary, Cor. Washington & Dudley Sts. Boston Highlands. "Alden's Apothecary Store" has been familiar to residents of Roxbury for over twenty years and ten years before Mr. Alden assumed control of it, it was carried on by Mr. Chas. H. Saville who gave place to Mr. E. A. Alden in 1867. The present proprietor, Mr. Edward F. Otis, is a worthy successor of those who have preceded him, and those familiar with the high standing this store has always held, know that this is no small praise. Mr. Otis came into possession in 1887, but was by no means a stranger to the establishment at that time, as he had been associated with Mr. Alden some years previously, while pursuing his studies in the Massachusetts College of Pharmacy. He is a native of New Hampshire and may be depended upon to give his establishment that strict personal supervision which ensures accuracy and the maintenance of a salutary discipline. The premises occupied comprise one floor and a basement, and there is carried a remarkably complete stock of Drugs, Medicines, Chemicals, Fancy articles, etc., employment being given to two competent and polite assistants. The prescription department is maintained in the most efficient condition and physicians' prescriptions are compounded with the utmost care, but without the annoying delay so common at some drug stores. Mr. Otis has made every provision his experience could suggest, for the accommodation of this branch of his business, and those who may have their prescriptions filled here may rest assured that the motto of the enterprise, "Scientia et Progressus" will be strictly adhered to. "Take nothing for granted." "Reject nothing because it is new." These are the true principles of scientific progress, and as long as they are adhered to, there need be no fear that either undue enthusiasm or over-conservatism will stand in the way of constant improvement.

James H. Lord & Co., Grocers, Fine Teas and Pure Coffees, 359 Warren Street, Opposite Metropolitan R. R. Car Station, Boston Highlands. We need not state our reasons for making prominent mention of the establishment of which Mr. James H. Lord is the proprietor, located at No. 359 Warren Street, for this undertaking has not been carried on during all the years of its existence, without becoming familiar to most of our readers at all acquainted with representative Roxbury business enterprises. As a Family Grocery Store, we believe the establishment in question to be unsurpassed,

and in some respects even unequalled in the entire city, and we are positive that in no store devoted to retail trade, either in groceries or any other articles is there more careful attention given to the wants of customers and more pains taken to fill every order expeditiously and satisfactorily. This is high praise, you say? No. it is not praise at all, it is a simple statement of fact, and for its truth we have only to refer you to any one of the many customers who have traded here year after year. Under such methods of management, is it surprising that a large business is done? That orders steadily increase from year to year, and that satisfaction is expressed on every side? Of course not. Such a condition of affairs is but the natural result, and although highly gratifying is still richly deserved. Mr. Lord carries a large assortment of carefully selected goods and employs a sufficient number of experienced assistants to enable him to handle his heavy trade without confusion or delay. His Teas and Coffees are of the choicest character and most delicate flavor, and especial attention is given to the handling of the best Creamery Butter, this being received at short intervals, fresh from the dairy, and offered at most reasonable rates.

Thomas Crosby, Dealer in Fresh, Salt and Smoked Fish, Oysters, Lobsters and Clams, 2219 and 2375 Washington Street, Boston Highlands. Mr. Thomas Crosby of No. 2219 and 2375 Washington Street, is undeniably one of the most enterprising dealers in Fish and sea-food in general, in this part of the city, and we are gratified to learn that his success has been commensurate with the efforts he has made to accommodate the public. One floor, of the dimensions of 25x45 feet, is occupied at the address given, and another store is carried on at No. 2375 Washington Street, that measures 20x50 feet in size. This latter establishment has been occupied as a Fish market for some forty-five years, but has only been under the control of its present owner since 1887. At both stores a heavy stock is carried, comprising Fresh, Salt and Smoked Fish, together with Oysters, Lobsters and Clams in great variety. Mr. Crosby claims to keep the best Fancy Oysters to be obtained in the market, and we think that no one acquainted with his resources, will be likely to dispute the justice of this claim in the slightest. All kinds of Fancy Fresh Fish are also dealt in and in the proper season there may be found, Cod, Halibut, Salmon, Haddock, Mackerel, Lake Trout, Brook Trout, Blue Fish, Sword Fish, Black Bass, Striped Bass, Spanish Mackerel, Fresh Herring, Tom Cod, Tongues, Pickerel, Perch, Eels, Smelts, Shad, Pike, and Pickled Salmon Trout. All goods are fully warranted to give satisfaction, and it is by the careful avoidance of anything that might be looked upon as "sharp practice" and the invariable habit followed of keeping faith with customers, that Mr. Crosby has built up the extensive business he now carries on. He is a native of this city and has a very large circle of friends in the community. His prices are as low as the market will permit and orders will be promptly delivered free of expense.

Wm. L. Sweet, Apothecary, 2907 Washington Street, Boston Highlands. An old established and well-known Apothecary store of high reputation, is that conducted by Mr. William L. Sweet at No. 2907 Washington Street, and it may truthfully be said that the large business done is not entirely the result of the many years the enterprise has been before the public, but is likewise largely due to the methods employed by the proprietor of the establishment. Operations were begun in 1870 by Mr. B. W. Gardner, who was succeeded by the present owner, Mr. Sweet, in 1874. The latter gentleman is a native of this state and is connected with the Grand Army. A most varied and complete stock of Drugs, Medicines and chemicals is constantly carried, and every provision is made for the prompt and accurate filling of prescriptions, for this is the most important duty of the retail druggist, and cannot be too carefully and thoroughly attended to. As a result of the special preparations made, and pains taken, to properly serve the public in this respect. A large prescription trade has been built up, for the public have found the service rendered at this establishment, is much more satisfactory and reliable than that extended at many other stores of a similar character. A fine assortment of Toilet articles and Fancy Goods in general, is also presented by Mr. Sweet, and his prices on the same are as low as can be quoted anywhere, on goods of equal desirability. Sufficient assistance is at hand to allow of prompt and polite attention being given to every customer and we commend this establishment to the favorable consideration of our readers.

Thos. F. Boleman, Chicago Beef Market, Dealer in Provisions, Fruit and Vegetables, in their season, 2227 Washington Street. Chicago Beef is known the world over, and the "Chicago Beef Market," although not quite so celebrated, is still as popular and well-known an institution of the kind as is to be found in the Highlands. It is located at No. 2227 Washington Street, and has been carried on as a market for about twelve years, but only since coming into the possession of its present proprietor in 1881, has it attained the reputation it now holds for fair dealing and liberal business methods. Mr. Thomas F. Boleman, the gentleman alluded to was born in this city and has a very large circle of friends in the vicinity. The store is 20x70 feet in size, and is at all times fully stocked with Meats, Provisions, Fruits and Vegetables, four assistants being employed and courteous and prompt attention given to every caller. Beef, Mutton, Lamb, Veal, Pork, Game in its season in short all kinds of meat are to be had here at bottom prices, and whether you want a sirloin steak or a pig's foot, Mr. Boleman can supply you without delay, and the same may be said if vegetables of any kind are wanted, as a full assortment of these are carried in their seasons, as well as foreign and domestic fruits, etc. A large and constantly increasing business is done, and our readers may feel assured that no similar establishment has more to offer, or is prepared to give more complete satisfaction.

D. L. Jones, Successor to S. Jackson, Trunks, Bags, Shawl Straps Hats, Caps, Gloves etc. 2251 Washington Street, Hall's Block, Boston Highlands. The choosing of a trunk is a matter of no small importance to one who has to travel a great deal, and even when journeys are not often taken, it is well to have a trunk that is capable of standing hard usage, so as to be prepared to start for anywhere at short notice. A perfect trunk must be strong, light, easy to handle and capable of fully protecting its contents from injury, and if it has all these good points, it is bound to have one more and that is—durability. Mr. D. L. Jones, of No. 2251 Washington Street (Hall's Block) carries a fine assortment of Trunks to choose from and the prices placed on the same are as low as can be named on articles of similar merit. Travelling and hand bags, shawl straps, etc., are also largely dealt in, and as a specialty is made of trunk and bag repairing, those having old or damaged articles of the kind would do well to give Mr. Jones a call. He is a native of Boston, and is connected with the Grand Army, having been a member of Co. K. of the 22d Massachusetts at a time when all was not "quiet on the Potomac." Mr. Jones assumed control of his present undertaking in 1887, succeeding Mr. S. Jackson who founded it some 27 years previous, Mr. Jones having been with him since 1865. A fine and complete stock is carried, comprising, besides the goods already mentioned, a full selection of Hats, Caps, Gloves etc. The most approved styles of these articles are recived as soon as put on the market and the most fashionable headgear is quoted at prices within the means of all

---

Hausman & Cook, Successors to Hausman Bros., Manufacturers and Dealers in Fine Confectionery, 2107 Washington Street. That there is an immense amount of confectionery produced and sold in this city daily, all are aware, but not everybody is in a position to appreciate the improvement that has been made in the quality of the candies offered to the public within the past few years. Inferior goods are no longer in demand here in Boston, for the consumers of confectionery have been taught to expect something better and hence insist upon being served with articles of standard merit. No doubt it is largely owing to their appreciation of this fact that the firm of Hausman & Cook, who succeeded Hausman Brothers owe their exceptional success, for although the store was only opened in 1887, a large, thriving and rapidly increasing trade has already been established. The gentlemen constituting this concern are natives of Cambridge and Boston respectively and are thoroughly acquainted with the various details of their business. The premises in use, are of the dimensions of 20x60 feet and comprise one floor and a basement, employment being afforded to four efficient assistants. Fine confectionery of many kinds is manufactured and dealt in very extensively, and a well-equipped and largely patronized Ice-Cream Parlor is carried on in connection with the enterprise. A specialty is made of supplying Churches and Families with the best Ice cream. Orders delivered at residences promptly and mail orders given special attention. Hausman & Cook's Cream is always evenly frozen, delicately flavored and made of the best materials, and as it is offered at very reasonable rates, it is no wonder that a very large business is done in this department alone.

Sawyer's Highland Crockery House, No. 2157 Washington Street. Everybody in the Highlands has heard of "Sawyer's Variety Store" under Hotel Adelphi, No. 2157 Washington Street, and it would be strange indeed if they had not, for its proprietor is the originator of the five and ten cent business in this section of the city, and like most originators, although he has many imitators he has no equals. Mr. William Sawyer is a native of Boston and a member of the Odd Fellows, becoming identified with his present enterprise in 1880. The premises he occupies are of the dimensions of 20x70 feet and comprise one floor and a basement, the store having elegant plate glass show-windows and belngone of the finest in Roxbury. Large as it is, it is literally packed with a stock of goods so varied, and at the same time so useful, that while a mere catalogue of them would more than fill our remaining space, there is scarcely an article contained in it but what is indispensable to every well-regulated household. It is in the selection and purchase of goods that Mr. Sawyer's ability and experience tell, and a call at his establishment will show to what he owes the great success he has won. Crockery-ware is given special attention and dinner and tea sets in great variety are at hand to choose from at prices that cannot fail to please. Glass, Tin and Wooden Ware are also very largely handled and in the line of tin-ware alone, Mr. Sawyer's assortment would furnish a complete stock to the average variety store. Then he offers Lamps, chimneys and Burners, Fancy Goods of every description including Vases, China Cups and Saucers, China Mugs, Pocket Books, Birthday and other cards, Dolls of every description, and hundred of other things that everybody wants and that everybody can purchase here at bottom prices. A magnificent and complete assortment of five and ten cent goods shows that Mr. Sawyer is better prepared than ever to meet all competition in this line, and in short his store is a place where it is safe to say genuine bargains and fair treatment are offered to all. He is also Justice of the Peace.

E. B. Pratt, Proprietor of the Economy Butter and Egg Store, 2232 Washington Street. Fresh Country Eggs, Choice Cream Cheese and Pure Milk. Like the man who "could eat crow but didn't hanker after it" the vast majority of civilized mankind doubtless could eat bread without butter, but it is safe to assume that excepting in case of unusual hunger very few would "hanker after it." Indeed the writer of this remembers that the chief deterring influence that prevented him going west when a boy and fighting "Indians," was a consideration of the fact that butter would have to be left behind when the "plains" were reached, thus butter helped him to grow up well "bred" and it is not surprising that an article considered of so much importance, should give employment to many hands in its production and sale. One of the most popular establishments handling butter at retail in the Highlands is that conducted by Mr. E. B. Pratt, at No. 2232 Washington Street, and since this gentleman began operations in 1857 he has built up a large patronage by the superior quality and low prices, which characterize this article as dealt in by him. He is a native of Mass. and well known, he employs an attentive assistant, who will deliver goods promptly and correctly. Fresh milk and cheese are also among the products in which he deals extensively. Patrons will find that he is always ready to advance their comfort and convenience by all practical means.

Alfred H. Howe, dealer in Boots and Shoes, 2179 Washington Street. Custom work a specialty. The establishment conducted by Mr. A. H. Howe at No. 2179 Washington Street, is one of the handsomest in this section of the city wherein it is located, and its beauty is only increased by an application of the time-honored saying "handsome is that handsome does," for the goods and prices are enough to delight the heart of the most careful buyer. The spacious show windows are fairly crowded with foot wear of every description, and whether a pair of slippers or a pair of boots is wanted; shoes for streets or pumps for party wear, here is the place to get them and here is the place where a great many people do get them. Altogether an immense stock is carried considering that a purely retail business is done. One floor and a basement are occupied and five assistants are employed, and all callers will have their wants attended to without annoying delay. All goods are guaranteed to be as represented. Mr. Howe is a native of Boston and has been in business at his present place since 1871. He belongs to the Knights of Honor and is well known both in business and social circles.

A. M. Richardson, Groceries, Choice Teas, Coffees, etc., 1951 Washington Street, corner Woodbury, Boston. There are about as many theories as to the best way of doing business as there are people interested enough in the subject to talk about it, but after all, no improvement has been made on the good old-fashioned plan of giving every customer a fair equivalent for his money and treating him in a manner that renders it not only profitable but pleasant for him to come again. Such has been the method pursued by Mr. A. M. Richardson of 1951 Washington Street. He began operations in 1884 as successor to Cobb & Co., who had occupied the premises since 1879, the dimensions of same being 20x60, with a large basement. Mr. Richardson is a native of Mass., and well known. His success has been pronounced and prominent enough to fully justify the pride he feels in his business. Groceries, teas, coffees, spices and flour are handled in both large and small quantities, the most popular brands being in stock and sold either by the bag or barrel, at but a small margin above wholesale rates. Good service is guaranteed as Mr. Richardson employs four experienced assistants.

13

Mrs. C. M. Hayes, Dealer in Fine Fruit and Confectionery, 116 Dudley Street, opposite Dudley Street Opera House. Fruit is generally either good or bad for there is but little of it that can be placed between these extremes. Good fruit is by no means hurtful to the health, nor is it of necessity expensive, that is to say, provided it is bought in the right place, and by the way, we know of none better than that carried on by Mrs. C. M. Hayes, at 116 Dudley St. The proprietress Mrs. Hayes was born in Boston, and is very well known and much esteemed by her friends. Business has been carried on by Mrs. Hayes at the above mentioned place since 1882, and her methods of doing it have been such as to have gained her the patronage of all lovers of fresh fruit and confectionery; fruits of all kinds in their seasons are largely dealt in, and rates are extremely low. One floor 20 x 50 feet is occupied and everything guaranteed as represented.

John F. Newton, Jr., Real Estate and Fire Insurance Agency, 53 Warren Street. The influence of an active, enterprising and energetic agent in real estate operations cannot fail to be beneficial in stimulating trade and calling attention to the natural advantages of a particular section, and this influence has been exerted to a very considerable degree by Mr. John F. Newton, Jr., since he began operations in 1886. As many of our readers doubtless know, Mr. Newton is a native of Boston, and has a very large circle of friends throughout this vicinity. His office is located at No. 53 Warren street, and those wishing to buy, sell, exchange or rent real estate, will do well to give him an early call. He is prepared to assume the charge of estates on behalf of non-resident owners, and only needs to be tried to furnish convincing evidence of his fitness for such duties. Those who have made use of his services in this capacity speak in the highest terms of his faithfulness and zeal, and all agree in ascribing to him a careful regard for the best interests of his customers. He has a number of valuable pieces of property to lease and for sale, which will suit all. Mr. Newton is also engaged in the insurance business, and acts as agent for the well known Hanover Fire Insurance company of New York. This company has a cash capital of $1,000,000, and a net surplus of $310,003.07, having on the first of January, 1887, total assets amounting to $2,546,674.95. Thus it will be seen that the ability of the Hanover to honor every obligation is put beyond a doubt, and that its insurance is insurance that may safely be depended upon.

W. J. Barta, Shirt Maker, and Dealer in Gent's Furnishing Goods, 143 Dudley Street, Boston Highlands. The establishment conducted by Mr. W. J. Barta at No. 143 Dudley Street, is very popular with the gentlemen of this section for it is certainly known to every young man residing in Roxbury, who desires to dress correctly. Mr. Barta began operations in his present line of business it 1878. One floor and a basement are occupied, 25 x 60 feet in size, and a stock is carried that is so extensive and varied that no description of it is possible in these columns. It comprises every article generally handled by a first-class men's outfitter, and the very latest styles and most approved fashions are always fully represented. Mr. Barta has made it a point, from the inception of his business, to let his customers know just what they are buying, and all representations made by him or his assistants may be fully depended upon. He keeps himself perfectly informed in regard to the usages of the best society as far as the costume and its accessories are concerned, and his advice in matters of dress will be found valuable and always in accord with the dictates of refined taste. One of the most important departments of the business is the making of fine shirts to order, as Mr. Barta is an experienced draughtsman in this line, and a very heavy patronage is enjoyed, as perfection of style and fit is guaranteed. Gloves, Fancy Hose, Underwear, and all the many articles required by gentlemen are obtainable here at moderate prices, and Toilet Articles, Perfumery, etc., are also largely dealt in. Employment is given to two efficient assistants, and courteous attention is extended to every caller. The fine custom shirts which he is manufacturing to order, embrace Fine White Dress, French Cambric, Pesangs, and English Cheviot. At short notice, and at lowest prices possible, for the very best quality of goods and fine workmanship.

Glen Laundry, 160 and 162 Dudley Street, S. K. Poore, Proprietor. Widely known and largely patronized is the establishment known as the "Glen Laundry," of which Mr. S. K. Poore is the proprietor. Notwithstanding the competition there is in this branch of business, Mr. Poore has succeeded in establishing a large and enviable trade. His work has always proved satisfactory, both in the way it is performed and in the prices charged for same. The work-rooms are all equipped with the latest and most approved appliances for carrying on the business, which is conducted mainly under Mr. Poore's personal supervision. All work is called for and delivered at the shortest possible notice. Special attention is given to fine laces, embroideries, etc.; dresses of the finest texture being laundried equal to new. Orders for carpet cleaning received, and promptly attended to. Mr. Poore, who is a native of Boston and well known, is fully competent to carry on the business he has undertaken and so successfully conducted for the past six years. He employs seven efficient assistants, and occupies at 160 and 162 Dudley street one floor 30 x 50 feet in dimensions.

G. E. Gray, Photographer, 1068 and 1070 Tremont Street. Old and Faded Pictures Copied and Enlarged. All work done by the Instantaneous Process. Since the time that the great French artist discovered the art of daguerreotyping, photography has been making rapid and continual advances, until today it occupies a position of commanding influence. Mr. G. E. Gray opened his photographing studio at 1068 and 1070 Tremont Street, in 1883, having been previously located on Hanover Street for four years, and the popularity and success which have attended his subsequent progress, speak most conclusively for his skill as an artist, and the good taste of the people of this section of the city. Mr. Gray occupies at the above address three floors, each 20x90 feet in dimensions, where he is prepared to offer his patrons the most satisfactory work in all branches of fine photography. All work is done by the Instantaneous Process. Old and faded pictures copied and enlarged, and special attention given to life-size portraits, also to pictures of children. Three skilled and artistic assistants are constantly employed. Mr. Gray has the contract for the photos for the entire baseball league. An examination of his work, and the testimony of his large circle of patrons, will confirm all he claims for his talents and workmanship. Mr. Gray has made many friends in our midst by his thorough and uniform courtesy and trained skill as an artist.

Thomas Carey, Plumber, and dealer in Plumbing Material, Jobbing done on the most reasonable terms. Contracts faithfully executed. No. 1186 Tremont Street. The Plumbing business is extensively carried on in this city, by Mr. Thomas F. Carey, whose business premises are located at No. 1186 Tremont St., and who is a practical and thorough workman in all kinds of sanitary, and house plumbing. He carries also a complete assortment of plumbers' supplies. Mr. Carey who has enjoyed a long experience, established himself at his present location in 1880, and is regarded as a leading representative in his line of trade in this neighborhood. His successful and steadily increasing business necessitates the employment of eight skilled workmen and every order is promptly and efficiently attended to. The favorable prices and the skill displayed in all work, combine to make this establishment one in which the utmost confidence can be placed. Mr. Carey is a native of Boston, he is genial and affable in his dealings with the public, and highly esteemed in this community as an energetic, enterprising business man, and worthy the confidence of all with whom he may be brought into business relations.

G. A. & S. W. Brackett, Jobbing Masons, Whitening and Coloring a Specialty, Office, No. 147 Dudley, corner Warren Street. The average citizen may not have occasion for the service of a mason very often, but when he does want any work of this kind done, he finds it to his advantage to have it performed in a thorough manner, and as not every one who hangs out his shingle is competent and anxious to fill orders in a first-class manner we take pleasure in calling attention to a firm who are, G. A. & S. W. Brackett, located corner of Dudley and Warren streets, make a specialty of jobbing orders, and are fully prepared to attend to them at short notice and in an entirely satisfactory manner. The business experience of these gentlemen, having been of great length, enables them to be prepared to meet all emergencies that may arise, and avoid all unnecessary expense and annoyance to their patrons. Ten skilled workmen are employed, whitening and coloring are given special attention, and we can unreservedly recommend this firm to all who may wish first-class masonry done.

Cunard Market, Provisions and Country Produce, Wholesale and Retail, by J. C. Kingsley, 1060 Tremont Street. So old and historical a city as Boston has of course many business houses identified with it of long establishment and unblemished reputation, and among these is the house popularly known as the Cunard Market, located at 1060 Tremont Street. The inception of the enterprise alluded to occurred fifty years ago and has been under the management of Mr. J. C. Kingsley since 1877. An extensive wholesale and retail business is transacted in provisions and country produce of all kinds. The premises cover an area of 22x50 feet. Employment being given to only capable and experienced assistants, and the entire establishment is conducted in a thoroughly systematic business manner. The position held by this house enables it to procure goods at the lowest rates and on the most favorable terms and these advantages are shared by its customers to the mutual benefit of both parties. Mr. Kingsley is a native of this city. He is a reliable and conscientious business man, and these attributes have had an important influence in extending his trade.

C. E. Beane, Artist Photographer, 2228 Washington St., corner Warren St. Of the many photographic establishments in the Highlands none have gained a reputation for more uniformly artistic and reliable work than has that conducted by Mr. C. E. Beane at 2228 Washington St. cor. Warren, founded nearly a quarter of a century ago. It early established a high record for its productions. The premises occupied are a reception room 20x20 and an operating-room 15x20. As two courteous and capable assistants are employed, all orders are assured prompt and satisfactory attention; the various instruments and appliances in use are all of the latest and most improved design and construction and this fact, together with the experience and skill possessed by the proprietor and his assistants sufficiently explain the large patronage enjoyed and the high artistic merit of the portraits made. All styles of pictures are made and while a good likeness is guaranteed, the retouching or finishing as it is called, of the portrait is so skillfully done that the best points of the features are brought out, and an artistic picture and not a mere photograph is the result. He also makes a specialty of crayons, pastels, India and water-color portraits. The prices will be found very reasonable and the delivery prompt.

Roxbury Novelty Works, Manufacturers of Odd Furniture, Fancy Boxes, Small Bureaus, Book Cases, Cabinets, and anything in wood, 1203 Harrison Avenue, between Dudley and Warren Streets. Special attention given to repairing all kinds of Antique Furniture. Repairing and Polishing a Specialty. Mr. O. J. Jorden, the manager of this business, is a native of Maine. He began business 36 years ago, removing here in 1878. He now has a very extensive custom as his long experience enables him successfully to undertake anything in that line of work from the making of a stool to furnishing an office. He not only makes all kinds of odd furniture to order—being a skilled cabinet maker—but he gives special attention to repairing. Among the different articles which he manufactures to order we would mention window and door screens, mantel shelves, book-cases, desks, tables, stands, drawer cases, signs, sashes, patterns, models, whatnots, order and letter boxes, counters, shelves, cornices, frames for mirrors, etc. The premises occupied are on the street floor and thus customers have no stairs to climb. The location at 1203 Harrison Av., between Dudley and Warren Sts., is very central and convenient. The shop occupied is 20x30 feet in size and is well equipped with all necessary tools and appliances for the successful conducting of the business. Two assistants are employed. The prices charged will be found very reasonable and the work guaranteed first-class.

Miss E. McDormand, Dealer in Stationery, Newspapers, Fancy Goods, Toys, Tobacco and Cigars, also Griffith's Laundry Agency, No. 2718 Washington Street, near Dale. The business carried on by Miss E. McDormand at 2718 Washington Street, was established in 1884, and the methods of this lady have been so liberal as to have gained her the good will and patronage of all residing in her vicinity. Her store which is of the dimensions of 20 x 50 feet, is stocked with a well-selected assortment of toys, stationery, fancy goods, and also a full line of the finest cigars and tobacco. Her trade in this line has grown very large, for Miss McDormand has used every effort to satisfy the demands of her customers. Toys of every description are constantly on hand, and a polite assistant serves customers who will find the price on everything offered for sale, as low as the lowest. Daily and Sunday papers are delivered at residences, and orders are taken for Griffith's Steam Laundry.

Henry Towle & Co., Dealers in first class Provisions, Oakland Market, No. 2714 Washington Street, Boston Highlands. The conditions attending the carrying on of a first class provision store have greatly changed of late years and these changes are too well known to require detailed mention here. The day when some dingy cellar with cobweb-covered windows and appearance of dirt and neglect could be occupied by a house catering to respectable trade, has we are happy to say, gone by, and in its stead has come a time when neatness is not only appreciated, but even demanded, and we may say that the establishment conducted by Mr. Henry Towle & Co., at No. 2714 Washington Street, is well worthy of careful study, by those who seek a model from which to copy. Mr. Towle founded his present business in 1882, and his success has been as prompt and decided, as his management has been liberal and far sighted. One floor and a basement are occupied, 20 x 50 feet in dimensions, and beef, mutton, pork, hams, and all kinds of fresh and salt meat are handled very largely. Two courteous and well-informed assistants are employed and all callers given early and polite attention.

F. S. Cate, successor to Mrs. E. A. Peiroe, Egleston Square News Depot and Circulating Library. 3107 Washington Street, Stationery, Cards, Toys and Confectionery; Daily, Weekly and Sunday papers delivered at Residences. The Egleston Square News Depot, so widely known for its honorable dealing and its prompt and polite attention to customers, desires to call the public's attention to its fine line of stationery and choice confectionery. It also has a large and well-selected assortment of toys, cards, etc., in their season. All goods are as represented and the prices as low as to be found in Boston. The Wollaston Steam Laundry, which does an excellent style of work, has an agency here and all orders in this department will be promptly filled. It is also a public telephone office which gives it great prominence. Telephone No. 3707. The circulating library is constantly having new books added to it, which with its present number of volumes furnishes a large variety of interesting reading. Articles are received for Lewando's French Dye House, the reputation of which is too well known to need further comment. Everything is first-class throughout and any new patrons who see fit to give us a call will receive the same courteous treatment as our former friends.

Andrew Littig, Dealer in all kinds of Beef, Mutton, Pork, Lard, Hams, Poultry, Eggs, etc. Also Fruit and Vegetables. No. 2 Pynchon St. Of the general business of Boston Highlands the meat and provision trade forms a very important part; many enterprising houses are engaged in it. Among these we are pleased to mention, for the benefit of our readers in this section of the city, the house of Andrew Littig, located at No. 2 Pynchon street, Boston Highlands. He conducts one of the best retail meat and provision stores in this locality, which is fully supplied with a well-selected stock of first-class provisions. This house was established as a market thirty years ago, and has been under the control of Mr. Littig since 1882, who was formerly at 1337 Tremont street for thirteen years. He has been successful in conducting a large retail trade, which requires the assistance of four capable and reliable clerks. The store occupied covers an area of 20 x 50 feet, and is well stocked with a large assortment of meats, etc., embracing all kinds of beef, mutton, pork, lard, hams, poultry, eggs, fruit and vegetables, while the prices are guaranteed to be entirely satisfactory to all who deal at this establishment. Mr. Littig is a native of Germany, and has established a reputation for fair and honorable dealings, and we commend his house to our readers who desire first-class supplies in the above-mentioned lines.

Frederick L. Rich, Bread and Pastry Baker, 170 Hampden Street. One of the best places in the vicinity in which it is located, to obtain good, wholesome bread, is the Bakery conducted by Frederick L. Rich, and located at No. 170 Hampden street. The business was inaugurated in 1883 by Mr. Eben Hoffman, but has never been more successfully managed than since the present owner has taken control of it which he did in 1885. One floor 20x70 feet in size is utilized, and all kind of fancy cakes, pies, etc. are constantly on hand. Hot rolls morning and night, which articles are made from only the finest flour. Mr. Rich has had a great experience in his trade and gives his customers the advantage of it. His prices are as reasonable as can be found in any other establishment. Three competent assistants are given employment, and polite attention is extended to all who may patronize this popular establishment.

C. C. Fuller, Carpenter and Builder, 21 Blue Hill Avenue, Boston. No person has striven with greater zeal during the time since his establishment to bring to the front that branch of industry in which they labor, than has Mr. C. C. Fuller, and he has been rewarded, for today he occupies a leading position in the building trade of Roxbury, and has acquired a fame for the reliable and substantial manner in which he fulfills his contracts. This business was established by its present proprietor in 1841, who is a thoroughly reliable and practical builder, and all work undertaken by him is accomplished under his personal supervision. The premises occupied by him are conveniently located at No. 21 Blue Hill avenue, and cover an area of 15 x 25 feet which is equipped with all the requisites necessary for wood-working of all kinds. Mr. Fuller gives employment to a number of skilled and experienced workmen,

and his business operations consist of the erection of buildings, and all kinds of carpenter work. It is a matter of the greatest importance that buildings should be erected with care and of good materials, and those contemplating building of any description will promote their own interests by consulting with Mr. Fuller before entering into contracts with other parties. Mr. Fuller is a native of this city and his long business career has gained him the reputation of being one of the most reliable builders in this section of Boston.

Miss E. Babb, 220 Dudley Street, next to Church, dealer in School Utensils, Toys, Confectionery, Periodicals. Also Select Employment Agency. It is hard to find a satisfactory substitute for experience in the carrying on of any industry or business establishment in which any pronounced amount of competition is met with and although material ability may sometimes do much when experience alone is to be contended with, it is only when the two are combined that the best results can be attained. A fine example of the truth of this statement is shown by the neat little establishment presided over by Miss Ellen Babb, at No. 229 Dudley Street. Miss Babb, who is a native of New Hampshire, but has resided all her life in Boston, has devoted considerable time to the supply of good help to families in need of such and has been successful without a doubt. She receives applicants for any kind of female help desired, and guarantees satisfaction. The hearts of all the children in the neighborhood are daily made happy by the supply of fresh confectionery which is to be obtained at the above-mentioned place. Toys and school supplies are largely dealt in and Miss Babb's endeavor is to please all who patronize her. Everything dealt in is of the best quality obtainable and her prices are very low.

HISTORICAL SKETCH

OF

DORCHESTER.

Of all the suburban towns and cities which have been absorbed in Boston, as she has spread her encircling arms further and further into the surrounding country, none have more strongly and notably retained their individuality than Dorchester. This has been the result of its long cherished memories and traditions which have seemed dear above most earthly things to the many old residents who still constitute the bulk of the people in the region, and not until many years have changed the people and their characters will the memory of their separate town-life be forgotten. The history of the town has been one of unusual interest even among the towns of New England and one of which its people may well be proud. It reaches back to the earliest days of this country, as Capt. John Smith of Virginia, first English settler, is known to have stopped here in 1614, and traded with the Neponset Indians. He found, moreover, that the French traders had been here before him, this being a favorite spot with the natives, and when one of the first settlers was digging the cellar for his log cabin, in 1631, he found French coins, which were doubtless a relic of a trader's visit. Capt. Smith quarrelled with the Indians here and took French leave, and the place does not seem to have been visited again until 1621, when a military expedition, probably under the command of Miles Standish, and of which a good idea can be gained from Longfellow's celebrated poem, came hither from the Plymouth Colony, now about a year old. They, however, soon departed and were followed in 1626 by the first regular settler, a gentleman by the name of Mr. David Thompson, who established himself on the island in the harbor now known by his name. He was the first recorded inhabitant of Boston Harbor, and carried on quite an extensive trading business with the Indians. A few other unknown wanderers settled in this vicinity before the arrival of the Massachusetts Bay Colony, under the leadership of John Winthrop, to which the real founding of the town must be ascribed. The Indians inhabiting this section were known as the "Neponsets," a branch of the great nation after which Massachusetts was named. At this time their chief was Checkatabot, generally regarded as the most influential chieftain around the bay, so that his friendship was greatly sought and valued. The deed of the region was obtained from him and his descendants. The Neponset tribe numbered at this time about one hundred men, which rapidly decreased, and after the death of Checkatabot, in 1633, it lost all unity and weight. They possessed large corn fields in the vicinity of Dorchester, which have long been cleared and cultivated, and which were a great advantage to the early settlers here.

That portion of the Massachusetts Bay Colonists who settled at Dorchester, were among the most honored and influential of them all. Rev. John White, was the original mover in obtaining the charter for the Massachusetts Colony, and no other beside Winthrop was more active or effective in getting together the company to whom so much of New England's growth is due. Mr. White was the rector of Dorchester, England, and organized the Salem company, which, under John Endicott, settled that town in 1628. In the following year was organized a body known as the Dorchester Company, consisting of about sixty families, two ministers of the gospel, two government officials, and three military leaders, so that in size, character and means the settlers of Dorchester had few equals among the early colonists. They arrived here May 30, 1630, and landed on the south side of Dorchester Neck. They immediately settled to work and soon had one of the most thriving settlements on the coast. Among the leading men were the Rev. Mr. Maverick and Rev. Mr. Wareham, Messrs. Rossiter and Ludlow, government officers from London, Capt. John Mason, Capt. Richard Southcote, quarter-masters John Smith, Henry Wolcott, Thomas Ford, George Dyer, William Gaylord, William Rockwell and William Phelps. Isaac Stoughton, George Minot, Roger Clap, George Hall, Richard Collicott and Nathaniel Duncan were younger men who were very active in every line of work

The center of the town was fixed at Allen's Plain, south of Old Harbor, and here the dwelling houses clustered about the meeting house and the fort, though the quiet attitude of the Indians rendered the latter unneeded. The first summer was attended by much sickness owing to scarcity of provisions, but the settlers soon conquered these difficulties in a large measure. They were said to have been the first settlers who set systematically to work at fishing, and in this were very successful. The town was divided into lots of from fifty to one hundred acres apiece. The Dorchester church was organized at Plymouth, Eng., before the company sailed, and was the oldest in the State, outside of the Pilgrim settlement at Plymouth. In all civil and military affairs, Dorchester for a long time took the lead in this vicinity. The right to use the name of Dorchester was conveyed in 1630, by the Court in London. Out of one hundred and eight freemen in the Massachusetts Bay Colony in 1630, twenty-four hailed from Dorchester. A visitor named Wood wrote in 1633 that "Dorchester is the greatest town in New England;" but its laurels were soon contested. A great deal of attention was early given to fishing and commerce. The Dorchester Record Book goes back to 1632-33, and is the oldest in Massachusetts. In 1633, the government which had been in the hands of the church and freemen, was vested in the form of a town, being also the first of its kind here, and followed soon by all the other settlements. The first selectmen were Mr. Johnson, Mr. Pomeroy, Mr. Richards, John Pierce, George Hull, William Phelps and Thomas Ford.

The first meeting house in Dorchester and the colony was erected in 1031 at the corner of the present Pleasant and Cottage Streets. In 1633 a sign of business progress is noted in the erection of a mill by Isaac Stoughton, and in 1634, a bridge over the Neponset was completed. The first general court of the colony met in 1634, Dorchester being represented by Isaac Stoughton, Wm. Phelps and George Hull. A burying ground was commenced in 1633. The tax for the whole colony for 1633 was $800, of which Dorchester paid the largest single amount, $80; Boston only furnishing $48. In 1633, a ship load of eighty persons and twelve kine arrived to increase the town at Dorchester.

A large part of the first settlers of Dorchester were led, in 1636, to emigrate to the valley of the Connecticut river, having heard of its fertile soil. Over sixty persons, among them Mr. Maverick and Mr. Warham, the minister, Mr. Ludlow and other leading men, went on this new expedition. But their places were taken by another company of about one hundred persons, under the leadership of the Rev. Richard Mather, who arrived from England in the same year. So the little settlement went on increasing steadily, despite loss and desertion. An interesting evidence of her advance is shown in the fact that a ship was built at Dorchester in 1642, one of the earliest in this country. In 1645, a sum of $235 was collected to build a new meeting house. The life of the town from now on through the century was that of the typical New England in its infant stage and growth. One of Dorchester and Massachusetts' leading citizens, Maj.-Gen. Humphrey Atherton, died here in 1661. In the following year the town of Milton was set off from Dorchester. The unsettled state of affairs in England in the last part of the 17th century, caused great anxiety here, which was however soon overpast. The first actual touch of Indian fighting at Dorchester occurred in 1675, at the outbreak of King Philip's war when there was considerable bloodshed all around. Fourteen men enlisted for the war, of whom two were killed and two wounded in the final and decisive battle of the war in Rhode Island.

The town was much interested in the witchery troubles in 1681, though it did not go so far as to disgrace itself by any actual executions. In 1695, a party under the leadership of the Rev. John Lord, left here and founded the town of Dorchester, South Carolina. The expedition was for a religious purpose, and is said to have been the first missionary company that ever left the shores of New England. By it was planted the first Congregational church in the south, as formerly Dorchester people had founded the first church in Connecticut. These early Dorchesterites seem to have been great originators. An interesting movement, reminding one of the present century, was a religious association formed by the young men of Dorchester in 1697, at that time a unique and marked step. Lt.-Gov. Wm. Stoughton, one of early Dorchester's most able and distinguished men, died in 1701. His epitaph is one of the most beautiful and expressive of its kind ever written. Several earthquakes were felt here in 1727, it being a very remarkable year for natural phenomena, storms, etc. The year 1740 was remarkable for the visit of the Rev. George Whitefield, who made a great impression and did a great work for good.

The war of Independence first began to be thought of here in 1701, and no place was more enthusiastic in its endeavors and preparations. In 1771, the town drew up resolutions to the British government, vigorous and bold in plain statement of cold facts, and at the same time appointed a committee of correspondence, as follows: Capt. Lemuel Robinson, Capt. John Hemans, and Samuel How. At Lexington, Concord and Bunker Hill, it was nobly and largely represented, and the great critical movement of the seige of Boston was made here; March 16, 1776, the night expedition passed through Roxbury, and worked all night in the fortifications on Dorchester Heights. Unable to destroy or attack it, the British troops were obliged to rapidly evacuate, March 18, 1776, as the possession of this place left Boston at the mercy of the Continental cannon.

The census of the town was taken in 1776, when it was found to number 1550 persons; 1515 white, and 85 negroes; number of families 291. The town offered large bounties for enlistment, and not only did seventy-nine soldiers go out from this town, but they even came from other towns to enlist on account of the large bounty. £5,343 were paid out by the town in one way and another to the soldiers, and their patriotism and generosity never grew cool throughout the whole struggle. Many distinguished soldiers hailed from Dorchester, among them Col. Samuel Robinson, and Lt.-Col. Samuel Pierce. In 1780, £40,000 was raised by the town for the hiring of soldiers, more than was spent in all the other years of the war put together. Some fifty men or more went from this town in 1787 to aid in the suppression of Shay's rebellion. The year 1801 was rendered memorable by the occurrence of a duel, the only one recorded in the town, between a Mr. Miller and a Mr. Rand, over a love affair. The latter gentleman had first shot, but failed to hit. Then Mr. Miller wanted it decided without bloodshed but Mr. Rand would not consent and so was killed. As early as 1803, prominent citizens of Boston began to agitate the annexation of Dorchester Neck to that city, and in spite of vigorous opposition on the part of Dorchesterites, a bill was passed by the Legislature granting it in 1804. In the following year the South bridge from Boston was completed at a cost of $56,000. The old meeting house was so shattered by the severe gale of September, 1815, that a new one had to be built the following year. The town took an earnest and active interest in the war of 1812-15, and contributed a full quota of men and money. The population kept on steadily increasing as follows:

1790	1,722	1840	4,458
1800	2,847	1846	6,500
1810	2,930	1848	7,386
1820	3,684	1850	7,968
1830	4,064	1855	8,357

The town has always taken great interest in educational matters, and one of its first public movements was the ordering of a tax to maintain a school in Dorchester. The Rev. Thos. Waterhouse was the first school-master, and the first building was erected at the corner of Pleasant and Cottage streets. Gov. Stoughton of Dorchester, left at his death in 1701, the sum of £150 to the schools of Dorchester, which was carefully applied. The funds allotted to the schools by the town, increased steadily with its growth, being in 1805, $1650; in 1806, $1900; in 1807, $2,000; in 1812, $2,700; in 1821, $2,877; in 1857, $28,622.98. Since that time the schools have steadily advanced with the times, and are now on a level with the best in the state. The town has always taken a great interest in Harvard, almost all its school teachers and leading professional men having graduated there. Several hundred, among them some of Harvard's greatest men, have been graduates of that University.

The union of Dorchester and Boston, in 1869, was one of the great eventful occurrences in its history. After discussion for many years and not without some struggling, the act of union was passed by the Legislature in 1869, and this was accepted by both places in January, 1870. Since that time the growth of the place has been rapid, though absorbed in that of Boston. It has come to be one of the most popular and delightful district anywhere in the vicinity for residences, and a great number of beautiful rural mansions have been erected in recent years. The accessibility of Dorchester, as well as its topical and scenic advantages, have contributed to this result. The main thoroughfares through the district, are

AN ELM HILL RESIDENCE.

Washington, Bowdoin, Hancock and Boston streets, and Dorchester avenue. Commercial interests are very largely centered about these and off from them in every direction lead beautiful avenues lined by extensive, park-like grounds and charming villas. Savin Hill is one of the spots especially famed for its surpassing beauty, being a lovely height, with commanding view of the water on three sides, and with its beauty of decoration and residences visible for miles around. Landscape gardening is an art much practiced, and unrivalled effects and triumphs in horticultural art are achieved. Elm avenue, near Grove Hall, is noted for its fine residences.

There are several fine parks in the Dorchester district, the best known being the old square on Meeting House hill, which, although careful attention is given to its culture and adorning, still retains exquisite touches of antique charms. The old colonial days are brought to mind by historical memorial and the proud traditions of the town are tenderly revived and cherished. It is charmingly situated and in every respect a delightful spot. The soldiers' monument which has been erected here by the people of Dorchester to the memory of their honored dead, adds a touch of modern splendor to the old-time spot. The architect of the monument, was Mr. B. F. Dwight, and he has succeeded in producing an admirable and substantial effect, well in keeping with the red Gloucester granite of which the monument is composed. It is after the form of an obelisk, and including the pedestal, is thirty-one feet high, and eight feet square at the base. The names of the fallen heroes are inscribed in tablets on the pedestal. It was dedicated in September, 1869. Of other pleasant parks in this district are, the square on the top of Mount Bowdoin, and the one at the corner of Church and Bowdoin streets, known as Eaton Square, both elegantly laid out.

UPHAM'S CORNER (DORCHESTER), IN 1883.

Upham's Corner is one of the most interesting spots in this old, yet progressive town. Nowhere else can be better seen that blending of the old and the new than here. About this spot the very earliest settlements were made, and it has always been a leading center of Dorchester, both in business and social life. The old burying-ground here contains tombstones with older inscriptions and dates than any other place in this country, with one possible exception in Virginia, can show. One can linger for hours in this old spot among the treasured memorials of the very earliest days of our country. Since the union with Boston, Upham's Corner has made great advances in the commercial and now contains a number of large and beautiful buildings representing some of the leading houses in this vicinity.

Grove Hall has gained a fame all through this country and others as occupying a unique and unrivalled position in the treatment and cure of a disease hitherto regarded as incurable. The originator and manager is Dr. Charles Cullis, and under his able direction this institution, incorporated in 1870, has grown steadily until it has attained its present preëminence. It has relied entirely on voluntary contributions, and from this source a round $600,000 have now been received, and nearly 2,000 patients have received treatment. The main building, known as the Consumptives' Home, is a large and elegant mansion, capable of accommodating eighty patients. There are other buildings, including two homes for children, one for those suffering from diseases of the spine, and a free chapel. When we remember that this great work was begun entirely without funds, and that no solicitation for aid has ever been made, but what has come has been voluntary, no wonder that Dr. Cullis calls it "a work of faith," and believes in answer to prayer. The system which has been maintained since the beginning has been that of the famous Orphan Asylum of Müller, and it admits all poor persons sick with consumption, without home or friends, whether white or black, old or young, foreign or native. The success and fame of this noble work is no less an honor to Dorchester, than it is an unmeasured blessing to thousands suffering from this scourge of New England which has been combatted so unsuccessfully in the past. That it will continue to grow in prosperity is no less the desire than the assurance of all who have known it.

Among the oldest and most influential churches in New England is the First Parish Unitarian Church of Dorchester. It was organized May 20, 1630, just previous to the departure of the Dorchester settlers from Plymouth, and the first services were held in June, 1630, in the open air. The church has only had twelve successive ministers in more than 250 years. Among the most famous of these were the Rev. Richard Mather, who served 33 years, John Danforth, 48 years, Thaddeus Mason Harris, 43 years, and Samuel J. Barrows. The present structure was built in 1866, and is one of the most interesting objects in the town.

The second church of Dorchester was founded in 1808, with a membership of 64, and its size and influence have steadily increased since that time. In course of its eighty years it has had but three pastors: John Codman, D.D., James H. Means, D.D., and E. U. Packard, D.D. It has been a great power for good as the place has grown, and its influence has ever been on the right side. Dorchester is rich in charitable works and institutions, among which is the Industrial School for Girls, a noble work founded in 1855. It is situated on Center street, and capable of maintaining about thirty girls annually. The annual expense is over $5,000, met by legacies and subscriptions. In every department of its life, religious, educational, commercial social and philanthropical, Dorchester is fully alive and widely active, giving numerous evidences of being one of the most energetic sections in this lively city. Its popularity and adaptability for suburban residences must surely increase for a great many decades yet to come, and it will ever remain one of the most beautiful and healthful regions within the city bounds.

H. G. Allbright, Provision Dealer, Winthrop Hall, Upham's Corner. What may fairly be called the representative establishment of its kind of the section in which is located, is that of which Mr. H. G. Allbright is the proprietor, situated in Winthrop Hall building, Upham's Corner (see illustration on page 203). The inception of this well-known enterprise dates back a quarter of a century, for it was inaugurated in 1853 by Wm. H. Park, Jr. In 1870 the firm name became Park & Allbright, and in 1877 Mr. H. G. Allbright became sole proprietor. He is a native of Dorchester, and one of the best known business men in this section, being a member of the Odd Fellows, the Knights of Pythias, Ancient Order of United Workmen, and Royal Arcanum. Mr. Allbright is a justice of the peace and is owner of the beautiful building in which his store is located. This was erected in 1885, and is a credit to its designer and an ornament to the vicinity. It is a brick structure of the Venetian style of architecture, and no expense was spared to render it a perfect edifice in detail of design and architectural finish. The upper part of the building contains several public halls, and the Winthrop hall, which is a most elegant hall for parties and receptions. It is equipped with a good sized stage, large enough for the use of scenery and the staging of a play. A large stairway leads to the hall, and a good sized waiting-room, clothes closet and toilet room, and also a ticket office, tend to convenience the arrangements for parties, entertainments, etc. The next floor contains the gallery of the theater, and waiting and smoking room. On the next is a lodge room handsomely furnished, in which ten different societies hold their meetings, and the floor has every convenience in the way of waiting rooms, toilet rooms, clothes closets, children's room, etc. The store is a model of perfection. It has two large plate glass windows; the interior is finished in light hard wood, the ceiling being highly polished. In the center of the store are large marble tables for the handling and cutting of meats. In the rear we find a large ice chest having a capacity for the storage of four tons of ice, and another large chest for the storage of corned beef, tongue, salt pork, etc., and the fish and oyster department, which is of large size and equipped with a spacious ice chest. Four wagons are used for the delivery of goods. A good-sized brick stable is also here, and a carriage house. The stable is equipped with four stalls, and has a good hay loft overhead. In the store, employment is given to six efficient and courteous assistants. A large and select stock is carried, and those at all familiar with Mr. Allbright's business methods need not to be told that it contains nothing but reliable goods, for much of the abundant success this gentleman has won, is due to the fact of his handling nothing that could not be conscientiously guaranteed. Another popular feature of the management is the celerity and accuracy with which orders are filled and those sent either by telephone, or by other means, will receive the same prompt attention as though given in person. Mr. Allbright quotes no fancy prices, but supplies first-class goods and prompt service at low rates, giving full equivalent for every dollar taken.

J. H. Upham & Co., Upham's Corner, Dorchester, Office also at 21 South Market St., Boston. If some of the grocers, who did business in Boston fifty or so years ago, should return to the city and note the changes that have occurred in some of the methods of carrying on trade, the chances are that they would be both astonished and displeased. We say displeased, because the old idea was, that business was so sober and serious an undertaking that even the appearance of frivolity or anything approaching it must be sedulously guarded against. Hence their stores were gloomy and ill-lighted, dark and meagre in appointments and inconvenient and cramped in arrangement. Contrast with such a store, that occupied by Messrs. J. H. Upham & Co., at Upham's Corner. This firm, although one of the most progressive in the city, and quick to adopt any modern improvement, is concerned in the management of one of the oldest grocery enterprises in town, for the business was founded over three quarters of a century ago by Mr. Joseph Capen, who was succeeded after many years of faithful service by Mr. Amos Upham, who in 1843 admitted his son Mr. J. H. Upham (the present senior partner) to the firm, this latter gentleman having been brought up in the business and by that means, acquiring that perfect knowledge of its every detail for which he is noted. A little more than a score of years ago Mr. J. H. Upham became associated with Amos Upham jr. and Richard C. Humphrey and later Dexter Humphrey and this co-partnership continuing for six years and terminating with the death of Amos Upham jr. and Dexter Humphrey. As now constituted, the firm is made up of Messrs. J. H. Upham, J. F. Williams, who purchased the interest of Richard C. Humphrey, and Edward P. Upham, and was never better prepared to carry on operations to the entire satisfaction of all concerned. Every resident of Upham's Corner is of course familiar with the building recently completed for the use of this concern, and we will only say in regard to it, that no expense has been spared, either in its design or its appointments to make it the equal of any similar establishment in New England. It is illuminated both by gas and electricity, and is sufficiently spacious to accommodate even the enormous stock carried by this firm, without crowding. As for the business-methods in vogue here, they speak for themselves. No enterprise could have attained and could retain the popularity accorded to this, were it not carried on in a liberal, fair and far-sighted manner, and no house in the city takes more pains in the filling of orders than the one under consideration. The articles on sale at this store are first-class in every particular and are sold at the lowest market rates on goods of similar character. Four teams are utilized in the delivery of orders and courteous attention is guaranteed to every caller. This is truly a representative enterprise, and no account of the resources of Upham's Corner would be complete without extended mention of it.

SEE ILLUSTRATION OF BUILDING ON PAGE 203.

Charles A. Rutledge, Home Bakery, 755 Dudley Street. In every large city the question of food supply assumes considerable importance, for where hundreds of thousands of people are gathered together, an enormous amount of sustenance must daily be provided. The great bulk of this is uncooked of course, for each family does its own cooking to a greater or less extent; but one kind of food is being prepared at home less and less every year, as the facilities for its public production are gradually improved upon. We refer to bread, and it is a well-known fact that bakeries are increasing, owing to the growing demand for the commodities they supply. Some of these establishments are unfortunately unworthy of patronage, and as good bread is a necessity, let us call attention to a place where it may be obtained at the lowest market rates and of guaranteed quality. We refer to that carried on by Mr. Charles Rutledge at No. 755 Dudley Street, and have no fear but that those who may give this store a trial will never regret having done so, for Mr. Rutledge handles only reliable goods, and the Bread, Cake and Pastry sold by him can not fail to suit. Ice Cream supplied by the quart or gallon; special attention given to large orders on which very favorable terms will be made. He is a native of Boston and has been identified with his present undertaking since 1885. Mr. Rutledge served in the navy during the Rebellion, and was with Farragut in the operations about Mobile. He has many friends in Dorchester who wish him the abundant success he deserves.

———

M. M. Griswold, Provisions, Meats, Poultry, etc., Fruits and Vegetables, 757 Dudley Street, Dorchester. Although many men complain that it is hard to get a living nowadays, we suspect that in most cases the fault is with them and not with the times, for there are abundant instances on every side going to show that provided you thoroughly understand your business and are not afraid of work, you will find no difficulty in gaining a livelihood. As an example, suppose we call attention to the enterprise conducted by Mr. M. M. Griswold at No. 757 Dudley Street. This was inaugurated in 1886, in November, so that it is now not two years old, yet it has taken its place among the most thriving undertakings in this section, and its present large patronage is steadily increasing. Now Mr. Griswold did not win this success without effort, but on the contrary, worked hard to bring it about, and as he had a complete knowledge of his business, he knew what the public wanted and took pains to supply their wants. Mr. Griswold is also proprietor of a store in South Boston, and is a native of this city and a member of the Red Men and of the Royal Society of Good Fellows. He employs eight competent and courteous assistants, and handles Meats, Poultry, Provisions, Fruits and Vegetables very extensively, delivering all goods free, and quoting the lowest prices possible on first-class articles. His customers have learned that all representations made at his store can be strictly depended upon, and therefore they put the utmost confidence in the enterprise and recommend it to their friends.

I. H. Allard, Livery and Boarding Stable, 71 to 75 Hancock St. There's many a cure for disease not to be found in any apothecary store, and it may be added that the same may be said of preventives of it. Fresh air, rapid motion, and the exhilaration attending driving are oftentimes more potent than any drugs in straightening a man out, and if more frequent use were made of them by our overworked business men, some of our physicians could safely take a holiday. We believe that people are beginning to appreciate this fact; and to guide such as may feel uncertain as to where they can secure a desirable team at a fair rate, we would suggest a visit to the establishment of Isaac H. Allard, located on Hancock Street. Mr. Allard is possessed of the means to assure his patrons the best of service in every respect. He takes a pride in furnishing such horses and carriages as no one need feel ashamed of, and although he does not pretend to have a Maud S. in his stable, still he does strive to furnish good roadsters as well as stylish appearing animals. The premises in use offer the best of accommodations to horses, and the most intelligent care is promised. Reasonable rates are adhered to, and satisfaction is assured.

Gould & Co., Dealers in Choice Family Groceries, 104 Washington Street, Corner Eldon. Among the many Grocery establishments carried on in this city, that conducted by Messrs. Gould & Co., at No. 104 Washington Street, Corner Eldon, Dorchester District, deserves particular mention, for in some respects this enterprise has no parallel in the vicinity of Mount Bowdoin. The individual members of this firm are Mr. J. B. Gould and L. S. Grant, both natives of Massachusetts and thoroughly acquainted with every detail of their business. They began operations here in 1888, and have already succeeded in establishing a thriving trade. They are dealers in Choice Family Groceries of all kinds, in which they offer inducements to patrons difficult to equal elsewhere. The stock carried is a very large one, and so far as variety and fineness of quality go, certainly leaves nothing to be desired. Messrs. Gould & Co. are very careful and experienced buyers, and as they enjoy the most favorable relations with the large wholesale importing houses and also with producers, they are enabled to offer standard articles at positively the lowest market rates. Customers are always served with celerity and courtesy, and orders will be acted upon without delay and delivered accurately as directed. Messrs. Gould & Co.'s business is a

constantly growing one, and they fully deserve the success they have already attained.

Burke Brothers, Carpenters; Window Screens and Screen Doors made at short notice; all Jobbing promptly attended to. No. 27 Hancock Street, Upham's Corner. Upham's Corner, and in fact all the surrounding neighborhood, being a growing section of the city, there is a wide field presented for the operations of a competent firm of carpenters and builders, and this field is admirably occupied by the well-known and representative house of Burke Brothers. These gentlemen began operations in 1882, the firm being made up of Messrs. W. E. & H. W. Burke, both of whom are natives of Nova Scotia, the former being connected with the Odd Fellows. The premises occupied are located at No. 27 Hancock street, and comprise two floors, employment being given to twelve efficient assistants. A steam-engine of six horse-power is utilized to drive the machinery in use, and wood-working of various kinds is extensively carried on. Window and door screens being made to order at short notice, and jobbing of all descriptions given prompt and careful attention. Messrs. Burke Brothers enjoy unsurpassed advantages in their line of business and are able to meet all competition, either as regards the character of the work turned out or the prices quoted on the same. They use reliable stock and employ competent help only, thus being able to guarantee their work in every respect. If any of our readers are thinking of building, they would do well to consult this firm, for any desired information will be cheerfully given, and contracts will be entered into for the prompt and satisfactory carrying out of building operations of any kind.

William H. Purnell, Restaurant and Ice Cream, 98 Hancock Street, Upham's Corner. If one may judge from the scarcity of good Restaurants and Ice Cream Parlors in this, and in fact in every other large American city, it is as difficult to run an establishment of this kind successfully as it is to keep a hotel, and those who have had experience know how few and far between good hotels are. But when found they deserve, and generally receive liberal patronage, and this being as true of restaurants as of hotels, it is not surprising that Mr. W. H. Purnell has built up quite a business since he began operations in the latter part of 1887, for he is an experienced caterer, and his Restaurant and Ice Cream Parlor is well worthy of appreciation and support. It is located on Hancock Street, Upham's Corner, and those who want excellent food, well cooked, promptly and neatly served at low rates (Table Board by the week at special rates) might go a great ways farther and fare a great deal worse. Mr. Purnell is a native of Philadelphia, and is a member of the Free Masons. He served during the Great Rebellion in the Burnside Expedition, and is, we believe, connected with the Grand Army. Employment is afforded to three assistants, and close personal attention is given by Mr. Purnell to catering for Parties, Weddings and other occasions. Church Fairs and Festivals supplied with Ice Cream of all flavors on very reasonable terms. The premises occupied measure 33 by 46 feet, and are very conveniently arranged.

Geo. P. Brooks, Apothecary, 782 Dudley Street, Upham's Corner, Boston. We have heard a great deal of "Mind Healing." "Christian Scientists," "Cures without Medicine," etc., within the past year or so, but as we have not noticed an unusual number of failures in the Drug business, it is to be presumed that the old-fashioned methods of treatment are not yet entirely superseded. Some people may be able to convince themselves that as, philosophically speaking, there is no such thing as disease, they cannot be diseased in the least, and therefore have only to *think* themselves cured to be cured; but the average man cares more for facts than he does for names, and when he finds himself losing strength or showing other signs of illness, he prefers being made to feel like himself by the judicious use of medicines, rather than allowed to grow steadily worse on the theory that he has no business to feel ill at all. Consequently Drug stores are as much of a necessity as ever, and being a necessity and a great public convenience as well, we take pleasure in calling attention to one of the best managed establishments of the kind with which we are acquainted, that conducted by Mr. Geo. P. Brooks at No. 782 Dudley Street, Upham's Corner. The store is 25 by 50 feet, and is one of the handsomest in New England. The floor is of French tiles, the woodwork of mahogany, and the elegant stained glass and French plate windows, the beautifully frescoed ceiling and the Tufft's soda fountain, all combine to make a very attractive store. One floor and a basement are occupied, and a skillfully selected stock of Drugs, Medicines, Chemicals, etc., is constantly carried, together with such Toilet Articles and Fancy Goods as are usually found in a first-class City Drug Store. Mr. Brooks founded this undertaking in 1881, and has built up a large trade by close and conscientious attention to business. He is a native of Salem, Mass., and is connected with the Royal Arcanum. Employment is given to two efficient and polite assistants, and all orders are promptly filled, especial attention being paid to the compounding of physician's prescriptions, only the best and purest ingredients being used, and the prices put at the lowest figures consistent with a reliable service.

Henry Steeger, Merchant Tailor, 778 Dudley Street, Upham's Corner. The art of dressing well is worthy the attention of every man, and it will be found that a neat and fashionable appearance may be presented at a comparatively small expense if one only goes to work in the right way to secure such a result. It is not the most pretentious establishments that offer the most advantages, and if a house is patronized that occupies a magnificent store in an expensive part of the city, it is not surprising that the customer has to pay accordingly. On the other hand, where the expenses are comparatively small, the prices are apt to be the same, and if you want proof of this, just visit the establishment of which Mr. Henry Steeger is the proprietor, located at No. 778 Dudley street, Upham's Corner, Dorchester District. Mr. Steeger has carried on his present establishment since 1884, and has had many years of experience as a practical tailor. He is a native of Germany, but has lived in this country for twenty years and is connected with the Knights of Pythias and the Ancient Order of Foresters. Mr. Steeger is prepared to furnish custom-made garments at short notice and at very reasonable rates. He employs about eight skilled assistants during the busy season and guarantees satisfaction in every respect—fit, trimmings, finish and general workmanship. Drop in and inspect his stock of Foreign and Domestic Fabrics, and depend upon it if you favor him with an order, you will have no reason to regret it.

M. F. Farwell, Dealer in Dry Goods, Small Wares and Fancy Goods, No. 769 Dudley Street, Upham's Corner. Although not making any extensive pretensions, still the establishment conducted by Mrs. M. F. Farwell at No. 769 Dudley street, Upham's Corner, is a decided public convenience, and this view of the matter is taken after learning the estimation in which the enterprise is held by those residing in the vicinity of its location. The stock carried is surprisingly complete; consisting of dry goods, small wares and fancy goods in great variety. These articles are sold in accordance with the lowest market rates, and not the least gratifying feature of the management of the business, is the fact that everything sold is guaranteed to prove as represented, every precaution being taken to handle none but reliable goods. Novelties of various kinds are to be found here as soon as they make their appearance in the market, and in short the proprietress exhibits enterprise as well as reliability in her business methods. Callers are assured prompt and polite attention, and orders sent by children or other messengers will be filled with as much care as though given in person. This establishment was opened nearly a score of years ago, and has from the inception, proved itself to be worthy of the most liberal support.

J. F. Woods, Plumber, Hancock Street, Upham's Corner. It makes no difference how healthful the situation of a house is, how freely exposed it is to light, air, etc., if its drainage and plumbing are defective the house is not fit to live in. No more fruitful source of disease exists than defective plumbing, and it is well that people are beginning to appreciate this fact, for it will result in incompetent men being driven out of the plumbing business. There are plenty of skilful and well-informed sanitary plumbers to be found now if they are looked for in the right place, and we feel confident that none are more thoroughly competent and careful in their dealings than is Mr. J. F. Woods, doing business on Hancock street, Upham's Corner. Mr. Woods has had an extended and a varied experience and understands his business perfectly in every detail. Although he employs skilled and pains-taking assistants, he does not depend entirely upon their reports of what has been done, etc., but makes it a rule to keep himself personally informed as to the progress of any work of any importance which he has in hand. As a consequence, he is enabled to guarantee that his patrons shall be entirely satisfied, and his reputation for thorough and neat work is steadily and rapidly growing

Mr. Woods carries a sufficient stock of plumbers' materials, etc., to enable him to attend to all orders at short notice. Jobbing is made a specialty, and repairing of all descriptions is done after the most approved methods and at prices that are as low as can be quoted on first-class work.

Daniel F. McCormack, Horse-Shoer, Cor. Hancock and Columbia Streets Ward 24.

A horse is something more than a machine, and even if he were a machine, and a strong one too, he would be very apt to break down at times under the abuse to which he is subjected. Probably more suffering and injury to horses are caused by defective shoeing than by any other one thing, and no horse owner can afford to let his animal be shod by a man who is not thoroughly experienced and competent in every respect. Try it yourself. Put on a pair of shoes unfitted to your feet, too small or too large, or having nails that penetrate your skin. Go out on to the cobble stones and drag a carriage or a wagon after you and see whether you can stand it or not. Horses shoes should be a protection; in too many cases they are a positive injury. Hunt up a skilful horse-shoer, it is well worth your while, for it may save you the price of a valuable animal, to say nothing of the humanity which should make every man worthy of the name hate to see a dumb beast suffer. We can help you in your search for we can direct you to the corner of Hancock and Columbia streets, Ward 24, where you will find the establishment conducted by Mr. Daniel F. McCormack, it having come into his possession in 1881 after having been started by Mr. C. A. Wells in 1875. Mr. McCormack is a native of Prince Edwards Island and controls one of the best-appointed horse-shoeing and blacksmith shops in the city. It measures 100 x 60 feet, contains four forges, and employment is given to six careful and efficient assistants. A large business is done, but orders are very promptly filled, and the charges made are very moderate. Horse-shoeing is given special attention, and the hoofs of each animal are carefully fitted.

A. H. Copley, Pharmacist, No. 45 Hancock Street, Upham's Corner.

Upham's Corner is well known as one of the most beautiful sections of the city, and its desirability for residential purposes is greatly heightened by the fact of there being a number of first-class stores of various kinds, located where they are easily accessible to those living in this portion of the suburbs. Every prudent man of family, likes to have a first-class pharmacy within a short distance of his home, for reasons that are too obvious to require mention. A few moments delay in the procuring of a remedy may cause serious results, and even more grave consequences may ensue if drugs or medicines are procured of incompetent dealers. Therefore, the desirability of having a pharmacy, not only near but under proper management, and in this connection we may well mention the establishment conducted by Mr. A. H. Copley (who was formerly with T. Metcalf & Co.) at No. 45 Hancock street, Upham's Corner, for its location is very convenient and no similar enterprise in the city is more carefully and conscientiously managed. The interests of customers are protected at all times, and those leaving physician's prescriptions here to be compounded, (a branch of the business to which Mr. Copley gives special attention) may depend upon their being filled with the utmost care and accuracy, and at most reasonable rates. A fine stock of drugs, medicines, etc., is carried, all needful facilities are at hand, and ample and efficient assistance is employed. Fancy and toilet articles, cigars, etc., are very extensively dealt in, and in short, everything obtainable at a first-class pharmacy is to be had of Mr. Copley.

Lewis Hall, Livery Stable, Boston, near Hamlet Street, Upham's Corner.

It is being more clearly demonstrated every day that fresh air and plenty of it is one of the most powerful agents that can be found to assist in the maintenance or the regaining of health, and that while drugs and medicines are all very well in their way, still they by no means possess the virtues that were long ascribed to them. No better way of regaining strength and vigor than to ride behind a good horse as much as possible. You get change of scene as well as pure air and agreeable occupation by so doing, and as a means of "getting up an appetite" driving is way ahead of all the "stomach bitters" that were ever concocted. Of course, however, you want a horse that don't make a practice of going to sleep on the road, and to be sure of getting a good animal as well as a stylish and comfortable vehicle, we should certainly advise you to visit the establishment of Mr. Lewis Hall, located on Boston Street, near Hamlet, Upham's Corner. Mr. Hall not only knows a good horse when he sees it, but takes pains to supply his customers with such animals every time. He can furnish a horse suitable for any lady to drive that will get over the road in lively style without urging, and his carriages are of late pattern and are easy riding. Mr. Hall is very moderate in his charges, considering the quality of the accommodations he supplies, and gives every order prompt and painstaking attention. His stable is one of the most popular in the Highlands, and the character of his patronage is very high.

14

H. J. Burrows, Dealer in Fresh, Salt and Smoked Fish, Oysters, Lobsters, Clams, etc., 759 Dudley Street, near Upham's Corner, Dorchester. A really first-class fish market is one of the most useful establishments which any community can have located in its midst, for the demand for fish is a universal one, and all are interested in having it supplied in the proper manner. Mr. H. J. Burrows has won much commendation and built up a large and growing business by the enterprise and energy he has shown in catering to the wants of the public since he opened his present store in May 1887, at No. 759 Dudley St., and visitors will find that he carries a very complete stock of fresh, salt, smoked and pickled fish, and in fact of sea food of all kinds. Mr. Burrows was born in Leyden, Mass., and is connected with both the Knights and Legion of Honor. He gives close personal attention to his business and is always on the alert to improve the service to customers in one way or the other. The most improved facilities are at hand for the storing and preservation of the stock, and fresh supplies are received daily. Among the more important fish handled may be mentioned: cod, haddock, halibut, bluefish, mackerel, salmon, whitefish, striped bass, shad, sword fish, smelt, perch, together with trout, pickerel, black bass and other game fish. In the way of salted fish should be mentioned pickled salmon, salmon trout, shad, mackerel and herring and oysters; clams and lobsters are also handled largely and furnished at prices that will compare favorably with those quoted elsewhere.

A. D. Marcy, Druggist and Apothecary, 453 Blue Hill Avenue, Grove Hall. It seems to us as if the responsibilities attaching to the business of the druggist were not properly appreciated by the general public, but a little thought will serve to show that those who pursue this branch of trade for a livelihood must have an opportunity to realize that eternal vigilance is the price of success. A single and apparently trivial error in the filling of an order may have serious consequences, and all our readers know that years of faithful service are seldom admitted in extenuation when such a mistake is made public. An establishment whose management may be truthfully characterized as being both conservative and enterprising is that conducted by A. D. Marcy at No. 453 Blue Hill Avenue near Grove Hall, and we can assure our readers that they may rely upon receiving uniform care and consideration when having dealings with this house. Mr. Marcy began operations in 1885, and has already been honored with a full share of the patronage of the public. He employs courteous and efficient assistants, and carries a stock of Drugs, Medicines and Chemicals that is carefully selected, and is so complete in every detail as to warrant the assertion that Mr. Marcy has exceptional facilities for the filling of physicians' prescriptions. Such orders are promptly and accurately filled, and no exorbitant rates are charged, either for Medicines or for Toilet and Fancy Goods of which a fine assortment is offered.

W. A. Swan, Dealer in First-class Provisions, Choice Butter, Eggs and Produce, No. 456 Blue Hill Avenue. No one can blame a man for wanting what belongs to him, and therefore no one can blame anybody for trying to find an establishment where all agreements made are steadily adhered to, and where honor and fair dealings prevail. We can render our readers efficient help in finding such an establishment, for these are precisely the kind of business methods that have given the store conducted by Mr. W. A. Swan at No. 456 Blue Hill Avenue its present popularity, and we feel convinced that they will be steadily continued. Mr. Swan was born in New York state and began operations in his present field of usefulness in 1885. He occupies a store 23 x 45 feet in dimensions and carries as choice and varied a stock of provisions, etc., as anyone could wish to see, for it is all selected under Mr. Swan's personal supervision, and will be found strictly first-class in every respect. Choice butter, eggs and produce are given special attention, and those who want "gilt edge" goods at moderate prices, should by all means give Mr. Swan an early call. He is prepared to give all orders prompt and accurate delivery, and we feel sure that none who may favor him with their patronage will have the least reason to regret it. Four polite and experienced assistants are constantly employed, and the most minute detail of the business is most ably handled. Mr. Swan is a member of the Odd Fellows, Iron Hall and A. O. U. W.

E. W. Jordan, Dealer in Fine Family Groceries, Choice Butter, Cheese, Eggs and Produce, Kitchen Furnishing Goods, etc., etc., No. 459 Blue Hill Avenue. An enterprise that has been successfully carried on for the past three years, certainly deserves mention in our columns and as that conducted by Mr. E. W. Jordan at No. 459 Blue Hill Avenue, Grove Hall, was founded in 1885, it will be seen that it has pronounced claims upon our attention. Mr. Jordan is a native of Augusta, Maine, and of course is thoroughly acquainted with every detail of the retail grocery trade, for even if he were entirely ignorant of the business when he began (which was not the case), he has had ample opportunity to master it in every part. The premises utilized are of the dimensions of 23 x 45 feet, and comprise one floor and a basement. We do not know the precise value of the stock carried by Mr. Jordan, but it must reach a high figure, for not only is the assortment on hand very extensive, but it is composed to a considerable degree of unusually choice articles. In fact, this store has a well-earned reputation in this vicinity for containing as desirable a selection of Fine Family Groceries as is to be found in this section, and we can assure the most fastidious of our readers that they can here find goods suited to their tastes. The prices quoted are remarkably low considering the uniformly, superior character of the commodities handled which consist of fine family groceries, choice butter, cheese, eggs and produce, and as employment is given to three active and obliging assistants, callers may depend upon receiving courteous treatment and having their orders promptly filled. A full line of garden tools, kitchen furnishing goods, tinware, etc., etc., is carried and supplied at low prices.

COR. BLUE HILL AV. AND WASHINGTON ST. GROVE HALL, DORCHESTER.

E. Reynolds, Meats, Provisions, Vegetables, etc. Grove Hall is a very desirable section of the city to live in in more respects than one, and the gentleman whose card we print above has done his share toward adding to its desirability, first by building a fine brick structure containing six commodious suits for the the accommodation of tenants, and second by occupying a spacious and well appointed store in the building and furnishing the choicest meats, provisions, vegetables, etc., at the lowest market rates. Mr. Reynolds is by no means new in this line of business, on the contrary he has been identified with it in Grove Hall ever since 1871, and no business man in that section is better known or more highly esteemed. Of course, having been so long before the public, Mr. Reynolds has built up a very large trade, which is constantly and rapidly increasing, for his relations with producers and wholesalers are of the best and he gives his customers the full benefit of the advantages he enjoys. A heavy and carefully selected stock is carried at all times and although the best class of trade is catered to, exorbitant prices are carefully avoided and the most economically disposed can trade here with profit and pleasure. A noteworthy feature of the management is the fact that misrepresentation is not allowed or practiced under any circumstances, and therefore purchasers know just what they are buying and are assured of receiving the full worth of their money in every case. Space forbids a description of the stock, and we will simply say that it comprises every article usually found in a first-class establishment of this kind, and should be inspected by every careful buyer.

E. S. Davis, Dealer in Hay, Grain, Coal, and Wood, 467 Blue Hill Ave., Grove Hall. In spite of the manifold and surprising uses to which steam has been put, and in spite of the numerous and ingenious devices in the shape of bicycles, tricycles, etc., that have been produced to enable people to travel about swiftly and safely without the aid of horse power, it still remains a fact that horses are becoming more and more important every day, and it is still true that modern business would be seriously interfered with and in some cases utterly ruined were the supply of horses to be suddenly cut off. Such indispensable animals deserve the greatest care and consideration, and in no way can these be more satisfactorily and humanely shown than by making it a point to see that your horse is fed on proper material and is given enough of it. Naturally it would be well for them if every dealer would handle only such products as are dealt in by Mr. E. S. Davis, located at No. 467 Blue Hill avenue, Grove Hall. This gentleman carries a large stock of hay, grain, coal and wood, and strives to handle none but reliable goods. As his enterprise has been before the public since 1881, and his reputation is equal to the best, it is safe to conclude that he succeeds in his efforts. The store is 35 by 112 feet in dimensions, and the stock on hand is very large and complete. Three assistants are employed and customers given immediate and polite attention. Mr. E. S. Davis is a native of Massachusetts, and is well known in social as well as business circles of this city, being a member of Grand Army Post No. 26, also of James Warren Commandery of Knights Templar, Mt. Vernon Chapter, Roxbury Council, Washington Lodge.

HISTORICAL SKETCH

OF

JAMAICA PLAIN.

No suburban region of Boston has acquired a wider fame for its beauty of land-scape and of stately residences than that part of West Roxbury known as Jamaica Plain. Early recognized by observing and enterprising men of Boston as unrivalled for quiet and lovely homes, easily accessible to the city, its advantages have been extended and improved with generous foresight, until now its name is synonymous for the highest architectural and horticultural art as well as natural beauty of high order, and the value of its real estate has arisen to an extremely high figure, such as only the wealth of a great city can produce. The history of Jamaica Plain has been mostly quiet and uneventful, merged invisibly in that of the surrounding region, so that there is not much in this line for the historian to specify.

When the first settlers began to know the region round about Boston well enough to name it, this particular part was for some time called "Pond Plain" on account of its large and beautiful sheet of water. It formed the "end" of the town of Roxbury but was not so quickly settled as the region nearer the sea. About the year 1667 it was named, by whom it is unknown, by its present cognomen, in honor of the Island of Jamaica, in the West Indies, which was captured from the Spanish by Oliver Cromwell at this time. The soil was unusually rich and fertile so that as the colony grew it came to demand a higher price and was mostly taken up by the richest men of Boston and vicinity. This accounts for the fact that it has been more sparsely settled than any other place around Boston, and this has made it particularly adapted for large villas. The Warren and Loring estates are good examples of the old-time manors. Jamaica Plain shared in all the movements of the colonial and revolutionary periods as a part of Roxbury, so that its history is contained in that of the latter town. During the siege of Boston, the Plain was used as a camp by the Rhode Island forces under General Greene.

When the town of West Roxbury was incorporated it became a part of it, and continued under its local government until it was annexed to Boston in 1878. At this time the valuation of West Roxbury was $22,148,600, of which Jamaica Plain furnished no small share. Jamaica Pond has several other uses than purely ornamental. In 1795 a company of Boston men were incorporated as an aqueduct com-

SQUARE OPP. DEPOT, JAMAICA PLAIN.

pany to supply water for the city, and Jamaica Pond was selected as the source of supply. Modern science had not then enlightened the ways and means of such enterprises, so that the pipes used in conveying the water from the pond to the city were made of pine logs. Though financially unsuccessful at first, the company was eventually put upon a paying basis, and about fifteen hundred city families were supplied. An improvement was introduced in 1820, in the shape of an iron main, ten inches in diameter, which was laid through the whole length of Tremont street to Bowdoin square. This served by largely increasing facilities of supply until about the middle of the century, when it became evident that the city would need a larger source than Jamaica. Lake Cochituate was then decided upon, and in 1851 the city paid the Jamaica company $45,000 for its property and franchise. Since the aqueduct business was removed, the only practical end which the Pond has served has been the production of ice, for which it is a favorite center in this vicinity. A large number of extensive store houses have been erected, especially on its southern side and an immense quantity is taken off and stored every year, making a considerable industry here during the winter and summer. But Jamaica Pond is even more famed as a skating-pond than for its water and ice. Great numbers from the city and suburbs flock here during the winter season and the Pond presents a beautiful and animated scene. There is also a famous drive around it which is considered one of the most beautiful sights of Boston. Many very costly and palatial residences are situated near and within sight of its shores. In summer also it is largely patronized for all sorts of aquatic sports, and in addition to the pleasure, rowing and sailing regattas are occasionally held.

Ride where you will among the charming hills and vales, park-like avenues or country roads, you cannot find a spot which is not distinguished by some beauty. The place is surrounded by hills on all sides, forming a sheltered plain, which is always cooled by the breezes from the hills, yet always protected by them from the storms.

It is safe to say that nowhere in this country has the art of making beautiful homes and placing them in the loveliest environment reached a higher stage than in this charming suburb of Boston. Matthew Arnold, when he was last in this country, said that the Americans were lacking in the beautifying arts, such as architecture. Had he taken a drive through Jamaica Plain we are sure his criticism would have been modified. One great feature of Jamaica Plain is its extreme healthfulness, it being shown on the best of authoritative statistics that the death rate for many years has been only one in one hundred, a remarkably low proportion. The salubriousness of the soil, the perfect facilities for water and drainage, the sheltered position and splendid location have become widely known and have aided no less than the natural beauty of the place in its great upbuilding.

Among the prominent churches at Jamaica Plain we may mention the Central Congregational Church. This edifice, erected in 1872, is one of the most beautiful in the city, of substantial, yet graceful, Gothic style. The church was earliest known as the Mather Church, and has exercised a wide and increasing activity in every line of good work. The First Congregation (Unitarian) Church in Jamaica Plain is one of the leaders in its denomination and in the best thought and work of Boston. It separated from the Second Church of Roxbury in 1770, and among its best-known pastors have been the Rev. Wm. Gordon, Rev. Thomas Gray, Rev. Grindall Reynolds, Rev. James W. Thompson, and Rev. Charles V. Dole. The Third Church is also well known for its great benevolence and wide sympathies in all departments of christian work. Most of the leading denominations are represented here by strong and active societies.

A noble institution, and one that is ably conducted is the Bussey Institute, near the Forest Hill station. This part of New England has always been especially interested in horticulture, and this institution is an embodiment of that interest. It was organized in 1870, and its large and beautiful building of Roxbury pudding-stone was erected in the same year. It is 112 x 73 feet, three stories high, and elegantly finished off in Victoria Gothic style. It was established by bequest of Benjamin Bussey of Roxbury, and given by him to Harvard University, to found a department in agriculture and horticulture, in that great institution. In the main building are the offices, the library devoted to books on agriculture and horticulture, recitation and collection rooms, laboratory, store rooms and conservatories. The cost of the main and outlying buildings, among which there are several greenhouses, was $62,000. James Arnold, of New Bedford, bequeathed $100,000 to the university in 1872, which was to establish a professorship of tree-culture, and an arboretum containing all trees which will grow in the open air here, in connection with the Bussey Institute. This arboretum now contains about one hundred and forty acres and is very carefully and thoroughly conducted, containing an immense variety of valuable and rare trees. It forms a most beautiful park, and one of the most unique things in the country, having no parallel this side the water. For those interested in tree culture it contains an immense source of pleasure and instruction. The Bussey estate containing 360 acres is now entirely owned by the university, and all the work in connection with this department is admirably carried on under the direction of the Dean, Professor Francis H. Storer.

The West Roxbury Soldiers' Monument is another interesting feature of Jamaica Plain. It is placed at the corner of Center and South Streets, opposite Curtis' Hall formerly used for a town hall. It is thirty-four feet high, the shaft being of gray granite and the pedestal of dark Quincy stone. The whole is planned in the Gothic style, there being a pyramidal pedestal upon a broad square base supporting the figure of a soldier. On each of the four sides of the pedestal is an arch, over which are the names of Lincoln, Thomas, Andrew and Farragut, and within the vaulted chamber is a pillar of Italian marble, on which are inscribed the names of the West Roxbury soldiers who were killed in the war. Military trophies are elegantly carved on the pinnacles at each corner of the monument. W. W. Lommls was the talented architect, and the monument is in many respects unique among the large number of commonplace designs for this purpose which are seen throughout the north. At the dedicatory services which took place Sept. 14, 1871, Rev. James Freeman Clarke delivered an address.

Near the Bussey Institute is the Adams Nervine Hospital, a well-known scientific and benevolent institution. It was founded in 1877 by Seth Adams, of Boston, who gave to it $600,000, and it was opened in 1880. The estate contains twenty-four acres on which is situated a beautiful and commodious building capable of maintaining thirty patients. Its object is to furnish a place of retreat to residents of the state suffering from nervous exhaustion and debilitation, yet not insane, and has accomplished much good in its eight years of existence.

For decades and centuries it is safe to say that Jamaica Plain will remain a favorite resort for Boston people and an unsurpassed region for surburban residence. Its position and occupancy at present render it impossible to be seriously impaired by the inroads of Boston's great commercial interests. All the local departments of education, charity and religion are generously conducted. The business interests, though unostentatious, are thoroughly first-class, and everything about Jamaica Plain shows that it is almost entirely occupied by well-to-do and wealthy people. And it would not be possible to wish it any better destiny than to maintain its present admirable condition as a most beautiful place, pre-eminent for its model homes.

LEADING BUSINESS MEN

OF

JAMAICA PLAIN.

Peoples' Cold Blast Market. Thomas Decatur, Dealer in First-Class Provisions, Jamaica Plain; Telephone 8763. It is very close on to a third of a century since the enterprise conducted by Mr. Thomas Decatur was inaugurated, and those familiar with the locality will agree with us in giving this the leading position among similar undertakings in Jamaica Plain. But something besides age has, of course, been required to give the establishment in question its prominence, and this has been afforded by the skilful and liberal management that has characterized it from the first. Mr. Decatur was born in New Hampshire, but may fairly be called a Massachusetts man, by adoption at least, for he has long been closely and prominently identified with the advancement of the best interests of that portion of the Commonwealth located in Jamaica Plain and vicinity. His name is intimately connected with the history of the Roxbury Horse Guards, and away back in the early "sixties" Mr. Decatur was instrumental in organizing more than than one company to go to the front and battle for the Union. He has occupied his present premises about five years, being the owner of the building, the store measuring 60 x 60 feet, faces on two streets, is three stories in height and has large plate glass windows and other modern improvements. Mr. Decatur's establishment is known as the "Peoples' Cold Blast Market," and is worthy of careful study, for it contains the latest and most scientific apparatus for the preservation of meats and other perishable commodities, having been fitted up without regard to expense. The famous cold blast system of refrigerators is utilized by him, and it is possible to attain almost any desired degree of temperature, and to provide perfect ventilation without the admission of heated air. The meat-block is so arranged that waste portions drop through the floor, and in fact nothing is neglected to ensure neatness and serve the public perfectly. Both a wholesale and retail business is done, employment being given to six assistants, who will be found efficient, willing and courteous. Orders by telephone No. 8763 will receive prompt and careful attention, and goods will be delivered at short notice. The quality of the goods sold at this market is two well known to call for extended comment. Suffice it to say, that the meats and provisions furnished here are strictly guaranteed, and that the prices are such as to make it a "Peoples' Market" in fact as well as in name.

Cyrus White & Co., House-furnishing Goods, Hardware, Plumbing, Furnaces, Ranges, Stoves, Drain Pipe and Gas Fitting. Patentee and Manufacturer of White's "Tropic" Furnace, White's Block, Centre Street, Jamaica Plain. The enterprise conducted by Messrs Cyrus White & Co., in White's Block, Centre Street, Jamaica Plain, is truly a representative one, and has reached its present leading position after 22 years of active and faithful service. Business was begun in 1866 in a small shop on the lot adjoining that occupied by the fine building now utilized. "White's Block" was erected by Mr. Cyrus White in 1872, and the present store first occupied during the same year, the business being carried on under the firm name of White & Mayo. The existing style was adopted about 14 years ago and the firm of Cyrus White & Co., is unquestionably one of the best known of any in the trade. Mr. White is a native of Mattapoisett, Mass., and is the patentee and manufacturer of the celebrated White's "Tropic" Furnace. This furnace not only supplies an abundant amount of heat with a small expenditure of coal, but has also made it very "warm" for its competitors, as it would be hard to find an apparatus of the kind that is at once so efficient and simple in its design and so thorough and durable in construction. This furnace is sold and put into working order for a very reasonable sum and those who are dissatisfied with their present arrangements would do well to investigate the merits of the "Tropic" House-furnishing goods of various kinds are sold by the firm at bottom prices, and a fine assortment of ranges, stoves, etc., is kept in stock, the latest and most successful novelties being included within it. Gas fixtures, etc., are also dealt in largely and gas-fitting will be done in the best manner and at short notice, nine assistants being employed. Jobbing orders of all kinds are attended to promptly and skillfully.

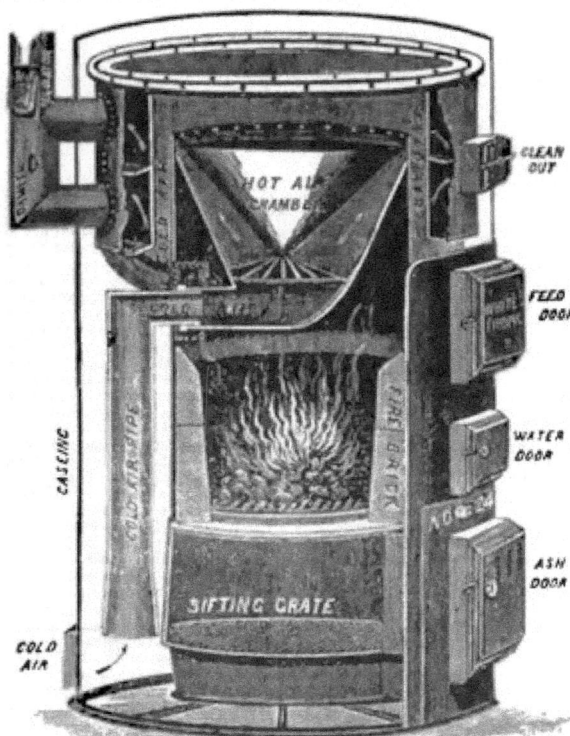

J. B. Moore, Dealer in First class Provisions, Centre Street, Jamaica Plain. The strictly first-class provision stores of Jamaica Plain are not so numerous as they might be, but still there are enough of them if they can but be found, to supply every customer, and one of the very best of them is that of which Mr. J. B. Moore is the proprietor located on Centre street. This establishment was founded December 1835, and has steadily gained in popularity and patronage until its present prosperous position was attained. A store is occupied measuring 20 x 85 feet, and the stock carried is such as to go far to explain why people like to trade with this house. Provisions of every description are included in the stock handled such as meats, vegetables, fruits, also poultry and game in their seasons, which are supplied in quantities to suit customers. Employment is given to three assistants and every patron is given such prompt and polite attention that this of itself would go far to build up the popularity enjoyed. All of the various goods dealt in are fully warranted to prove as represented, and while more attention is paid to quality than to quantity, still the prices are always as low as the state of the market will permit. Mr. Moore is a native of Nova Scotia, well and favorably esteemed in this community. He is a member of the Odd Fellows, Good Templars and Legion of Honor.

Albert H. Eayrs & Co., Manufacturers of all kinds of Surgical Elastic Bandages, for the support of Varicose Veins, Weak Joints, etc., Jamaica Plain Station. That some diseases and many weaknesses are best cured and most surely relieved by mechanical rather than by medical means, is well known to every person of intelligence, and as it is of the highest importance that whatever mechanical appliances are used should be of the most approved design and most honest manufacture, we take pleasure in calling attention to the productions of Messrs. Albert H. Eayrs & Co., as the goods made by this house are of standard quality and are designed and constructed with the most advanced scientific principles. The firm began operations in 1872, and are located at Jamaica Plain, occupying finely fitted-up premises and doing an extensive wholesale and retail business. Mr. Eayrs is a native of Nashua, N. H., and has made a life-study of the industry with which his name is connected. Surgical elastic bandages of every description are manufactured adapted to the support of varicose veins, sprains, weak joints, etc., and a noteworthy point in connection with these articles is the fact that they are made of the best materials obtainable, the finest imported rubber thread being used, and skilled and experienced labor employed. Thigh hose, knee hose, thigh pieces, knee caps, anklets, three-quarters hose, leggings, abdominal belts, suspensories, etc., are among the articles turned out, stout silk, fine silk, linen and cotton being used in their making. The firm take a just pride in the superiority of their goods, guaranteeing their elastic hose to be of the very best quality and made of the freshest English rubber, combined with a warp of new unmixed, highest grade silk or cotton, as represented. There is elastic hose in the market, made of inferior or deteriorated materials, but it is the most expensive to buy in the long run, and should be purchased by no sensible person. Elastic abdominal belts, for obesity, weakness, etc., and for use at any time when abdominal support is required, are dealt in extensively, and are so shaped as to combine entire effectiveness with perfect comfort, wristlets and armlets for weak or sprained wrists and for athletes' use are supplied at wholesale and retail, orders being given prompt attention. Special inducements are offered to physicians, a liberal discount being allowed them, and any original ideas which they may wish carried into effect, will be given immediate and pains-taking attention. This is a representative house in many respects, and we can, and do heartily commend it to the attention of our readers.

George Sauer & Co., Upholsterers and Interior Decorators, 4 Gordon St., corner Elm St., Jamaica Plain. Furniture, Curtain, Shade, Mattress and Carpet Works. While there is much work about a house that a careful housekeeper can do herself or have done under her own direction in the way of cleaning and renovation there is also considerable that requires special facilities and experience to do successfully, and here is where the services of a competent upholsterer and interior decorator becomes of value. We are aware that there are some claiming to be practical upholsterers who are utterly unworthy of the name, but there are others who may be trusted to perform all the work allotted to them with fidelity and discretion, and prominent among such are Messrs. George Sauer & Co., at No. 4 Gordon Street, Jamaica Plain. The individual members of this firm are Mr. George Sauer and Mr. A. Kretschmar, both residents of Jamaica Plain. They established their business in 1882, and for the past two years and a half have occupied their present premises, which cover an area of 35x60 feet, and every facility is at hand to perform all the work which may be received, at short notice, and in the same thoroughly first-class manner that has ever characterized the operations of this enterprise. Furniture will be made to order or repaired, curtains, shades, matress and carpet work of every description carefully attended to at very lowest rates consistent with satisfactory results. Three skilled assistants are employed and we can assure our readers that they will find it to their advantage to avail themselves of the inducements presented by Messrs. Sauer & Co., in the Upholstery and Interior Decorating line.

J. W. Goodnow, Baker and Confectioner, Ices of every Variety a Specialty, 710 Centre Street, Jamaica Plain. Branch Stores, 80 Boylston Street, Jamaica Plain, and 137 Warren Street, Boston Highlands. Twenty years is a long time to be sure, but even in twenty years there are very few who succeed in building up such a business in the baking and confectionery line as is carried on by Mr. J. W. Goodnow, who began operations in 1863. The secrets of this gentleman's success are no secrets after all, for it is evident to the least observing that the reputation held by him has been honestly gained by hard and intelligent work, and that any one who can produce such uniformly superior goods and offer such complete accommodation to his customers, will achieve equal success. But this, of course, is not an easy thing to do, and Mr. Goodnow has no reason to anticipate his present claim to a leading position being seriously disputed. He is a native of Vermont, and is connected with the Free Masons, Odd Fellows and Knights of Honor, and is known (by reputation at least) to a large proportion of the residents of this vicinity. His main establishment is located at No. 710 Centre street, Jamaica Plain, but he has one branch store No. 80 Boylston street, in the same section of the city, and another at No. 137 Warren street, Boston Highlands. The Jamaica Plain store is 20 x 65 feet in dimensions, and gives employment to twenty-two assistants, offering at each store fresh and desirable goods at low prices. Bread, cake and pastry, fine confectionery fresh daily, (made on the premises) and all the articles handled by a first-class bakory can be purchased at any of these establishments at the lowest market rates and a specialty is made of Ices of every variety, orders for which will be taken and the goods delivered with a guarantee of satisfaction, a specialty is made of catering for weddings, parties, etc. None but the choicest materials are used by Mr. Goodnow, and the high reputation of his products for purity and excellence of flavor is richly and honestly deserved.

Charles H. Nichols, Dealer in Hardware, Cutlery, Stoves, Ranges, Kitchen Furnishing Goods, etc., etc., 743 Centre Street, Jamaica Plain. Among the newly established but well patronized, and in short most truly popular Jamaica Plain establishments, due mention should be made of that of which Mr. C. H. Nichols is the proprietor, located on Centre street. At this store is to be found a very extensive assortment of general hardware, cutlery, stoves, ranges and kitchen furnishing goods, together with full lines of the goods usually sold in connection with the commodities included under this head; and if this assortment be examined, its quality learned and the prices named on the goods composing it noted, no further explanation of the large business done will be wanted by any reasonable person. Mr. Nichols thoroughly understands his business, having been engaged in similar lines for the past ten years, and therefore has a comprehensive idea of what is best suited to the wants of the class of customers to which he caters. He makes it an invariable rule to represent articles just as they really are, and as a consequence is not troubled by customers returning and demanding explanations. The most inexperienced buyer can trade at this store with the certainty of getting the full worth of his money every time; and under such a system of management it is gratifying to be able to state that the business done is rapidly and steadily increasing.

D. Keezer, Provision Market, Wolsey Block, corner Green Street, Opposite Depot, Jamaica Plain. One of the oldest established provision markets in this community is that conducted by Mr. D. Keezer, who now conducts business at the corner of Green street, (Wolsey Block) Jamaica Plain. Mr. Keezer has been in business for twenty-nine years and was formerly located on Centre street, and has occupied his present location since 1883. We can pay Mr. Keezer no higher compliment than to say that during the twenty-nine years his enterprise has been before the public, it has never been more skillfully managed and more truly popular than at present. Mr. Keezer's guiding principle seems to be, that people shall have what they pay for, and such of our readers as have had any experience in marketing, need not be told that this of itself would ensure the success of his enterprise, provided it is scrupulously carried out. Mr. Keezer strives as far as possible to make all customers permanent ones, by making it evident that fair treatment is assured to all. Employment is given to three reliable and experienced assistants. The premises comprise a store with a frontage of twenty-three feet and a depth of forty-five feet, where will always be found a heavy stock of meats, vegetables and fruit, together with poultry and game in their seasons. His prices are very moderate and all orders are promptly filled.

William Rooney, Dealer in Boots and Shoes, New Block, Centre Street, Jamaica Plain. Massachusetts is well known to be the greatest shoe manufacturing State in the Union, and therefore if you can't buy shoes to advantage here, you can't anywhere. But even in the old Bay State you are by no means sure to get your money's worth when purchasing foot-wear, and therefore we take this opportunity of calling our readers' attention to an establishment where Boots and Shoes are largely dealt in, and where you may feel perfectly sure of square dealing and polite treatment. We refer to that carried on by Mr. William Rooney on Centre Street, in his new building just erected, and it only needs a visit to this handsome store to prove to the satisfaction of any unprejudiced person that what we say concerning it is fully justified by the facts. Boots and Shoes of every description are to be had at bottom prices, for Mr. Rooney is an experienced and careful buyer, and knows that it will best serve his own interests to give his patrons a fair share of the benefit he gains by close buying. His stock comprises goods of all grades, as well as all sizes; but whatever grade is chosen, it is sold entirely on its merits, and no misrepresentation is ever practised. As for prices, those quoted by Mr. Rooney will stand the severest comparison with those of any other dealer, and if you give him an order once you will surely call again.

E. H. Fairbanks, Jeweler, Centre Street Jamaica Plain. Among the peculiarly attractive stores located in this section we desire to call attention for a moment to that carried on by Mr. E. H. Fairbanks on Centre Street, who has been here for a quarter of a century, as we are convinced that an investigation into the advantages offered to purchasers at this establishment will demonstrate the fact that they are both real and generous. To begin with, a stock is carried comprising all the latest novelties as well as a full assortment of staple articles, and it is therefore easy for the most fastidious purchaser to find something just suited to his or her tastes. Then the quality of the goods is unexceptionable, and the utmost confidence may be placed in every representation made by Mr. Fairbanks, as his reputation for the practicing of strictly honorable business methods is of the highest character. Engagement Rings, Wedding Rings, Seal Rings, etc. — all these are shown in great variety, and the stock of earrings, bracelets, etc., is also worthy of careful inspection. All the leading Watches may be bought of Mr. Fairbanks, and some decided bargains are offered in this department. Repairing is done neatly, strongly, durably and cheaply, and both Watches and Jewelry will be put in order in the most satisfactory manner, and guaranteed to prove just as represented. Courteous attention is given to all and goods are cheerfully shown.

C. B. Rogers, Druggist, 704 Centre St., Jamaica Plain. Taking into consideration its capacity for genuine usefulness, it may be truthfully said that no retail establishment is of more real importance to a community than a well-appointed and well managed pharmacy, and the residents of Jamaica Plain are to be congratulated on having so worthy a representative of this class of business enterprise as that conducted by Mr. C. B. Rogers, 704 Centre Street, which was established in 1870. A full and carefully selected stock of drugs, medicines and chemicals is carried in this store and every provision is made for the filling of orders with the promptness and accuracy so essential to the highest success in this line of business. Fancy and toilet articles, cigars, soda, etc., are dealt in to a considerable extent, but particular attention is given to the prescription department, and no pains is spared to make this the most important branch of the trade. Every facility is at hand to assist in the measuring of the ingredients called for in the prescription presented, and every precaution is observed that will tend to reduce the liability to error to a minimum. The drugs and medicines are procured from the best-known wholesale houses and other equally reliable sources, and in short, if any prescription fails in its effect, it will not be the fault of Mr. Rogers. Another gratifying and popular feature of the management is the low prices quoted on the goods handled. This holds good in the prescription department as well as in the sale of fancy articles, etc., and fair dealing is guaranteed to every customer.

Alan Burke, House and Sign Painter, No. 207 Green Street, near Washington, Jamaica Plain. It is always a safe rule to follow in the placing of orders for work of any description, to employ the best skilled labor you can get at a reasonable price, for although the job you want done may not call for a great deal of skill, still it is better to have it carried out by those who know too much rather than those who know too little and many annoying mistakes and delays would be avoided were this rule more generally followed. It holds as good in painting as in any thing else, and hence we take pleasure in calling our readers' attention to the establishment conducted by Mr. Alan Burke, at No. 207 Green street, Jamaica Plain, for we can assure them that while they may entrust the most difficult orders to Mr. Burke and depend upon having them filled as they should be, they may be equally sure that all due attention and care will be given by him to work of the simplest character. He started in business in Jamaica Plain about thirty years ago, and now occupies premises at the above named address, covering an area of 25 x 50 feet, giving employment to eight experienced assistants. He manufactures an excellent Furniture Polish Renovator which he sells for twenty-five cents a bottle. Painting of all kinds especially house and sign will be done at short notice and at very moderate rates, and attention will be given to the durability of the work accomplished, as well as to its appearance, only the best materials being used and the greatest care exercised in their application.

B. E. Murray, Funeral Director, Hotel Gordon, Depot Square, Jamaica Plain. From the very nature of things, those who commonly take charge of affairs at home, find themselves totally unable to manage in so perfect a manner as they desire, when affliction is upon the family and it becomes necessary to have a funeral and to attend to all the trying details which are connected with such a ceremony. This state of affairs has long been noticed of course, but it is only of comparatively late years that provision has been made to meet it, and to secure the good of all parties concerned by one person taking charge of every necessary arrangement. One of the best known, most experienced and most careful funeral directors of which we have knowledge is Mr. B. E. Murray, whose rooms are located in Hotel Gordon block, Jamaica Plain. This gentleman fully appreciates the dignity and responsibility of his position and having every facility at hand, is enabled to serve his customers with the utmost promptness and thoroughness. He is in a position to furnish everything required if it is so wished—caskets, coffins, robes, carriages—in short, to take upon himself the responsibility which must else be borne by some member of the family or near friend. Those who remarked the manner in which Mr. Murray discharges his onerous duties, speak in the highest terms concerning him, and we unreservedly recommend him to all wishing the service of a well-informed and thoroughly equipped funeral director. His charges are extremely reasonable and the character of the articles provided is of standard quality. Telephone connections.

T. W. Robinson, Harness maker and Carriage Trimmer, Collars made a specialty and Trunks Repaired, 607 Centre Street, Jamaica Plain. Honestly-made articles are none too common nowadays, we are sorry to say, and even in the manufacture of such important commodities as harness, methods are practiced by certain makers that cannot but affect their goods injuriously. To make a strong, light and durable harness the best of stock must be used, and as such stock costs money, unscrupulous parties employ inferior grades, and palm off dangerous productions on their customers as articles that are first-class in every respect. We say dangerous productions and mean just what we say, for no one at all acquainted with the tremendous strain brought on harness, will deny that the use of poor stock may result in breakage and consequent loss of life and property. But happily there are honestly-made harness to be had at reasonable figures if they are looked for in the right place, and one of the best of these places is that conducted by Mr. T. W. Robinson on Centre Street. Visitors to this establishment will find a choice selection of goods to choose from, not confined to harness alone but including horse-furnishings of various descriptions. Mr. Robinson is prepared to make harness to order and to fully guarantee it as regards both strength and durability. Although using uniformly reliable stock he does not put his prices away beyond the reach of common folks, but supplies a trustworthy article at a most reasonable figure.

William Anderson, Boylston Cash Grocery Store, Flour, Sugar, Tea, Coffee, etc., Boylston Street next to the Depot, Jamaica Plain. Everybody, at all acquainted with this locality, knows that Boylston station has increased wonderfully in population in the last eight years or so, and if any proof of this fact was wanted, it might be found in the growth of some of the business enterprises catering to local trade. Take for instance the "Boylston cash grocery store," located on Boylston street next to the depot, and owned and managed by Mr. William Anderson. This enterprise was started some six years ago, and already the store has had to be enlarged three times in order to accommodate the rapid increase of trade. It now measures 25 x 66 feet and is elegantly and conveniently fitted-up, containing an immense stock of choice staple and fancy family groceries, canned goods, flour, teas, coffees, sugar, etc., in fact everything in the grocery line and not a few things outside of it, for, as an examination of the long list on the back of Mr. Anderson's business cards will show, he handles such goods as shovels, spades, etc., as well as many others, a mere catalogue of which would more than exhaust our space. Mr. Anderson is a native of Boston and is connected with the Ancient Order of United Workmen and the Grand Army. We do not wish to convey the idea that he owes his success entirely to location for this would be far from the truth. The fact is, that he saw the possibilities of his business and endeavored from the first to so treat his customers as to make them come again and bring their friends. Confining himself to strictly legitimate methods, he has built up his own trade without seeking to destroy that of his competitors, and the result is to be seen in the standing he holds in the community. Employment is given to four competent assistants, and orders will be called for and goods delivered promptly in any part of Jamaica Plain. Nothing is sold under false representations, and while the goods are of uniform and excellent quality, the prices will bear careful examination and comparison.

L. Ernst, Bread, Cake and Pastry Baker, and dealer in French and American Confectionery, 175 Lamartine Street and 120 Green Street Jamaica Plain. On account of the localities in which his establishments are situated, it is obvious that Mr. L. Ernst, of Jamaica Plain, must handle only choice and desirable products or otherwise his enterprise would meet with but meagre encouragement instead of the liberal and rapidly increasing patronage it actually receives. This gentleman founded his present business in 1881, and having not only a thorough knowledge of the baker's trade in general, but also a keen appreciation of the probable demands of the class to which he proposed to cater in particular, it is not surprising that the result has been the building up of a very extensive business. The premises utilized comprise two stores each covering an area of 20x30 feet; one located at 175 Lamartine Street and the other at 120 Green Street, and employment is afforded to five men and three girls. Bread, cake and pastry are always to be had at these establishments, fresh, appetizing and carefully made,

and in addition to the above-mentioned products Mr. Ernst deals in French and American confectionery. He pays the strictest attention to the selection of the many materials he is called upon to use in the conduct of his business, and rejects all that are not fully up to the high standard he has established for his guidance. Customers may feel sure that the reputation already gained for uniformity and superiority of manufacture will be rigidly sustained. Mr. Ernst is a native of Germany and is very popular in his line of trade, and what is more, fully deserves the popularity he has attained.

Charles H. McCaffrey, Plumbing and Gas Fitting, 88 Boylston St., Boylston Station, residence 35 Boylston Avenue. Those who have availed themselves of the services of Mr. Charles H. McCaffrey since he began operations in 1887, need not be told that he is both willing and competent to undertake plumbing and gas fitting work of every description or that his shop contains all the necessary facilities for the carrying on of repairing and similar work to the best advantage. Mr. McCaffrey is well-known throughout Jamaica Plain and vicinity. The premises occupied for business purposes are located at 88 Boylston Street, and covers an area of 15x25 feet. Employment is given to efficient and reliable assistants and orders are attended to at remarkably short notice and executed in the most thorough and workman-like fashion. Mr. McCaffrey has given the subject of gas fitting and sanitary plumbing careful study, and has had years of practical experience in the arrangement and alteration of plumbing facilities. He is perfectly able to assume direction of such matters, and those who know how much the health of the occupants of a house depends upon the plumbing, drains, etc., being in perfect condition, will thank us for calling to their notice one who guarantees satisfactory work, and whose record proves him to be deserving of everything. We have written in his favor both as regards his skill and reliability.

E. G. W. Kraushaar, Ph.G., Apothecary, corner Boylston and Lamartine Streets, Boylston Station. It is of course convenient and desirable to have stores of all kinds within easy access of one's residence but it is particularly useful to have a well-conducted pharmacy near at hand, for such a state of affairs is not only convenient, but in some cases may be the means of saving life itself. Therefore the residents of Boylston Station and vicinity have reason to congratulate themselves on the existence of such an establishment as that carried on by E. G. W. Kraushaar, Ph.G., at the corner of Boylston and Lamartine Streets, for this pharmacy is well appointed in every respect and what is still more essential, is conducted by an educated, experienced, and in short thoroughly competent chemist. The store was opened in 1870 and has been carried on by a gentleman named Moisano, and afterward by Mr. Sprague, then by E. F. Morse, the present proprietor assuming control in 1884. He is a native of Germany and gives that close and painstaking attention to detail which makes his scientific countrymen the acknowledged authorities on all medical subjects requiring profound research. The premises utilized measure 15x40 feet and contain an extensive selection of drugs, medicines, chemicals, etc. Fancy and toilet articles are also kept on hand and offered at low rates, their quality being guaranteed. Kraushaar's Almond and Rose Cream is prepared at this pharmacy, and as its name implies, it is a soothing, healing and fragrant compound for those afflicted by or liable to irritation of the skin, sunburn, chapped hands and face, etc. It is prompt and lasting in its effects, and unlike many other preparations on the market, is very agreeable to use. Especial attention is given by Mr. Kraushaar to the compounding of physician's prescriptions and only the best and purest ingredients are used in the filling of such orders which are put up without delay at very low rates.

The Chicago Beef Market. Charles Burghard, Dealer in Provisions, Beef, Pork, Mutton, Lamb, Poultry, etc., 140 Green Street, opposite Depot, Jamaica Plain. Chicago is becoming known as the great distributing centre of the wholesale beef trade, and the Chicago Beef Market of Jamaica Plain is also coming to the front as the representative meat and provision store of that locality. Its proprietor and manager, Mr. Charles Burghard, is a native of Germany, and those acquainted with the thorough manner in which trades are learned in the Fatherland, need not be told that he is a master of his business in every department. Mr. Burghard is a member of the Royal Arcanum, and is extremely well known in this vicinity. The premises utilized by him are 30 x 50 feet in dimensions, and he carries a heavy stock of beef, pork, mutton, lamb, veal, poultry, provisions, etc., which he offers at the lowest market rates for goods of equal quality. All classes of purchasers can trade here with profit, for the assortment of goods comprises articles of all grades, and soup-stock and roasting pieces can be bought with equal facility. One thing that makes this market popular is the fact that all goods are warranted to prove as represented, and another thing is the promptness with which callers are served, three efficient assistants being employed. The store is centrally located at No. 140 Green street, opposite depot, and should you call there once you will call again.

J. P. Shaw, Carpenter and Builder, and dealer in Building Materials of all kinds, Lumber, Lime, Cement and Bricks, Glass and Putty, No. 102 and 164 Green Street, Jamaica Plain. Although it is doubtless true that there is much more anxiety, care and trouble connected with building a house for one's self than at first thought would be supposed possible, still there is much to be said on the other side of the question and it is not to be disputed that many of the obstacles and vexations met with are due to the want of exercising the proper care in the selection of a builder to undertake the work. Some builders will consult customers interests invariably and use as much discrimination as to

the avoiding of unnecessary expenses as though their own pockets were concerned, while others will, as everybody knows pursue an exactly contrary course. But the former class of men are quite easy to find in this vicinity, and one of the most popular of them is Mr. J. P. Shaw, doing business at Nos. 102 and 164 Green street, Jamaica Plain. He is a native of Maine and has conducted the business of carpenter and builder since 1870. When he began operations here, having been located here for fifteen years previously, and built up a very prosperous trade. The premises utilized at the above named address, cover an area of 75 x 300 feet, and in addition to the carpentering and building business which requires the employment of twenty to fifty experienced workmen. Mr. Shaw deals in builders' materials of all kinds, including lumber, lime, cement, bricks, etc. We can recommend Mr. Shaw to all who wish to avail themselves of the services of a strictly reliable carpenter and builder.

A. Papineau, Hack, Boarding and Livery Stable Keeper, Green Street, Jamaica Plain, near depot and Washington Street. There is

not a better known establishment in Jamaica Plain, than that conducted by Mr. A. Papineau on Green Street, near depot and Washington Street, for this gentleman has done business in the vicinity mentioned for a score of years, having inaugurated his enterprise in 1868. In December, 1879, Mr. Papineau removed to his present quarters which were built by him and which were fitted up expressly for the carrying on of his business to the best advantage. Some 11,000 feet of land is utilized and the building is three stories in height, the upper floor being used as a hall for entertainments, etc. The proprietor was born in Canada, but passed nearly all his early life in Vermont, to which state the family of which he was a member, removed during the famous Canadian "Landlord Rebellion." The Papineaus were very prominently identified with those opposing the landlord laws, and finally removed from a country where they could not remain with respect. Mr. Papineau gives employment to five men and boards about 30 horses at his spacious stables. His charges for boarding are very reasonable and the animals are assured the best of care at all times. Carriages will be furnished for weddings, funerals and other occasions at the shortest possible notice, and the drivers will be found to be careful and experienced men who are both civil and attentive. Orders by telephone are given immediate attention, and particular credit should be given this establishment for the excellence of its livery service, speedy and stylish turnouts being supplied at any time and at prices as low as can be placed on such accommodations.

Frank Ganter & Co., Dealers in Provisions, Butter and Poultry; Manufacturers of Sausages. Smoked Hams, etc., Boylston Station, Jamaica Plain, Mass. The important influence exerted by the food upon the health is becoming more and more generally recognized every day, and it may well be said that the poorest economy is that which tends to stint or cheapen the food supply. Mr. Frank Ganter of Boylston Station, Jamaica Plain, is one of the most active and enterprising provision dealers to be found in this vicinity, and we can confidently assure our readers that they may place their orders with him and rely upon having them filled without delay and at the lowest market rates. Mr. Ganter and his partner, Joseph Wittenauer, are both natives of Baden, Germany, and are members of the Royal Arcanum. Mr. Ganter established the present enterprise in September, 1872. Mr. Wittenauer entered the firm in 1835. The store occupied is 22 x 70 feet in size, and the building was erected in 1887 by Mr. Ganter. It also contains another store, and up stairs are six commodious suits of six rooms and bath each. The store is one of the handsomest we have seen, and embraces a very large and varied stock of Meats, Butter, Poultry and Provisions in general. Mr. Ganter also manufactures Sausages, Smoked Hams, etc. There are six efficient and courteous assistants in attendance, and all callers will be served promptly and politely.

HENRY LOVESY, Manufacturer of RUSTIC WORK,

Cor. Washington and East Concord Sts. (Under Station A.), Boston.

No. 12, Oblong Vase, Price $6.00.

Verandah or Croquet Chair, very pretty, Price $2

Price, $3.25, $5.00 and $7.00.
Very fine and roomy Vases.

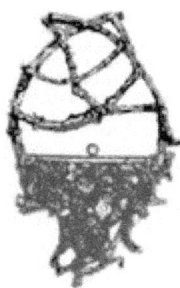

No. 14, Wall Pocket,
For hanging against the wall, Price, 75c.

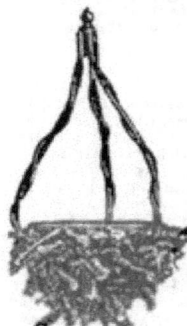

No. 7, Hanging Baskets,
3 sizes, 75c. to $7.